ALSO BY ALMA GUILLERMOPRIETO

Samba

The
Heart
That
Bleeds

The
Heart
That
Bleeds

LATIN AMERICA NOW

Alma Guillermoprieto

Alfred A. Knopf   New York   1994

THIS IS A BORZOI BOOK
PUBLISHED BY ALFRED A. KNOPF, INC.

All of the essays in this work were originally published in The New Yorker as
"Letters" from the various countries and cities in Latin America.

Library of Congress Cataloging-in-Publication Data
Guillermoprieto, Alma.
The heart that bleeds: Latin America now / by Alma Guillermoprieto. — 1st ed.
p. cm.
ISBN 0—679—42884—4
1. Latin America—Politics and government—1980– 2. Latin America—Social
conditions—1945– 3. Latin America—Economic conditions—1982– 4. Latin
America—Moral conditions. I. Title.
F1414.2.G77 1994
980.03'3—dc20   93-35488 CIP
Manufactured in the United States of America
FIRST EDITION

For Bob, and John

Contents

Introduction

THESE STORIES WERE WRITTEN over a four-year period, on assignment for *The New Yorker*. They are presented here in the sequence in which it occurred to me to write them, and in that order they represent a certain consistency—and evolution—in my own obsessions: violence, inequality, survival, the faithlessness of politicians, the faithful stubbornness with which people seek to believe. These topics occupy the attention of people in other regions of the world, of course, but it seems to me as a Latin American that for us they are such urgent issues, and so iescapable, that they surface in our dreams and in our needlework, in our love lives, our literature, and even in the way we dispose of our garbage. I am part of a violent and poor culture: Colombia has the highest rate of homicides for any country not at war; in Brazil, fifty-five out of every thousand children born die before they are twelve months old. These are shameful figures, and yet, to the extent that they indicate lives lived on the very edge of all precipices, I have no doubt that they are also part of what makes our world compelling: people from highly civilized countries travel to Latin America seeking passion and intensity; they find it, and stay.

Anyone who had anything to do with Latin America in the nineteen-sixties and nineteen-seventies knew another obsession: the revolution that, to both guerrilla groups and the death squads who opposed them, seemed just around the corner. Now that the Cuban revolutionary epic is staggering to its close, leaving behind neither heirs nor offspring, it is possible to see the latest failed encounter with redemptive apocalypse as one more aspect of a larger, ongoing, and unsolved discussion the continent has had with itself about modernity. The self-awareness acquired with independence from Spain, early in the nineteenth century, has been inseparable from a sense of backwardness and self-doubt, and the social upheavals that have swept through the region since then have at bottom been about the terms under which the Latin-American nations will accede to the modern era, about what aspect of their historical (old-fashioned) identities they will sacrifice in the process, and even about just which modern era it is they will be entering. For indentured peasants in Peru in the nineteen-seventies, to be modern meant simply not to be feudal; for the Lima-based owners of haciendas so large that some even minted their own coin, to be modern meant having the newest television set from Miami—and an indentured servant to provide manicure service during the news hour.

The questions not yet answered in Latin America have to do with a coherent future vision, not only of how the hugely unequal sectors of Latin-American society can all modernize themselves into the same century—or, in these times of catapulting technological change, into the same decade—but of how they can modernize each other into the same ethical standard and a rough consensus regarding what it is that a modern society owes its citizens, and what those citizens owe each other.

Lacking an appetizing alternative to the left's dream of a transforming, equallizing revolution, the Latin-American ruling classes of the nineteen-sixties came up with the idea of progress as a way of attaining modernity. The word was almost always linked to the notion of order, as in "Ordem e Progresso!," the credo written on the Brazilian flag, which the Brazilian military dictatorship took up as a battle cry. *Ordem e progresso* meant mega-highways and superconductors and workers marching off to the factory in serried, punctual ranks. The concept was so unappealing that it had to be imposed by force, and so in 1964 Brazil inaugurated the hemisphere's era of military rule with a coup—an era that ended only a little under three decades later and left a legacy of superhighways in shambles and devastated ecosystems, ruinous debt and workers no more punctual than they ever were, in large part now because the region's bloated cities simply cannot be traversed with any speed or order.

The military dictatorships' record is disastrous, but when the Generals withdrew from power throughout the continent nearly all of them reaped the sweet reward of media flattery and official glory, by calling for, and supervising, what became known as free and democratic elections. Here and in the United States, elections were taken as ultimate proof that modernity had arrived at last. Indeed, elections were even taken as proof that democracy had arrived at last. George Bush and the media applauded when Fernando Collor de Mello was elected President of Brazil, in 1990. Unhappily, it cannot be said that Collor was the sleaziest, most shameless con man ever spawned in the swamps of Latin-American politics, because the competition is too stiff. He was, though, according to the hearings that led to his impeachment, a major-league swindler, who betrayed higher hopes than had been placed in any Brazilian ruler before him. In the last four years—the period covered by this book—in Venezuela, Peru, Nicaragua, El Salvador, Guatemala, Paraguay, and Haiti elected governments have also been deposed or led their nation's economies to ruin, turned dictatorial, or failed to keep basic covenants with their electorates.

In a region in which fifteen per cent of the population is illiterate and the majority receive only the most meagre schooling, in which nearly thirty per cent has no access to basic health care, and the prisons remain crowded with detainees whose cases may never see trial, what are the terms on which the merits of electoral democracy can be discussed? And where is the ruler who can negotiate the niceties of formal plurality while dealing with a petty, retrograde ruling class, a restive and greedy military establishment, and recurrent economic cyclones that tear away jobs, erase the narrow spectrum of the middle class, and dump absurd rates of inflation on all? The strongman is back in demand. Alberto Fujimori of Peru, now a dictator, remains popular, not necessarily because he governs well but because he governs hard. He has only to lurch in the vague direction of his stated goals to provide his desperate constituency with a sense of movement, and therefore of progress, and of future.

In Latin America, the vast majority of people wish to be modern, because they would like not to be poor, and they know that the United States, which is modernity itself, is wealthy. But urban dwellers, who constitute the great majority of Latin Americans today, already *are* modern. They ride overcrowded subways or buses, watch television, fail to use condoms, suffer from noise pollution, and eat hormone-treated chicken, just like any put-upon New York resident. Unlike the average New Yorker, though, most Latin Americans have become urban only in the last forty years or so, and modernity has struck like a tornado in the arid shantytowns that ring the overburdened cities. It is disorienting to go virtually overnight from wearing traditional handloomed Indian costume to dressing in polyester, or from playing the violin with the town band to watching *Robocop II* on the VCR. The pervasive inequality that confronts the new urban citizens, their orphanhood vis-à-vis the state, and the sense that all past traditions and skills are worthless have set the newcomers frighteningly adrift. The search for meaning and identity has thus taken on some of the same industrious, resourceful, and urgent quality displayed by the garbage pickers of Mexico City as they sift for sustenance through the refuse of other people's lives.

The articles in this collection—the one about the drug culture in Medellín as much as the ones about religion in Brazil and the guerrillas of the Shining Path in Peru—are all about modernity. The reader may be distressed to find that they are also overwhelmingly about poor people, but that is simply on account of proportional representation. These are, in addition, stories reported and written from inside a culture, with no effort made to justify to a foreign (that is to say, English-speaking) reader what might appear strange or unappealing. On the other hand, they are also stories written with foreign—English—words, and so, inevitably, with a foreign (that is to say, non-Latin-American) state of mind. I write as a Mexican-born-and-bred journalist who learned the trade working for newspapers published in London and the District of Columbia, and as a New Yorker who prefers to live in Latin America. In these stories, I have tried to make my own biculturalism into a bridge for two cultures that are, through modernity, increasingly intertwined, although both sides might vehemently deny that union, and although each still appears to the other to be sometimes exotically, sometimes painfully foreign.

The
Heart
That
Bleeds

BOGOTÁ
1989

"This country feels as if someone had turned out the lights."

AMONG THE FEW PEOPLE to have benefitted from the current faceoff between the government and the cocaine traffickers are Bogotá's windowpane fitters. The other morning, at an apartment building that had been left glassless as a result of a nearby explosion, there were three teams of them, trotting from a lineup of flatbed trucks to the damaged building with enormous rectangles of glass in their mittened hands, maneuvering each one into place by means of suction cups, clambering back into an apartment through the nearest gaping window, and barely pausing to puff a little and ease their backs before picking up the next pane. "Every morning, we turn on the radio and wait for the announcement," one of them told me, "and then when we hear it we go, 'Bomb explosion! Let's get to work!' And we set out for whatever address they give on the newscast. There have been a lot of bombs, but there are a lot of glaziers, too, so it's not really *that* much extra work, but I've done four or five buildings already myself."

The man said his name was Carlos López, and added, as he and his partner eased another pane of glass out of their truck, that he expected to be extremely busy that day. Eleven bombs had gone off the previous night, most of them in this neighborhood, which is called Teusaquillo and is one of the pleasantest in Bogotá. It dates from the nineteen-thirties, and if the orderly rows of red brick houses with tile roofs don't quite achieve the English look that was so clearly intended, it is partly the fault of the vegetation—splendid purple-flowered *sietecueros* trees along the curved streets, and blood-red begonias and blue agapanthus crowded into the narrow front yards. There are a few modern apartment buildings here, several unpretentious brick churches, and—a blessing in a city plagued by noise and congestion—not much traffic, even though Teusaquillo is only a fifteen-minute drive from the downtown area, where Congress, the National Palace, and several government ministries are clustered. The major parties and a good many important politicians have their headquarters in Teusaquillo, so that when the cocaine traffickers decided to launch an attack on what is known here as *la clase política* it took only eight minutes, and two cars cruising down the neighborhood with several charges of dynamite, to devastate the campaign headquarters of nine politicians. Because the streets here are not very wide, the detonations shattered an inordinate amount of glass, some of it as much as two blocks away from the target sites. Thus Carlos López's euphoria as he saw himself surrounded by buildings full of business potential.

In the way Colombians have of taking all disasters in stride, López's prospective clients were neither hysterical nor outraged as they stood in clusters outside their windy apartments, comparing notes to see which glazier was offering the best price. One woman, still recovering from the fright of waking up a few hours earlier to the sound of ever-closer detonations, until an enormous one sent a storm of glass shards flying into her bedroom, was still amused to note how the window men had knocked at her door, offering cards and taking measurements, even before the clock struck seven.

The aftermaths of the first several dozen bomb attacks launched by the narcotics trade in response to the joint United States–Colombian anti-drug offensive have had in common this slightly festive air. At least, people seemed to be thinking, things weren't worse. At least there was only broken glass. No one was hurt. Indeed, given the relish and the creativity with which the drug traffickers have employed violence in the past, the bombs have seemed unimpressive; by Colombian standards, these last three weeks have been extraordinarily calm. Following the murder of the Presidential candidate Luis Carlos Galán, on August 18th, and President Virgilio Barco's use of his emergency powers to set up an extradition arrangement with the United States, Bogotanos had spent weeks in a stifling mood of depression and fear: The worst political assassinations of the last few years have been committed in the name of Los Extraditables, an ad-hoc alliance of drug traffickers whose slogan is "Better a grave in Colombia than a jail in the United States!" What horrible retribution would the traffickers plot as a response to Barco's extradition decree? Another individual murder—of a Cabinet member, perhaps? Or would a bomb be set off in a crowded supermarket, a cinema, a plane? Any of this may happen as of today, when the Supreme Court ruled that the extradition decrees are constitutional, but since September 2nd, when a massive bomb caused severe damage to the militantly anti-drug newspaper *El Espectador*, there have been no major assassinations, kidnappings, or truck bombs in Bogotá. Homicide and burglary rates are down by more than fifty per cent from their usual levels—a hiatus that was taken as a form of communication from the drug trade: people read in it the traffickers' restrained menace, their decision to hold off on the real stuff until the Supreme Court decision.

In the meantime, there were the bombs, a few small explosions a night. In contrast to Medellín, where a similar campaign against banks and restaurants, and even a country club, caused several injuries, the bombs here were almost always set off at times when no one was likely to get injured or killed. After three weeks of this, one of my neighbors took stock of the damage and wondered, "Is that all there is? Just a few little bombs?" And when I asked a member of one of Colombia's prominent political families whether the confrontation between the government and the drug traffickers could destabilize the government his reply was scornful. "These people don't even know where to put their bombs," he said. "They're so ignorant and provincial that they declare war on us, the leading class, and they don't know how to strike us where it hurts. They put a bomb in the Medellín country club, because Medellín is where they're from, but, I assure you, they don't even know where the Bogotá Country Club is. They don't even know that there is one."

This man thought the traffickers were floundering, and there is evidence that the Bogotá-based operations of one of the bloodiest and most sought-after of the traffickers, Gonzalo Rodríguez Gacha, have been nearly dismantled. But there is no indication yet that the drug traffickers as a group have suffered any damage to their strike capability. Instead, the bombs in Teusaquillo appear as one more episode in a purposeful and unhurried response to the joint Barco-Bush anti-drug offensive: the traffickers have simply decided to ignore the government's confrontational tactics, opting instead for their own version of low-intensity warfare, with low-cost, low-risk strikes against almost every area of public life. Telephone substations have been hit, putting forty-four thousand lines out of service at a time. Government savings-and-loan associations have put on extra security but are still being targeted. Movie houses are emptier now that a small bomb went off in the men's room of a neighborhood cinema. There was an escalation of terror last week, when a bomb in a hotel room in the resort city of Cartagena killed two doctors attending a convention. Here, a spate of weekend bombs at public elementary schools is keeping children home while repairs are made.

THE RELATIVE RESTRAINT—the delicacy, even—displayed by the drug traffickers in their choice of targets was in sharp contrast to their reckless use of violence in the months preceding Galán's murder. This is, after all, the year that opened with a direct challenge to government authority when two investigating judges (or district attorneys) and ten members of their team were ambushed and executed in the course of an investigation of drug-related murders in the countryside. The judges belonged to the Public Order Courts, which were set up by the government last year following the murder of Attorney General Carlos Mauro Hoyos and endowed with special powers to investigate and sentence drug- and guerrilla-related crimes. The Public Order Courts had been quite effective in building cases and issuing indictments against the major drug traffickers. The Army and the national investigative police, for their part, were pursuing an unusually vigorous offensive against major cocaine laboratories. The *narcotraficantes* struck back. In May, although a car bomb miraculously failed to kill General Miguel Maza Márquez, the head of the investigative police, six other people died. In July, another car bomb killed the governor of the *departamento* of Antioquia, whose capital is Medellín. Later that month came the murder of a Public Order judge who had issued an arrest warrant on the Medellín-based trafficker Pablo Escobar in relation to several mass murders last year. On August 17th, another judge who had charges pending against Escobar was killed, and then, on August 18th, gunmen assassinated the Antioquia chief of police. That evening, as President Barco was preparing to go on the air to announce a series of drastic measures against the cocaine trade, including the revival of extradition procedures and an expropriation decree aimed at the trade's luxury homes and cattle ranches, Galán, the clear popular favorite among six pretenders to the Liberal Party candidacy, and the reported choice of Barco himself, was shot at a campaign rally on the outskirts of Bogotá.

Public opinion immediately ascribed the murder to Escobar, and Bogotanos with any political or social prestige, money, or intellectual influence spent the ensuing days reviewing every detail and every rumor in an attempt to understand why Escobar had chosen to kill Galán at that particular time, their hope being thus to find an answer to a second, more pressing question: Am I next? Those were ugly weeks of expectation, but in the ensuing dead calm two more questions arose: How badly have the traffickers been hurt by the offensive? How will they strike next?

The most logically constructed explanation for Galán's murder is that the killing was plotted single-handedly by Pablo Escobar ("one of the twenty richest men outside the United States, according to *Fortune*," reporters cannot resist writing), who is said to have a thing about revenge. Reportedly, he has been unable to forget that it was Galán's political movement that drummed him out of Congress in 1984.

Galán, privately a soft-spoken and conciliatory man, was also scrupulously honest, and as a result he often found himself in situations that required him to play the role of firebrand or rebel. In Congress, his magnificent leonine face and old-fashioned oratorical style served him well, and, being pragmatic and occasionally eager to please, he could have progressed swiftly up through the Liberal Party ranks had he not spent the late nineteen-seventies denouncing his party's increasing corruption and cronyism. He finally broke with the Party leadership in 1980 and, together with a group of other intelligent, ambitious young politicians, founded a breakaway movement called Nuevo Liberalismo.

One of the co-founders was Rodrigo Lara Bonilla, another senator. Escobar had bought himself a great deal of popularity in the poor neighborhoods of Medellín by then, financing squatter housing and paying for things like funerals and soccer uniforms for people there. In 1982, under the sponsorship of an influential senator named Alberto Santofimio, he joined the Liberal Party and ran for Congress as an alternate representative for the *departamento* of Antioquia. The titular candidate, Jairo Ortega, won an easy victory, possibly thanks to generous amounts of Escobar campaign money. When Lara Bonilla was appointed Justice Minister in 1983, he launched an investigation of illegal contributions to political campaigns, and focussed specifically on Ortega and Escobar. Shortly afterward, the newspaper *El Espectador* published a story disclosing that Escobar had been arrested in 1976 as a minor cocaine trafficker, and he was publicly disowned by his one-time sponsor Santofimio. Less than two years after his election, Escobar was forced to withdraw from public life. A few months later, Lara Bonilla was murdered.

According to the revenge interpretation of recent history, Galán's murder was simply thorough-minded Escobar getting rid of one more Nuevo Liberalista, although a subrumor adds that Escobar had got wind of President Barco's plan to revive the extradition process and had decided to combine past and future revenge in a single blow: he struck against the man who had helped disgrace him, against Barco's program, and against the President's chosen candidate and likely successor.

This is a comforting version of events to most of those who might be wondering if they are on a hit list, because at this stage there are barely a half-dozen Nuevo Liberalismo founders still alive—among them, former Justice Minister and Ambassador to Hungary Enrique Parejo González, who survived a 1987 attempt on his life in Budapest, and Galán's widow, Gloria Pachón, who continued to receive death threats every half hour following her husband's murder and who is leaving for Paris as Colombia's envoy to UNESCO.

There is also an important, optimistic corollary to the revenge theory, and it holds that Escobar acted not only alone in ordering Galán's murder but against the wise counsel of the elder statesmen of the drug trade, the Ochoa clan. When members of "the leading class" argue that all drug exporters should not be considered equal, they invariably point out that the trafficking Ochoa brothers—Juan David, Jorge Luis, and Fabio, Jr.—come from "a good Antioquia family," meaning, among other things, that the Ochoas can be relied on for levelheaded business decisions. Although they have lately been at war with still other traffickers—the Rodríguez Orejuela brothers, based in Cali, who control most cocaine shipments to New York—rumor has it that the Ochoas and the Rodríguez Orejuelas in Cali are now willing to talk, to each other and to the government, because Escobar keeps ordering assassinations and the resulting government crackdowns are bad for the trade. The extravagant and particularly unnecessary murder of Galán, who was neither a law-enforcement official nor a pro-extradition crusader, exhausted the patience of the Ochoas and the Cali traders. Escobar and Rodríguez Gacha are now on the run, abandoned by their colleagues and with a two-hundred-and-fifty-thousand-dollar price on their heads. The strongest evidence that the government, the Ochoas, and the Cali traders are in some sort of agreement, the rumor concludes, is that the government is offering its quarter-

million-dollar bounty for information leading to the capture of
Escobar and Rodríguez Gacha and nobody else.

THE ROGUE-TRAFFICKERS-ON-THE-RUN theory could be in-
terpreted as a victory of sorts for the government; in the absence
of a real decline in the world demand for cocaine, or of a public-
relations coup like the capture of a major trafficker, it is hard to
judge what else could constitute measurable progress in the current offensive. It was easier in the early days, immediately after
Galán's murder, when the mood of fear was counterbalanced by
the excitement of intensive and well-publicized raids on property
owned by drug traffickers. Gold-plated bathroom basins and
white grand pianos, transparent acrylic dining-room sets and
mock-medieval architecture were on the news every evening.
There were daily tallies of ranchland acreage seized, a major policy speech on the subject of drugs by the President of the United
States, and detailed coverage of the capture and extradition, to
Atlanta, Georgia, of a middle-level cocaine-money launderer. But
none of this has added up to increased popular support for the
weakest President in recent Colombian history, and, despite the
Supreme Court's surprising decision in his favor this evening, it
is still very much a question whether Barco will have a mandate
to pursue a war with so many noncombatant casualties. I have
not talked to a single Colombian—of whatever income level or
political persuasion—who believes the drug traffickers can be
permanently defeated as long as the United States continues to
provide a market. In the face of this perceived invincibility, how
could the man the leading weekly *Semana* once described as "the
worst communicator among contemporary heads of state" persuade anyone that the cost of the war—the bombs, the murders,
the generalized fear—is worth paying?

    With his wispy hair and thin voice, Barco is singularly un-
gifted for public life; he is resented when he disappears from public view, which is often, and is mocked when he speaks. When
he is trying to sound cheerful, he comes off as flippant, and when
he is being serious he sounds peevish. Although his virtues are
grudgingly recognized—he is undeniably honest, persevering,

meticulous—they do not produce affection. Oddly, it was his weaknesses that helped get him elected: as mayor of Bogotá, his reputation as a first-rate administrator with no taste for politicking appealed to an electorate weary of President Belisario Betancur's bubbly charm and flamboyant political initiatives; Barco played Water Rat to Betancur's Toad of Toad Hall. But three years in power have in no way improved Barco's effectiveness as a politician. He has not been able to hold on to his Cabinet members, and following the mishandled firing/resignation of his Justice Minister, Mónica de Greiff, two weeks ago, and rumblings of discontent from the Interior Minister over the extradition issue, he is now looking for his ninth Justice Minister and fifth Interior Minister. Nor has he proved skillful at the pork-barrel handouts any President needs to keep his party happy in Congress, and now, with less than ten months left in office, he is a lame duck as well. All the luckier, then, that as the drug offensive appeared to be losing momentum the Supreme Court should overcome its historical dislike of extradition measures and grant Barco what is probably his most important political victory to date. Today's decision was a reversal of all previous positions—proving, a Colombian journalist at *El Espectador* said happily, "that the Court is no longer avoiding the burden of the drug crisis."

Extradition involved getting the Colombian government to override its own legislation and authorize the trial, sentencing, and incarceration of its citizens in a foreign country. There are powerful and logical reasons why the United States government should want this: there are reams of charges against the most well-known drug traffickers in the United States, while there are virtually no charges against them in Colombia. Few traffickers have ever been captured here, and none have been successfully held for more than a few weeks; the only major Colombian cocaine figure currently in jail is Carlos Lehder, who was captured in 1987—just before the most recent bilateral extradition treaty collapsed—and spirited off to Florida, where he was sentenced to a jail term of life plus a hundred and thirty-five years, no parole.

Colombian arguments against extradition are not so neat,

and to the degree that they come wrapped in intense nationalist feeling they make many United States listeners impatient. The first argument—defended for a long time by Conservatives like Betancur—is simply that citizens have an inalienable right to be tried in their own country. There are others, subtle and less popular: for example, that Colombia's historical weakness has been the lack of a strong central state capable of imposing the rule of law on its population, and that by abdicating this obligation through extradition the government will effectively usher in an era of lawlessness more dire and bloody than anything that has been known in the past. Another, put forward by students of the cocaine market, is that the capture of any major trafficker—or even all of them—will have absolutely no long-term effect on cocaine supply, that the United States' cocaine problem will be solved only when its citizens stop demanding cocaine, and that it is arrogant for the United States government to demand a measure that produces so little result, at the price of so much pain to the people of a country it otherwise cares so little about.

Even so, no one here dared criticize extradition in the aftermath of Galán's murder. There was a consensus that an extraordinary situation called for extraordinary measures, and it was clear that Barco had a unique chance to obtain a favorable ruling from the Supreme Court, which—quite independently of the many threats against it and the murder of one of its members over the issue—has historically looked askance on extradition. The aloof Barco reportedly took the uncharacteristic step of sounding out the Court before staking his political future on the emergency decrees. "It's my understanding that he consulted, and was told that the decrees would not be rejected out of hand," a legal expert with friends on the Court told me. When the last bilateral extradition treaty with the United States was knocked down by the Colombian Supreme Court, early in 1987, it led to a pause in the horrendous killings with which the traffickers had sought to intimidate proponents of extradition. When, after Galán was shot, President Barco announced that he was sidestepping constitutional limits on his right to legislate and single-handedly reviving extradition procedures for traffickers facing charges in the

United States, the response was the bombing of *El Espectador*—whose previous editor, Guillermo Cano, had campaigned in favor of the extradition treaty and was murdered in December of 1986 as a result.

NOW, AS WE AWAIT the cocaine exporters' reaction, the question remains whether, despite the Supreme Court's backing, Barco has the strength to command the war he declared on drugs. In the absence of popular support, he needs to be able to fall back on a strong government, but the institutions of rule in Colombia are notoriously frail.

Three weeks into the big offensive, Barco's Interior Minister, Orlando Vásquez Velázquez, asked to address a session of the Chamber of Representatives, the lower house of Congress, in order to explain the emergency anti-drug decrees and to obtain a vote of confidence from the representatives. When he arrived to deliver his scheduled address, he found the Chamber's doors locked. At the suggestion of the vice-president of the Chamber, the representatives had decided to hurry away and postpone a discussion on the delicate subject of drugs.

"This is a bad moment to judge what the state is capable of, because we are at the end of an administration," the dean of one of Bogotá's several law schools mused a few days after the congressional incident. "Of course, that means that this is not the best time to attempt a principal and dangerous offensive. But there are also limitations that have nothing to do with the effectiveness of the President himself. The legislative branch, for example, is worthless. It's frightened, and when an entire branch of the state shows that it is intimidated this is very serious. But, unfortunately, this is a chronic problem, and not Barco's to solve: Congress has been ineffective for the last twenty-five years." But, the dean acknowledged, even by its own unimpressive standards the Chamber of Representatives' fear-induced boycott of the Interior Minister's anti-drug presentation was unheard of. It was true, he went on, that the judicial branch was powerless as well. "It is prostrate, lacking the most minimal capacity to react." There was no exaggeration in this: for lack of staff and resources, an estimated eighty per cent of all crimes are not prosecuted; of those that are, a million seven hundred thousand cases are currently awaiting sentencing each year. Less than three per cent of these receive verdicts. The country's twenty-five thousand judicial employees are not only underpaid and overworked but terrified; a hundred and twenty of them, including thirty-five judges, have been killed in the last few years. On a salary of under four hundred dollars a month, it is not every district-court judge who can afford a bodyguard.

In the dean's opinion, the high judicial death rate is in itself evidence that the system is not fundamentally corrupt. With adequate training for the judges, an adequate salary, better physical protection, and computers and other equipment vital to efficient criminal investigations, it would be possible for the courts to make significant progress against the drug trade's overwhelming impunity. But in its current economic straits the Colombian government will have to rely almost exclusively on United States assistance to finance improvement in its judicial system. Of the sixty-five-million-dollar aid package announced by President Bush last month, about eighty-five per cent is earmarked for the military and the rest is for the police. A separate five-million-dollar grant this spring largely went for emergency protection for the judiciary—bulletproof vests and armored cars—but the aid is barely more than symbolic; there are more than four thousand judges in Colombia, and the national justice system's employees association estimates that one out of five is under threat. At thirty-five thousand dollars per armored car, it would cost about thirty million dollars to provide protection for all of them. Given the circumstances, the law-school dean had to conclude that if the Cali traffickers and the Ochoa clan could be persuaded to deliver the corpses of Rodríguez Gacha and Escobar the country would be well served. Like everyone else, he did not think that talk of eliminating the cocaine trade was realistic as long as ravenous United States and European demand continued to create a market: "No democratic government can completely eradicate crime," he said. "But it can reduce immorality to its tolerable dimensions. The government can strike significant blows against crime, do away with two or three big traffickers. The trade will continue to exist, but we can control its destabilizing effects on society, on the economy, and on political life. The problem is that drug crime has spun out of control. The will to rein it in does exist, however, and I think that, despite everything, the judicial and executive branches together have enough strength to do it."

This is what could be called the New Pragmatism among the power élite, and one of its problems is that it reduces the idea of a drug offensive to rhetoric, while the cocaine traffickers consistently pursue a course of all or nothing. Of course, there are many people, including former members of Barco's inner circle, who think that the current offensive *is* rhetoric, on both the Colombian side and the United States side. George Bush declares a war on drugs and sends some fifty-five million dollars' worth of surplus—and inadequate—military equipment. The Colombian Army goes on an offensive and fails to launch a single significant strike against the cocaine exporters based in Cali, who probably account for the largest volume of cocaine shipped to the United States. "This is absurd, completely absurd," a former close adviser to President Barco said. "All this—the emergency decrees, the U.S. trainers, the military offensive, the political risks—just to capture Escobar and Rodríguez Gacha?"

"YOU KNOW WHAT really gets me?" a journalist friend of mine from *El Espectador* burst out a couple of weeks ago. We were watching a television newscaster announce that in Washington the Drug Enforcement Administration had just confirmed the extradition to the United States of a second-level cocaine-money launderer who was captured here in the first days of the raids. In expectation of immediate retaliation from the cocaine trade, the members of the paper's staff had been advised to lock themselves indoors. "What really kills me," my friend said, duly locked away, "is that we're now stuck with the extradition policy, whether we like it or not, and, for lack of a better policy, we're honor bound to defend this one. You know perfectly well that someone is going to die—something dreadful is going to happen—as a result

of this extradition tonight, and it won't even be for the sake of
any really major figure. All this destruction will take place just so
the United States can have its symbolic bringing to justice, even
if it's of some second-rate flunky who's worth nothing to it."

The visceral charge of this reaction was typical. Anti–United
States sentiment is not overt here (as the local saying goes, "From
Miami, you can see Heaven"), but it is a volatile constant in the
national mood. (This is the country that lost the Isthmus of Panama during an uprising instigated by the United States.) There
have been anti-extradition rock-throwing incidents sponsored by
the left and, after the press leaked the names of congressmen who
are no longer allowed entry into the United States—including
one-time Escobar associates Alberto Santofimio and Jairo Ortega—a series of fiery counterattacks by the injured parties,
charging the C.I.A. and the Drug Enforcement Administration
with Galán's murder. None of this goes very far, but if anti-
Yankee rage becomes an issue for the first time during a Colombian electoral campaign this year, it will largely be because
Colombians feel their government's arm is being twisted on the
extradition issue.

How any campaign at all will take place is difficult to imagine
at the moment: What will dispirited voters make of the array of
candidates, who are supposed to represent hope but seem shell-
shocked? There is the personable Conservative Party candidate
Diego Pardo Koppel, for example, whose headquarters was the
one most badly hit the night of the Teusaquillo bombs, and
whose private secretary, Alvaro López Acevedo, has received
"about nine" death threats over the phone since Galán's murder.
Sitting in the rubble the morning after the bombing, López
affirmed that Pardo Koppel's campaign for the Senate would
continue, but said five minutes later, with no apparent sense
of contradiction, that "there is no climate for political campaigning now." How will Pardo run a campaign if it's impossible to
have one?

And how will voters respond to the Presidential candidacy of
César Gaviria, former Interior Minister and the late Luis Carlos
Galán's campaign coördinator, who sobbed at his candidate's

funeral and was sworn in as his replacement a month after the murder? Gaviria, a skillful backstage politician and an efficient administrator, completely lacks his predecessor's popular appeal. Are Galán's followers being asked to vote for his ghost? Will they?

They could decide to vote instead for the normally ebullient Ernesto Samper, also of the reformist wing of the Liberal Party. He has been slowed down a little since last March, when eleven bullets kept him hospitalized for two months with near-fatal septicemia, but he says that his survival vindicates a lifetime's worth of optimism. Yet his demeanor is often solemn these days— brooding, even—and prospective voters, contemplating his campaign team, his security apparatus, and his recent past, could also find themselves sinking into a certain gloom.

Eight months ago, as Samper was waiting to check in for a local flight at the Bogotá airport, he spotted José Antequera, a representative for the city of Barranquilla, standing in another line. Antequera, a member of the leftist Unión Patriótica party, was well liked by many Liberal and Conservative politicians. He was open-minded, pragmatic, exceptionally bright, and possessed of the essential political talent for forging alliances. At a time when nearly eight hundred members of his party had been killed—by Gonzalo Rodríguez Gacha's right-wing *narcoparamilitares*, according to all indications—Antequera was trying to protect the Patriotic Union by distancing it from its guerrilla origins and strengthening its congressional links with the other parties. He had been quite successful at this, but when Samper went over to say hello to him at the airport he found Antequera tense. "He told me that he was under very serious threat," Samper recalled on a recent afternoon. "And that he was going to Barranquilla for a rest, because he was feeling very anxious. As he was saying that, I heard the first shots." A *sicario*, or hired assassin, was emptying his machine gun into Antequera, and a spray of bullets hit Samper in the lower abdomen. He was saved by his wife, Jacquin, who threw herself across his body and screamed at his stunned bodyguard, "Kill the *sicario!*," which the bodyguard did. Antequera was already dead, but Samper, who saw blood on his finger and thought he had been wounded only in the hand, hung on to life. His wife dragged him behind the check-in counter, onto the luggage conveyor belt, and out onto the tarmac, where she flagged down an airport van and instructed the driver to race for the nearest hospital.

When Samper had recovered, he resumed his campaign. Horacio Serpa, who is one of the most seriously threatened men in Colombia as a result of his outspoken denunciations of the *narcoparamilitares*, resigned his post as Attorney General to act as Samper's campaign manager. This week, Mónica de Greiff, who as Justice Minister received meticulously detailed threats against herself and her family, announced that she was joining the team. When Samper and Serpa go campaigning, as they did this week-end to Medellín, they wear bulletproof vests and are protected by a security detail of more than four hundred men. Samper has taken to joking that the current campaign is not about who will be selected for the Liberal candidacy but about who will survive to claim it, and he could add that voters may well make their choice not on the basis of which candidate they prefer but of which one is likeliest to live out his four-year term.

Two weeks ago, when Samper arrived at his campaign head-quarters for a scheduled interview, he was preceded by a body-guard, who had the candidate wait outside while he went through every room in the house, automatic gun in hand, looking for strangers. When he had finished his search, a second body-guard inspected the candidate's office, checking in the closets and under the sofa cushions for bombs. Finally, Samper was ush-ered in, and a bodyguard closed the door and remained waiting in the hall.

"It's very difficult, you know," Samper admitted, with a sigh. "We had to move our headquarters this month, because we re-ceived serious threats that they were going to bomb it, and the house was on an exposed corner. It was hard to find anyone will-ing to rent to us. These last weeks, I've felt, for the first time, that people are afraid of being near me, because I'm a politician. The neighbors in my apartment building would like me to leave, and I understand why. The first thing their children see when they go to school in the morning is six men with machine guns. Of course they're scared!" As for the campaign itself, now that most of the candidates had decided to keep open-air appearances to a minimum, Samper said, "It's almost impossible to find anyone willing to rent you a meeting hall. My wife and I decided to raise funds with an art auction, and we hired the Gun Club"—an elegant private club. "We paid for it, mind you, and signed a contract, and everything. But the day before the auction was going to be held somebody called and said they knew about the auction and they were going to bomb it. When the Gun Club cancelled on us, I told them they were committing a profoundly undemocratic act. We held the auction somewhere else at the last minute, and, of course, it was a complete failure. Now, where is someone like me, who is hated by the *narcotraficantes* and not particularly liked by the big interest groups, going to find funds to campaign in this country if it's impossible even to rent a hall?"

I remarked to Samper that he was not sounding optimistic.

He disagreed. "You can't get into a Presidential race if you're pessimistic," he said. "I'm not out for martyrdom. I think I can win, and I think I know what has to be done. There are still moral, economic, and institutional reserves to draw on in Colombia. But there is no doubt that we are facing a huge task. The problem is that we let violence and the drug traffic go too far before we reacted. Just as there is a climate of tolerance in the United States with regard to drug use, there has been a climate of tolerance among us for the traffickers—a certain predisposition to live alongside them."

And now there was the immediate problem of getting voters to overcome their fear. "People are afraid," he said. "This country feels as if someone had turned out the light."

If Samper has a new awareness of the depressive atmosphere, it is because he is tuned in to the changes in mood of the middle class, a natural constituency he shared with Galán. The country has recently enjoyed a construction boom and a phenomenal expansion in the luxury-service sector—restaurants, boutiques, hair salons, and travel agencies—which benefitted the upwardly mobile. All this was financed largely with drug money, while the trade's seamier activities—mass murders of left-wing peasants, gang warfare, corruption of government institutions—barely touched the middle class, whose reaction to the drug problem in the past has covered the range of indifference. But Samper's accidental shooting shook his followers, and Galán's murder has brought home the implications of terror to people who had previously had no reason to consider themselves targets, and therefore enemies, of the drug exporters. Galán's funeral was attended by multitudes, in a rare explosion of collective middle-class outrage, but it is not clear how this all-important sector of the population will react if a full-blown terror campaign with human casualties gets under way now that the extradition decree has been ratified. The reaction of the middle class will be a weathervane of sorts, and will strengthen either the lonely Barco or those who would like to see an increased role for the military in making government decisions or, yet again, people like the mayor of Medellín, a Conservative, who believes that, in the absence of legalization of the drug trade, a settlement of some sort with its illegal traffickers is necessary. The mayor, Juan Gómez Martínez, is not alone in his opinion: the president of the Chamber of Representatives, having announced earlier that he has always favored dialogue—"even with my enemies"—quietly let it be known last month that he had had two "brief, respectful, and threat-free" phone conversations on the subject with Rodríguez Gacha and Pablo Escobar. How any deal could be made in the face of vehement United States opposition is an unaddressed question, but the talk being bandied about is of an arrangement that would allow the traffickers to stand trial here for minor crimes, say, and to put their badly needed money into the regular economy.

There might as well be a curfew, so empty are the streets and restaurants after dark in this normally night-loving city, and as of this evening the tension is perceptible even in the dead silence all around. Anything could happen: deaths, major drug arrests and extraditions, Presidential fumbling. But what could also happen over the next few months is that Colombia could remain more or less as it always has been—with the government neither victorious nor defeated, the situation neither settled nor chaotic, the country neither at war nor at peace. "Something like that is what will happen," the man who belongs to what he calls "the leading class" said recently. "And that will be the best thing. What people here haven't understood is that this war isn't against the drug trade but against the drug traffickers—two of them. The other war has to be won in the United States, not here. But if we get rid of Escobar and Rodríguez Gacha—and they have to be killed, because if they are captured alive the consequences will be extremely bloody—everything can go back to the way it was before."

"That would probably be the saddest solution of all," the law-school dean said. "It would mean that Colombia has once again shown its capacity to adjust to everything."

THERE WAS A BOMB two Sundays ago on one of the major avenues, at the point where it crosses an upper-middle-class residential area. The bomb itself was not unusual—it was only one of the forty or so that have gone off in the last three weeks. What was startling was the fact that it exploded almost exactly in front of the spot where a car bomb nearly killed General Maza Márquez, the police chief, in May. The car-bomb explosion opened a crater in the pavement five metres across, left six dead and more than fifty wounded, shattered almost every windowpane within a two-block radius, and thoroughly terrified the residents of the tall apartment buildings along Carrera Séptima. To hit the same spot twice seemed mean even by narco standards, but there it was: the shattered glass sprayed all over the street, the collapsed façade of a travel agency on the corner where the bomb was placed, the winking red lights and nasty wail of the police vans, the startled, shivering residents standing on the sidewalk again, staring.

They were getting used to it, though, they said. Enrique Sánchez and his wife—two kids who looked hardly old enough to be married—said that only two days before they had gone for a walk through Chapinero, a nearby shopping district, and got home in time to hear an explosion at a corner they had just

walked by. "We were in the elevator, and it shook," Señora Sánchez said, giggling. And then the Thursday before there had
been another bomb, and they'd heard that, too. Enrique Sánchez
said that the explosions weren't the half of it. "I went for a run
the other evening, and the Army stopped me, said I looked like
I could be carrying a bomb. And just yesterday they stopped me
in the car, because I drive a jeep—I guess like a lot of traffickers.
They asked for my papers and saw that I was born in the town
where Rodríguez Gacha had his headquarters; so they questioned me for a couple of hours. Can you imagine? We get the
bombs, and they think we're the bombers!"

His wife, who thought all this was terribly funny, hugged
him tightly.

I asked how they had reacted to the newest bomb, the one
that had exploded just a few minutes ago, virtually under their
feet.

"It's really not that scary," she said. "Once the explosion is
over, everything's fine."

MANAGUA
1990

"The future is ours."

WHEN THE POLLS OPENED at 7 a.m. on Sunday, February 25th, the long lines of waiting voters did not know that they were about to decide the end of a ten-year-old one-party regime, and in the extraordinary thirty-four hours that elapsed between 6 a.m. Monday, when President Daniel Ortega appeared at a televised press conference to concede defeat, and his reappearance in public at a Sandinista rally on Tuesday the country came to a complete halt while the stunned people of Nicaragua contemplated the magnitude of what they had done, and tried to imagine the unimaginable consequences of their act.

February marks the height of the dry season here; on that Monday morning, only dust inhabited the streets, rolling through the city in brown clouds. Everywhere, there was dead silence. The era of Sandinismo had ended; for the first time in the country's history, a democratic transfer of power had been announced, and a great many people were fearful that the first result of this gift could be civil war.

It is now general knowledge that when the voting stations closed Sunday evening President Daniel Ortega was calmly writing his acceptance speech, having been lulled into unfounded optimism by a series of polls that gave him a huge percentage lead over his opponent, Violeta Chamorro—a lead about as large as the one he would soon learn he had lost by. At 10 p.m., the Sandinista National Liberation Front's campaign workers were still setting up their victory celebration—huge loudspeakers, balloons, ska and salsa music, and all the other trimmings that had for months drawn immense crowds to their rallies. At 11 p.m., with the promised "quick count" results still unannounced, the Managua headquarters of both Ortega's F.S.L.N. and UNO, the coalition backing Mrs. Chamorro, were electric with rumors, as was the new Olof Palme Convention Center, in the ruins of what had been downtown Managua until the devastating 1972 earthquake. Most of the thousand or so foreign reporters covering the election were waiting here for someone to come out and say something. At the nearby Bambana night club, where UNO supporters were waiting for Mrs. Chamorro, no preparations for a celebration seemed to be under way, but a spokesman, Danilo Lacayo, was brimming with cheer. "We are very tranquil," he told skeptical reporters. "Believe me, there will be surprises tonight." At 2 a.m., the head of the Supreme Electoral Council, Mariano Fiallos Oyanguren, announced the results of the first 5.6 per cent of votes tallied. His voice was broadcast over the Sandinista loudspeaker system to thousands of youths who had gathered at a bandstand outside F.S.L.N. campaign headquarters and were still waiting for something to celebrate. As Dr. Fiallos, a former rector of the National Autonomous University and a longtime Sandinista, droned out the results region by region, the teenagers gradually stopped chattering as they began to realize that the count was against them.

Inside the Party headquarters' V.I.P. room, the President's wife, Rosario Murillo, a poet who likes to wear miniskirts and shoulder-length earrings, broke a dreadful silence by bursting into Sandinista song, her eye makeup running as she led half a dozen followers through a series of off-key verses. In a corner, Bianca Jagger and Régis Debray stared at the scene. Outside, an announcer told the stunned crowd that the show would continue, and four couples in nineteen-fifties Cuban-style dance outfits went through some demure gyrations. Before the reality of defeat sank in, a few teen-agers actually joined the music and danced.

The scattering of adults in the crowd milled about in shock. "But the polls," people kept saying. "The polls."

In fairness to the pollsters, the complexities of the population's relations with the guerrillas who took power at the head of a popular insurrection in 1979 might have confused almost anyone trying to call the results of an election that was essentially a plebiscite on the Sandinista regime. When the Sandinistas toppled Anastasio Somoza Debayle, the last of the Somoza family dynasty installed forty-three years earlier by the United States, and rode triumphantly through Managua in their ragged uniforms, they appeared scrawny, heroic, unbelievably young. They embodied the best of everything that three and a half million people who were used to seeing their nation treated as a fourth-rate banana republic might dream of. Inspired by the guerrillas, they, the people, had brought to an end the tedious, repetitive history of occupations and manipulations by the United States and its longtime protégé, and the Sandinista anthem that the Nicaraguans then bellowed fullheartedly said it all:

> The future is ours.
> Our people are the owners of their history,
> Architects of their own liberation . . .
> We fight against the Yankee,
> The enemy of humanity.

The self-image of heroic defiance, martyrdom, and abnegation lived on in a steadily growing core of members and sympathizers of the F.S.L.N., parallel to the wearying, everyday reality of life with the Sandinistas. Over the decade, the ex-guerrillas built and destroyed so much, empowered and offended so many people—enlightening and repressing them in almost equal measure—that by the time the elections were held it was hard to know which of the Sandinistas' many contradictory attitudes and policies people would choose to remember in the privacy of a voting booth.

HOW COULD ONE JUDGE, for example, the peasants on the outskirts of Estelí whom a trio of us reporters interviewed shortly

before the elections? I had first visited Estelí, a drab little city
in the cool northern hills of Nicaragua, in 1978, following the
Sandinista takeover of the National Palace. The takeover had
sparked the first nationwide insurrection against Somoza, and a
small Air Force plane was strafing the city that day. The only
person we found at the entrance to Estelí was a wiry old man,
one of those swamp-green-eyed people whom Nicaraguans call
"cats." He offered to take us into the combat zone, and when
we asked, rather doubtfully, if he was armed he displayed that
combination of recklessness, theatrical flair, and innocence
which has seduced so many visitors to this land. "This is the
weapon I will defend Nicaragua with to the last drop of blood!"
he declaimed, his ragged shirt fluttering in a heroic wind that
seemed to have just sprung up around his chest, and, thrusting a
hand into the air, he brandished a table knife.

Now, a dozen years later, two Estelí men, also in their care-
worn fifties—one a "cat"; the other brown-eyed, and pale-
skinned below the shirt collar; both missing a few teeth—talked
to us and to a woman known everywhere around Estelí as Chepita, the leader of the local unit of the all-purpose Sandinista
Defense Committees that have at various points in their history
served as emergency civil-defense organizations, neighborhood-
control apparatuses, and, in their most recent transformation,
support centers for community projects. Chepita had volun-
teered to take us on her rounds that day, and now we listened as
she helped the two men, Ernesto Delgadillo and Juan Blandón,
organize the inauguration of a two-room school building that
had just been completed.

"Is there music?" Chepita wanted to know.

There was: a couple of guitar pickers and a violin.

"Good. We'll bring the loudspeakers. Dancers for the dance
contest?"

There were four child couples and four adults.

"Other cultural activities?"

The two men looked blank.

"Other activities to fill in the program after the ribbon-
cutting," Chepita insisted.

"Someone told us about a burlap-sack race that's supposed to be a lot of fun," Blandón said. "Does that count?"

Chepita frowned. "Compañero," she said, "how about things to make the community aware of its history and its values? A joke-telling contest, or a storytelling contest by some of the oldest men in the village."

The elders agreed to try, and Chepita went on to explain to the women present how they could use red and black ribbon— the Sandinista colors—to make decorations.

Delgadillo—whose home, a rudimentary three-room hut, we were sitting in—said he and Blandón had learned to read during the 1980 literacy campaign, which mobilized tens of thousands of Nicaraguan teen-agers in an exhausting but exhilarating five-month drive. "Basically, we just got familiar with the letters," Delgadillo said. "We resisted the learning at first, because one gets used to living in the torment of ignorance and thinks that reading won't make a difference, but, of course, it does. For example, at seminars, when at the end they hand out questions, and you have to write down the answers."

Seminars! Since when had cracked-footed peasants with gawky smiles been going to seminars in Nicaragua?

"Oh, since the revolution," Blandón said casually.

There are now seminars on planting and livestock-insemination techniques, on coöperative management and public health, held both in local urban centers and in Managua, and the most active community leaders can even aspire to a trip to Havana or Belgium. Just imagine what Delgadillo could dream of for his children! "They're going to have a different style," he said, spreading his arms enthusiastically. "Because we cast off the slavery of the Somoza days, when he didn't even give us permission to dream of a future."

Still, for the present things hardly looked positive. Delgadillo's hut represented the lowest rung of Latin-American poverty: dirt floors, no windows, wide gaps between uneven wall boards, a wood-burning hearth for cooking corn and beans. There was little else. Delgadillo, who had been bursting with eloquence just a few moments earlier, was suddenly taciturn when we asked him about his house, and admitted only after much prodding that his family's life was difficult—desperate, in fact. "It's the war," he said. "It takes resources from the state, so we don't get any help." Then we noticed that the head of the village's Sandinista Defense Committee had come in and was standing directly behind us, listening carefully.

We found out more at another hamlet near Estelí, which would also soon inaugurate a school. Chepita had wandered away to talk to a group of women, leaving us with a man who was sifting sand for cement at the construction site. "Some are happy, some are not," he answered with an equivocal smile when we asked about the economic situation. Eventually, he explained that most families were planting only subsistence crops, and were surviving on a cash income of nearly zero. There were no credits, he said. Hadn't been for several years now, and since 1988, when the government finally decided to link the interest rate on bank loans to the outrageous rate of inflation—thirty-six thousand per cent that year alone—peasants had refrained from even asking for loans. The situation was so bad that several families had left, and the ones that remained lived in fear of the Contras, who were still operating just on the other side of the hill.

Even though the United States officially suspended military aid (but not maintenance assistance) to the Contras in 1988, you can still see the war in much of northern Nicaragua. On the road between Estelí and San Rafael del Norte, our attention was caught by a couple of dozen brand-new prefabricated houses set in orderly rows in a lovely valley below. It was a *cooperativa armada*, one of dozens of such settlements established by the Sandinista Army as military/civilian obstacles, barring access to the local garrisons. The place seemed deserted, and a woman nursing a sickly baby explained why. "Since the Contras came and burned this place down, no one wants to come and live here," she said. The Contras, it seemed, had descended on the place in 1984, setting fire to the original village and all the machinery, and seven families had fled.

Several of the *cooperativa's* twenty men were out in the fields, using a burned-out tractor and husking the season's meagre crop.

The men were not really farmers. They had come here from the outskirts of Estelí in exchange for the promise of land, and the results of their inexperience were evident: worm-infested cauliflower, runty corn. The Contras were all over, they said—in the hills within walking distance of where we were standing, and in the valley just beyond. There had been some shooting in the vicinity the previous Sunday, but the farmers felt relatively safe: the local Army commander had been fighting in those hills ever since he was a Sandinista guerrilla, and he knew his business. Whenever the Contras got too close, the captain would come and tell the men to drop their work and get their guns.

In general, the *cooperativas* are well armed—with AK-47s, like the Contras—and they have privileged access to farm equipment and loans, so within the general grimness of the situation the men we talked to seemed calm and unswerving in their Sandinista loyalty. Besides, the Army captain's military skills were obviously matched by his political tact. "He has let me keep my boy here, helped me hide him from the draft," one man said. "He knows there aren't enough hands here to work the land if the boys go. He's a very good man. In exchange, we let him have a little bit of land at the entrance to the valley, so the troops can grow some food."

There are figures that give some idea of the war's damage. For example, by 1985, following the worst year of fighting, local research centers had tallied forty-eight schools destroyed and five hundred and two others closed down in combat areas; forty-four thousand hectares of forest burned; and four million dollars in gold lost in the principal mining centers. There were also four thousand dead, including five European volunteer workers and seven hundred and thirty-three farmers, and there were four hundred and twenty-five thousand displaced persons, some inside Nicaragua and some abroad. It is hard to compute the almost complete disruption of agriculture, the effects of allocating around thirty-five per cent of the eight-hundred-million-dollar national budget to the Army, the huge cost of treating the war-wounded and providing for their families. The Sandinistas brought suit against the United States at the International Court

of Justice in The Hague for twelve billion dollars in war reparations in 1988, and the Court has agreed to try the case. An eventual ruling in their favor would gain them nothing; Washington
refused to recognize the Court's jurisdiction when it condemned
the Reagan Administration for mining Nicaragua's ports. The
Sandinistas were not able, in their tallying of the destruction and
damages, to factor in the effect of the Contras on their own hold
on power, although many of the Sandinista blunders and political
defeats were a direct response to the army of rebels organized,
trained, supplied, and promoted by the United States.

Who knows, for example, whether the *cooperativa* members
would have seemed so disposed to vote for Daniel Ortega if the
local captain had not agreed to let their sons evade the draft? If
the Sandinistas and their opposition can agree on anything, it is
that the government lost the elections on the critical issue of the
draft. It proved beyond a doubt that the war against the Contras,
for which the draft was indispensable, did not move Nicaraguans
as a whole to the extremes of patriotism and sacrifice which the
Sandinistas had just naturally expected from their people, and
which those people had displayed inexhaustibly during the insurrection against Somoza.

A FEW KILOMETERS OUTSIDE Managua proper is a dismal,
sprawling township that has been known since the revolution as
Ciudad Sandino; earlier, when the Somoza family and a close
associate parcelled it out to victims of the 1972 earthquake (at a
price), it was called Open Tres. During the 1978 uprising and the
final anti-Somoza insurrection, in 1979, almost all the male teen-
agers in Open Tres left it to join the guerrillas, and Somoza's
National Guard attempted to arrest the remainder one night, so
closely was the area's youth identified with the rebellion. Less
than a dozen years later, Ciudad Sandino voted against the Sandinistas nearly three to one, and shortly before that happened I
spent a few days there, to see how some of the poor who constitute the vast majority of Nicaragua's population lived and what
they did with their spare time.

They didn't do much. After privation, the overwhelming reality of Nicaragua is boredom, a reality so pervasive as to explain the crowds at almost any campaign event at which the Sandinistas appeared with their loudspeakers and salsa music, and of those there were many in Ciudad Sandino. The campaign kicked off in December when Daniel Ortega, who used to be an amiable, nondescript type of guy, arrived in Ciudad Sandino wearing new, flashy shirts that his campaign designers had found for him, to pose with babies for Polaroid pictures and hand out caps and T-shirts with the Sandinistas' red-and-black logo.

The teen-age daughters of Alonso and Rosa Ramírez still wear the T-shirts—partly because they like Daniel, as he is universally known, and partly because they have hardly any other clothes. Their parents, like most of the population, have seen their standard of living decline over the last several years, and that means they must support three children still living at home on a combined income of less than a hundred dollars a month. Rubén, the youngest child, is nine, and never drinks milk. The family subsists on rice and beans and a few tortillas (they're expensive) and very sweet black coffee. They sleep on metal cots overlaid with salvaged bits of foam rubber, and careless sleepers soon find different parts of their bodies wedged between sagging wires and knocking against the floor. The house has no kitchen, and not even a sink, but only a hose in the yard, with the running water the revolution brought; a washstand; and a latrine next to a tiny pen where a pig is kept. There is no electrical appliance except a radio. An automobile's sideview mirror serves the family for grooming, and is stowed away carefully after each use.

Before Alonso Ramírez lost his job at a state-owned cheese factory, his salary actually came to less than he now earns by picking up construction work here and there, but when he was taken off the payroll he had no way of knowing that people would come to trust his honesty and reliability and sweet temper enough to keep him almost steadily in demand. The factory shut down a year ago, after years of corruption and mismanagement, which began when a program to halt inflation led instead to an inflation rate so wildly out of proportion to government-controlled wages that consumption of most goods virtually stopped. Demand for the cheese soon dropped so sharply that it started to fester in the vats. Rather than admit to a production setback, the factory manager gave orders that the stuff be dumped secretly at night behind the Cuesta del Plomo—the sharp rise off the shore of Lake Managua where Somoza's National Guard used to drop the mutilated corpses of Sandinista sympathizers. Eventually, much of the cheese started disappearing into the black-market network, but there was still an excess, and it was still disposed of at the dump site. A high-ranking offficial from the Ministry of Agrarian Reform, which owned the factory, visited it after hearing of the crisis. "And he was really angry," Ramírez said. "He told us that our boys fighting the war would have been grateful for just a little cheese at the front, and that at the very least we could have distributed the cheese among ourselves. So for a while we were all taking lots of cheese home, and some was going to the border"—the border with Honduras, where the Contra war was being fought. "There were still black-market sales, though," he added. And the official had said nothing about generating profits, so, despite determined efforts by the union to get rid of the manager, the factory was eventually closed down, the manager was promoted, and Ramírez was dismissed.

Amazingly, both Alonso and Rosa Ramírez voted for Daniel Ortega. Rosa, who works as a maid and washerwoman for less than thirty dollars a month, likes him, and she does not seem to associate her extreme poverty with the Sandinistas' erratic economic policies. She told me that she thought the President was a good man, with much better intentions toward the poor than his opponent's, but she didn't know what she would have done if she had had a draft-age son. She does know that she had fought tooth and nail to keep her older daughter from joining a coffee-picking brigade. "No one can like the idea of her daughter going off someplace where she can be raped or lost," she said. "I told my neighbors that since none of us agreed with this situation we should get together and tell the head of the Defense Committee, so he could at least get our complaint down on paper and show it to those farther up. But people were scared to talk. Privately, they complained, but in public no one said a word. That's what's happened to the Sandinistas. There's a lot of dissatisfaction they didn't know about." She thinks it's a pity that communication between "the people" and Ortega has been sabotaged by what she calls "his administrators": the middle-level Party cadres and bureaucrats who were hastily put in place by the guerrillas to manage a country their own small numbers could not hope to control.

Rosa's neighbor across the street, Enrique García Avilés, once attempted unsuccessfully to hide his son from the draft, and the draft is only one of a long list of grievances he has against the F.S.L.N. He remembers that when the Sandinista Defense Committees were formed, to watch over him and his neighbors, enforce calls to voluntary work sessions, and mobilize people for rallies, the woman who had performed similar tasks for Somoza emerged as the head of the local organization. García, who then considered himself a Sandinista, loathed her. Eventually, he grew to hate the Sandinistas, too, with a passion that did not diminish when the woman was replaced by a more reasonable neighbor, and it has not diminished since. "They are drastic, totalitarian," he says. "That woman stood here in the street and burned *La Prensa*"—the opposition newspaper. "A lot of people didn't like that, but there was pressure on us to go to those things. If we didn't, she could cut our rations."

García is a shoemaker, affiliated with the Cooperativa Kojak. "Only the *cooperativas* got materials at one point, but if you refused to go harvest coffee or sugar on the government farms they cut back your supplies," he complains. "I still feel my blood boil when I remember those things. And what about what they did to Father Bismarck Carballo? Anyone can have a slipup, but to set a trap for him with a woman like that and run him out naked into the street! And then to have the shamelessness to show this on the nightly news! They think we don't remember things like that, but the people never forgot."

The Sandinistas did run their election campaign as if no one in the country had any memory. In the past, whenever international or domestic pressure against a particular policy—harassment of the conservative sector of the Catholic Church, say, or censorship of nongovernment news media—became unbearable,

the policy was simply dropped. In the campaign stops I wit-
nessed, Ortega made no reference to recent history; he never
attempted to explain to his audience what had happened to the
economy after the worst of the Contra war was over, what mistakes had been made by the Sandinistas themselves, or what
measures were being taken to correct policies that had proved
unworkable. There was no discussion of why Cardinal Miguel
Obando y Bravo had once been a principal object of ridicule in
the official press and why his homilies calling for peace are now
quoted respectfully. For Sandinista supporters and detractors
alike, the message was simple: UNO, the coalition backing Mrs.
Chamorro, was "the National Guard–UNO." And for the Sandinistas the message was that, following Ortega's inevitable reëlection, *"Todo será mejor"*—"Everything will be better." The speeches
usually lasted about fifteen minutes, and then the loudspeakers
switched to salsa music, while Ortega threw autographed base-
balls out to the crowd.

A lot of F.S.L.N. people agreed even before the election that
the Ortega campaign had about as much content as the literature
on a box of breakfast cereal, but, they said, the President had
already got a deeper message across in the weekly televised
question-and-answer sessions known as "De Cara al Pueblo"
("Face the People"). "In the beginning, to be perfectly honest, the
sessions were staged," the mayor of Managua, Carlos Carrión,
told me two days before the elections. "We'd make sure someone
in the audience asked this question and someone else that one.
But it made us uncomfortable. The President, especially, wouldn't
put up with it. So 'Face the People' became the place where the
real issues could be debated, and they always ended with a long
explanation by the President of the issue that seemed to be most
on everyone's mind."

Carrión's underlying assumption was that the Sandinistas'
spiritual link with the people was so strong that it could override
any temporary romance with the opposition, so that UNO and
F.S.L.N. sympathizers alike would turn up at the lively question-
and-answer sessions, allowing the Party to keep accurate track of
the pulse of the nation. Although there was no reason that this

should be the case, the conviction appears to have been shared by the whole of the F.S.L.N., and it explains why, a few days after a disturbingly large UNO rally in the city of Masaya, Ortega's campaign organizers decided to turn a scheduled "De Cara al Pueblo" into yet another Sandinista sound-machine presentation. The session was to be held in the Indian enclave of Monimbó, which, like Ciudad Sandino, is considered a cradle of the revolution. By the time Ortega was scheduled to arrive, the crowd was not nearly as large as UNO's had been, but Justo González, a shoemaker and a local leader of the anti-Somoza insurrection, was insisting that nothing was wrong. "People will show up at the last minute," he said. "This isn't supposed to be a rally anyway. The people of Monimbó have been asking for a 'De Cara al Pueblo' for a long time, to discuss their problems, and that's a much smaller affair." González said that the community's main problems were lack of water—they had just spent two weeks without any—and lack of raw materials for the hammocks, Indian clothing, and leather goods that Monimbó traditionally lives off. But when the "Dannymobile" arrived Ortega spent almost two hours posing with babies for Polaroid shots and then gave the standard, content-free speech. UNO won Masaya two weeks later by a margin of ten per cent.

It seems that sometime in the course of the Sandinistas' long showdown with the United States, avoiding bad news became a Party tradition. At the grass-roots level, bad-news bearers were stigmatized as Contra allies or weaklings. The lower-level Party cadres and militants, eager to please in the pressurecooker atmosphere imposed on them by the demands of a war and of a barely consolidated government, filtered out the negative from their reports. "In January our own internal polls showed a sharp decline in our popularity," a Sandinista member of the National Assembly told me after the elections. "So we sent out our regional campaign supervisors to check with the local committees. And they said that they had been back to the block organizations, and that they were willing to put both hands and both feet into the fire, that we were way ahead, and that on February 25th they would deliver the votes." As a result of this encouragement, and of the impressive turnouts at most rallies (made possible by government logistics and considerable peer pressure to attend), the F.S.L.N. leadership decided that it did not have to make the announcement annulling the draft, which affected teen-agers, primarily those that the F.S.L.N. considered its natural constituency: the sixteen-year-olds, who had been granted the vote, free schooling, and great political weight by the government. There is a general feeling now that many of those teen-agers were actually undecided voters, who waited until the Party's closing campaign rally, on February 21st, for an announcement on the draft. More than two hundred thousand people turned out for the affair, and the younger part of the crowd stayed through the endless song-and-dance part of the festivities in order to hear Ortega's speech. Probably on instructions from his imagemakers, the President made strange prancing movements across the stage before launching into an unusually long and thoughtful talk, in which he announced a program of national reconciliation and specific economic improvement following the elections. He also discussed how the confrontation with the United States was draining Nicaragua, and predicted that an overwhelming number of votes in the Sandinistas' favor would legitimize the regime in United States eyes and lead to better relations. Everything will be better, he promised. But he didn't announce the end of the draft.

THE HUGE Olof Palme Assembly Hall was full at 6 a.m. on the day following the elections. A great many foreign reporters were on hand, quite a few of whom were living in Nicaragua and were in sympathy with the revolution or were working with the alternative press. There were also lots of *internacionalistas*, foreign volunteers who had somehow learned that Daniel Ortega would be speaking now that the vote tally showed UNO to have gained a resounding triumph. They were the first to rise to their feet when the doors opened and Ortega walked in, at the head of a crowd of F.S.L.N. candidates for the National Assembly. Miguel d'Escoto, the Maryknoll priest who is also the Foreign Minister, was with them, too, wearing a red-and-black kerchief around his neck, and so was Interior Minister Tomás Borge. As the novelist and historian Sergio Ramírez, who has served as Vice-President under Ortega, moved into the hall, he looked as if he had just had a death in the family. He and Ortega walked toward the microphone and raised their arms in greeting as a wave of applause rolled over them.

The Sandinistas were unique among Latin-American revolutionary organizations in their ability to project a heroic image and, time and again, overcome their own limitations as a radical movement from a small, backward nation in order to make the grand gesture. No matter that most of their leaders had never been outside Nicaragua before their 1979 victory, or had much beyond a high-school education. Never mind that the F.S.L.N.'s first eighteen years were spent in clandestinity and bred the sectarianism and paranoia inevitable in an underground movement, or that the desperate war with the United States reinforced the leadership's provincialism, rigidity, and general siege mentality. Now, as Daniel Ortega spoke in a sorrowing voice of the Sandinistas' deep love for Nicaragua, it seemed that no one could doubt him, and when he said unhesitatingly that his government would respect the people's vote one could almost feel listeners' memories welling up—of how the Sandinistas, organized in 1961, had endured in all but unbearable circumstances, carried on an all but hopeless struggle against the region's most firmly entrenched dictatorship, survived the torture and death of their most valuable and beloved leaders, wasted much of their lives in jail, nearly starved to death in the jungle, and at last led a suicidal charge against Somoza that ended in a confounding, delirious victory. And now the majority of the population wished them gone, and they were leaving.

After the sobbing in the audience had ended, the journalists filed quietly out. In the bright sunlight, the convention center's clean tropical architecture stood out against the rubble and overgrowth of post-earthquake Managua. I remembered how, a few weeks after Somoza's downfall, a well-known Latin-American Trotskyite had burst into the lobby of the Hotel Intercontinental here, just off a plane from Mexico, his face alight with discovery. "I understand!" he bubbled. "It seemed impossible that a guerrilla group could force the collapse of a state so quickly, but I've just driven here from the airport, and, let me tell you, Nicaragua was not a state. It was a hacienda—Somoza's private hacienda! And the National Guard were not an army, they were his private watchmen!" He was right: Nicaragua was not a state until the Sandinistas made it one. The telephone book (one two-hundred-page book for the entire country) used to list the sites of the public phones—less than a dozen in all of Nicaragua. And I once counted the elevators in Managua: three in the Intercontinental, two in the Bank of America building, three more in the old Central Bank building where the President now has his offices, two in what is now the Interior Ministry. It was a ten-elevator country.

All through the Contra war, the United States' trade embargo, and the catastrophic drop in prices for Nicaragua's principal exports—coffee, sugar, and cotton—the Sandinistas persisted with single-minded determination in their efforts to build a state, despite the barely three million dollars in cash and $1.5 billion in debt they inherited from Somoza. Its presence is now everywhere. There are traffic police who do not take bribes, modest but gracefully designed children's parks, public trash bins, and there are literacy, vaccination, and infant-anti-dehydration campaigns that work. There are, among a good many bureaucrats and Party munchkins, competent technical teams in every ministry. Above all, there is an institutional ability to organize, mobilize, and deliver, and it allowed the Organization of American States and the United Nations to set up electoral guidelines that would have been exacting by European standards, let alone Latin America's. The F.S.L.N. has trained so many young people in the Party discipline of punctuality and responsibility that, with UNO having to scrabble for months to dig up enough polling supervisors for Election Day, the Supreme Electoral Council had to staff most of its regional centers with Sandinistas. And, following their instructions from the Supreme Electoral Council to the letter, the regional-center heads went right on tallying and reporting the votes after they became aware that their party was losing.

• • •

THE PRESIDENT-ELECT of Nicaragua, Violeta Chamorro, claimed victory at 3:30 a.m., after Mariano Fiallos announced that thirty per cent of the votes were in and UNO had maintained its nearly fifty-four per cent of the total. Mrs. Chamorro, a stately woman with a high regard for the proprieties, had reportedly wanted to wait until after Ortega conceded, but as the night wore on and no word came from the Sandinistas it became clear that UNO had to lay claim to its spectacular victory or risk losing it. The Bambana Club was already bursting with campaign workers and an even larger number of reporters, and the UNO leadership had been celebrating on the dais for a couple of hours, when Mrs. Chamorro made her entrance, arms aloft, silver hair shining in the spotlights. There is no question among the people who voted for her or in the coalition that supported her candidacy that Mrs. Chamorro is a symbolic figure—she has trouble remembering the names of heads of state, and reads her prepared speeches with difficulty—but as figureheads go she's a pretty good one, and never had she been better than she was on that happy night. Radiant, she dropped the hectoring tone that dampens the spirits of her admirers at rallies. ("We are not rabble!" she will admonish a too enthusiastic crowd.) She spoke loudly and clearly, and, after months of a campaign that was nearly as bitter and divisive as the Contra war, she spoke generously of peace and reconciliation. "All Nicaraguans have triumphed today," she declared. "We have given the world a magnificent example of civic spirit. . . . Among all of us, we have achieved the first democratic election in the country's history . . . and we will, God willing, produce a peaceful change of government."

Violeta Chamorro is the widow of Pedro Joaquín Chamorro, a combative newspaper editor who was assassinated—almost certainly on Somoza's orders—in January, 1978. The country was then already in ferment, and his murder added coals to the insurrectionist fire the Sandinistas were fanning. Because he belonged to the moneyed élite, and because the record of that sector's fight against the Somoza dictatorship is skimpy, there has lately been an effort to appropriate Pedro Joaquín as a leader of the private sector, which he actually looked down on, and to present his murder as the single outrage that ignited the anti-Somoza insurrection. But this is a version of events that not even his immediate family can agree on: the Chamorro son Carlos Fernando and daughter Claudia, who are high-ranking F.S.L.N. members, vehemently refute it. Pedro Joaquín Chamorro was nevertheless so important to the insurrection that his widow was invited to join the Sandinistas' first coalition junta. She is said to have felt slighted and manipulated in that role, and to have been shocked by the F.S.L.N.'s secret socialist agenda. When she resigned, in 1980, she immediately went over to the opposition, where another son, Pedro Joaquín, Jr., was drawing the battle lines at *La Prensa*, the family newspaper.

She made sure she would not suffer similar vexations when she agreed to lead the campaign of fourteen tiny, squabbling parties that initially formed UNO: her daughter Cristiana's husband, Antonio Lacayo, became her campaign director; Antonio Lacayo's brother-in-law Alfredo César led the list of candidates for the National Assembly; and Pedro Joaquín, Jr., who had served as a director of the Contras, was an adviser. Thus securely supported, she grew in confidence as the campaign progressed. It is hard to imagine that UNO would have had its victory without Violeta Chamorro's energy, striking looks, and moral authority.

They were all on the dais that night—Lacayo, César, Cristiana, and Pedro Joaquín, Jr., laughing with and embracing former Contra leaders, like Azucena Ferrey. The embraces included even Vice-President-elect Virgilio Godoy, a temperamental man, whose relations with the Chamorro clan are notoriously poor. (The tensions came to a head on February 4th, when Godoy's chief campaign adviser, in full view of the television cameras, punched Lacayo in the stomach in a dispute over precedence.) Godoy is the head of the Independent Liberal Party, one of the larger minority parties, with representation in the National Assembly, and after a long struggle it was decided to give him the Vice-Presidency over Enrique Bolaños, the former head of the Private Sector Supreme Council. Bolaños thereupon took off for

Miami, and he withheld the Council's endorsement of Mrs. Chamorro until the last minute. He still refuses to shake hands with Godoy.

"There were months of arguing and fighting to create the coalition," I was told by a diplomat who monitored UNO's evolution closely. "And then more arguing over the platform. They couldn't agree on whether they should settle first on the candidate or on the platform. They tried to set up platform committees for a while, and that didn't work. They were always late for the deadlines set by the Supreme Electoral Council, and sometimes they missed them. Everything evolved in a very 'Nica' way." But the diplomat was not worrying about how Mrs. Chamorro would preside over her unruly group, or how the unlikely alliance of orthodox Communists, Christian Democrats, and aging Conservatives would share power and govern. "UNO at this point is Violeta," he said.

"I am in charge here," Doña Violeta has taken to saying in press conferences and interviews, but one wonders. She certainly has authority over her immediate family, but there is no question that most political decisions, large and small, continue to be made by her son-in-law, Antonio Lacayo, and who elected him? Then there is the issue of her health: Mrs. Chamorro suffers from advanced osteoporosis and has been in a wheelchair ever since she broke a knee in January. She stopped campaigning altogether that month while she went to Houston for treatment, and she left for Houston again last week. Will she be able to take real command of the government on April 25th?

The Sandinistas are hoping that she will. In the blinding light of the reality forced upon them on Election Day, they have decided they like Mrs. Chamorro and her family, particularly Antonio Lacayo. He is not a politician, they say, and that is precisely the advantage he has over the real UNO crowd: "He is moderate, pragmatic, efficient," one Sandinista official told me. "He is one of the most successful businessmen this country has ever known." Unlike his brothers-in-law Alfredo César and Pedro Joaquín, Jr., Lacayo never joined the rubber-stamp leadership of the National Resistance, as the Contras eventually came to call themselves.

He stayed in Nicaragua and added to the family fortune with a diversified portfolio: agroindustrial complexes here and in Costa Rica and Mexico, the oil-processing firm Gracsa, which is a successful mixed-capital operation, and a share in one of Managua's most popular restaurants.

"We think he is aware of how dangerous the situation is, and we think we can work with him to defuse the bomb we are all sitting on," this same Sandinista official said, echoing many others. In fact, there is hardly anyone in the country who is not aware of the dangers involved in completing a transition of power before April 25th, and of the equally grave situation the new government will have to face; one reason the UNO victory celebrations have been so low-key is that even its most furiously anti-Sandinista supporters know how little there is to be happy about. A few days after the election, I went to talk to a Latin-American ambassador with firsthand experience of the ruin a government can come to when it is unable to meet a desperate population's impossible hopes—the food riots and general popular insubordination, the military pressures, and the foreign-debt burden that can make a country ungovernable. "There are reasons to be pessimistic," he said. "It's not as if this is a transition of power between two parties that believe in the same basic system and agree on the rules of the game. We're dealing with two different concepts of what Nicaragua should be. To the degree that the Sandinistas perceive that their essential conquests—everything that gave their struggle meaning and content—are questioned, modified, or altered, they will react very strongly. The Army, for example. The Sandinista Army is partisan, and during their rule this broke with a long Latin-American tradition of an autonomous Army that can step in with a coup at any point. For the Sandinistas the Army is essential, but from UNO's point of view it is intolerable."

So far, the F.S.L.N. has seemed willing to replace much of the military top command, including Defense Minister Humberto Ortega and Interior Minister Tomás Borge, if suitably neutral substitutes can be found, but they could backtrack at any moment. "You can't ask the Sandinistas to reduce the size of the

Army without a parallel reduction of all the Central American military," the ambassador said. "Doña Violeta seems amenable to the idea, but the United States has to be willing to help, too, by reducing its levels of military assistance in the region. Will they be willing to do that in El Salvador?"

Above all, the ambassador thought, the transition teams headed by Antonio Lacayo and Humberto Ortega (brother of the President) will have to find a formula that takes into account both sides' fears and insecurities, "and in that sense the United States will have to send a very clear signal to the effect that it will respect the true results of the elections: UNO's victory and the Sandinistas' presence as the largest and most coherent party by far. This hasn't happened yet." It would be dangerous, the ambassador went on, to try to ignore or provoke the Sandinistas. "There is a sense in which the F.S.L.N. didn't really lose, considering that they got forty per cent of the vote in an economic situation that very few governments could have survived."

Of course, whatever happens in the next twelve months in Nicaragua will be determined largely by factors beyond the direct control of any of the players. Even if Congress approves the half billion dollars in aid that Mrs. Chamorro's team requested and the Bush Administration has agreed to press for, the country's economy will still be desperate. How will Nicaragua replace the hundred and sixty thousand tons of oil provided every year by the Soviet Union? Who will step in with money for public housing like the thousand units now being built by Cuban construction workers in hurricane-struck Bluefields? The UNO economic plan calls for reprivatization of the thirty per cent or so of agricultural lands now in government hands. Where are the buyers quixotic enough to invest in this unstable, economically devastated country?

The key to the new government's stability lies with the Sandinistas, as the Latin-American ambassador pointed out. They can be a loyal if difficult opposition, or, if they feel their existence threatened, "they can be savage." The blanket amnesty announced this week covering virtually every official crime that might have been committed during the last ten years—from em-

bezzlement to murder—and the rush to legalize property seized
from Somoza and the private sector (homes for the Party leadership and tens of thousands of small plots for squatters) are further
examples of how recklessly incoherent the Sandinistas can be
when they feel threatened: calmly discussing the restructuring of
the Army at one moment, subverting the very idea of legality at
the next.

FOR DAYS NOW, the country has been in a post-earthquake sort
of daze, and the situation is so precarious that wherever people
gather the talk is of whether April 25th will arrive peacefully, or
whether there will be still more fighting. For the Sandinistas,
whose very survival as an organization is at stake, the stress has
been almost unendurable, and never greater than in the official
silence following Daniel Ortega's 6 a.m. speech. Radio Sandino,
the official Party voice, did not stop broadcasting during those
hours, however, and a steady stream of strident cries filled the
airwaves as lower-level cadres from all over the country called in,
begging the President to annul the elections, bring in the Army,
and summon the Sandinistas to defend the revolution.

Finally, on the Tuesday after Election Day, it was announced
that the F.S.L.N. National Directorate was meeting with its top
cadres, and that President Ortega would address the press corps
afterward. Immediately, Sandinista delegations from all over Managua converged on Omar Torrijos Plaza, outside the convention
center. When the plaza was filled to overflowing, it seemed just
like old times. The faithful were sucking in desperately needed
strength from their own numbers and the spectacle of their red-
and-black flags and insignia. The questions that had floated so
heavily in the air (What will happen to my job? What will become of the kindergartens? Is this the end of the party that has
meant my life and my purpose?) were soon replaced by chants.
There were vivas to the Sandinista Army and oaths of loyalty
to The Struggle. The prodigious loudspeakers materialized, and
Sandinista music blared to the rooftops. Daniel Ortega appeared.
"The change of government by no means signifies the end of the
revolution!" he shouted, and the crowd gave a vast roar of relief.

And then, for long minutes, he tried to say something he had never said during the campaign and that the crowd now did not want to hear: "We are certain that the majority of the people who gave their vote to UNO did not do so because they are counter-revolutionaries," he insisted, while the plaza filled with cries of "Down with the National Guard–UNO!" Ortega went on, "They did so because they thought they could improve their situation with the opposition." In a divided country, Daniel Ortega was trying to speak of reconciliation to his most radicalized supporters, and he had a hard time shouting them down. Mrs. Chamorro will no doubt face similar difficulties with her UNO supporters at the beginning of what will be, if Nicaragua is lucky and both sides are uncommonly wise, a long, delicate, dangerous process of national rehabilitation.

Postscript, Nicaragua

AT THIS WRITING, Violeta Chamorro is into the third year of her six-year term. Her son-in-law, Antonio Lacayo, continues as de-facto Prime Minister. In a stunning reversal of roles, the Sandinistas have been until very recently Mrs. Chamorro's primary allies. Although Humberto Ortega resigned from the directorate of the Sandinista National Liberation Front in order to continue in his post as head of the Army, it is obvious to everyone that this was a formality, and that the Sandinistas retain full control of the Army and significant control of the police.

Most of the President's one-time coalition brethren in the UNO are now bitterly opposed to her, and yet, despite occasional riots and constant *sublevaciones* by disaffected Army members and embittered Contra fighters, the stability of the Chamorro administration has never been seriously in question, because the Sandinistas have been behind it in all their strength. They have the weapons and, with the help of a handful of UNO *diputados* who remain faithful to Chamorro, they also control the legislative assembly. Astonishingly, despite bitter and deep disagreement within its ranks, the Sandinista Party remains formally united, making it, still, the most powerful political force in the country.

Nicaraguans, whose numbers grew from 2.6 million to four million since the overthrow of Somoza, now have the second-lowest per-capita income in the hemisphere, after Haiti. A long campaign waged by Senator Jesse Helms in the United States Congress successfully held up most of the reconstruction money promised by the United States to help repair the damage of the Contra war. It was finally released this year—some six hundred million dollars, which will not go very far. There is simply no economic activity to build on, unless one counts a few car dealerships and supermarkets, and the multiplying numbers of street venders. According to the Washington Office on Latin America, sixty per cent of the population is unemployed or underemployed.

In the weeks immediately following their electoral defeat, before Violeta Chamorro took power, the Sandinistas proceeded to loot the state in a frenzy of revenge, fear, and sheer greed that is now remembered by every Nicaraguan as "the piñata." Sandinista revolutionary leaders and apparatchiks exchanged every shred of their painfully won *autoridad moral* for a car, a house, a computer, or a plot of land. Within the Party, the failure to come to terms with this event is the source of the deepest divisions. Outside the Party, it leaves the Sandinistas' electoral future very much in doubt. After the devastating years of revolutionary turmoil and U.S.-sponsored war, the best the widow of Pedro Joaquín Chamorro and the party of Sandino had to offer their followers was a little stability. It is probably the most that could realistically have been hoped for in this gutted, demoralized country, and it is not nearly enough.

MEXICO CITY
1990

"This is not a healthy place."

GARBAGE HAS BECOME an obsession for the inhabitants of Mexico City, spawning any number of fantastic stories, all of them true. There is, for example, the story of the open-air garbage dumps that spontaneously ignited one day in July, spreading fire and toxic fumes over acres of refuse stacked twenty yards high. There is the story of the cacique who controlled more than half the city's seventeen thousand-odd *pepenadores*, or garbage pickers, demanded sexual favors from the garbage pickers' daughters, and also took all his workers off to Acapulco on vacation once a year. There is the story of a sixty-square-mile garbage dump that the city government decided to turn into a park, complete with picnic tables—tables that have since been sinking gently into the settling layers of trash and loam.

Then, there are the rats. One of the most memorable stories dates from the beginning of the decade, when an evening paper announced above the fold that a "giant mutant rat" had been discovered floating dead in a sewage canal. The article said that the rat was the size of a Volkswagen, and in the accompanying photo one could verify the caption's claim that the beast had "the face of a bear, the hands of a man, and the tail of a rat." Two days later, a morning paper explained that the corpse belonged to a lion owned by a three-flea travelling circus. The old thing had finally died, but before throwing the corpse into the sewage canal the owners had decided to skin it, in case the pelt proved salable. Purists among those who collect accounts of Mexican trash dismiss this story on the ground that it turned out to be false, but the point is not that the mutant rat was a figment but that in the general state of decay and disrepair of one of the world's most overburdened cities many of us who read the story assumed at the time that it was true. The fact is that once started on the subject most city residents can come up with giant-rat stories of their own, and few are more convincingly told than the one offered by Iván Restrepo, a genial scholar of garbage who directs a government-financed institute for ecological research called the Centro de Ecodesarrollo. Five years ago, in Chapultepec, the city's most popular public park, Restrepo and his center mounted an exhibit on the subject of garbage. A tent, designed by an artist, had a long, dark entrance, filled with giant illustrations of microbes and garbage-related pests, from which the public emerged into "the world of garbage." One of the exhibits, Restrepo said, was "the most gigantic rat we could find."

Dr. Restrepo was telling his story in one of Mexico City's best restaurants, and he interrupted himself briefly to order roast kid, guacamole, and a millefeuille of poblano chilies and cream. "It was huge!" he went on, gesturing enthusiastically. The rat, one gathered, must have been about the size of a large cat. "It weighed almost eight pounds. But we had a problem. We began to realize that the rat was dying on us. It wasn't used to the nice, healthy pet food, or whatever it was, that we were feeding it. So we went out and collected fresh garbage for it every evening. Kept it happy. And that was important, because thousands and thousands of people came to see the garbage exhibit, and the rat was the absolute star of the show."

If *capitalinos*—the residents of Mexico City—flock to an exhibit on garbage featuring large vermin, it is because the subject is never very far from their minds. The problem of waste disposal may be only one of the critical aspects of the city's ongoing public-services emergency, but it is certainly among the most pressing. One of the world's three largest urban conglomerates, the city never had a proper service infrastructure to begin with and has been growing too much too fast for too many years. Figures from the 1990 national census show that although the Federal District, or capital proper, has a relatively stable population of 8.2 million, the surrounding sprawl in the neighboring state (also called Mexico) brings the total urban population to sixteen million. This is triple the 1965 estimated total, and the rate is not slowing. By the year 2000, if current trends persist, the urban area will be home to twenty million souls, all clamoring for services that are already strained to the breaking point in some areas and nonexistent in others.

Not only are services dangerously insufficient but there is almost no way to expand them. Water is now piped in from as far as fifty-five miles away. Ringed by mountains, the urban area is also gasping for fresh air. At least fourteen tons of waste, including lead, carbon monoxide, and what is known euphemistically as the products of "open-air fecalization," now floats in what the city breathes every day. Visibility has improved markedly since late last year, when the government passed a law restricting circulation of a fifth of the city's 2.5 million vehicles each weekday, but, because public transport is also in an awful state, car owners are now buying spare vehicles to use on the day their regular cars aren't allowed out. The poor, who can't afford any car at all, can spend as much as four hours a day travelling between the outlying shantytowns and their urban workplaces: the metro system, which has seventy miles of track and provides more than four million rides a day, serves only a small part of the Federal District, which covers some five hundred and seventy-nine square miles, and the same is true of the crowded, aging buses that spew their fumes along the city's uncharming streets. Twelve million more rides are provided by a network of *colectivos*—privately operated minivans and small buses—which clog traffic and gouge working-class salaries. And the deep-drainage system—nine miles of cavernous tunnels and thousands of miles of pipes, hailed as an engineering marvel when it was inaugurated, barely fifteen years ago—is now hopelessly overloaded, as anyone knows who saw the sewers backing up during each of this summer's downpours.

Bad as the city's public-service difficulties are, most of them appear to have fairly straightforward solutions: build more subways, install more phones. Not trash. The question is not how to put more of anything in but how to reduce the sheer bulk of what exists. The poor, who constitute the vast majority of Mexico's population, have lately produced almost as much waste as the rich; eager initiates into the world of junk consumerism, they find some consolation for their fate in the First World's plastic-encased gewgaws. And although the city has so far heroically managed to keep more or less abreast of the growing tonnage of waste, cleanup-service problems merely have their beginning in the dumps. Here Mexico's First and Third Worlds meet and fester. Rats are the least of it. There is pollution and, above all, the tangle of human misery and political intrigue represented by a peculiar sector of Mexico's body politic—the thousands of *pepenadores*, and their leaders, who stand in the way of neat solutions.

CONTEMPLATING THE LOVELY CITY of Tenochtitlán, rising from the now vanished waters of Lake Texcoco, the conquistadores marvelled not only at the personal cleanliness of the inhabitants but at the immaculate streets that fanned out in an orderly grid from the great plaza, now occupied by the National Palace and the Cathedral. The Aztec people could hardly conceive of waste: they used cornhusks to wrap food in and inedible seeds to manufacture percussion instruments. All organic waste went into the compost-filled rafts with which the Aztecs compensated for their lack of agricultural land. Each street was swept clean every morning, and the day's cargo of excrement was deposited in a special raft tied at the street's end.

By contrast, colonial Mexico was a filthy place, but the long-term accumulation of waste did not really become a problem until after the 1910 revolution, which yanked the Indian population out of self-sufficient subsistence economies and into the world of buying, selling, and discarding. In the nineteen-forties, when the economy finally stabilized after the long devastation of civil war, consumerism made its first inroads. Waste multiplied. Each month, thousands of peasants abandoned their land and came to the capital looking for a better life. By the nineteen-sixties, urban prosperity had proved to be a mirage, but the situation in the countryside was infinitely worse, and the mass urban migration continued. The newcomers settled in shacks along the roads leading into the city, stole their electricity from the highway power lines, and made do without running water, drainage, or garbage-collection systems. The communities grew at such a rate that one of them, Ciudad Nezahualcóyotl, is the country's fourth-largest city. Thoroughly integrated by now into the consumer economy, its million-plus inhabitants carry their groceries home in plastic bags, use their spare change to buy hair spray, splurge at United States–based fast-food chains on soda pop served in plastic-foam cups, and pour milk for their children from plastic-coated-cardboard cartons. The intractable accumulation of mixed waste—rotting, toxic, and non-biodegradable—generated by this fraction of the Third World's urban poor can be contemplated at the Bordo de Xochiaca municipal dump, on the southern edge of what was once Lake Texcoco, and a few blocks away from Nezahualcóyotl's city hall. Not many who pass by it linger; the stench causes motorists to accelerate way past the speed limit, and in their haste they may fail to notice what is most striking about this vast expanse of putrefaction. Scarecrow-like figures can be seen moving slowly over the dusty mounds, poking methodically. The garbage is inhabited.

The best view of Bordo de Xochiaca is from the driver's seat of a tractor that is used all day long to flatten out the incoming loads. From this vantage point one can look north across the clay-colored lake bed to the volcano-ringed horizon. In the opposite direction, the garbage dunes recede for half a mile to Ciudad Nezahualcóyotl. A few people work the edges of the dump, and a few others live in plastic-and-cardboard shanties there, but most of the dump's activity takes place in a clearing in the center—where people try to sift through a newly deposited truck-load of garbage before the tractor runs over it—and in an

expanse just to the west of this clearing, where Celestino Fernández Reyes, the dump boss, weighs and purchases the scavengers'
daily take of glass, rags, tin, cardboard, wood, plastic containers,
animal bones, and other recyclable materials. Behind the scales
and Celestino's headquarters, a row of shacks marks the beginning of the living quarters—scores of lopsided houses, some of
them quite large, that are built of and on rubbish, along reeking
alleys and paths with names like Virgin of Guadalupe Lane.

It proved a little difficult to get into Bordo. At a sentry gate
set between two small hills of garbage, a stocky man in dark
glasses, jeans, and cowboy boots waved in a procession of trucks
and quite a few mule-drawn carts—the latter belonging to the
Nezahualcóyotl municipal service and decorated with the red-
white-and-green logo of the nation's ruling party, the Partido Revolucionario Institucional, or PRI. The sentry said there was no
access to the public. As I argued with him, loaded trucks continued to file by, and the drivers of trucks not belonging to Nezahualcóyotl's municipal fleet stopped to press the sentry's hand,
which then flew to a pocket in his quilted vest. During the seconds required for these transactions, children climbed up on the
trucks' back wheels and then onto the loads of refuse, and as each
truck moved past the gate the children scrabbled frantically
through the load, throwing things overboard; they would return
to collect them as soon as the truck reached the dumping site,
which is invisible from the gate, being hidden by hills of piled-
up trash. Eventually, the sentry agreed to let me in for a brief visit.

After a week of rain, the pickers were working ankle-deep in
a thick slush; it was tinted blue or bright red in patches, and these
exhaled a mist of choking chemical fumes. Oblivious of the
smell, a cluster of children crouched in a blue puddle, poring over
a small pile of plastic comic-book figures—the Joker, Superman,
and the like. The children did not want to talk to a stranger (indeed, they avoided even looking at me), but after I made a couple
of tries the tallest boy answered a question, saying that he and
his friends wanted the toys not to play with but to sell. Nevertheless, as they salvaged the few dolls that had no arms or legs miss-

ing they deployed them in a brief, soundless mock battle before tossing them into a scavenging sack.

One of Celestino's overseers waved each arriving truck to a spot on the edge of the clearing, where a family or a team of friends was waiting, each member equipped with only a long-handled pitchfork, and no boots, masks, or other protective gear. The team began sifting through the waste even before the truck's shower of refuse ended, expertly plucking out the salvageable bits with their bare hands. The fork was designed to help the pickers separate the mounds of trash on the ground, but an elderly man in faded blue overalls said that since the tractor had been brought in there was hardly any time for the garbage to pile up, so a lot of salable material was left unsalvaged. (The tractor was somebody's idea of a landfill operation, but since the garbage wasn't covered with anything after being flattened out it seemed to serve no practical purpose.)

The garbage pickers proved to be a closemouthed lot, especially when I asked their names or put questions about Celestino, but the man in overalls was willing to explain the various stages of trash-picking. "You have to know what to select," he said, working with precision and delicacy as he talked. "For example, this pair of trousers is good, because the buttons and zipper can be removed and sold. If they were made of natural fibre, like cotton, you could sell the cloth as rag. There are a lot of tennis shoes in this pile, but they're not good enough to sell to the secondhand-clothes dealers." He was picking through a revolting pile of what seemed to be the refuse of a very large family, but by the time the things he had chosen to keep reached his sack they looked almost clean. He waved toward a point in the rubbish heap which I found indistinguishable from its surroundings. "That's my spot," he said. "When I'm through for the day, I take my sack over there and sort it. It's not enough just to pick the garbage. We have to put work into it afterward to make it salable."

A truck unloaded a pile of refuse from what someone said was an open-air market—a cascade of burst tomatoes, crushed bananas, empty egg crates, clear plastic bags, and wadded-up vegetable peelings. None of it was rotting yet, but, according to a group of women and children investigating the pile, there was nothing of any use other than a score of orange halves that had had most of their pulp pressed out of them, and that one woman picked up and immediately began eating.

I struck up a conversation with another member of the team, a woman with long gray braids who was wearing a clean checked apron over a faded dress. She told me that in general market waste was virtually worthless, except for an occasional pile of butcher-shop bones, which gelatin and bouillon-cube manufacturers would buy. Other pickers were saving the organic waste for pigs they kept along the edges of the dump, but she said she didn't own any. While quite a few of the garbage pickers looked filthy, her clothes, I noticed, were not only clean but crisply ironed. "I used to wash clothes for a living," she explained. "But now my arms can't take being in the water so long." The sun was directly overhead, and hitting hard, so the smells around us—acetone, vegetable rot, used disposable diapers—ripened and concentrated in the heat. Several of the workers had stopped for a noonday snack at a lopsided tent made of bits of plastic and wood, but the woman told me she would not buy the potato chips or lemonade available there. "The younger people make more money, but I can only clear about five or six thousand pesos a day," she said. Six thousand pesos is about two dollars. "I get here at ten or so, and work as long as my arms and legs can stand it. Then I eat when I get home." Soon, she said, she would carry her sacks, one at a time, to the weighing area and collect her pay from Don Celestino. Then she would try to make the hour-long walk back to her squatters' community before the afternoon rains started.

Others told me they lived near the weighing area, in shacks made of salvaged cardboard, plastic, and tin. Mexico's continuing economic crisis is constantly expelling residents from Ciudad Nezahualcóyotl, where they can no longer afford to pay rent, mortgage, or utilities. Many are emigrating to the edge of the urban sprawl, where they must begin life over again, as they did two decades ago in Ciudad Nezahualcóyotl—in bare fields, with no lights or other services. Some of the poorest, or frailest, of these exiles appeared to be ending up in Bordo. I walked away from the picking fields in the general direction of the dump's headquarters with a woman carrying a sack of glass jars which was almost as tall as she was. She lived a few blocks away, she said, but she couldn't afford the payments on her plot of land now that her husband was out of a job. Soon, if Don Celestino would permit it, she would move to the dump with her family. There was no electricity here, and the nearest public water faucet was a half hour's walk away, but at least it was free, and she wouldn't have to pay for transportation to get to work. "He's a very nice man," she said of the dump boss. "He doesn't charge anything for letting you live here. All you have to do is ask permission to come in, and promise to sell your material exclusively to him."

THOUGH IT IS ESTIMATED that some seventeen thousand people work in Mexico City's garbage dumps, no one has tallied the number that work in Bordo de Xochiaca and the other dumps in neighboring Mexico state—dumps that are for all practical purposes part of the same urban area, and so are often used by capitalinos. Like the cigarette peddlers, the street-corner fire-eaters and cartwheel turners, the windshield washers and parking space finders, the pot menders, the sidewalk violinists and portrait painters, the curtain-rod fixers, and the outright beggars who swarm through the city, the pepenadores are a result of Mexico's constant failure to find a social space for its very poorest. But, unlike millions of their fellows who also have to forage for each day's bread, they are a geographically stable population, tied to the arrival of a loaded truck. Their stability makes them easy to organize—a fact that the PRI, which has now been in power for sixty-one years, could not fail to notice. Throughout those years, the PRI has demonstrated a scavenger's genius for wasting nothing and no one, and a truly pre-Hispanic vocation for building pyramidal social organizations. Not long after Mexico City started producing serious amounts of garbage, the scavengers who flocked to it became small but extremely useful cogs in the PRI's political machine. Men like Celestino Fernández Reyes, who as a member of the PRI's Confederation of Popular Organizations became Bordo's overseer, make sure that the relationship between the Party and the scavengers is a smooth, productive one.

"Do you think I'm here for the pleasure of it?" Don Celestino asked me. "This is a terrible way to earn a living! Pickers can make good money—up to two hundred and forty thousand pesos a week. A lot of them have saved enough to move out of here and set up a little business on their own. Me, I have the thankless part. I have to fight with the buyers, keep prices up, go offering the pickers' wares from factory to factory. Plus, I'm a sick man, a diabetic, and this is not a healthy place. I would never have chosen to come here—I was doing fine buying glass from the dump—but the Party asked me to come and establish some order. 'Celestino, we need you here,' they said. So I came." Don Celestino is rumored to be a wealthy man, but his office is a one-room, tin-roofed brick house in the heart of the dump, furnished with a cot, two rusting metal chairs, and a makeshift desk. A small, trim man with extraordinarily liquid dark eyes, he dresses neatly but unostentatiously in a white guayabera and sporty blue slacks, and, until he relaxes, he moves and talks with meticulous humility. Our interview took place somewhat earlier than I had hoped. While I was wandering through the dump's residential area, trying to estimate the total population, and, to my surprise, discovering further paths and alleyways at every turn, a horse pulled up just behind me with a loud snort. Riding it bareback was a very beautiful youth with long hair and cold eyes. He demanded my business. I answered that I was looking for Don Celestino, and he said firmly that he would escort me to him.

In his dilapidated office, Don Celestino gradually lost his air of subservient courtesy as he explained the garbage market. He made it clear that the *pepenadores* were utterly dependent on him. "It's not that they can't transport their salvage to the factories," he said. "A lot of the buyers have warehouses right across the highway from here. But who's going to pay any kind of price for a dozen empty bottles?" In his own eyes, he was the community's benefactor. "I brought a doctor in here to look after the pickers full time. She charges for the visit, but who do you think pays for the medicines? Me!" He didn't smoke, he didn't have the face of a heavy drinker, and he kept a close watch on prices and profits. "Times are hard!" he exclaimed. "It used to be that factory owners came after me looking for things to buy, but ever since Salinas de Gortari"—the nation's President—"came up with his free-trade policies we've been getting undercut by United States waste products. There's trains and trains of them coming in! And, you know, American products are always better. The gringos are selling clean, nicely tied-up cardboard, and they're selling it cheap. Who would want ours? Now buyers are complaining that it's dirty, that often half the weight is moisture. I bought cardboard at three hundred pesos a stack the other day, and I couldn't get rid of it for a hundred and fifty. I tell you, I don't know how I let the Party talk me into this."

IN THE PAST, the PRI provided similar encouragement and support to Rafael Gutiérrez Moreno, a former garbage-truck driver who, in 1965, took over from his father as leader of the Mexico City garbage pickers. Gutiérrez Moreno turned his constituency into a rapid-response force at the service of his political sponsors. In the late nineteen-seventies, he also served briefly as an alternate member of the Chamber of Deputies, but after one term he chose to return to the political sidelines. Whenever a show of support was needed for the capital's appointed mayor, or for the President, or for a foreign head of state, Gutiérrez Moreno, known to his followers as El Líder, saw to it that his people were there, waving green-white-and-red paper flags or, it has been rumored, wielding billy clubs and metal pipes as part of the notorious Halcones (Falcons), who operated against strikers and student demonstrators in the early nineteen-seventies. In exchange, the authorities looked the other way as he tightened his hold on the pickers. In 1983, city officials ordered Gutiérrez Moreno to close down his fiefdom, the vast dump of Santa Cruz Meyehualco. A fire that had raged there for five days in 1981 and reports that toxic chemicals were leaching through the trash into the city's water supply contributed to the decision. Gutiérrez Moreno negotiated room for half his followers at the city's second-largest dump, in the western part of the city, and moved the rest to land he had acquired east of Santa Cruz, in the district of Santa Catarina. El Líder, who was reported to distribute as much as ten million pesos a day in bribes around the city bureaucracy, built himself an extravagantly appointed house on the Santa Catarina grounds; he also built housing there for the workers which was significantly better than the garbage hovels at the old dump. He paid for drinks and decorations for yearly fiestas, and it was he who took everyone off once a year for a beach holiday. All that, however, did nothing to diminish his reputation as a singularly heartless exploiter of the garbage pickers' penury. He punished them if they left the dump grounds, by cutting back on their allotment of garbage or by beating them, and—again, according to published rumor—assassinated those who questioned his leadership. In pursuit of his declared goal of fathering a hundred and eighty children, he took his pick of the community's teen-age girls, including his nieces. (Forty-five offspring have been legally recognized so far.)

Héctor Castillo, who wears a ponytail and plays drums with a pretty good rock band, is a social scientist, and he has spent a considerable amount of time trying to figure out how garbage communities and their caciques come into being. He began his research on the man he describes as "the most powerful of all the country's urban caciques" a decade ago, by sneaking past watchmen into Gutiérrez Moreno's dump several times, and he has since worked and drunk with the *pepenadores* often. At the heart of the problem, as he sees it, is Mexico's finely wrought system of intermediation between the ruling party, the government, and the citizenry. "Mexico's system is patrimonial, and that means that it operates through concessions, from top to bottom," Castillo says. "The garbage-collection concession is granted to the Federal District's Sanitation Department. From that point on, a number of subsidiary choices have to be made: whose trucks are going to collect the wealthiest garbage—the residential-zone garbage, with its mattresses and wine bottles and discarded clothes—and who is going to drive those trucks, because, of course, these things are scavenged by the truck crew long before they reach the dumps. At each step in the process where there is money to be made, a concession is granted, and at the end of the line are the garbage caciques, who tie the whole system together securely, and declare that the garbage is in its place, that the city is clean, and that its politicians are even cleaner."

This is probably a fair description of a system that is now dying: for most of the century, the PRI has ruled Mexico through the web of patronage and concessions that Castillo describes. His account, though, leaves out the layer of commitment to social change underlying the regime's all-embracing populist rhetoric. For all its inefficiencies and other faults, the patrimonial system worked well enough to pull a largely rural and illiterate population into the twentieth century, insuring levels of education, health care, public services, and social mobility which comparable societies (Peru, Brazil, and Colombia, say) never achieved. For decades, Mexicans appeared to take equal pleasure in mocking the state—for its corruption, its verbosity, its ruthlessness, its endlessly scheming system of privilege—and in boasting of it to outsiders who failed to appreciate the subtleties of its achievements. The wily old PRI might have endured even longer in its pristine corporatist form except for three devastating blows. One was the economic bonfire provoked by José López Portillo, who, as President from 1976 to 1982, promised to "administer the prosperity" generated by Mexico's newfound oil wealth. With the glee of a nouveau tycoon leaping into a pool full of naked women, López Portillo plunged the whole country into a reckless and corrupt spending binge, which came to a disastrous halt only with the collapse of the international price of oil, in 1981. By the following year, Mexico's eighty-three-billion-dollar foreign debt was draining the government budget, and even the money to pay for things that Mexicans had come to consider their right—things ranging from adequate schools to cheap public transportation—was scarce. Then came the 1985 earthquake, in whose aftermath the government appeared merely corrupt and inept, while tens of thousands of citizen volunteers rescued the concept of an engaged society from the rubble. And then there were the 1988 elections, in which, largely as a result of the previous two crises, the PRI lost enormous numbers of votes to a new left-wing coalition. Many members of the foreign press who travelled through the country think that the PRI may actually have lost the election, but government officials angrily dismiss the charge as "nonsense." Still, the PRI certainly lost Mexico City, and even Ciudad Nezahualcóyotl and the area around it, where Gutiérrez Moreno had his power base.

The combined result of these crises has been to open the doors for a new élite, whose head and symbol is President Carlos Salinas de Gortari. He and his youthful band of highly trained economists and statisticians take pride in representing everything that the old-style *priistas* do not—they scorn the pork-barrel theory of politics, disdain bribetaking as lower class, play squash regularly, and sound reverent only when pronouncing the word *modernidad*—but they remain, for better or worse, members and leaders of the party that brought them to power. The tensions between the old-time corporatists and the new neoliberal technocrats may ultimately split the Party; for the moment, the two sides remain united, because neither can rule the country without the other. The newcomers need to keep the country running on a day-to-day basis while they implement a devastatingly painful program of structural economic reform. The Old Guard, for its part, senses that its methods may be bankrupt, but it must somehow start delivering results again if the Party is to avoid any more losses like its crushing electoral defeat in the capital's "circle of misery." As a result of such convergent renovating impulses, officials were desperately maneuvering to get rid of the lord of Mexico City's garbage pickers even before his death, in 1987, at the age of forty-eight.

Rafael Gutiérrez Moreno was shot to death in his own bedroom late one night, and his wife was sentenced to twenty-five years in prison for the crime. Gutiérrez Moreno had beaten her brutally ever since their marriage, ten years before, and had raped her sisters and nieces. She had many motives for attacking her husband, but so did any number of his subjects, and when the murder finally took place the only wonder was that someone had not done in El Líder long before. Héctor Castillo points out, however, that a community capable of fighting back could hardly have let itself become so abject in the first place. "Most of the garbage pickers have never known a different way of life," he says. "There are people here who are third generation. The pickers are born and grow up in the garbage fields. They have almost no schooling, and they know that their position in society is extremely weak." After Gutiérrez Moreno's death, the pickers proved incapable of choosing themselves a new leader—a situation that set off a battle for his political inheritance.

A colleague of Héctor Castillo's, Rosalinda Losada, has been following the succession struggle. She is a friendly, energetic woman who once spent some time picking garbage as part of the research for her graduate thesis, and she has struck up something of a friendship with El Líder's principal rival, the rather more genial Pablo Téllez. "When Gutiérrez Moreno had to move from his original power base to Santa Catarina, he sent nearly half of the other *pepenadores* to a dump at the opposite end of Mexico City, Santa Fe, then dominated exclusively by Téllez," she explained. "As his stand-in there Gutiérrez Moreno delegated someone known as El Dientón." (The name translates roughly as Bigtooth.) Téllez cannot have allowed El Dientón into his site willingly, since the partition effectively cut his own take in half, but he was almost certainly persuaded to do so by Gutiérrez Moreno's allies in the local government. "When Gutiérrez Moreno was killed, everyone thought El Dientón would replace him," Losada continued. "But then one of Gutiérrez Moreno's former wives appeared, out of the blue, to claim his inheritance. This wife—named Guillermina de la Torre—didn't even live in the dumps, and no one knew very much about her, but she seemed to have the support of a lot of local officials. Now the Gutiérrez Moreno *pepenadores* are divided into Guillermina's followers, at Santa Catarina, and El Dientón's, at a place called Prados de la Montaña, in the northwest of the city, built in the winter of 1986 to replace Santa Fe, which was overflowing by then."

Officials in the new city administration who are trying to

keep Mexico's garbage problem under control tend to get huffy
in the face of insistent questions about garbage picking, for they
have plenty of critical issues to worry about besides scavengers
and the leaders who control them. There is the ecological problem represented by the old, unplanned dumps, which may still
be polluting the groundwater and air in their vicinity. There is
the logistical problem of transporting garbage across the enormous, chronically congested capital city. And there is the question of the increasing volumes of garbage generated by what
Professor Restrepo defines as "this poor, underdeveloped society's
penchant for consuming like a first-class industrial power, with
everything wrapped in more and more layers of plastic." The director of Urban Services, José Cuenca Dardón, has his own list
of hurdles: "We are behind in every aspect of sanitation, including the concept of what the service should be and the legislation
surrounding the problem. If you add to this the social problem of
people whose livelihood for generations has consisted of garbage
picking, the issue becomes doubly complex. And we have to try
to solve it with our municipalities' extremely weak financial base,
historically backward infrastructure, and very poor citizen awareness." Politically, Cuenca represents the PRI's transitional stage; he
is not upper class or foreign-educated, and he deals comfortably
with the city's caciques, but he is a legendary compulsive worker,
who can speak about garbage with unremitting intensity for
hours at a stretch, reeling off figures and achievements that include the total number of kilometres of roadways swept clean
every night, the percentage of garbage processed by the city today versus the percentage a decade ago, the total number of trips
saved by a new system of transfer points. "We have learned," he
says, eyes shining. "Now we know how many sweepable surfaces
every main thoroughfare presents, and how many man-hours are
needed to sweep two- and four-lane roads."

CUENCA PACKED ME OFF on a tour of the city's garbage infrastructure, beginning with a visit to the new transfer points, where
small garbage trucks unload into trailers six times as large, and
including a new landfill, whose main virtue, the engineer in

charge of it said proudly, "is that it is garbage-pickerless." But
the garbage itself *was* being picked through, at every stage of its
collection and dumping, by Urban Services employees sensible
enough not to let anything go to waste. Along the noisy thor-
oughfares, I saw orange-clad street-sweepers busy setting aside
cans and bottles. A garbage truck pulled into a transfer point with
a six-seat sofa tied neatly across its bow. The point's supervisor
beamed. "We have very good-quality garbage here," he said. "It
comes from first-class neighborhoods." Spontaneous recycling
was taking place throughout the city. Then what was being left
for the real pickers?

"Practically nothing," said Luis Rojas, Bigtooth's second-in-
command, at my last stop on the official garbage tour. "The truck
drivers are stealing us blind, no matter that it was El Líder who
got them out of the dumps and onto the trucks in the first place.
Now they want to forget where they're from, and we're at war."
At the gate of the new Prados de la Montaña dump, I and a travelling escort of Urban Services officials had been met, in what is
known here as the best *oficialista* style, by a lineup that included
plant managers, chief engineers, Rojas, and Pablo Téllez, the man
who had been Rafael Gutiérrez Moreno's fellow-cacique and lifelong rival. Téllez turned out to be a bouncy, loquacious man, who
clammed up only when he was questioned about the practical
aspects of his business—how much he pays, and how he weighs
the pickers' merchandise. (Some time ago, Rosalinda Losada revealed in an article the unsurprising fact that the scales he uses
are fixed.) He shook hands amiably and chatted about the nice
new dump facilities. Standing next to him, and looking stead-
fastly in the opposite direction, was Luis Rojas. He wore a torn
pink-and-green polo shirt, with a heavy gold chain around his
neck and a few diamond rings on his fingers. He was uncomfortable talking in the presence of Téllez, with whom he was apparently not on speaking terms, but he did loosen up enough to
describe the truck drivers' unfair scavenging advantage and Bigtooth's betrayal by El Líder's former wife. And as we left he made
a little goodbye speech, saying that he had been pleased to see
us, particularly since this visit represented yet another instance

of coöperation between city officials and the pickers. "Because if that coöperation ceased to exist," he went on, "there's no way you could have got past the entry gate." The city's top sanitation technicians, who just moments ago had been so full of talk about sweepable surfaces and pickerless landfills, now nodded and smiled gently. A barrel-chested thug was proclaiming that they were at his mercy, and they stood there and took it, because he was right.

The true extent of the garbage lobby's power, which enables it to pervert official goals, was only too evident at our earlier stop, which represents Urban Services' most ambitious attempt at change: the vast new landfill is supposed to take over in five or six years as the city's only dump site. Although scavenging there is strictly forbidden, no alternative arrangement exists for making the site economically viable through an industrialized recycling operation. "We didn't really have time to put one in," a site engineer explained apologetically. "In reality, we decided to open this site very quickly to give ourselves some kind of negotiating leverage with Rafael Gutiérrez Moreno, who was getting a little out of hand. Once he saw this site, and understood that we were planning to do without him, he became more manageable."

"The fact is that there are two or three things you can't mess with in Mexico City," a city official remarked to me reflectively. Young, Harvard-educated, and as clean-cut a representative of the PRI's new whiz kids as can be found, he nevertheless seemed to have taken a crash course in pragmatics. "You can't touch the metro, the deep-drainage system, or garbage. Because, for better or worse, those things work, and the proof is that in this city, which is built on a lake, we've never suffered a major flood. But can you imagine what would happen if the sewer-system workers went on strike? It's the same thing with garbage. All things considered—that this is a Third World city in the middle of a financial crisis, that there are sixteen million people throwing tons of trash away every day—this is a clean city. But what would happen the day the garbage pickers shut down the dumps on us? Or if the truck drivers, most of whom have family ties to the pickers, went on strike? And you can't just solve the problem by removing the leaders; you have to find a way to replace them, or you'll have people killing each other just to get their own little garbage concession. We have to change things slowly, with the people we have."

Sometime in the not too distant future, if the Mexican economy improves, if desperate communities of scavengers cease to rise on the fringes of Mexico's cities, if the PRI relaxes its hold on power, the *pepenadores* and their rulers will vanish as one of the most shameful blemishes of this society. In the meantime, Mexico City's garbage *líderes* have played old-time PRI politics in masterly fashion, not only to ward off the unemployment that poses a threat when any significant modernization of the waste-disposal system is undertaken but also to obtain benefits for their constituencies which the garbage pickers at Ciudad Nezahual-cóyotl's Bordo dump—or at dumps in Bogotá or Santiago de Chile, for that matter—cannot yet dream of. A city official who was privy to all the talks between Urban Services and Gutiérrez Moreno and Téllez once told me that Téllez built his power base in city politics by playing good guy to the intractable Gutiérrez Moreno. While El Líder's people protested the move from the old Santa Fe dump nearby to the new Prados by setting fire to government property, Téllez decided to make a deal. Out of that negotiation came what is now the pride of the Urban Services Department: a *colonia*, or residential neighborhood, for some five hundred pickers and their families, just across the street from the dump. It has a kindergarten, a grade school, a market, and houses with electricity and running water, all of which are shared by Téllez's people and Bigtooth's people.

As we wandered through the immaculate stands of the *colonia*'s new market, admiring the produce and taking in the smell of freshly cooked tortillas at a stand operated by two former pickers, an Urban Services dump-site manager was obviously filled with pride. He had been involved in the move to the new housing compound from the beginning, he said, and he still couldn't get over the fact that at first the pickers had refused to move in, preferring to sleep in their old hovels and use the new houses as storage rooms. "Then they moved in and started scavenging the

houses," he went on. "They unscrewed everything that was re-
movable and sold it. They used the toilets to wash clothes in. We
decided to bring in a team of social workers, and they helped the
women adjust. They taught them things like home management,
personal hygiene, and how plumbing works. One day, we noticed that the families had actually begun to settle in, and several
of them had even bought real furniture to set up housekeeping
with." The grade school and kindergarten are now at least partly
occupied, though Luis Rojas is ambivalent about the dump's new
restrictions on child labor. "I suppose my children will do something different," he said, when I asked if he thought there would
be a fourth generation of *pepenadores* in his family. "Because, thanks
to the gentlemen you see here"—he pointed to the Urban Services officials—"our children under the age of ten are no longer
allowed to come in to work with us."

The brand-new *colonia* is the Mexican system at its old-time
patrimonial best and also at its most typically inefficient: the investment to build it was not small, but when the dump reaches
the scheduled end of its useful life, in two or three years, the
housing complex will probably become obsolete. This seemed a
quibble, though, on a recent sunny morning when I stood with
María de la Luz López in the living room of her two-bedroom
house and watched her point proudly to her kitchen, her bathroom, and her dining room, with its matched furniture and hard,
dry cement floor. Her two small children were watching television peacefully, and a washing machine was giving off a comforting hum. She was born in a garbage dump twenty-one years ago,
she said, and what she remembered most about the nineteen
years she spent there was the older women's horror whenever rats
climbed through the rubbish into the huts to bite the babies'
cheeks and fingers. Now she hoped that her own children might
study through ninth grade, and she was happy to stay home and
take care of them, because her husband earned enough at the
dump for all of them to get by on. "This house is very solid," she
said when I asked what she thought its chief merit was. "It doesn't
collapse." She waved goodbye to me from the doorway, next to
riotously blooming geraniums that an Urban Services social

worker had shown her how to plant, and I remembered a rather long lunch with the sociologist Héctor Castillo when he had said that the obsessive question for him was whom to blame for all the garbage pickers' misery. In the bright light of Mrs. López's home, an even more disturbing question arose: whom to thank for her new surroundings? Among the ghosts rising up to take a bow stood El Líder.

LIMA

1990

"They were like gods, hitting us and destroying everything."

LIMA IS PROOF that there are no knowable limits to what people will put up with. This desert city was not always noted chiefly for ugliness; throughout the centuries in which the Spanish viceroys of Peru sent thousands of tons of gold and silver to the ravenous mother country, Lima was frequently described as a garden. Squinting, on days when the weather is good, one can almost see the ways in which this place could have been lovely. A few carved wooden balconies still float above the bazaars of downtown Lima. The massive doorways of remaining colonial palaces, now converted to shabby arcades, hint at how cool the silence in their courtyards must have been. These days, though, there is only noise: the cries of money changers and street venders, the howl of traffic, the mighty blast of radio music coming from every store, and, beneath it all, the insistent rumbling of portable electric generators that are switched on during blackouts. Noisy and chaotic, the city cannot even be described as colorful. A persistent fog keeps the sky gray most of the year. Despite the humidity, everything is covered with a thick monochrome coating of dust, for it almost never rains here, and when it does the rain is a polluted drizzle that merely turns the dust to grime. "Lima the Horrible," the poet César Moro called it forty years ago, and that was before the desperate poor had begun their mass flight from the Andes and carpeted the city with their misery, invading the parks and public plazas of the most elegant seaside neighborhoods with anxious offers of cigarettes, Sublime chocolate squares, handknit magenta-and-blue striped socks, alkaline batteries, contraband Chilean wine, fake Inca funeral urns, four rolls of toilet paper for the price of one.

It is not only the poor who are concerned with survival; one result of Peru's current economic breakdown is that all Limeños have become obsessed by money—not by wealth or finance or by business deals but by plain cash, the way members of other consumer societies are obsessed by sex. Money sells, and is omnipresent. There are bank advertisements on television and in the press whose central image is not an attractive man or woman but simply a sheaf of dollar bills. Thousands of money changers occupy the city's busiest intersections, tying up traffic as they race from car to car proclaiming their rates. To attract clients, they wave a pocket calculator in one hand and a thick stack of money in the other, and a driver who thinks he has just heard a particularly good price quoted will bring his car screeching to a halt, the way comic-book characters used to do for blond bombshells. In restaurants, when a group of men gather for lunch an eavesdropper will find that the conversation is most frequently about how much the dollar exchange rate with the inti is likely to be next month, and whether a mutual acquaintance has discovered a new way to transfer money abroad. Two women who had obviously met for a long, comfortable lunch conversation at the table next to mine one recent afternoon soon found themselves discussing their electric bills in lengthy detail, and apologized to each other with wry smiles when they realized how they had been spending their time.

Peru has gone broke in a way few societies ever experience— a precipitate impoverishment that makes almost every aspect of daily life here continuously stressful. Many government employees have not received their salaries for weeks now. Members of Congress who want to use the official messenger service must pay for the gasoline for the motorcycles themselves. Lima's largest department stores are no longer open mornings. Traffic lights are missing their colored filters. When you turn on a faucet, you may get water and you may not. Food prices have climbed to the point where people will quote the price of chicken to each other and burst out laughing, but anyone who hoped to save money by buying food in bulk and putting it in a freezer has made a bad investment; blackouts, which are an everyday occurrence here, often last long enough to defrost the most icebound freezer. In any event, most of the population can't afford to buy food in bulk, much less an appliance to put it in: four out of every five Peruvians lack a steady job. According to the government, about eight million Peruvians—more than a third of the population—require emergency food assistance in order to survive.

Devastated by drought and unpredictable weather, ransacked by successive governments, bankrupt and inflation-ridden, Peru is not a place where the imposition of further economic hardship would have struck most people as a logical course of action. Yet last August 8th, twelve days after being sworn in as President of Peru, Alberto Fujimori did just that, with a *paquetazo*—"violent package"—of economic measures which has left the country reeling. Price subsidies that had been in effect for decades were ripped away overnight. The price of gasoline went from about thirteen cents a gallon to about three dollars and fifty cents. Food prices were allowed to float—thus the funny chicken, and the equally hilarious noodles, which zoomed from about forty cents a pound to more than a dollar. As a result of these measures, inflation, which had averaged an already intolerable 38.4 per cent a month for the preceding seven months, shot up to four hundred per cent for August. Meanwhile, the minimum wage (which most Peruvians, being unemployed, cannot aspire to) was fixed at the equivalent of forty-eight dollars a month. As one columnist wrote, the country had been put on a regimen of "Japanese prices on African incomes."

THERE IS NO INTENTIONAL cruelty in the government's program: the *paquetazo* is intended as a tourniquet for Peru's economic hemorrhage, which is the result of four and a half centuries of pillage and reckless mismanagement by all its previous rulers, in-

cluding the most recent, President Alan García, who tried to expand a receding economy by increasing government spending,
without covering the additional expense through higher taxes.
García, who is now in exile and facing corruption charges in
Peru, also took on the international banking community in 1989
by announcing that Peru would not meet its debt-payment obli-
gations. At the end of his term, Peru had been declared ineligible
for further international loans, its per-capita gross national product had shrunk by 13.7 per cent, net government reserves were a
hundred and forty-two million dollars in the red, and the yearly
inflation rate was twenty thousand per cent. Although these are
dismal figures, they are by no means unique to Peru. Throughout
Latin America, there are similar crises, and, for lack of a better
option, variants of the structural economic-reform program that
is now stunning Peru·have been tried in Bolivia, Venezuela, Argentina, and Brazil. The programs, which are referred to here by
the English word "shocks"—as in electroshock therapy—have
been designed and supervised largely by a handful of economists
from Harvard, the University of Chicago, and M.I.T. The aim of
a shock is to solve inflation by drastically raising prices and thus
reducing demand—a simple and natural idea in the United
States, perhaps, where crash dieting has become part of a culture
that regularly binges. In Peru, the impact and the consequences
of a sudden diet are somewhat different.

A woman I will call Amalia Huaycán lives on the other side
of the river that separates the main body of Lima from the squalid
townships of Rímac, San Juan de Lurigancho, and Canto Grande.
I met her in the Lurigancho municipal center—an uncommonly
cheerful place, in the shape of a large market courtyard, where
the various government offices are set like bustling shops around
a central area that boasts real grass, and even a couple of hibiscus
bushes. Beyond these grounds Lurigancho consists of bleak miles
of dusty paved streets that turn to unpaved roads and finally, as
they reach the desert hills that mark Lima's natural limits, to
nothing—no network to connect the dust-covered hill shacks
made of woven mats where the most recent squatters live. The
simple change of environment from such surroundings to the *mu-*

nicipalidad visibly lifts the spirits of most visitors as they enter, but on the day I met Amalia Huaycán she had remained severely upset. To counter the impact of its economic measures, the government had announced a new Social Emergency Program, known by its Spanish acronym as the PES, which was designed to provide assistance to the 7.6 million people who had been identified as "extremely poor." The new program called for a system of *ollas comunitarias*—community pots, or soup kitchens—to be run by local women with government-supplied ingredients. To start an *olla comunitaria*, however, one needed at the very least a pot, and a group of a dozen or so women who had gathered in the office of the vice-mayor, Ésther Rojas, were complaining loudly that large pots were going for thirty million intis wholesale, or about ninety dollars, and that even for those who already had pots to cook in, and stoves or kerosene burners to cook on, there was nothing to *cook*. The PES was completely disorganized, and no food donations at all had reached Lurigancho since the *paquetazo*.

Señora Amalia's situation was different. For the past six years, she had been administering a *comedor popular*, or people's cafeteria—one of more than a thousand community-based centers in Lima which depended on Caritas and other international charity organizations for donations of nonperishable foods. (The number has swelled to nearly seven thousand since August.) The *comedor's* sixty-odd members supplemented the donated oil and rice, and some other grains, with fish and vegetables that they bought with their own pooled resources. They sold the food they cooked, in a communally owned kitchen, at a price of about seven United States cents a plateful to members and twelve cents to outsiders. This system had not only nourished hundreds of thousands of people each day for several years but also provided the women running it with a forceful sense of self-sufficiency: they might be destitute, but they did not consider themselves beggars, and they were not powerless. Señora Amalia's *comedor* had pots, a large stove, and a working organization, put together with tireless effort over the years, but now she was afraid that her group was about to split apart, with many of the members lured to the government-sponsored soup kitchens by the offer of free food. Besides, the supplies that her *comedor* had been regularly receiving from Caritas in large amounts had dwindled to zero. Following the *paquetazo*, Caritas had been overwhelmed and almost paralyzed by the increased demand for donations: in Lima alone, demand had soared from five hundred thousand to one and a half million rations a day. When I called on Amalia Huaycán at her home, a few days after our first meeting, she was a nervous wreck: the need for the *comedor's* meals was greater than ever, but in its communal kitchen, across the road from her house, I counted eight carrots, twelve onions, half a small pumpkin, and five dozen small fish; with this, the *comedor* was supposed to feed between two hundred and fifty and three hundred people.

Amalia Huaycán is a Quechua, thirty-eight years old, and she is austerely beautiful, with sorrowful eyes and the Quechua people's etched features. The only time I saw her smile was when I asked if I might see her petticoats. In authentic Andean style, she wears four of them—two of plain cotton, two of flannel, all trimmed with crude lace—under a gathered felt skirt. Although the rest of her dress is modern and nondescript—a snug knit jacket, thick stockings, and sturdy boots—the effect is traditional. She speaks Spanish imperfectly and with a very strong accent; she says she learned it only six years ago, when she left her home, in the department of Ayacucho, and arrived in Lima as one of many thousands of refugees fleeing the war between the government and the guerrilla organization known as Sendero Luminoso, or Shining Path. Although Shining Path's leaders are not Indian, it found its first mass base of support in the Quechua-speaking native communities of the Andean highlands, where Ayacucho is situated. As a result, the region has taken the brunt of government repression.

Shining Path is a frightening quirk in the annals of guerrilla struggle. It is profoundly isolationist and sectlike. Its leader is a former university professor who calls himself Presidente Gonzalo; that is as if in the United States a messianic movement of fundamentalists armed with guns were led by somebody named President Fred. His followers are guided by the principles of Marxism-Leninism, Maoism, and something called Gonzalo

Thought—a web of exhortations and formulas so dense that its adherents are reduced to desperate initializing whenever they attempt the simplest report. "The EGP has been reduced to an FP, failing in its relationship between the MS and the power. The FP has been reduced, the FL sidestepped, and the FB contained." So went a recent complaint, confiscated by the police and reproduced in the local press. Typical Shining Path operations include selective assassinations, generally of minor local officials; lightning takeovers of isolated rural enclaves; and mass executions of hostile villagers. Its urban forces are known principally for their skill at dynamiting electric pylons—actions that account for those blackouts not provoked by system breakdowns and shortages. The movement has retained from its early days a remarkable appetite for cruelty, and one consequence of this is that its support appears to have dried up most quickly in areas where it was actually able to establish temporary rule. Some analysts think that Shining Path may already have reached the natural limits of its growth, peaking at around six thousand members, but its core group of supporters remains strong. Indeed, in the struggles between guerrillas and government Señora Amalia did not give an impression of neutrality, much less of sympathy for the official side. By this time, the question of whether she became impenetrably hostile to the government before or after she became a refugee is almost irrelevant: the fact is that at some point she became hostile enough to refuse to vote in the recent Presidential elections, even though refusal to vote is against the law and has deprived her of a validated voting card, the most common form of identification in Peru.

Amalia Huaycán says she lost a brother, a brother-in-law, and a cousin in 1986, during massacres in the nearby Lurigancho prison and in the offshore penitentiary known as El Frontón, when two hundred and eighty inmates who were Shining Path members or suspected sympathizers were killed by military forces following an attempted uprising. By the time that happened, she says, she herself had spent a year and a half in a succession of the country's prison facilities, having been shuttled from rank municipal jails to various federal prisons while the file

on her case was lost, reprocessed, and, finally, annulled. "The police landed with guns and helicopters," she told me, recalling her
arrest on her Ayacucho farm. " 'Where is your husband?' they
said. 'If you don't tell us, we'll kill you and throw you in the river.'
We wept, but they were like gods, hitting us and destroying everything." After her release from prison, where her youngest
child was born, she came to Lima. "At home, we had corn, beans,
sheep, cattle, goats," she said. "Here there was only dust and
straw huts. I spoke only Quechua. Little by little—conversing,
weeping with the other women, asking 'Why are you here?' and
'Why have you come?'—we discovered that all our stories were
alike. We took part in the land invasions"—as squatter activities
are called—"and formed our communities here, and the *comedores*.
Our *comedor* is principally for the wives and mothers and widows
of political prisoners and the disappeared, and for orphans."

Not surprisingly, Señora Amalia thinks that the aid cutoff for
her *comedor* is politically motivated, and also that it is the result of
a long battle of whites against Indians. "That's why society in
Peru doesn't progress," she said. "People aren't allowed to work
independently. There's always domination. We in the highlands
didn't belong to any institution, and so the government began to
push us aside. Here in the community, it's the same thing: 'Those
people from the mountains, we're going to get rid of them. Those
Indians, those *cholos'*—citified Indians—"'let's get them out. Limeños are going to be in charge here.'"

Juan José Alva, who is a Limeño, said that the vast majority
of some forty thousand people who have settled in this corner of
Lurigancho are war refugees, like Amalia Huaycán, but he himself constitutes evidence that in Peru one does not have to be an
Indian to be penniless. He is the local director of a government
antituberculosis program, and as we talked, in a minute room that
serves as the program's medical headquarters and administrative
center, he frequently interrupted himself to dispense medicine or
advice to one or another of about thirty people under his care,
performing his duties so efficiently and knowledgeably that I assumed he was a doctor. He laughed at the suggestion, and said
he was a nurse's orderly—and, like everyone around us, a squat-

ter, who in 1984 had been part of a pioneer group of "invaders" of the land where he now lived, with his wife and two children. Following the *paquetazo*, his net income after taxes came to nineteen million intis a month, slightly more than the minimum wage. "That is six hundred and thirty thousand intis a day," he said, and he ticked off some figures. "Ten small bread rolls for breakfast and dinner cost a hundred and fifty thousand. The litre of kerosene we use for cooking is thirty thousand. When the water truck comes by, we fill our tank with two hundred litres of water, and that lasts about four days—that is, seventy-five thousand intis' worth of water a day. That leaves three hundred and seventy-five thousand intis—about eighty cents—for the four of us to prepare three meals a day with. I am poorly nourished, and I am in daily contact with people infected with tuberculosis. My wife can't help out with our income, because she doesn't have a job. She couldn't get one if she tried—there's no work even for professionals, much less for those of us who are nothing."

The suffering imposed by the government on people like Señora Amalia and Juan José Alva may be inevitable, but the point for them, each said, is that when people cast their vote for President Fujimori last June they did so precisely because the other Presidential candidate was proposing a program similar to the one they are now enduring, and, whatever the greater economic logic of such a measure might be, they wanted nothing to do with it.

ALBERTO FUJIMORI'S unsuccessful opponent happens to have been Mario Vargas Llosa, who, it can be argued, has, through his writing, brought his country more prestige than any other Peruvian, living or dead. When and why Vargas Llosa decided that being President of Peru was a worthier task than producing fine novels is a matter of debate, but from the moment his unofficial candidacy was floated, in 1987, until a month before the elections, there was little doubt here or abroad that he would achieve his goal. The saga of the unravelling of his candidacy, and his spectacular defeat by a complete political novice, is extraordinary, and all the more so because the strength of feeling

against the elegant writer and his neoconservative political program might have been foreseen by someone who understands
Peru as well as his novels suggest that he does. In fairness to Vargas Llosa, it must be said that even the people who ended up
voting en masse against him appeared willing to support him for
a while. His unofficial campaign began with a political meeting
in September of 1987; Vargas Llosa was one of a group of prominent conservatives who gathered in downtown Lima's Plaza San
Martín to denounce Alan García's attempted nationalization of
the banking system, but when, dark-eyed and well groomed, he
stepped to the microphone to talk about democracy, and how
the bank takeover would be the beginning of the end of democracy, it became clear that the event had been only a backdrop
for his political début. Cynical onlookers found his speech less
remarkable than the way his upper-class supporters rented suites
in the plaza's Hotel Bolívar so they could observe the event without having to rub shoulders with the *cholos*. Yet once the official
campaign got under way, in August of last year, the novelist came
out well enough in the polls. After all, there really was no one
else. In February, a survey by Datum, a Lima polling firm, showed
that Vargas Llosa had a forty-two-per-cent approval rating. Luis
Alva Castro, the candidate of APRA, which was the ruling Peruvian
party, and had been hurt by the disastrous rule of Alan García,
placed twenty-seven points behind him. One leftist candidate,
Henry Pease, was having trouble getting his campaign off the
ground, and another, Alfonso Barrantes, who had been a highly
popular mayor of Lima in the mid-nineteen-eighties, was going
down in flames. Potential voters barely registered the existence
of a series of lesser candidates—including a self-styled prophet
called Ezequiel, and an agronomical engineer of Japanese descent—giving them, lumped together as "others" in the poll results, three per cent of their favor. That was less than eight weeks
before the election.

"You know how when you walk into a cloud of mosquitoes
you hear nothing but the buzzing?" Hernando de Soto said
to me. "That's how I heard the name of the next President in
the streets. Everywhere, it was 'Fujimori, Fujimori, Fujimori.' " De

Soto, formerly a key adviser to Vargas Llosa and now a key adviser to Alberto Fujimori, has a good ear, and he listens to a sector of society which most people as wealthy and powerful as he pay little attention to: he has made his living and his considerable reputation by studying what he defines as the "informal sector" of the Peruvian economy—that is, the poor who live by their remarkable wits. While Vargas Llosa's ratings were still up in the polls, de Soto said, he sensed a dangerous vacuum in the campaign: "All the parties that had governed this country were burned out, and none of them were in a position to form a coalition." The lower-income voters he studies weren't really convinced by the leading candidate, who started out with an independent image but gradually became identified with the old-money political establishment. "Vargas Llosa simply appropriated a neoconservative program," de Soto told me. "And people saw that coming. They felt that he didn't identify with them, that he was having his picture taken holding hands with the oligarchy." He went on to recall how startled he was when he realized that a political nonentity—a nisei, or native-born Peruvian of Japanese parents—who didn't belong to any party and was running a campaign with no funding, was about to fill the void. "Vargas Llosa said he was going to liberalize the economy, impose stern measures, and Fujimori didn't say anything," de Soto said. "But people don't vote according to what they're told—they vote according to how they feel. People identified with Fujimori."

Fujimori, a reserved, stern-faced man, is hardly a gifted politician, even compared with the aloof Vargas Llosa. In different circumstances, or in a different country, his campaign might have evaporated swiftly. But Peru is a country marked by racism and class hatred, in which to the great majority of the population the fact that he was an Oriental meant, above all, that he was not white, and was therefore one of them. And, to a large degree, he was. Alberto Fujimori was born fifty-two years ago in a working-class neighborhood in Lima. His parents started out in Peru as shopkeepers. He graduated (with honors) from the Universidad Nacional Agraria in Lima, which is not where the élite study. He then taught at his alma mater, living modestly and apparently harboring no political ambitions, even though he rose to become rector of his university, in 1984, and then, in 1987, thanks to a gift for listening and a talent for reconciling interests, president of the National Assembly of University Presidents. In fact, he did not have Presidential ambitions when he decided to run for President. In late 1988, he had started a movement of professionals and businessmen and academics like him—self-made men who knew that they had something to offer the country and were being kept out of the insiders' club. The movement, called Cambio '90 ("Change '90"), wanted to modernize Peru. The current president of the Senate and First Vice-President of Peru, Máximo San Román, who might be seen as the embodiment of Cambio '90, told me, "We wanted to put an end to the enormous state bureaucracy and put Congress back in the hands of people with practical experience; to make legislation more flexible; and to modernize the administrative apparatus. We wanted to make the government more responsive to the interests and the potential of small-business men in particular and of the enterprising middle class in general."

San Román is a bulky, dark-skinned man whose first language was the Quechua of the highlands, and when I met him he looked refreshingly out of place in his ornate Senate rooms, and gleefully astonished at his surroundings. San Román owns a small but very successful factory that uses homegrown technology and recycled machine parts to manufacture industrial equipment for bakeries. In his role as an innovative small-business man, he was introduced to Fujimori in mid-1989. The forthright manufacturer and the reserved academic hit it off, and, one day in October, San Román got a call. "Alberto wanted us to get involved in politics, but I told him that I was a businessman," San Román recalled. "He said, 'Max, we can register the movement in the Senate race, and we can put ourselves on the Presidential ballot.' 'But who would be the candidate?' I asked, and he said, 'Me.' 'Fine,' I told him, but then Alberto said he wanted me to run for the Senate. I turned to my wife and said, 'Just listen to the crazy thing this man is proposing. He wants to run for the Presidency, and he wants me to be a senator.' And she said, 'Oh, that's a good idea!' That's how I got into this."

Fujimori's advisers say that between November of last year, when Cambio '90 put itself on the ballot, and the April elections, when Fujimori and Vargas Llosa got 24.6 and 27.6 per cent of the vote, respectively—results that led to a second electoral round—the Fujimori campaign spent a total of a hundred and twenty thousand dollars. (The novelist's campaign, which included the pricey services of Sawyer/Miller, a New York–based political-consulting firm, is believed to have cost around ten million dollars.) In the beginning, San Román and Fujimori flew out to the provinces and headed for the markets, where the future President would borrow a stool or a bench to stand on and make his campaign speech. Once, they sat in an airport lobby and watched Vargas Llosa's huge entourage file by. The Cambio '90 candidates ate in the marketplaces, but soon they weren't paying for their meals. "The market-stall restaurants gave us free food," San Román recalls. "Then people began bringing us presents— beets, potatoes, carrots." Although at the beginning the candidates made their speeches in narrow streets, because they couldn't fill a plaza, by March the crowds had taken to carrying Alberto Fujimori on their shoulders through the towns. He gave simple speeches, promising to fight corruption and bureaucracy, and spoke in a flat voice that was neither seductive nor artificial. To spread the news of his candidacy, he relied to a great extent on word of mouth provided by Peru's flourishing Evangelical Christian community, with which he had had the vision to establish a political alliance. What little money there was for publicity was spent on radio spots written by a little-known, self-effacing P.R. man named Roberto Morán, who devised a slogan that was pure genius. It was "Alberto Fujimori: Honesty, Technology, and Work": a Peru free of sharklike politicians, a Peru full of computers, a Peru where sweat would be honored and remunerated—in short, a modern, efficient, industrious Peru.

It was a dream to vote for. Peruvians knew their politicians well enough to know that they could be expected to fulfill no dreams, and in that profound cynicism and the need to dream once more lay Fujimori's strength. As his campaign flourished, political analysts made much of the fact that he was gaining ground *despite* the fact that he was a complete unknown. It was the other way around, as the leftist Senator Javier Diez Canseco discovered, with some pain. Diez Canseco, who, as a member of the Izquierda Unida, or United Left, is part of the militant left that has traditionally won over twenty per cent of the vote in all national elections, went campaigning in the city of Arequipa for his reëlection and for his party's Presidential candidate, Henry Pease. His partner on the Izquierda Unida slate was his good friend Hugo Blanco, a peasant organizer from the nineteen-sixties who was running for the Senate for the first time. Blanco had been in Arequipa not three weeks before and had found a warmly receptive audience. Now, as Diez Canseco and Blanco entered the city's market plaza, the battle-worn organizer raised his head and sniffed the air. "Brother, something's changed," he told Diez Canseco. The market people gave the two leftists a cool reception. Bewildered, Diez Canseco approached a vender who had a poster of Fujimori tacked up on her stall, and asked, "Señora, why are you voting for him?" The woman looked Diez Canseco in the eye. "Because he hasn't done anything yet."

What a lot of people remember about the press conference held by Mario Vargas Llosa on April 8th, immediately after it became known that the vote counts for him and for Alberto Fujimori were close enough to force a runoff election, is that he answered the first question in French. "He looked so relieved to be doing it, too—as if by speaking French he could get out of Peru at least as long as the question lasted," I was told by a middle-class friend of mine who might have been expected to vote for him. Vargas Llosa must have been intensely relieved two months later to be through at last with the whole painful process, even though it had been his choice to stay in the race rather than admit defeat to Fujimori. He was three points ahead in the first round; in the second, he lost by a humiliating twenty points. "It was like watching someone commit suicide by slitting his wrists rather than by shooting himself," another friend said. During the runoff campaign, Vargas Llosa's supporters in the media and on television carried out a rabidly classist, xenophobic drive against Fujimori. The Catholic hierarchy staged a special procession, headed by the statue of the Lord of the Miracles; society women started prayer chains ("Three Hail Marys so Fujimori doesn't win, pass it on"). And still the novelist went on sinking in the polls. "You'd keep asking, 'Is he dead yet?' " my friend said of the prolonged political agony. "And the answer would be 'No, he's going to another rally.'"

In the end, it was not the novelist but his supporters who lost the election for him. He cannot be faulted for being honest about the recessionary, monetarist program he saw as the only way to drag Peru out of the abyss, and he might even have been forgiven his white turtlenecks and love of French—this was, after all, the café-society Mario everyone already knew. What he was savaged for on Election Day was not knowing how to choose his friends. His friends called his opponent El Chinito—the affectionate diminutive being a favorite recourse of Latin-American racism— and the dark-skinned people who had heard themselves addressed forever as *indios* and little *indios* and *cholos de mierda* liked Fujimori better each time they heard the nickname. (He had the good grace to use the term himself, shouting "El Chinito has arrived!" on his first campaign tours, when there was nobody to do advance work for him.) For its election-week issue, the news magazine *Caretas* ran a cover that featured Fujimori wearing the *indios'* peaked wool-knit cap with earflaps and holding a llama on a leash, with his campaign slogan—"A President Like You"— punctuated as a question. The intention behind it was vicious, but if the cover had come out a few weeks earlier it could have served as Fujimori's best campaign poster.

"The mathematics of Fujimori's triumph were very simple," his publicist, Roberto Morán, told me. "What are there more of in Peru? Rich people or poor? Indians or Europeans? Limeños or provincials? Ideologues or nonideologues? There is no mystery to this, but still the other side never figured it out." On Election Night, as Vargas Llosa made a graceful, conciliatory concession speech, hysterical upper-class women outside his campaign headquarters shouted for a coup. They embarrassed many of their fellow-conservatives, but they showed an understanding of what an unreconstructed upper class needs in order to stay in power. In the end, Mario Vargas Llosa had been merely an instrument.

"FORTUNATELY, GOD IS PERUVIAN!" a prominent industrialist exclaimed last month. He is the chairman or a member of the boards of many important industries here, and I had wanted to talk to him because the financial support of men like him had been vital to Vargas Llosa's candidacy. I wanted to know how the business sector was taking its defeat, but this man turned out to be buoyantly optimistic about the new President, for Fujimori had undergone a full-fledged political conversion shortly before his inauguration. That happened in New York, at the hands of the International Monetary Fund's Michel Camdessus, the World Bank's Barber Conable, the Inter-American Development Bank's Enrique Iglesias, and the United Nations' Javier Pérez de Cuéllar. The ubiquitous Hernando de Soto, scholar of the informal sector and friend of the mighty, helped set up the all-star meeting. Fujimori brought one of his campaign economic advisers to this session, who argued for a gradual approach to inflation, involving price-indexing and a progressive reduction of subsidies. "He was talking about Howdy Doody, and the others talked to Fujimori about the facts of life," a dismissive participant recalled. The President-elect emerged from the meeting convinced that the only feasible approach to Peru's economic recovery—or to renewed I.M.F. and World Bank help, at any rate—involved a monetarist shock treatment. That was at the end of June. The *paquetazo* was delivered to the country in August. By the time I talked to my industrialist acquaintance, a month later, he felt that such an extreme program would never have been accepted by the population at large if it had come from what he called "the palefaces." Like all the other Peruvian businessmen I've talked to since August, he seemed convinced that Fujimori was bringing them the best of both worlds: the economic program that the country needed and a palatable politician who could push it through without getting them lynched. "Right after the trauma of Vargas Llosa's defeat, we felt as if we'd received a huge blow, but now, the way things are turning out, we can see that it's all for the best. Because—let's say that our candidate, elected President, had come out with an edict that we didn't like. We could have said among ourselves, 'Don't worry, I'll drop in on him tomorrow and discuss it with him,' or 'My wife will arrange to have lunch next week with Patricia' "—Vargas Llosa's wife. "But it would all have had to be very delicate, very restrained, because of the respect we feel for him and because we are so closely identified with him in the public mind. Whereas with El Chinito, every time he puts his foot in it we can yell, 'Chinito, don't do that!' And he'll correct himself."

One of the striking things about this business leader's statement was his faith that his community understands what is wrong with the country and knows how to fix it. I thought about that after waking up to yet another day without electricity, getting into a taxi that was a 1966 Volkswagen, buying a bunch of five locally manufactured pens for thirty cents and discovering that none of them worked, walking through San Marcos University, where the average professor earns fifty dollars a month and every inch of wall space is covered with oaths and exhortations by Shining Path and rival guerrilla organizations, and then having lunch at the home of a wealthy and hospitable foreign couple. They were delighted to show me their rambling garden—truly a luxury in this desert city—but a little embarrassed to confess that among the maintenance requirements of a garden here is not only an extravagant amount of water but the time it takes the houseboy to wipe dust off the greenery. In the polished garden, with the barren hills looming just behind, and the money changers and chocolate venders waiting just beyond the guard posts of the residential enclave, and with the houseboy now ducking his head deferentially as he brought out a trayful of drinks, the question was suddenly overwhelming: How much faith did one need to believe that Peru could be fixed?

I asked the industrialist who was so pleased with El Chinito how, once inflation had been stabilized, his sector was planning to get Peru back on its feet, and he said their main hope was foreign investment. ("You'd have to have a riverboat gambler's instincts to invest in Peru," an executive for a transnational corporation had commented to me earlier about that option.) I asked what he thought would happen six months after the initial *paquetazo*, when the Social Emergency Program is scheduled to run out, and he said he could only rely on the Peruvian people's native patience. In answer to those two questions other businessmen sighed and shook their heads, or said things like "We have to hope for the best." They are not economic planners.

Richard Webb, who is one, didn't groan, put his head in his hands, or look to Heaven when I asked about the approaching end of the emergency program. "In the first place, that's a poorly put question," he said softly. "There *is* no emergency program, and if we're lucky it will just be starting up six months from now. But what has that got to do with anything?" Webb was the chairman of Peru's Central Bank from 1980 to 1985, during the conservative Presidency of Fernando Belaúnde Terry (who was not much more successful with his economic policies than his successor, Alan García). He now produces *Cuánto*, an extraordinarily clear, didactic monthly publication about economics, and has pulled off the even more astonishing feat of being well spoken of in almost every sector of the Peruvian élite, whatever its political persuasion. He was putting the latest issue of *Cuánto* to press when I interrupted him, but he listened to questions and answered them courteously, chewing on aspirin as he talked. "It's very hard to cut through the declarations and beliefs about economics to see what is really there," he said. "The reason you're asking if foreign investment will come in great amounts is that people tend to believe that the country will sink without it, but, historically, foreign investment has been a very small percentage of the total. We probably won't have very much, but there will be a significant amount in petroleum, and perhaps in mining—if people start to trust Peru again. And it's foolish to speculate about what will happen with the economy in the future until we bring inflation under control. Right now it's stabilized, but if it starts up again things are going to be very, very bad. In order to prevent that, there's two or three years of recession ahead of us, and the government will have to rule with a very hard hand, imposing even more drastic measures than the ones we have now."

Measures more drastic and socially unjust than raising electricity rates by five hundred and twenty per cent?

"What's the point of keeping electricity so cheap that those who have it waste it, while the electric company doesn't make enough profit to expand the service to those who don't have it?" Webb retorted. "You say we can't impose too much hardship, because the guerrillas will benefit, but the fact that there are guerrillas is no excuse for running a country wastefully. On the contrary."

PERHAPS PERUVIANS will give the shock treatment the time it needs to achieve its desired effects. In that case, three or four years from now Peru will have a stabilized currency and a sound budget. Perhaps the cocaine trade will continue to provide an estimated eight to twelve hundred million dollars in foreign currency a year—an amount that in more normal economic circumstances can contribute greatly to a stable foreign exchange. With any luck, there will be good international prices for Peru's petroleum, copper, silver, and tin, which will allow the country to start rebuilding itself. But it will then be an even poorer nation than it is now, with even more desperate social needs like those which in the past the private sector has never been willing to pay for through higher taxes. At this stage, the only alternative to that grim scenario is continued economic chaos, and President Fujimori, who has no party or nationwide political base to keep his hand firm, is particularly vulnerable to strong-arm lobbying tactics that could make the shock program fall apart. He has already lowered prices of fertilizers and chemicals for this year's planting season (how could the Andean farmers be expected to plant otherwise?), increased the minimum wage by about eight dollars a month, and agreed to make electric bills for August payable in January. (No one knows when the January bills are supposed to be paid.) With the trade sector foundering and small industries going under—a thousand are estimated to have done so thus far—the National Confederation of Merchants is already asking the government to ease up on the shock treatment.

The one sector that might recover slightly in the short run is the middle class, even though it has probably lost more proportionately than any other during the crisis. Juan Buccio, my occasional taxi-driver—he's the owner of the 1966 Beetle—is good at providing clear explanations of this and other economic questions. A silver-haired, fine-boned engineering-school graduate who was never able to find a decent-paying job, he is also the only remaining Vargas Llosa supporter I met. The businessmen I talked to think that now that they've got Vargas Llosa's monetarist program they can do without Vargas Llosa, but Buccio thinks that Fujimori is applying the program mechanically, with no real understanding of its logic and no competent advisers to help him with the fine-tuning. Still, he clings to the hope that the program will have some positive effect. Buccio's car reaches cruising speed at thirty miles per hour, which is a nice speed for ruminating, and whenever he hits a little bump of understanding he chuckles to himself and shakes his head before passing the idea on. "This is what I've just figured out," he said the other morning as we were rolling down the Lima speedway. "There are two bureaucrats in this country who have me to thank for their health and sustenance. What's the minimum wage for bureaucrats? Twenty million intis, or two million per workday. How much gasoline do I put into my car every day? About four million intis' worth. Most of that is taxes, and most of *that* goes to pay for the bureaucracy. So my gasoline is paying for salaries for two of them!"

Ever didactic, he explained that this wasn't just the government's way of stopping inflation by squelching demand but also the most accessible way it has of pouring money into its depleted coffers. After another pensive stretch of driving, he asked me if I thought Peru could be fixed. I told him I couldn't quite understand how, but I was thinking about the eight million people at the bottom, and about an extremely nice, thoughtful businessman who told me apologetically that he wished he could perceive Indians and *cholos* as his equals but that in truth he couldn't help noticing that they stink. "I think things can improve," Buccio said, more focussed on his own situation. "We don't need much. All I need is a stable currency so I know what I can rely on. Then I can take out a loan for another car and have two cars to work. People here have extraordinary initiative; we're always inventing all sorts of little business deals. Without inflation, we'll get by."

And what about the people who voted for Fujimori in the first place? Everyone here is wondering anxiously how much more they can take, and although the historical evidence is that they can take almost anything, the question arises because, to a bizarre extent, poor Peruvians today are an unknown quantity— a new composite. They are the new *chicha* culture, the migrants in the shantytowns who have abandoned their native costumes and the flute music of the Andes for bluejeans and harrowingly monotonous songs about sex with a tropical beat. They are the leftist masses who have voted for socialist mayors in any number of urban centers and yet turned their backs on the socialist candidates for the Presidency. They are the "informal sector" whose capacity for hard work and spontaneous forms of capitalist organization Hernando de Soto has charted admiringly—who can rise to the top, like Vice-President Máximo San Román, or, at the bottom, continue peddling rusty car exhausts and disposable razor blades and simply refuse to give up. They are the ones nobody bothered to consult, or even advise, or try to soothe in connection with the drastic economic program they had voted so firmly against. According to Felipe Ortiz de Zevallos, a canny political analyst, "they are pragmatic, oriented to television, somewhat committed to democracy but critical of its formalisms, urgently concerned with their immediate problems, and in need of day-to-day solutions." They are the *cholos de mierda*, and they are the new Peru. With them, all bets are off.

THERE WAS A DEMONSTRATION the other day, much like dozens of other demonstrations that have taken place in the center of Lima during the last several months. A few people were kicked or beaten by the police, many more were teargassed, and, in the end, some of the complaints were heard. This particular demonstration was one of the largest so far, and it was organized by the women who administer a community-based food-relief program for children called Vaso de Leche, or Glass of Milk. Like so many other programs for the very poor, it depends on donations from Caritas and had suffered from the agency's sudden overload following the *paquetazo*. In addition, serious tensions had arisen between its administrator, who is appointed by the mayor of Lima, and its president, who is elected from among the women who run the program. The women I met in the municipal offices of San Juan de Lurigancho had told me that all the neighborhood Vaso de Leche participants would be marching together from the *municipalidad* to the center of the city, and had invited me to come along.

On the morning of the demonstration, a half-dozen women met early in the *municipalidad* to prepare their march; by the time I got there, they had finished cutting out a stack of letters made of yellow paper and were about to start gluing them on to a large red banner. The women were all middle-aged housewives, and they readily agreed that a few years ago they would not have been caught dead at a demonstration, or even in the *municipalidad*. "I thought it was wrong to be seen outside my house," a short, lively woman named Matilde Valenzuela told me. "But we needed the help, so I began coöperating with Vaso de Leche. I would ladle out the milk with one hand and cover my face with the other, I was so embarrassed. But I got elected head of my block and then regional coördinator for the settlement, and then general coördinator for our forty settlements. The organization has been so successful that now our men want to get into it, so we're bargaining. We'll let them in if they'll let us into theirs. They don't want that. They're jealous. They say we're hoarding the food for political purposes, and stuff like that. Our own men! But it's just because they know that political organizing around food is important, and that the only thing they do is talk."

The other women were laughing at this story, but I was beginning to feel apprehensive about what lay ahead. Surely they had seen on television what happens to demonstrators? The teargassing? The police ganging up on one person and clubbing him to the ground? Surely they were nervous?

"No way!" a woman with frizzily permed hair said. "We've got demonstration calluses."

"We've got protection," another said, and she slyly pulled the Lurigancho version of a gas mask out of her cardigan pocket: a handkerchief, moistened and wrapped in a bit of plastic. It turned out they had all been getting teargassed for years.

Were the effort and the risk worth it? Could they point to any concrete positive result they had obtained from their previous marches?

"Of course," the frizzy-haired woman said. "After we march, they deliver the milk. If we don't, they don't. The last time, they were sending us industrial-grade wheat instead, and we had to go protest to straighten things out."

In any case, another woman said, there probably wouldn't be any problems today. Unusually, the Lima mayoralty had granted the Lurigancho vice-mayor—these leftist women's leftist leader—permission for the march, and she had sent someone downtown to pick up the authorization slip.

When the banner was ready, the group headed for the main road, where a couple of hundred women were waiting between the market stalls and the bus stop, on an open patch of ground separating the four-lane highway from the two- and three-story buildings of downtown Lurigancho. I walked from the back of the crowd to the front, hoping to find Amalia Huaycán, who had told me she would be there. There were many women dressed like her—in wide skirts, with bright-colored handloomed shawls around their shoulders—and many dressed like Matilde Valenzuela, in plain cotton shifts and thin sweaters, with wool socks to protect their legs from the cold. As the march began, several women went on with their knitting, and chatted placidly with their neighbors, needles clicking while they walked. I saw the banner being raised, and then I stumbled as the crowd lurched backward in a single reverse motion. Just ahead of us was something I hadn't noticed earlier: two rows of riot police in gas masks, lunging for the front line of demonstrators and wielding billy clubs as they charged. There were screams and a series of short, sharp detonations, and I found myself gagging and blind from tear gas. There was shouting everywhere, and the sound of stampeding feet. The clearing where the demonstrators had gathered was now empty, and the women were regrouping in clusters around the market stalls, whose owners had not so much as bothered to run. Upwind of them, a last cannister on the ground spewed a long plume of tear gas. The fumes were asphyxiating, the sight of the masked policemen terrifying, but the women who were now racing toward the back alleys to dodge past the police blockade and continue their march downtown were not at all panicky. In fact, they were laughing uproariously.

MEDELLÍN
1991

"We're all going to die."

EVERYONE HERE KNOWS that if you get shot, run over, or knifed the place to go is the Policlínica, an emergency clinic run by the San Vicente de Paúl Public Hospital: the surgeons and internes who staff it on weekend nights have intensive on-the-job practice and a reputation for performing miracles. Security is tight; there have been instances of frustrated murderers who finished off their victims in the recovery room, so now guards at the entry gate check to see that only the wounded and their relatives or friends go in. Standing at the gate on a recent Saturday at midnight, I watched a man emerge unaccompanied from a taxi, with blood seeping from a large hole in his chest. He could still walk. He needed to, because there are no hospital orderlies to help patients in at the gate, and although I saw five taxis screech to the entrance and deliver five severely wounded men in less than ten minutes, not a single ambulance arrived. Metal stretchers were wheeled out and operated by the victims' friends or relatives, but the man with the chest wound was alone. "How about that?" the gatekeeper said, watching him stagger past. "Maybe he'll survive." He was not being cynical; he knew from experience, he told me, that on weekend nights about ninety such men appear at the Policlínica, and between twelve and twenty die. Another taxi pulled up, and the driver helped a hysterical woman drag out a young man with a gunshot wound through his back and haul him onto a stretcher. He appeared to be dead. The taxi-driver matter-of-factly mopped up a pool of blood on the back seat and drove away. The driver of the taxi that later took me home explained that picking up wounded passengers is part of the job. "How can we leave someone to die on the street like that?" he asked. "Most of the time, we lose the fares, because those people are in no position to pay, but we do it anyway, out of charity."

On nights like these, one can have the impression that Medellín is about to drown in its own blood. Over the past decade, the level of violence here has risen so far above what is rationally conceivable, even in a country as violent as Colombia, that statistics make no sense: What does it mean, for example, that last year, the most violent in Medellín's history, more than three hundred police officers were killed, along with some three thousand youths between the ages of fourteen and twenty-five, or that in the first two months of this year the rate had increased? When I first came here, in mid-1989, that year was already on record as being the most violent to date; I met a judge, a woman who had become anorexic because she was receiving constant death threats, and a few weeks later I saw in the papers that she had indeed been killed. Then, there was the radical left's representative on the municipal council—a bustling, courteous man I had also interviewed—who was assassinated in his office by a young man who had walked straight past the security guards. I talked to a man who had survived six attempts on his life and was waiting for the seventh wearing a bulletproof vest, not certain he would make it. The young, highly popular governor of the *departamento* of Antioquia, of which Medellín is the capital, was murdered by a car bomb on his way to work. Things only became worse after the joint United States–Colombia offensive against the drug trade got under way, in August of 1989, and the mood of the *paisas*, as the inhabitants of Antioquia are called, swung from stunned disbelief to a kind of hip cynicism. In the offensive's fourth month, a few weeks before Christmas, the police announced that they had surrounded the most wanted of Colombia's drug traffickers, Pablo Escobar, in one of his many Antioquia country estates, and that his capture was imminent. The general assumption was that he would not be taken alive. That night, I had dinner here with some friends at a restaurant that was unusually crowded and cheerful. "I can't imagine it!" a woman in our group, a chic and lively socialite, burst out. "I can't imagine a future without Pablo Escobar. I can't understand what it's going to feel like to live without fear, but the mere possibility makes me so happy that I feel like decorating the Christmas tree with little red coffins."

That mood has now passed—swept away by an avalanche of events that did not include Escobar's capture—and has been replaced by a wave of depression and self-doubt that permeates every conversation: How is it that the *paisas*, the proud vanguard of enterprise and innovation, the architects of Colombia's industrial future, the most punctual, God-fearing, and family-bound citizens of an otherwise slapdash country, have come to this? The question has even spawned a new breed, called *violentólogos*—researchers who try to make sense of the madness that has overtaken Antioquia, and who have a hard time just keeping track of who has killed whom. The proliferation of warring groups is staggering: in addition to Escobar's brigades, which continue their attack on the government, there are drug gangs, street gangs, death squads, "militias" (left over from guerrilla groups that passed through Medellín in the mid-nineteen-eighties, now operating on their own), paramilitary squads, and extortion brigades—all of them up in arms against the police and against each other. And now that bizarre truces and deals are being worked out between the central government, in Bogotá, and the illegal traders who have made Medellín the drug capital of the world, an even more sobering question is how the city will cope with a problem that only a short while ago appeared to belong exclusively to the drug trade but currently seems beyond the very considerable abilities of even a Pablo Escobar to control.

Viewed from densely populated hills known as the northeast and northwest *comunas*, the heart of the city—its gleaming white skyscrapers and brick office buildings—seems as remote as Oz.

The hillsides are as much Medellín as the bustling, cheerfully venal commercial district in the valley, but not even the citizens of the ghettoized *comunas* see it that way. The "real" Medellín has factories, travel agencies, video stores, and probably more commercial square feet of clothing boutiques than any other city its size. On the hills, the spreading network of improvised housing is mottled with tiny grocery stores, an occasional school or movie house, and, here and there, a church. Half the population of Medellín lives there—about eight hundred thousand people—in brick and concrete houses that may slant a little but are nevertheless stable, with water and electricity that the municipal government has provided to even the most outlying areas. Yet when the people who live in the *comunas* describe their neighborhoods they often say there is nothing there, because there is nothing there that counts. No wealth, no prestige, no self-respect—only a gnawing resentment of the Medellín of shopping malls and nine-to-five jobs.

This is Pablo Escobar's power base. He was born, in 1949, a little farther uphill, in the misty, densely wooded mountains that surround the Medellín valley, into a family that seems to have been the embodiment of *paisa* pride: a farmer father, and a mother who was a schoolteacher—the kind of folks who keep their farmhouses immaculately whitewashed and then deck the porch with so many pots of hanging orchid and geranium plants that the whitewash barely shows through. Of all the stories Escobar might like to tell if he is ever captured, one of the most fascinating would surely be the account of his transition from respectable farmer's son to small-time hood. Certainly he was imaginative from the first: he found a way to make a living by reselling gravestones he'd stolen from a Medellín cemetery and sanded flat. He was ambitious: in 1982, as soon as he had made enough money from drug trafficking to build up a power base, he got elected to Congress as an alternate representative on the ticket of the Liberal Party. He was also vengeful: his leap to notoriety came in 1984, when he masterminded the assassination of Justice Minister Rodrigo Lara Bonilla, who had exposed Escobar's connections with the cocaine trade and forced him out of office just months before. From that time on, Escobar operated on two fronts: he created what narcotics officials believe was the largest and most efficient individual world network for the production and delivery of cocaine, and he waged a single-minded war against anyone in Colombia who spoke out against the cocaine trade, focussing on the justice system, and on anyone who supported the extradition of traffickers to the United States, where the long arm of corruption could not spring them.

After dozens of political assassinations, and after twenty months of what must be the most determined manhunt ever mounted by the Colombian government, Escobar, although militarily weakened, remains not only at large but in control of most of his business operations—sound evidence of a vast network of loyal supporters. Escobar nurtured that support carefully—with jobs, housing, and interest-free loans for the people of the *comunas*. He built on a belief his admirers once shared with almost everyone in Colombia—that drugs were the United States' problem. He exploited the business-loving *paisas'* inability to resist a good deal; there are plenty of people here who have learned to hate him but still cannot be completely persuaded that there is anything wrong with selling merchandise—any merchandise— for which there is a market. Mostly, though, Escobar prospered and survives because through the cocaine boom and his private war he has enabled thousands of dead-end kids to make the leap from the *comunas* to the otherwise inaccessible city beyond.

ALONSO SALAZAR, a slight, mustachioed young man who has about him an air of almost preternatural alertness, is one of the most original of the new *violentólogos*. He drifted through the faculties of veterinary and journalism schools until someone urged him to collect a series of oral histories he had been taking and turn it into a book. It is called *No Nacimos Pa' Semilla* (*We Weren't Born to Bear Seed*), and it is selling out all over the country, because the oral histories were provided by the *comuna* youths known, variously, as *pistolocos* (crazy guns), *los muchachos de las bandas* (gang members), and simply *sicarios* (hired assassins). Salazar started collecting the boys' stories in 1988, when the extraordinary

amount of criminal activity going on in the *comunas* brought them
sharply to the "real" city's attention. One series of interviews,
with someone he has called Toño, was recorded as the boy was
dying of gunshot wounds in a bed at the Policlínica. "He was so
bad, so evil," Salazar said to me one afternoon when he and I
were sitting in a dusty, garbage-strewn plaza in the northeast *comuna.* "You could almost see him salivate when he told the stories
about all the people he'd killed." Still, it makes Salazar sad to
think of him, because the boy came to depend on his visits, and
was grateful and proud that anyone would think he was important enough to be listened to. It was the same with all the
interviews. "To have their lives become a word, a line of text,
thrilled them," Salazar said. "They all wanted so badly to find a
place in the world."

Salazar isn't baffled anymore by the combination of vulnera-
bility and murderousness in the kids he interviews. The first thing
that happened to him when he started out, he says, was that his
view of the world turned upside down. Partly, it was because the
boys were so nice, so amiable, that he found he couldn't keep the
concept of evil in the forefront of his mind as he worked with
them; and partly it was because the stories he heard were so similar. There is, it seems, a process at work—a series of events, some
known, some still mysterious—that has produced a generation
of hopeless suicides, whose particular form of self-destruction
happens to be murder. Salazar believes that the first crime wave
was partly provoked by the massive economic crisis that hit
Medellín in the mid-nineteen-seventies, when the textile factories that were the heart of the city's economy closed down or
fired thousands of workers. As it happened, that was also the period when the nascent cocaine trade consolidated into several
cartellike formations, one of them headed by Pablo Escobar.
What Salazar still hasn't managed to understand is why these two
phenomena coincided with a runaway increase in all forms of
violence. Ever since the Conservative-Liberal civil war known as
La Violencia came to an end, in the late nineteen-fifties, Medellín
had been relatively peaceful. "But suddenly there was a burst of
kidnappings," Salazar said. "You could argue that this was the

drug trade's way of accumulating working capital, but the number
of rapes and homicides also shot up. It seems that the whole society began to shred then." Recent figures show the trend: in 1980,
there were seven hundred and thirty violent deaths in Medellín;
in 1990, there were fifty-three hundred.

The gangs put together by the traffickers went largely unno-
ticed in the early part of the drug era, because they were used
mostly for internal business—collecting bills, eliminating stool
pigeons, and so forth. It wasn't until Escobar was drummed out
of Congress by Justice Minister Lara Bonilla that the *bandas* acquired a paramilitary structure and a political role. Escobar put a
young man named David Ricardo Prisco in charge of Lara's murder. With four of his brothers and several cousins and close
friends, he formed a gang known as the Priscos, which was Escobar's most effective terrorist squad for the next six years, which
was as long as it lasted. "Thanks to that murder, the Priscos were
the first band to become notorious," Salazar says. "They became
the prototype of a series of highly organized bands with close
links to the drug lords. Their center was the family, and the barrio, with its network of family relations and loyal friends. A *sicario*
from one of the bands could earn as much as twenty million pesos"—about two hundred thousand dollars—"for a single job,
buy a luxury condominium in an upper-class neighborhood,
and—this is fundamental for people in this culture—provide a
better life for his family. At the height of their power, the bands
emulated Escobar: they helped out the community with money
and public works, and were considered benefactors. In peace-
time, they organized street festivals, and they often had a police
escort when they rode around the neighborhood."

Since early last year, when the Medellín police underwent a
thorough purge of their ranks and a complete overhaul of the
high command, they have been waging war on the drug trade,
and the department is now fond of providing *organigramas* that
show dozens of *bandas* neatly spread out in a series of networks
leading straight up to Escobar. Salazar thinks that only about
thirty per cent of the Medellín gangs have such formal links to
the drug world, and that it's the remaining seventy per cent that

are at the heart of the current wave of violence. They are the *chichipatos*, or small-time hoods; the *basuqueros*, or consumers of *basuco*, a highly addictive cocaine derivative; the *punketos*, still devoted to the music of the Sex Pistols and The Clash. What Salazar calls the "countercultural gangs" don't last very long as such, nor do the individual youths who join them. They are somehow free of the middle-class aspirations that gave discipline and structure to the now extinct Priscos and their spinoffs; the Priscos made a pact with destiny which had clearly defined goals—a short life, yes, but, in exchange, a B.M.W. and a penthouse for one's mother, say. The *punketos'* minds are too frayed for such orderly planning. Maybe it has something to do with their distance from the "real" Medellín. The Priscos came from Aranjuez, a well-established working-class neighborhood just up the road from Medellín's main drag. The *desechables*, the throwaway kids, come from much farther uphill. They have only recently been translated from the strict, hardworking world of rural Antioquia that their parents fled, and they are caught between cultures. They don't want their parents' thankless lives, and, to judge from a thirty-five-per-cent unemployment rate in the *comunas*, the city doesn't want them.

ON A NARROW STREET in the northeast *comuna*, just uphill from a plaza in the Guadalupe barrio, the kids had gathered in large numbers the other day, sullen and fashionable in their funky haircuts, baggy Bermudas, and high-tops. Virtually all the neighborhood women and a good number of unemployed and elderly men had also crowded into the street, because word had flown around the barrio that Jesus Christ was manifest and visible there. He had appeared to a bus driver, who noticed that what seemed to be a damp spot near the bottom of his bathroom door was in fact a miraculous likeness of the face imprinted on the Holy Shroud. The driver, Ricario Hernández, was sitting in his empty, rattletrap bus, honking furiously at the crowd to move aside so he could park and have lunch. He and his family had tried to keep the apparition a secret, he told me, but in a matter of hours the entire community had somehow found out, and the crowds, in their eagerness to see the face, were on the verge of knocking down the driver's front door. Almost as exciting as the miracle itself was the fact that the local media had taken note of it: when a TeleAntioquia crew showed up with a camera, people in the crowd went nearly berserk in their eagerness to be filmed. "At last!" someone in the crowd exclaimed. "They're going to show something good about us!" A young woman explained why she was so happy. "Even if it turns out to be a fake, we'll have something nice to talk about," she said of the image on the door. "All we ever get to comment on is who went crazy from too much *basuco,* or who got killed. 'So-and-So's lying in a pool of blood on the corner,' they'll say, and we all go running over and stare."

Having failed to see the miraculous bathroom, I walked back downhill with the young woman and with her rotund and lively middle-aged neighbor, whom I had met earlier and whom I'll call Doña Violeta Mejía. The women pointed out a pretty young girl who had been thrown out of her house because of her hopeless *basuco* addiction, and the corner where the son of Doña Violeta had been shot down a year ago. Doña Violeta's son, it seemed, had a bad *basuco* habit, and stole, and probably also hired himself out as a killer, to support it. Eventually, he died at the hands of former playmates in the neighborhood. Weeping, Doña Violeta said that she spends hours trying to figure out what she and her husband did wrong. "My husband would take him aside, and say, 'Talk to me as a friend,' but he would grab his head between his hands and say there was nothing to be done," she said. "In the end, he would come home so stoned, so crazy, that he would bang his head against the wall until we grabbed him and held him back. We'd tell him he was going to kill himself, but he would say that was what he wanted. He wanted to die, he'd say. He wanted to rest. There was this great anxiety inside him, and we never figured out how to get to it."

There are so many kids in the neighborhood like that, the women said. They want too much, they want lives they can't have, they have no patience, and they are seriously hooked on *basuco.* I asked the women what they thought of Pablo Escobar, and they said that he and the other traffickers had done a great deal of harm, buying kids off and turning them into murderers, and bringing *basuco* into the world. But when we reached Doña Violeta's house, and settled down in a comfortable living room, her husband, Don Jaime, who was about to set off for his noonday shift at a plastics factory, said that the neighborhood was also much to blame. There was a woman up the hill who, ten years ago, became the first person in the neighborhood to sell *basuco*. The Mejías and other neighbors remonstrated with her, Don Jaime said, but she answered, "I have my children to bring up." She had two sons then. Now one was dead, killed in a fight, and the other was hooked on *basuco*, but she was still selling the stuff. "We *paisas* are sometimes too interested in money," Don Jaime said. And yet, he added, if he had his life to live over again he would do everything the same way. Not Doña Violeta. She had come here with her husband a quarter of a century before "from the last village on the last road in Antioquia," she said. If they had stayed in the countryside, she believes, she would still have her son. But Don Jaime used the word *fracaso*, which means a shattering failure, to refer to what would have happened to him if he had stayed on as a day laborer on the coffee *fincas* of southwestern Antioquia. Here he had a house with four bedrooms and real tile floors, good food, a telephone. His three youngest children seemed to be doing all right, he thought. How could he have stayed in rural Antioquia?

The Mejías went through the list of the kids in the neighborhood who had died or were on drugs. On some streets, they claimed, every household had at least one addicted son or—less frequently—daughter. They said that their nephews suffered the same uncontrollable anxiety as their son, partly caused, no doubt, by the death squads that had started operating in the neighborhood. Because the men who roamed the streets at night, with brown kerchiefs tied over their faces, were brawny and not very young, the Mejías were convinced that they were cops. The men killed *basuqueros* and petty thieves, but sometimes missed their mark. Don Jaime and Doña Violeta pointed out the bullet holes in the façade of the house next to theirs, made one evening when the masked men started shooting aimlessly up and down the

street. There was no place in the entire neighborhood where one
could feel safe.

Later, I chatted briefly with their surviving son, a taciturn kid
named Jorge Mario who smokes a great deal of marijuana but
stays away from *basuco*. It was only midmorning, but he already
looked as stoned as the kids in front of the bus driver's house,
who, with joints dangling from their fingers, had been waiting to
see the miracle. I asked Jorge Mario what he wanted to do with
his life. "I'm a bum," he answered. "What's the point of making
plans if I'm not going to get anywhere anyway? All the kids
around here are getting killed. We're all going to die. It's useless."
Then he went out to sit on the stoop and stare down at Medellín.

A PANORAMIC SHOT of the distant city is a recurrent motif in
the work of the filmmaker Victor Gaviria, who has succeeded in
presenting Medellín as if filmed through the eyes of the *pistolocos*,
for whom he feels an obsessive, painful tenderness. Gaviria has
dedicated most of the last five years to documenting the violent
lives of these kids; his first feature film, *Rodrigo D: No Futuro*, is a
fictionalized account of the lives of the punks who acted in it.
(One of them was Doña Violeta's son.) In the movie, filmed in
1986, Rodrigo D tries to recover from the pain of his mother's
death, fails to make it as a drummer with a punk-rock group, and
remains alienated from his neighborhood friends, all of whom are
living a drug-and-adrenaline high—staging holdups and playing
with guns. In the end, Rodrigo throws himself from the window
of one of the skyscrapers that are inescapably in view from the
hills. The title role was played by Ramiro Meneses, an aspiring
musician from the *comunas*; he is the only one of the cast of boys
who did not have a criminal record, and the only one who has
been able to make the transition to an acting career in Bogotá.
All the other actors are now dead.

I had lunch the other day with Gaviria, whom I have known
for some time, and asked him to talk about the boys from the
comunas. He was in the process of preparing a Colombian version
of a television documentary on the deaths of his various actors,

which he had made for German television, and he was still recovering from the death of his co-scriptwriter of *Rodrigo D*, a talented twenty-one-year-old named Ramón Correa, who was not able to star in that movie because he had been arrested and sentenced to prison for armed robbery just as filming was about to start. (On being released from prison, Ramón Correa travelled with Gaviria to present *Rodrigo D* at the Cannes Film Festival, but apparently found the experience more threatening than pleasurable. He despised the food, and seemed to feel that it was his duty to pick up the wallets and watches left lying so carelessly on the beach. Back home, he tried to do some serious writing, but he never made it. He died in January, shot to death in front of his mother's house.)

Gaviria said that he was drawn to the *comunas* by the same questions that haunt all Medellín: How could this city produce a generation of murderers for hire? How could all our values go so wrong? Despite the fact that he is now in his mid-thirties, there is something wide-eyed and vulnerable about him, a kind of inner adolescence that makes him sympathetic to the *punketos'* harsh music, their morally flat view of the world, their fascination with drugs. "I fell very much in love with the lives these boys lead, and we began a dialogue that in reality was between the two cities that coexist in Medellín," he told me.

His first encounter was with a teen-ager named John Galvis, who was killed a couple of months later. "When he walked into my apartment, he said it was the first time he'd been in an apartment building for a purpose other than stealing," Gaviria recalled. "Then he talked about his love for his mother. He told us how sometimes when he was feeling upset he'd go for a little walk with her, and smoke a joint, and then he would feel better. I began to see that this was all part of the *paisas'* intense devotion to their families. I understood that the most extreme acts of terrorism had their origins in kids' inability to see their families suffer, or fail, which is what always happens in these neighborhoods—the sister starts turning tricks, the brother gets hooked on *basuco*. I spent a long time recording interviews before I knew that I had to make a movie. It was because the phenomenon came to seem so *normal*, so much a part of everyday life, that I felt I had to leave a record of what I'd seen."

Gaviria, who is usually full of good-natured banter and, in white sneakers, a T-shirt, and bluejeans, always looks bouncy and clean-cut, was now talking in dead earnest, brushing aside interruptions while he let his food get cold. "For the kids, who in their lives have never known the slightest power, delinquency is a way of looking for power. No one pays attention to them, no one notices their lives. They're living N.N.s"—the "No Name" that identifies paupers' graves here. "Some of them have fathers with relatively structured lives, maybe even factory or construction workers, but these men are completely defeated—they have values that are useless in Medellín. The kids fall in love with whoever has power—you know, young people like values that involve some heroic element, some ability to achieve great things. Killers can do that—the kids have seen it on television, where the heroes have guns. That's why you can't explain the *sicariato*"—the culture of the hired assassin—"as an individual pathology. It's something else. Medellín is the capital of fashion, Colombians say, and fashion is the present. Medellín is the present. You go a few miles outside Medellín and it's all the past; it's all dusty roads, and farmhouses, and they've never even heard of the Gulf War there. These kids who have no place in the world, whom nobody has ever made room for, look at least for a place in time, in the present, through fashion. It's vitally important to them to look right. When they get money from a job, they spend it immediately on something for their mothers and on clothes. Of course they're not going to have any respect for their fathers, in their shabby old backcountry suits!"

Gaviria was a poet before he taught himself to make movies, and he has paid close attention to his actors' zigzagging, hazy, humorless speech. Through their words he has come to believe that in the *pistolocos'* fragmented world their essential relationship with reality is magical. "You see it in the language," he said. "At first, they used the word *traído* to refer to the things they 'found,' or stole. *Traído*, meaning 'that which is brought,' is a term we *paisas* use to refer to the Christmas gifts that the baby Jesus leaves on the table, so they would say, 'Look at this motorcycle, or this watch—what a *traído* I found!' Then the word became its opposite: *traído* referred to an enemy, and then to a corpse. That is, *traído* refers to everything that appears in front of one, which in the end is always death." An essential part of the magic involves turning everyone into an enemy, to ward off surprises. "Once John Galvis and another boy pulled guns on my producer and me, and yelled '*Quietos!*'—'Freeze!' That's another word. There's a children's game in which you point and yell 'Freeze!' and turn the others into statues. Now the kids refer to their holdup or murder victims as *quietos*. When they pulled guns on me, they were turning me into a *quieto*. You turn your potential enemies to stone, and they can't threaten you. The kids spend their days looking for enemies, spotting them, making them up. The point is to kill them before they kill you."

In the documentary for German television, Gaviria traces the swift deterioration of his actors into *basuco* addiction and, eventually, death. In the opening shots, the boys complain that times are hard, that there is no work anymore, and, bitterly, that they don't even have the money for a decent pair of bluejeans. Then, one by one, they drop away. With one notable exception, all of those who were killed died at the hands of other boys in the neighborhood—boys whose relatives they might have killed, or boys with whom they might have shared a gun or a joint or been blood brothers just days before. "I think that in the end the kids kill just to see what it's like," Gaviria said. He is now working on a script about a fifteen-year-old killer he knew, who had held a wounded friend's head in his lap in order to watch him die. "I think they want to know how their own passage from one world into another will be," he said.

The exception who did not die at the hands of his peers was a boy known as El Alacrán—The Scorpion. It seems that his death was a consequence of one of Pablo Escobar's ongoing efforts to take revenge on the state for its pursuit of him. Escobar has been severely hurt by the anti-drug offensive that started in the summer of 1989. His chief associate, the rather bloodier and more reckless Gonzalo Rodríguez Gacha, was killed in December of that year. Escobar's principal commercial subalterns have also been killed, and on the military side of his operations he has seen the Prisco band wiped out. He is said to be cornered and to have cash-flow problems, and to a large extent all this has happened because the restructured Medellín police have managed to keep him on the run. Accordingly, Escobar sent word around the *comunas* last April that he would pay more than four thousand dollars for every cop killed. El Alacrán, who told Gaviria and his crew that he had once been gang-raped by a police squad, was more than eager to take up Escobar's offer. According to what are necessarily unreliable reports, El Alacrán killed a few cops, and then, one day last October, was chased down by police in a patrol car and shot to death.

Whether the Medellín police pursuit of the drug chiefs has degenerated into a private war between cops and gangs has become an openly debated question in the last few weeks, largely as a result of a car bomb that went off here on February 16th, and the bomb's aftermath. The car bomb, the signature weapon of the drug trade, exploded outside the Medellín bullring that Saturday afternoon just as people were emerging from the ring into the improvised fair that sets up after *corridas*. Twenty-four people were killed and more than a hundred were seriously wounded. Of the dead, ten were members of the Medellín police force. After the rubble from the bomb was picked over, and the victims were identified, police officials explained what had happened: the car bomb was placed near a supporting pillar of a viaduct underpass—an area that is used as a parking lot on days when there are bullfights. Someone then phoned the police and reported signs of terrorist activity near that spot. When the police had got close enough, the car bomb was detonated by remote control.

On February 17th, police spokesmen declared that the bomb was the work of close friends of the last remaining Prisco, Conrado, in revenge for the death of his last surviving brother, Armando, during a shootout with the police in January. According to the police, Conrado was a typically evil member of the family who went by the nickname El Médico—The Doctor. The following day, Señora Leticia de Prisco announced the disappearance of her son, and when his body was found, two days later, the staff of the Metropolitan Institute of Health declared that Conrado Prisco had been a practicing physician—a hardworking doctor, who spent his free time in volunteer work and at the staff soccer games, and had no connection that anyone knew of to the violent world of his brothers. It seemed that somewhere a mistake had been made.

It is typical of Medellín's upside-down ethical universe that the New York–based human-rights group Americas Watch has found itself having to document claims initially made by Los Extraditables, as Escobar and a group of his associates like to be called, of police torture and arbitrary execution of drug suspects, and that Los Extraditables now routinely champion the cause of human rights in their communiqués. It is also typical of the bizarre, contradictory, and confused relations between the state and the drug trade that in Bogotá the Attorney General has opened an investigation into these charges. There are several reasons for his doing so, one being that there is serious evidence that the police routinely take the law into their own hands. It is also true that Escobar is using the cause of human rights as part of a campaign to obtain status as a "politico-military organization" similar to two guerrilla groups that were able to turn in their weapons and rejoin civilian life within the last two years. To the degree that the government is considering Los Extraditables' allegations of human-rights violations, it is signalling that political status—or some satisfactory equivalent—is not impossible. But if Pablo Escobar and his Extraditables can get a hearing from the Attorney General it is mostly because they are already a political reality and a social force whose demands the establishment can no longer ignore.

SPANISH IS NOT a language that lends itself to neologisms, and they're somewhat frowned upon in Colombia, where part of the self-definition of the élite involves a commitment to guarding the purity of the language. Nevertheless, the drugs and the violence in Medellín are so far beyond the scope of the Real Academia dictionary that new words are forever cropping up: there's *basuco*, from *pasta base de cocaina*; there's *pistoloco, violentólogo, paniquear* (as in the English verb "to panic"); and there's the ever-growing list of words prefixed with *narco-*, among them *narcocondominio* and *narco-congresista*. Old words also come to be used in curious ways. There is, for example, the "democratization" of wealth that the drug trade has brought Colombia, which means the ability granted to working-class people suddenly in the possession of drug money to rub it in the faces of the rich. Apologists for the drug trade often argue that the upper classes and the political establishment in Bogotá would never have opposed the drug trade if it had not enabled former punks and small-time hoods to buy property in the posh neighborhoods, and they may be right. In the nineteen-seventies, when Escobar was making his fortune, dealing in co-caine was still looked upon by many as a questionable but harm-less occupation, and I know society women whose mothers went on international shopping trips with Escobar's mother and thought the experience was a giggle. It wasn't until the consoli-dated drug trade emerged, in the mid-eighties, as an economic and paramilitary power capable of overturning the normal way of doing business in Colombia that the establishment reared back in alarm. But by then the traffickers had multiplied in numbers and in strength. Men like the Ochoa brothers and Escobar, in Medellín, and Gilberto Rodríguez Orejuela, in the city of Cali, about two hundred miles south of Medellín, are now prob-ably the country's most daring and successful entrepreneurs. The Ochoas ran—and probably still own—state-of-the-art cattle ranches, complete with solar-heating systems and other alternative-technology innovations. Rodríguez Orejuela has made handsome profits from radio stations, drugstore chains, and soccer teams he owns. Even Escobar, despite a funny greased-down hairdo and a lower-class belly, has put on airs. The 1988 bomb set by his rivals that literally blew open the luxury apart-ment building where he then lived revealed an apartment de-scribed as tastefully, and even soberly, furnished, stuffed with a first-rate art collection that appeared to include everything from Chinese porcelain to paintings by Fernando Botero.

At this stage, drug money has so pervaded agriculture, commerce, and real estate that, according to an estimate by Salomón Kalmanovitz, dean of the economics faculty at the Universidad Nacional, the wealth could account for as much as seven per cent of the gross national product. The members of what is known as the "leading class" have always been pragmatic—that's one of the reasons Colombia has remained institutionally stable and economically healthy despite constant turmoil—and there is among them a deep-seated conviction that, however repugnant the drug traders may be, they are now too powerful to be successfully challenged. Consequently, throughout the succession of government anti-drug offensives and drug wars there has remained an undercurrent of conciliation.

In 1984, former President Alfonso López Michelsen met in Panama with Pablo Escobar and Jorge Luis Ochoa, who offered to bring their money back to Colombia and turn over their laboratories if the government proved willing to grant them an amnesty. Five years later, when world consumption of cocaine had doubled, an intermediary for the Medellín group made a new offer, this time in a series of meetings with President Virgilio Barco's private secretary, Germán Montoya. The Medellín group was again offering to get out of the business, but this time they were asking for more. This time they wanted extradition declared unconstitutional. They also wanted to make sure that the country's various guerrilla groups—which had made a practice of extorting "war taxes" on ranch land, including the very considerable holdings of the narcotraficantes—would be defeated. Talks between Montoya and the Medellín intermediaries ended the week after the Presidential candidate Luis Carlos Galán was assassinated and the Barco administration declared war on the drug trade. But by then there were a number of members of the establishment—like Juan Gómez Martínez, the publisher of the daily El Colombiano and also, at the time, the mayor of Medellín—who were willing to go on record as stating flatly that the only way to bring the violence in the country to an end was to negotiate with the traffickers and legalize the cocaine trade. People familiar with the thinking of Barco's successor, President César Gaviria, say that he was convinced long before he took office, last August 7th, that a negotiated way out of the drug crisis was unavoidable and indispensable. One of his first acts was to issue a decree that would eliminate extradition—the principal focus of the traffickers' anti-government campaign—if they turned themselves in. In addition, the government offered a major reduction of their sentences to traffickers who took up this offer. It is Gaviria's political misfortune that Pablo Escobar decided to strengthen the Presidential resolution with a series of kidnappings of prominent Colombians which began a few weeks after Gaviria's inauguration.

Two hostages now remain in captivity: one of the heirs to Colombia's most powerful publishing family; and the sister-in-law of Luis Carlos Galán, the Presidential candidate who was murdered on the day the 1989 anti-drug offensive started. Also in the initial group of hostages were Marina Montoya, the sixty-five-year-old sister of Germán Montoya, who is now Ambassador to Canada, and forty-year-old Diana Turbay, the cherished only daughter of former President Julio César Turbay Ayala (1978–82), who is an immensely powerful man. Sometime last October, when Los Extraditables had collected ten hostages, they announced that they would like to bargain, and this time they offered much less favorable terms than any in the past. The government immediately issued a few modifications of its original extradition decree; for instance, it allowed a trafficker who may be facing serious charges in the United States to avoid extradition by confessing to only one (presumably minor) crime here. Polls showed that the public supported the unacknowledged negotiations, and so did the Archbishop of Bogotá and the leftist leader and the two former Presidents—Misael Pastrana and Alfonso López Michelsen—who occasionally form a negotiating body with the drug traffickers and the guerrillas. As a sign of the drug traffickers' good will, there was quiet in Medellín for a few weeks, which gave rise to a type of story that appears once or twice a year in the local press under headlines like "Medellín Resurgent!"

An image that filled the television screens late in January, of former President Turbay leaning over the coffin of his dead daughter, Diana, is likely to remain with Colombians for some time. Turbay is not a popular man here, particularly among liberals and the left. During his administration, the military were given a great deal of money and free rein in their endless war against the guerrillas, and it was in those years that Amnesty International issued its first damning report on Colombia, detailing the military's systematic use of torture. I watched the television report on Diana Turbay's funeral with a leftist friend for whom loathing her father was almost a matter of principle, but the sight of the heartbroken old man muttering endearments into the coffin made my friend blink and turn away.

"It's the democratization of pain," the *violentólogo* Alonso Salazar commented later on that scene. "It used to be that only the poor of this country had to feel that kind of sorrow." It was a botched show of force by the police at a farm on the outskirts of Medellín, where Diana Turbay was being held, that enabled her captors to shoot her before their escape. In the following hours, Diana's mother, Nydia Quintero (she is divorced from Julio César Turbay), added to the national commotion by blaming President Gaviria for her daughter's death. He should have kept the police away, she said, and she went on to ask that he make peace with the drug trade as quickly as possible. That, then, was the national mood two months ago: the cocaine traffickers are too powerful to take on; let's settle with them quickly, bring them into the mainstream, and put a stop to the bloodshed.

However, when President Gaviria went on television the following week and announced that further lenient modifications of the narcodecrees were being studied and would soon be announced, the speech did not sit well. "How much did the government give in?" *Semana*, the leading newsweekly, asked. On January 30th, the day after Gaviria's speech, a communiqué from Los Extraditables announced that before Diana's unfortunate death they had ordered the execution of another hostage, and that it was probably too late to cancel the order. The body of Marina Montoya was identified on January 31st. Seventeen days later, Fortunato Gaviria, a cousin and close friend of President Gaviria, died in the course of an amateurish kidnap attempt, which appeared to have been contracted out by Escobar. When Gaviria's government minister then affirmed that the new narcodecrees would stand, quite a few people thought that the President was looking craven.

Against that charge, Gaviria's defenders affirm that the decrees are part of a strategy to continue armed attempts to stop the drug trade while offering the traffickers a bloodless way out. They point out that Jorge Luis Ochoa, Medellín's second-biggest trafficker, has surrendered, along with two of his brothers, and is peacefully awaiting trial in Medellín. They don't point out, although they could, that while Pablo Escobar may be on the run, and cocaine seizures are at an all-time high, the big 1989 anti-drug offensive has hardly been a success, despite having taken the military approach to the drug problem about as far as it can go. Except for Gonzalo Rodríguez Gacha, Escobar's terrorist associate, not a single head of a drug-export ring has been caught, and Rodríguez's share of the market has simply been reapportioned among a group of up-and-coming traders. United States narcotics officials believe that partly as a result of the drug war, which has been directed mostly against the traders in Medellín, a group of traders based in Cali has been able to overtake the Medellín group in terms of their share of the export market. Meanwhile, the overall production and export of cocaine from Colombia are estimated to be up slightly from what they were when the offensive began. Under the circumstances, a negotiated surrender by the drug traffickers might make sense, but a member of the diplomatic community pointed out that the government has opted for a conciliatory approach "at a stage when the judicial system doesn't seem up to the task." The roles of judge and prosecutor are combined under the country's Napoleonic Code, and those judges capable of refusing a bribe often do not have the resources to gather evidence that will stick against even the

most notorious traffickers. Someone here who was closely involved with the Ochoas' surrender told me that at this stage the
government has no charges against any of the brothers, and that,
even with evidence provided by the United States of charges
against him there, the likelihood is that Jorge Luis Ochoa will
get off with a three- or four-year sentence.

As for Escobar, this person thought that he was waiting to
see the results of some of the Ochoa trials before turning himself
in. Opinion is divided on this. Some diplomats here think that
Escobar will settle for nothing less than recognition of Los Extraditables as a politico-military organization, which could conceiv-
ably entitle him to run for Congress again in a few years. Others
think that he will never put himself in a Colombian jail, where a
legion of his enemies could get at him.

NO MATTER WHAT HAPPENS to the founders and leaders of the
cocaine trade, however, no one seems to have any idea of what
to do with the gangs they are leaving behind. There doesn't seem
to be any way that even Medellín's comparatively generous
municipal-services structure can stretch itself to the dimensions
of the crisis at hand. There aren't enough ambulances, clinics,
teachers, and efficient policemen to go around, and, anyway, it's
unclear at this stage whether even the most judicious efforts by
law-abiding cops and enlightened social workers could bring
measurable short-term relief. I talked to a man involved from the
social-services point of view in the city's efforts to cope with the
violence, and he went on about municipal plans to unify the various existing plans, and about joint housing-rehabilitation programs with international nongovernmental organizations, and
about the redirecting of budget expenditures, until I interrupted
to ask whether he had ever been on the hills, and whether, having
been there, he thought that any of his proposed measures would
do any good.

At that, he threw up his hands and heaved a great sigh. "You
would have to change the society altogether for the problem to
disappear," he said. "*Paisas* are adventurous by nature. You know,
Antioquia was colonized only in the last century, and the people

who came here were mostly gold miners. We're a migrant people, enterprising, and fond of wealth and risk. The tragedy was that in the nineteen-seventies, when the private-enterprise system was crashing to the ground in Antioquia, the traffickers showed up with an alternative, and in a stratified society like this one it was very appealing: the traffickers said 'You, too, can have a swimming pool, and you don't even have to work for it. Work will never make you rich.' The fundamental thing is that we can't offer better prospects. We know of a lot of companies here that fire their good workers—the ones who last—at the end of their ninth year of employment, because after ten years they have a right to half a pension. How can you convince a kid that there's a future in being a good citizen and working a steady job? I don't see any real change in the situation for this generation."

I asked this man if the city's job would be made any easier by Escobar's capture or surrender.

He looked at me in amazement. "Don't you see that part of the reason things are so bad now is precisely that Escobar is so much weaker than he used to be?" he said. "There's tremendous unemployment among the drug gangs now, and they're all fighting for the available crumbs. Also, there are all sorts of old scores that are getting settled, now that there's no one to keep the lid on things. Everybody's free-lancing; there are the death squads and the pseudo-revolutionary groups. An awful lot of teen-agers have weapons. This city is going to be in dreadful shape for the immediate future."

I MET A YOUNG MAN, about twenty-five, whom I shall call Johnny. (The English name is a favorite here.) When Johnny was ten, his father, who was an alcoholic and travelled the countryside doing odd jobs, finally settled, with his wife and their six children, in the northeast *comuna*. By the time Johnny was twelve, he had learned to contribute to the meagre family income by begging. When he was eighteen, the military press-ganged him, along with dozens of other youths, in a noonday sweep through the streets of the downtown district. Following this forcible conscription, which Johnny describes as a "waking nightmare," he served out the mandatory eighteen-month draft term, acquiring an extensive knowledge of weapons and then an honorable discharge. He returned home and found a job as a security guard for a downtown office building. An overwhelming desire to "improve my mother's life" made him single out a friendly-looking executive and sneak some time from his duty hours to wash and polish the executive's car. His hope was that the executive would notice this, be pleased, and offer him a better-paying job as a bodyguard, driver, or carwasher. What actually happened was that Johnny's supervisor caught him in the act and immediately fired him.

Eventually, Johnny was able to find another job, as a messenger, but the work pained him. Above all, he says over and over, he has always wanted desperately "to do the right thing, to improve my situation, to be a *persona decente.*" He wanted to furnish his mother's house with matched dining- and living-room sets, and have a job in which he was not faceless and nameless, but he couldn't see his way from here to there, from messenger work to being called Señor. Nevertheless, he worked steadily for almost seven years, because he had found more consuming activities, which made his daytime hours seem pale and secondary. First, he ran into one of the many guerrilla groups operating in the *comunas,* and eagerly joined its clandestine game of hide-and-seek with the military, but after several months the Army moved seriously against the neighborhood and the guerrillas swiftly withdrew, leaving Johnny and his friends to take the heat. Johnny lay low for a while, and then, through what he calls "a pioneering innovation," he found his lifework: he founded a *grupo de autodefensa,* or death squad, and he believes that it was the first of its kind in Medellín.

What got him started was the experience of seeing his younger brother Tony wounded in the course of a *banda* holdup at the corner grocery store in his neighborhood. The *banda* kids were attacking an old man, and Tony asked them to lay off. At this, one of the boys cracked a beer bottle in half and lunged at his throat, wounding him seriously but not fatally. Johnny says that he watched the assault and felt unbearably humiliated by his own impotence, and that that emotion is what guided him to the idea of an *autodefensa*. What is more likely is that, after a lifetime of systematic humiliation and terror with no possibility of retribution, Johnny understood that he was finally facing an enemy he could actually take on.

Johnny has talked with reporters before, and he easily agreed to talk to me. We met in a small, crowded coffee shop downtown, and no one paid any attention to Johnny—a nondescript young man in bluejeans and a baggy T-shirt—even though he got noticeably tense, occasionally rhetorical, and at times almost giggly as he talked.

"I formed the *autodefensa* with a neighbor who had a wife and two kids and was sick of violence, too," he said. "We didn't know how the two of us would manage to defeat more than two hundred kids who would be our sworn enemies, but we agreed that it was a risk we had to take. We recruited two other boys and started out on this endless task. On my block, one out of every three families had a son or a relative who was a *banda* member. We decided that the thing to do was to clean up the block first, and spread out from there. My idea was that we had to strike terror to the heart of the community in order to be effective. We went around and borrowed black shirts and trousers from some older men around the block, and a girl we knew stitched black hoods together for us. Then, one evening, around ten o'clock, we walked up to our first chosen victim, who was sitting on a stoop drinking beer, and we did it. We executed him. Then we ran around the corner, took our hoods and shirts off, and came back to help the family take the body away."

Johnny seemed both terribly frightened and amused at this part of the story. It was, he thinks now, an act of brilliance to remain in clandestinity while the kids from different *bandas* grew paranoid and started blaming each other for the wave of murders. In the first three months, he said, the *autodefensa* eliminated some thirty "undesirables." Then the work got easier, because the undesirables started eliminating each other, and those who didn't fled the neighborhood in terror. These days, he said, his barrio is a nice place to visit. It's *tranquilo*, calm, no problem.

Was his work finished, then?

"Oh, not at all. I don't know what makes these kids so perverse, but there always seem to be a few who like the bad life.
Right now, there's a little spurt of activity, and, regrettably, I think
we're going to have to take measures."

Shortly after my conversation with Johnny, a communiqué
was delivered to the parish priest of Barrio Santa Cruz, in the
northeastern *comuna*, with the information that someone would
be at the Sunday sermon to make sure that the priest read the
communiqué to the congregation. (He did.) The communiqué
was signed by a group calling itself the GAM, or Grupo Amable
Medellín, which translates as Nice Medellín Group. It said, in
part, "We alert all parents and the community in general that they
should dialogue with their sons so that they will not continue
smoking *basuco*, since this is harmful to their health and a bad
example to growing children. . . . There will be a general
cleanup, and neither sex nor religion will be respected. We will
shoot anyone who does not obey this letter."

A few days later, on February 27th, a group that signs itself
Robocop took credit for the recent murder of nine teen-agers,
who were rounded up when they were playing soccer in the
northwestern *comuna*. Because they share a common target, one
might conclude that groups like Robocop, Nice Medellín, and
Johnny's *autodefensa* are friendly to the police, but there is no indication that these groups are linked to the police or even to each
other. In fact, when I asked Johnny if he approved of the police's
alleged involvement in the killing of the Prisco brothers and
other murders, he was emphatic. "Cops are murderers," he said.
"They massacre everybody. I'm a Christian, and I only take human life when it's absolutely necessary. Besides, there are some
very respectable *bandas*—like the Priscos were, for example.
They don't attack their own communities but only work outside.
We don't touch them."

After our conversation was over, we left the coffee shop together. It was the height of the afternoon rush hour and I had
trouble keeping Johnny in sight—an insignificant kid from the
comunas without even a trendy T-shirt to stand out in. But Johnny

knows perfectly well that he is an important person in Medellín, and I have seen pimply kids approach him on the street to seek his help in putting together death squads of their own. He is in demand, just like the numerous guerrilla leaders in Colombia whom journalists climb over mountains to get to. He makes guerrilla-like statements, as he did to me when he told me he had never been in love. "I preferred to devote my love to my homeland," he declared, holding himself very straight. He is a person of consequence, and he will continue to be so as long as he holds life-or-death power over a sizable number of people here. It's the only power he has, a power he shares with the punk killers who are his enemies, and it's enough to keep them all going for a long time—for as long, at least, as they live.

BUENOS AIRES
1991

"People follow me because I am a transgressing President."

DANIEL CAPALBO listens to two radio stations at the same time, lights one cigarette with the burning stub of another, and bites his fingernails ferociously. He is a reporter, and he resembles a stock character from *The Front Page* in so many ways that one keeps looking for his fedora. The stories he has to assign and cover these days in Argentina really belong on the stage: the President won't travel without his private hairdresser and is passionately fond of driving a red Ferrari at twice the maximum legal speed; he kicked his wife out of the official residence; his sister-in-law and former appointments secretary is under investigation, for having allegedly carried suitcases crammed with cash from New York to Buenos Aires at the behest of the cocaine trade. In true Argentine fashion, Capalbo looks mournful whenever he's asked how he's doing, but the fact is that he's having the time of his life with this stuff. The early-winter sun shines here in the season's perfect blue sky, soccer stadiums fill to the top for the local championship games, as does the grand Teatro Colón, where the opera season packs the audience with solid rows of tuxedos and diamonds. Ice-cream parlors stay open past midnight. Night clubs are full of gorgeous men and kinky women. What's best, though, is to stock up on newspapers and magazines and repair to a sidewalk café to absorb the latest scandal.

There are newsstands all over the city—sometimes four to a corner. Van-size, they are papered on all sides and filled to eye level with publications: newspapers, poetry journals, specialized porn, foreign decorating magazines, a Yiddish weekly, a German daily, and even a monthly devoted to the semiotic and political analysis of local and foreign comic strips. None of these are cheap—the daily papers cost the equivalent of about seventy-five cents—and, despite the sold-out opera evenings, not all that many Argentines have cash to spare these days, but sales are brisk. Mostly the boom is due to something even the chronically gloomy *porteños,* or inhabitants of this port city, recognize as an unqualified positive achievement of the years since 1983, when the military dictatorship came to an end: before, newspapers and magazines were thick with pictures and almost devoid of information, but now people say, "With the press free, we get to find out what's going on." What's going on, at least in the media's telling of it, is breathtaking.

There has been no lack of stories since President Carlos Menem took office, two years ago, but Daniel Capalbo dates the symbolic anniversary of the scandal era to a week last July, when the magazine he was then working for, *Noticias,* ran a cover photograph of the head of the state telephone company, María Julia Alsogaray, wearing nothing more, apparently, than some draped fur and an enticing smile. The image was resonant for reasons beyond the fact that senior government officials are not supposed to appear in public in provocative states of undress. María Julia, now forty-eight, was familiar to her startled observers. Stocky, dark-haired, and invariably dressed in sombre colors, she had enjoyed for much of the last three decades a reputation not for flightiness but for ruthless loyalty to the cause of her father, the ultraconservative politician Alvaro Alsogaray. The elder Alsogaray got less than seven per cent of the vote in his last try for the Presidency, but those million and a half votes were powerful: the military establishment and the moneyed élite are the source of much of his support.

Because Alsogaray has made a career of opposing the populist caudillo Juan Domingo Perón (1895–1974) and Perón's politi-

cal successors, the first but not the greatest shock for followers
of the family's political fortunes came in July of 1989, when the
Peronist Carlos Menem, newly sworn in as President, appointed
the father to the ranks of his political advisers and put the daughter in charge of privatizing the state telephone company. The
situation was odd—a Peronist President asking a relentless political adversary to sell off a company that Perón himself had appropriated for the state. The photographs that soon began appearing
in the press were odder still: María Julia and the President together at numerous state and social functions; María Julia showing off a mane of newly red hair and an increasingly shapely
figure; María Julia laughing enchantingly, leaning so close to the
President that her cheek nearly brushed his bushy sideburns.
Still, nothing had quite prepared the public for the interview that
accompanied *Noticias'* cover photograph. "What do I feel for the
Prez? . . . I love him very much," María Julia confessed, but she
added, "Menem doesn't seduce me as a man, he's not my style."
The story was perfect: it involved a rich and powerful person
flouting convention, it touched on the Presidency, it had hubris
and sexual innuendo, and it was all designed for, and exploited
by, the press. An extra run of that issue of *Noticias* had to be
printed less than twenty-four hours after the first printing hit
the stands.

The peculiar convergence of the Menem era and an uncen-
sored and rowdy press makes for great entertainment but for less
than satisfying politics. Although Argentina has now had a civilian government for eight consecutive years, a span unequalled
since 1933, the present boisterous circus is not really the kind of
democracy that people had in mind back in 1982, when the
bloody dictatorship collapsed as a result of its defeat in the Falklands War. This city, from its Frenchified boulevards to its most
cherished rituals—five-o'clock tea, a visit to the analyst four
times a week—is the embodiment of a national longing for Europe and its rational forms of civilization; it is Bonn, say, and not
Caracas, that people here have in mind when they talk about
democracy. The sense that Argentina happens to be on the
wrong continent is pervasive. A local cartoon strip has been fea-

turing the story of an about-to-be-born baby who refuses to leave the womb until he can emerge in Europe. Comparisons with the rest of Latin America are often taken amiss and often intended venomously: the term *carnaval carioca*—"Carnival in Rio"—is used to describe an incompetent mess. A former Air Force chief of staff was just sentenced to thirty days in jail for saying that the government's likely cancellation of a missile-development program threatened to turn the country into a "banana republic." And yet, the dream of sober grandeur notwithstanding, Argentina's real history lurches forward in episodes that veer from the ludicrous to the shameful.

Capalbo, who is well acquainted with both, is thirty-five. In 1981, when he graduated from a state university with a degree in history, journalism was an almost extinguished profession. Many of the country's best reporters and editors had died in the torture camps set up by the military regime that took power in 1976. Most of the survivors were in exile. Self-censorship and toadying compliance with the policy of terror were the norm. A small literary magazine that Capalbo started back then with a few friends was clandestine of necessity. "There was nothing that could be legally written at the time," he says. "We set up the magazine because we wanted to have something to read. We wrote it, printed it, and distributed it by hand to a few friendly kiosks. It was really a way of trying to get in touch with people who felt and thought the same things we did."

After the dictatorship fell apart, Capalbo was one of the bright young men who joined Jacobo Timerman's rejuvenated version of an old establishment daily, *La Razón.* That was the time when Capalbo, too, entertained dreams of democratic journalism as a kind of platonic forum for the free and generous discussion of politics and ideas. The country had just elected Raúl Alfonsín, a President who seemed the embodiment of everything that Argentines aspired to be: He was modest, moderate, fair. Not being a Peronist, he did not come bearing that party's tradition of politics as revenge. He had not behaved cravenly during the years of dictatorial terror, and he had not indulged in the left's guerrilla lunacy. He was in every way the antithesis of the recent past, and so, Capalbo says, "he represented above all freedom from the fear of being killed." The new President was respectful of the press, and Capalbo characterizes the media's reciprocal behavior as levelheaded and boring. This peaceful interlude lasted about five years. In 1987, *La Razón* became involved in a financial scandal, at a time when its circulation was sinking. Timerman left the country in disgust, Capalbo quit, and, not long after, the Alfonsín administration began its slow and painful collapse. The century's most hopefully elected President had to leave office five months ahead of schedule—in July of 1989—defeated by an unrealistic economic program that was supposed to rescue Argentina from the financial pit the dictators had dug for it but was instead buried under an inflationary avalanche that reached a record 196.6 per cent monthly.

The Alfonsín era is ended and, with it, the national effort to be well behaved. In the new era, Capalbo's editor at *Noticias* advised him to "let his id mesh with his superego" when he sat down to write a story about Menem; in the Freudian jargon that pollutes the conversation of middle-class Argentines, that meant he should write the wildest story he could, as long as he could provide the evidence. I had lunch with Capalbo a few weeks ago, shortly after he quit *Noticias* for a better job at a daily, and I asked him to go over some of the more memorable stories he had covered or supervised for the magazine in the spirit of his editor's exhortation.

During Easter week of last year, after a series of relatively minor scandals involving the possibility of corruption at high levels of government, Capalbo said, the city's walls were covered with posters calling for "loyalty to the President but not to the corrupt ones," and naming four officials, including Menem's brother Eduardo, who is the Senate chairman, as wrongdoers. Menem's wife, Zulema Yoma, a tempestuous woman whose marriage to the President has rarely been happy, and whose relations with her in-laws are openly hostile, was widely accused of financing the poster campaign. Capalbo thinks that the posters had a great deal to do with the fact that on May 4th a year ago Menem quietly moved out of the official residence in Olivos, a

Buenos Aires suburb, and into a friend's house. This was followed by a long Presidential trip abroad, presumably timed to allow Zulema a seemly departure from Olivos and the marriage. It was not to be. She threw a lunch for the press corps at Olivos, to prove that she was still very much around ("She served us broiled beef for the main course and tangerines for dessert, to show that she was poor," a guest recalled), and stood her ground. Menem returned to Buenos Aires on June 11th, but not to Olivos. Two days later, Zulema found her way to the front door barred by men under the direct command of the brigadier in charge of Menem's security. The moment was recorded for nationwide viewing by a slew of reporters Zulema had brought along for the confrontation, having been alerted by her twenty-year-old son, Carlitos, that something was up.

Cameras also recorded Carlitos and his sister Zulemita emerging from the residence and embracing their distraught mother. That evening, Carlitos burst onto the set of a live television talk show, where the man who had drafted the Presidential decree expelling Zulema from Olivos was being interviewed, and demanded equal time.

"I know your father," the interviewer said. "And he must be crying as he watches this on television."

"All my life I have suffered, I have wept, for the two of them," Carlitos replied, looking near tears.

On July 2nd, Menem threw a huge sixtieth birthday party for himself in his home province, La Rioja; the celebration was reportedly organized by his constant companion María Julia Alsogaray. The *Noticias* cover story on her ran three weeks later.

A relative lull followed, which continued through December, when an abortive military uprising shook the country. Then, in January, came allegations that one of Menem's in-laws was involved in an extortion. This scandal, far from going away, has snowballed, to a point where the lull is remembered fondly now, as, in a way, are the good old days when the most one could gasp about was the President's wife banging on her own front door in full view of the nation. Similar stories have followed, of course; Capalbo can list the President's hot-rodding to the beach in the red Ferrari (a gift from some Italian-industrialist admirers), his subsequent weekend of photographically documented spiritual retreat at a Trappist monastery, and also his weekend of undocumented retreat in the bosky south of the country, from which he emerged with a swollen face that was explained as a reaction to a wasp sting. (*Noticias* gleefully tried to demonstrate that it was actually the result of a face-lift: the magazine produced witnesses who saw Menem enter a famous plastic surgeon's clinic late that Friday evening, and witnesses who saw the surgeon arrive at Olivos the following week, but the President's associates vigorously denied that any surgery took place.) Meanwhile, Menem has acquired a three-hundred-thousand-dollar bachelor pad in downtown Buenos Aires, and Zulema has filed for divorce, on the ground of infidelity.

THE MOST IMPORTANT STORIES in the headlines now, however, are not about flings and eyelid tucks but about drug trafficking and unfettered corruption—stories that Capalbo thinks would threaten the survival of a government in any European country or in the United States. But there are two reasons no one is questioning the stability of the Menem administration at this stage. The first is that, while the scandals so far have involved Presidential in-laws and Presidential appointees—and, in the most explosive cases, Presidential in-laws who are Presidential appointees—Menem himself has not been accused of any criminal activity. The second reason has to do with the experimental nature of democracy here—nobody knows what the rules of the game are, and no one knows what is supposed to happen if the game folds. Nevertheless, the stories that are appearing almost every day in the press must make unhappy breakfast reading in government circles.

Most of the worst stories involve Zulema Yoma's brothers and sisters. She has nine of them, and they all maintain close ties with Syria, from which both Menem's and the Yomas' parents emigrated early in the century. One sister, Delia, lived in Damascus for nearly thirty years, and is married to a retired Syrian Army officer. A brother, Karim, who runs a leather-import business in

Madrid, was Secretary of Special Affairs in the Argentine Foreign Ministry after Menem took power. Another brother, Emir, runs the family leather-processing factory, and was until recently a Presidential adviser. The youngest sibling, Amalia, who is known as Amira, served as Menem's appointments secretary. She lived in Syria for several years and is reportedly a member of Hafez al-Assad's Baath Party. Amira used to be married to a Syrian national, Ibrahim al Ibrahim, who served briefly under Menem as an "overseer" for customs at Buenos Aires' Ezeiza Airport. He was removed from the post in March, shortly after the Spanish press broke the scandal that has become known, inevitably, as Yomagate.

The scandal involves allegations that Karim Yoma, Amira Yoma, and Ibrahim al Ibrahim were all part of a multinational money-laundering ring, in which the key Argentine operative is said to have been Menem's former head of the federal water system; this man is currently under arrest in Buenos Aires. The story first appeared in print in March, in the Spanish magazine *Cambio16*, when, as a result of a Spanish government investigation, one of the alleged participants in the laundering operation turned state's evidence, implicating the Yomas. The Spanish government's witness, Indalecio Iglesias Cruz, who was arrested following the seizure of five hundred and thirty kilos of cocaine on a ship docked in Cape Verde, told the Spanish federal prosecutor in the case how previous drug-money profits had been shipped from New York to Ezeiza Airport and from there to Uruguay and, presumably, Europe. Ibrahim's was among the names mentioned, along with those of a number of Cuban, Panamanian, and Uruguayan operatives, one of whom has since been arrested in Montevideo and is facing extradition to the United States. Iglesias said he had been told by his Argentine control to contact Karim Yoma in Madrid, because Karim had already performed some money-laundering services for the ring. More damningly, he said that he and two associates had once gone to Ezeiza Airport to meet Amira Yoma and Ibrahim, who turned over four suitcases they had just brought from New York. Iglesias then verified that the suitcases were full of United States currency. Amira Yoma has been on leave from her post on Menem's staff since shortly after the scandal broke. (She has not been charged with any crime in either Argentina or Spain.) At the request of the Spanish prosecutor, Ibrahim has been indicted in Buenos Aires on charges that he used his position as Presidential appointee at Ezeiza Airport for money-laundering purposes.

According to people who know the Yomas well, by far the most intelligent and ambitious member of the family is Emir. He is Menem's longtime financial backer and ally—so much so that even during two lengthy separations between Zulema Yoma and Menem Emir remained friendly with his brother-in-law. He was a go-between in each of the couple's unsuccessful reconciliation attempts: once in 1982, after an initial four-year separation, when Menem ran for reëlection as governor of La Rioja, and then again in 1988, following a second four-year estrangement, after Menem won the Peronists' Presidential candidacy. On taking power, Menem appointed Emir a Presidential adviser, and in December of 1989 named Erman González, Emir's former accountant at the leather factory, Economy Minister. (González was shifted from Economy to the Defense Ministry last February.) Emir Yoma, who has not been implicated in the money-laundering case, was dismissed from his advisory post in January, as the result of another scandal, still unfolding, in which he is accused of participating in an extortion scheme against the Swift-Armour transnational meat-packing corporation—a scandal known now as Swiftgate, which could end up implicating the highest levels of government in a criminal cover-up.

Like nearly all the most significant Argentine stories of the last twelve months, the one that may yet be the undoing of the Yoma clan first saw print in *Página/12*, an upstart daily that has just finished celebrating its fourth anniversary, and whose circulation has climbed in that short time to the No. 3 spot. It doesn't look like a major daily, and it certainly doesn't act like one. For one thing, Jorge Lanata, the editor-in-chief, is barely thirty-one, and his idea of business attire is bluejeans, a tweed jacket, and a neon tie. The Government House (Casa Rosada) correspondent, in charge of covering Menem, is an ebullient twenty-five-year-old who could pass for seventeen. The paper looks and reads like what one would expect from such a crowd—a literate rag for Latin America's most literate and literary population. The tabloid format is cluttered with overambitious graphic design; the paper's scope is narrow, focussing almost exclusively on Menem, capital politics, and the military. The back pages are full of ads for Lacan workshops and rolfing therapy. It is unabashedly of the left, and conscientiously provocative.

Readers love it. They talk about the savage cartoon that appears every day on the front page and repeat the punning headlines, which Lanata is usually responsible for, and which he freely admits are often dreadful. On Corrientes Avenue, where the newsstands and secondhand bookstores stay open all night, one can enter any café at 2 a.m. and see a group engaged in an intense discussion of the general hopelessness and hilarity of events as presented in the latest *Página*. Months after a given event, *porteños* of every political leaning summarized their own reaction to it for me by describing *Página*'s front page. There was the time the paper responded to Menem's accusation that it was engaging in "yellow journalism" by printing the entire edition on bright-yellow paper. There was the front page for the first day of the World Cup soccer tournament last year, in Milan: it was written entirely in spaghetti Italian, including the front-page joke and an account of an outburst from Zulema Yoma (*"Explosivi declarazione di Zulema: La Prima Donna"*). There was the time when the Planning Minister announced an inflation index far below what consumers had measured on their supermarket bills, and Lanata turned the tabloid format sideways to make room for the Minister's nose, which the art department had lengthened to match Pinocchio's.

Irreverence edged with anger is what makes *Página/12* fit in so nicely with the spirit of the times, but what keeps it journalistically viable is its muckraking. Its most signal achievement so far has been its coverage of the Swiftgate scandal, which, together with Yomagate, has transformed the President's normally easygoing charm into irritability. Swiftgate began on January 6th, when the paper leaked a letter from the United States Ambassador, Terence Todman, addressed to the then Economy Minister,

Erman González. In the letter Todman informed González that certain high Argentine government officials had asked Swift-Armour, which has had significant investments in Argentina since the beginning of the century, "for substantial payments in order to provide the necessary documents to import machinery." (In fact, what Swift was requesting was a standard tax exemption, worth four hundred thousand dollars, on equipment already at customs.) Three days later, *Página* and two other dailies stated that the man extorting payment from Swift-Armour was none other than Emir Yoma, the President's brother-in-law and the former boss of the Economy Minister. Although the President initially accused *Página* of being a "journalistic delinquent," Todman confirmed that the letter was authentic. There followed a burst of tension in the normally smooth relations between the Menem and the Bush Administrations, and a federal-court inquiry. Ambassador Todman predictably declined to appear in court. The Swift-Armour official who had been asked for the bribe did testify but declined to identify his extortioner. The reporter who wrote the original *Página* story refused to reveal his sources, and, for lack of evidence, the investigation was provisionally closed down on May 3rd.

There was also a separate investigation by a standing body of government attorneys, which Menem asked to trace how the story found its way into print. The investigators failed to uncover the mysterious extortioner's identity, but in their report to the President they did conclude that Raúl Granillo Ocampo—the man who had drafted the Presidential decree expelling Zulema Yoma from Olivos—was the source of *Página*'s leak.

Granillo Ocampo, who is well groomed, good-looking, and fond of wearing dark glasses, is a powerful member of Menem's inner circle. Like Menem and the Yomas, he is from La Rioja. It is hard to know what to make of the fact that at last report he was continuing to play a weekly game of tennis with the President, or of the fact that after the investigators named him as the leak he told *Noticias* that if the government continued to accuse him he would be morally obliged to tell what he knew before a court. (There are reliable indications that he was not in fact the source of the *Página* leak.) The workings of the inner circle have always been hard to decipher; it is small, goes back a long way, and is held together by conflicting but unswerving loyalties. Granillo Ocampo is probably the man whose political judgment Menem trusts most.

There has been speculation in the press that the whole Swiftgate affair was engineered by the anti-Yoma faction in Menem's inner circle to force Menem to break with his embarrassing in-laws. Others see the hand of Menem himself behind the scandal. A foreign diplomat speculated that Swiftgate was actually a way of driving a wedge between the Menem and the Bush Administrations at a time when the Argentine government is seeking what its Foreign Minister Guido di Tella refers to as "carnal relations" with the United States. (In pursuit of that goal, Argentina sent two warships to the Gulf War, sided with the United States in a human-rights vote against Cuba at the United Nations, and keeps in such close touch with Ambassador Todman that he is commonly referred to here as "the viceroy." Bush, for his part, played tennis with Menem on his state visit last December.)

For whatever reasons, Granillo Ocampo retained his friend-ship with the President and simultaneously indicated that he would spill the beans on Swiftgate. Taking the hint, the judge in charge of the federal investigation reopened the case on May 10th. Granillo Ocampo reportedly met with Menem and told him what he was planning to testify, but very few other people had an inkling of what he would say. The day after the inquiry reopened, I went by the *Página/12* offices to ask Lanata, who is facing several libel suits, what would happen with Swiftgate. "Nothing" was his unhesitating reply. "Our reporter will be questioned again and refuse to reveal his sources. Granillo Ocampo will be called in again and deny everything, and that will be the end of that."

With certain exceptions, trials and court proceedings are secret in Argentina, and no one knew what Granillo Ocampo had said until the following week, when *Página* published a devastating account of his testimony, based on undisclosed sources. According to the *Página* version, the question of Emir Yoma's alleged bribe-taking had been discussed at a Cabinet meeting on January 11th, five days after *Página* leaked the Todman letter. Menem chaired the meeting, and the then Foreign Minister, Domingo Cavallo, who had met with Todman earlier, told the President and the rest of the Cabinet that Swift-Armour's extortioner was indeed Emir Yoma. After Cavallo allegedly finished reporting what he was said to have learned from Todman, *Página* went on to say, Yoma was called in; Cavallo told him that Todman's source for the damning information on him was a Swift-Armour official. Yoma denied everything.

There are those who would argue that within the national context of crime, which in the recent past has included officially sanctioned torture and murder and the merry embezzlement of uncounted billions of dollars, Emir Yoma's alleged involvement in an extortion bid is a relatively minor affair. As Menem's next-oldest brother and acting appointments secretary, Munir, put it, talking with a reporter about the dollar value of the tax exemption Swift was seeking, "they're uncovering a case worth barely four hundred thousand dollars. That really isn't an amount to get alarmed about." The fact is, though, that most people here—and particularly the working-class people who voted for Menem—have to struggle to earn a decent living and are often kept awake at night by the fear that the monster of hyperinflation could reappear at any moment to devour their income. Tens of thousands of state-enterprise workers have been laid off since Menem took power, as part of his ambitious free-market plan to restructure the economy and ease the state's lopsided burden. For weeks now, retirees have been camping out in front of the federal-court building, angrily demanding an increase in their pensions, which are a hundred and twenty dollars a month. These are the people who are at the core of the Peronists' traditional base of support, and soliciting a bribe worth four hundred thousand dollars—no matter which government officials were involved—looks greedy indeed from their perspective. Menem is not accused of taking the money, but in *Página*'s telling of the Cabinet-meeting episode he appears clearly implicated in a cover-up. The story does not sit well with the citizenry.

So far, though, the consequences of the revelations are nebulous. Menem would probably have suffered substantially greater political damage if the day before the *Página* story he hadn't publicly announced that he would rid the country of corruption, "no matter who's involved." No heads have rolled yet. Although all the government officials present at the Cabinet meeting have been called in to testify in the court's ongoing Swiftgate investigation, only Granillo Ocampo has commented publicly on the case. He has upheld *Página*'s story. It is reported that Emir Yoma has also been called in to testify, but leaks are getting harder to come by these days, and no one at *Página* knows what he said. Yoma does not give the impression of a man in disgrace, though: Menem was the guest of honor at the baptism of Yoma's only son, and Yoma spends much of his time in the private office of the President's chief of staff, Eduardo Bauzá.

THE MAN WHO BROKE the Swiftgate story and most of *Página*'s other big scoops is Horacio Verbitsky, a work-obsessed forty-nine-year-old reporter who comes out of what he calls "the militant, rancorous, aggressive, unforgiving tradition of the nineteen-seventies," and is delighted to have his natural tendencies tempered now by the more lighthearted kids at *Página*. Typically, having said this, he looked almost offended when I commented that he was indeed looking very happy these days. "Happiness is for more serious things," he retorted. As a reporter, at least, Verbitsky is blessed with an almost complete inability to see the good side of any situation. For him, the press's current freedom is only a sign that "the bourgeoisie is feeling very strong, and so the press is a luxury it can allow itself." He thinks that *Página*'s high circulation is possible because the collapse of the dictatorship and, above all, the humiliation of the Falklands War created what he describes as a new, less arrogant moral climate, in which people finally needed to hear the truth about themselves. He is not at all sure that the new humility will last, though, or that Argentina will be able to refrain from undertaking another wild adventure in the near future. "If Argentines aren't marching to the clash of cymbals, we're not satisfied," he says. "We always need to go riding to glory."

I went to see him one recent Monday, the day after *Página* ran a four-page story of his which moved several people I know to phone each other for comfort after reading it. The story was about a Chilean immigrant named Luis Jaramillo, a forty-one-year-old factory worker whose passions were classical music and mechanical inventions, who was never a militant of the union in the boiler factory where he worked for sixteen years, and who was respected by both his co-workers and his supervisors. He was "disappeared" one day in 1976, along with seventy other workers, not long after the Peronist Montonero guerrillas kidnapped a factory manager, and in the midst of an escalating series of demands by the union. The management of the factory had called in the military to set up operations inside the factory grounds and deal with "the labor process and the terrorist process." The disappearance of Jaramillo and the other workers was a result. At the time, military operations of that kind were called cleanups. Now they are what Argentina remembers as the Dirty War.

It lasted six years; left at least nine thousand dead, nearly all of them kidnapped, or *desaparecidos;* taught an entire generation of soldiers that torture is a legitimate weapon; destroyed what there was of Argentina's feeble civic tradition; and went on under the willful indifference of much of society. Theoretically, it was designed to extinguish the Montoneros and the members of the People's Revolutionary Army, or E.R.P., whose combined numbers could not have come to more than three or four thousand in the groups' heyday. The Montoneros had been formed, with Perón's equivocal consent, to fight for his return from an eighteen-year exile in Franco's Spain. The Marxist E.R.P. was fighting for socialist revolution. Perón returned, aging and addled, in 1973, and easily won the Presidential elections, with his third wife, the former cabaret dancer María Estela Martínez, or Isabelita, as his Vice-President, and with her spiritual adviser, the sinister ultra-rightist José López Rega, as the regime's éminence grise. Perón died in 1974, and under Isabelita the country slipped into chaos. López Rega organized death squads against Jews, Montoneros, and suspected leftists, laying the groundwork for the terror that began when the military finally stepped in, in 1976. Isabelita and most senior Peronist officials were placed under arrest then. (One of them was Menem, who at the time was governor of La Rioja province.) Intellectuals, journalists, and men like Luis Jaramillo were suddenly prime targets of a war they never knew they had been recruited for.

The things the military did to people like Jaramillo during the Dirty War have been well documented since, but Verbitsky's story in *Página/12* was different, because he had found a former manager at the factory where Jaramillo worked. This man had not been able to shake off his guilt over the part he had played in the workers' fate, and he was willing to describe the decision-making process that led to management's invitation to the military to operate within the factory, in full knowledge of what was likely to happen. Verbitsky thus provided what is probably the only existing firsthand account of the private sector's significant role in the military's bloody national purge.

Verbitsky's reconstruction of Jaramillo's captivity and execution was made possible by the patient work of a group of young men and women who call themselves simply the Argentine Forensic Anthropology Team. Started seven years ago by a United States forensic specialist, Dr. Clyde C. Snow, the group has been systematically digging up Argentina's awful past, in the form of mass graves where the Dirty War soldiers deposited their dead. The forensic team excavates the graves with archeological precision, sorting and numbering the bones, so that the real history of Argentina may be known, and so that families may one day properly bury their dead. It found Jaramillo's remains late last year and, through the network of *desaparecido* survivors and relatives, was able to give Verbitsky an account of Jaramillo's passage through various camps, with their routine of torture, beatings, and starvation. Prisoners who were held with Jaramillo have testified that they were fed twice a month and were allowed to drink water every four or five days, and that the bodies of those who died from this treatment were left to rot among the survivors. Jaramillo survived for a few months in the camps, and then he was taken out somewhere and shot—twice in the back and once in the head.

When I talked to Verbitsky again, not long ago, he was in a pensive state, bemused by the unexpected consequences of his story, which were still unfolding. On the one hand, he said, the forensic team had been flooded with calls from readers who had *desaparecido* relatives, who had never felt they could trust a government official with this information, and who now wanted the team's help. On the other hand, his management source had met with the factory's principal owner, who wanted to know only one thing: Who was the competitor who had paid *Página/12* to print this damning information about his company?

Dealing with the recent past does not come easily here. The press, the justice system, and human-rights groups like the forensic team have been largely responsible for uncovering whatever truth surfaces, and even today their efforts remain unwelcome in many official circles. (The forensic team, for example, operates exclusively on foreign funding.) The process of coming to terms with the past has been made more complicated by Menem's decision to grant a blanket pardon to all those who were tried and sentenced under the Alfonsín regime for their participation in the Dirty War, the Falklands War, or the three military uprisings against Alfonsín himself. The first batch of pardons was issued on October 8, 1989, and not even *Página* had the spirit for a joke: its front page that day was completely blank. Polls showed that more than two-thirds of the population disapproved of the final set of pardons, signed a year later, which included absolutions for former President Jorge Rafael Videla—the Army general who overthrew Isabelita and masterminded what he called the Proceso de Reorganización Nacional—and a few of the more notorious torturers, and also for their stated enemy, the Montonero leader Mario Firmenich, who some people believe was an Army intelligence operative all along. This set of pardons was signed on December 28th, which is the local equivalent of April Fools' Day.

Less than three weeks earlier, Menem had had to face *his* first military uprising: by the *carapintadas*, or painted faces—ultra-nationalist right-wing officers who like to get themselves up in camouflage gear and makeup and declare themselves patriots at war. Many of the *carapintadas* involved in December's uprising against Menem had been pardoned by him a year before. Since there was no public support for the pardons, and not even any great pressure from the military hierarchy to grant them, the people I talked to in the justice system and in the press speculated that the pardons had been an attempt by Menem to mollify the *carapintadas,* their supporters among the moneyed élite, and their leader, Colonel Mohamed Alí Seineldín, with whom Menem shares certain key backers. During the 1989 election campaign, Seineldín, who had been imprisoned for his role in the anti-Alfonsín uprisings, spoke favorably of Menem, and subsequently received frequent visits from the President's associates. None of this, however, was enough to prevent another rebellion.

The uprising against Menem last December 3rd was rather more serious than the three earlier ones against Alfonsín. During the 1987 uprising, the journalist Daniel Capalbo recalls, he stayed up all night in the rebel barracks arguing politics with an officer, who ended up in tears over the miserable farce that was the Falklands War. Nobody argued about anything on December 3rd. The *carapintadas* took to the streets and occupied the military national-headquarters building, just two blocks from the Casa Rosada. By the time the fighting was over, thirteen people were dead and twenty-five had been severely wounded. Fifteen principal conspirators in the revolt, including Seineldín, are currently on trial in federal court, in a case that, like earlier public-order trials, has been declared open to the public.

Perhaps the most striking thing about the trials is the extent of public indifference to them: it appears to be total. When I attended a morning session recently, in an ornate but gloomy courtroom, no one was there to listen to the testimony except

the fifteen accused officers, neat and straight-backed in their uniforms, and their relatives and a few reporters.

"During the Dirty War trials it was different," a member of
the prosecution staff told me. "But people are cynical now. A lot
of the people Menem pardoned in the first round took part in the
December 3rd uprising, so this trial strikes some people as futile.
There is also a sense in which people now feel some respect for
the *carapintadas*. These guys are willing to stand up in court and
say, 'I take responsibility for the uprising.' Nobody ever takes responsibility for anything here—we see stories of corruption every day in the press, and political leaders never keep their word.
We're not used to people who stand up for their actions, and we
wish our leaders would. By comparison, the *carapintadas* come out
looking good."

I asked this prosecution-staff member whether she thought
that the trials could eventually help make the military a more
democratic institution.

She leaned back and sighed, and said, "Who's democratic?
The sector of the military that remains loyal to the President isn't
loyal because it's democratic. It's loyal because it's absolutely authoritarian, and because it happens to agree with Menem's free-
market program. It isn't easy for an institution that has had life-
and-death power over all of us to transform itself. It's hard for
everyone. Am I democratic? I don't know. I've never lived in what
I consider a democracy, and the dictatorship closed off all alternatives—unless you were one of those who were willing to risk
their lives against it. You can't reconstruct a civilian society very
quickly after such experiences."

Like many of the reporters I talked to, this woman said she
was facing a new and unexpected dilemma as a result of the freedom, given her by democracy, to hunt for information that could
result in the fall of this administration. "Now that the press is free,
we get to discuss everything that happens absolutely openly," she
said. "But we talk among ourselves all the time here about another
problem: What if we investigated and found that the President
was involved in wrongdoing? We would face a choice between

resolving the case with little or no justice—covering it up—or provoking the fall of another President. We have no idea what the consequences of that would be."

THE SECOND CHAPTER of the Swiftgate scandal marks the first time that Menem has appeared to be directly implicated in any wrongdoing. If the court were eventually to ratify the allegations that Menem presided over a meeting in which his own Foreign Minister stated that Emir Yoma was an extortionist, and then failed to take action on the case, he would be held responsible for a large cover-up. It would be hard for Menem to persuade public opinion that he was ignorant all along of the other questionable events that have taken place during his time in office. The questions of what Menem knew and when he knew it are not being posed either to the President or in press stories, and when I asked reporters why not they replied in the same terms as the prosecution-staff member: "What if he falls? What then?" Despite the fact that Raúl Alfonsín—faced with three military uprisings, with waves of hyperinflation that brought food riots to Argentine cities for the first time ever, and with so crushing a defeat for his party in the 1989 elections that his ability to govern was threatened—decided at last to resign five months ahead of schedule, the transfer of power to Carlos Menem still counts as an orderly succession, the first from one elected civilian President to another in more than half a century. That would not be the case if the effects of the Yomagate and Swiftgate scandals, possibly combined with a resurgence of hyperinflation, forced Menem to leave office before the 1995 Presidential elections.

In government circles, the most dreaded scenario is one in which a wave of hyperinflation strikes just before the congressional and gubernatorial elections this coming October, the Peronists therefore lose resoundingly, and more damning information surfaces. There is general agreement that under those circumstances Menem would have to resign. Constitutionally, power would then pass to the Vice-President, Eduardo Duhalde, but, given that a glamorous talk-show hostess once asked him point-blank if he was, as rumor had it, the head of the Buenos

Aires drug mafia, it is unlikely that he would have the political credibility necessary to take firm command of a country in uproar. (This is a particularly bizarre rumor, because Duhalde has tried to stake his reputation on an anti-drug stand.) Next in the line of succession is the Senate chairman, but he is Menem's brother Eduardo. After that comes the head of the Supreme Court, who is an old man. A triumvirate that could lead the country to early elections is mentioned as a possibility, but this kind of speculation is seen as getting way ahead of a game that people desperately want to finish out by the rules.

In La Rioja province on the day after the second part of the Swiftgate story appeared in *Página/12*, I went up to the President as he was finishing dessert at a banquet in his honor and asked him to comment on the story. He was visiting his native province as part of festivities commemorating the four hundredth anniversary of the founding of the city of La Rioja, and he had arrived before the Swiftgate story appeared. I was expecting tight security, many flacks with prepared statements, and a cloud of reporters. Instead, I found open access for anyone who cared to take a seat at the banquet table in a local hotel (the tables eventually filled up, but there was no rush), and the only reporters I saw were two Casa Rosada correspondents, from *Página* and from the leading daily, *Clarín*. Menem, a short, dapper sixty-one-year-old with Levantine features and the trim figure of a man half his age, looked a little startled when I approached and put my question, then apologized for refusing to answer. As if I might doubt that he would prefer not to talk, he pointed to the two correspondents. "Ask those two girls over there," he said. "They'll confirm that I'm not even giving them interviews, and they're friends of mine."

Before becoming President, Menem spent his entire political career in the province of La Rioja, a desolate-looking place that produces some textiles, significant amounts of leather, and a little wine. (The Menem family has its own, inexpensive label.) There aren't many people in this rugged, hilly land that is supposed to resemble the Syrian countryside Menem's parents and thousands of other Rioja settlers came from. The city of La Rioja has a hundred thousand inhabitants, and the entire province only as many more. Goats occasionally wander onto the airport's one landing strip and keep the plane waiting. On the outskirts of the city, workers ride their bicycles past a long string of abandoned warehouses to the few factories that remain open. In town, orange trees shade the narrow sidewalks, pomegranates and rosebushes bloom in the yards, and grape bowers surround the doorways. On Sundays and holidays, the better-off families pile into their cars, drive around the downtown area until they're dizzy, and then head home so the fathers can tend to their card games.

On the day I arrived in La Rioja, the Fourth Centennial Commemorative Parade was providing an exciting break from routine; spectators lined the sidewalks for blocks, and, for more than three hours, enthusiastically applauded every one of the horseback gaucho delegations and school bands. Then they surged onto the parade route and toward the reviewing stand, where Menem shook hands tirelessly and asked well-wishers about their relatives, their grocery stores, their government jobs. He knew many of them as friends and also as former constituents from his days as governor. Menem was first elected governor of the province in 1973. He was a fervent Peronist then, and the famous sideburns are proof: he swore to let them grow full-length, in the style of La Rioja's nineteenth-century caudillo Facundo Quiroga, if Perón was ever allowed to return from his long exile in Spain and rule again. Perón did, and, despite the chaos that followed, and five years that Menem spent in prison after the coup Isabelita and the Montoneros had brought upon themselves, he kept the sideburns. They have been diminishing steadily since his Presidential campaign, though.

An old friend of the Menems in La Rioja, who often visited the governor in prison with baskets of supplies, remembered him lying in his cell and swearing that he would get back at the military by becoming President. The friend's husband said he thought that Menem had set this goal for himself long before. He remembered that Zulema Yoma always said that Carlos Menem had become a convert from Islam to Catholicism early in life in order to comply with the Argentine constitution, which bars non-Catholics from the Presidency.

Whenever the ambition seized him, the Presidency was a seemingly impossible goal: in Buenos Aires and in the seaside resort of Mar del Plata, which Menem has frequented for years, upper-class Argentines spoke of him fondly but not without condescension as the *loco divino*—an engaging, cordial eccentric from the provinces, whose brand of Peronism did not seem to include the defiant populism that set the élite's teeth on edge, but who certainly could not be considered *presidenciable*. His standing within the Peronist Party—which is officially known as the Partido Justicialista—was not much higher. He was not part of the inner circle of labor bosses and Party lifers, and he did not participate much in Party politics. He did something else: he travelled constantly throughout the country, visiting thousands of *unidades de base*—neighborhood Party headquarters—shaking hands, remembering names, himself unforgettable in a caudillo getup consisting of sideburns and red poncho. When he decided to run for the Party chairmanship—and thus for the Party's Presidential candidacy—he was considered such an unlikely threat that his opponent hardly bothered to campaign against him. Antonio Cafiero—experienced and crafty, solidly established in the Peronist hierarchy—lost the candidacy by a large margin to Carlos Menem in July of 1988.

The campaign that followed had messianic overtones. The novelist and journalist Tomás Eloy Martínez, whose splendid historical fiction *The Perón Novel* was published in the United States three years ago, remembers Menem dressed all in white, riding in a "Menemobile," raising his hands to the crowd as if in blessing. The candidate exhorted the Argentine people to "rise and follow me," but he also continued to play a hard tennis game, stay late at parties, and eye attractive women. Somehow, the combination did him no harm on Election Day. "The thing about Menem is that he is as contradictory and unpredictable as the country," Martínez says. "It's an integral part of his attractiveness." Although the candidate of the Unión Cívica Radical, President

Alfonsín's party, would have had little chance of winning under any circumstances, the unlikely Peronist candidate won by a landslide—ten percentage points. In an extraordinary interview in the gossip magazine *Gente* last December, Menem showed that he understood the source of his appeal—the identification with the national spirit that Martínez describes. The *Gente* interviewer was inquiring about the effects on his public standing of his "numerous sporting accidents, the divorce, the public statements."

"Things happen to me, and I do the things that any normal person does," Menem replied. "I'm frank, and everything is visible. What people wouldn't forgive me for is hypocrisy, falseness, or demagoguery. People are tired of rulers who have lied all their lives about the government or about their private life. The same things happen to me that happen to everyone, and I talk about them. Or they become known."

A quibble might be that it doesn't happen to everyone that he gets to be President, or that the directors of an Italian motorcycle company decide to make him a present of a Ferrari—a gift that was much on the public mind at the time of the interview. The reporter asked Menem if he intended to keep the car.

"Of course," he answered, a little testily. "They gave it to *me*. Why are people scandalized?"

The reporter pointed out that official presents are part of the national patrimony, and Menem said that if that was the case he "had no problem" in turning the car over eventually. "But what I'm telling you is that nobody can tell me what to do with something that was given to me." Having made that statement, he proceeded a few weeks later to drive the car at over a hundred and thirty miles per hour to Mar del Plata, in the continuing conviction that, as he said in another interview last year, "people follow me because I am a transgressing President." (He finally had to put the car on the market in May. So far, there have been no takers.)

People also follow him—or, at any rate, were willing to vote for him—because, no matter who Menem may be as an individual, politically he is a Peronist, and that means he belongs to one of the largest and most militant parties in the Western world.

Despite the many horrors that Peronism has brought to Argentina—the tradition of politics as confrontation, the dreadful,
boundlessly corrupt years of Isabelita's rule, the death squads
founded by her spiritual adviser López Rega, the terror imposed
by the Montoneros—perfectly reasonable people are still reluctant to renounce Perón, seventeen years after his death. Guillermo Saccomanno is a case in point. He has short, wiry hair and
a face that crinkles easily into a smile, which comes with a shrug
and a shake of the head whenever he has to confess that, despite
everything, he is not only a Peronist but a former campaign
worker for the man he now calls Méndez. Saccomanno and thousands of other Argentines call Menem Méndez, because they are
convinced that the President is *mufa*—that associating with him,
or even pronouncing his name, can bring extreme bad luck. As
evidence, Saccomanno cites the dubious penalty goal that cost
Argentina the World Cup last year after Menem attended the
opening ceremonies in Milan; the death of Menem's first Economy Minister within a week of the man's taking office, and, only
months later, of the man who replaced Menem as governor of La
Rioja; and the fact that recently, after a long evening Saccomanno spent with friends bewailing the Menem Presidency without taking the Méndez precaution, one of the friends had got
two traffic tickets on the short drive home. Saccomanno is a
writer—he has published two prize-winning novels—but he also
free-lances as a scriptwriter for the arty adult comic books that
Argentina exports to France and Italy, and as a campaign copy-
writer, whose clients tend to win elections.

Saccomanno can go on at some length about his perception
that Méndez is a clowning, irresponsible, self-centered offense
to the office of the Presidency. He didn't feel so strongly about
the matter two years ago, but he wasn't enthusiastic, either. Nevertheless, he agreed to sign on for the campaign. "I'm a Peronist,"
he explains. "I had to do it." For him, "Peronism of the first
stage"—the years in power from 1946 to the time Perón was
overthrown, in 1955—represents the closest thing Argentina has
ever had to government for and by the people: together with his
legendary second wife, Evita, Perón defied the landed oligarchy

by making the despised "black heads" and "no-shirts" (the *criollo* migrants from the provinces and the working-class European immigrants in Buenos Aires) the center of his attention and the real beneficiaries of many of his programs. He treated them like citizens, Saccomanno says, and they responded in kind: the no-shirts joined his party, voted massively for him, argued politics, and acted as if they had a role to play in history. Others say that Perón and Evita ransacked the wealthy Argentine state's coffers for their personal gain, and planted the seeds of the current economic disaster by putting the state in charge of everything from telephones to shoe factories. Saccomanno thinks that Perón had this century's only enlightened social policy: he built schools and hospitals and left behind one of the continent's most progressive labor codes. "My father is a lifelong socialist, and he could never have imagined that his son would become a Peronist," Saccomanno says. "But the left in this country is a failure—it's élitist, mechanistic, and corrupt. Peronism represents the interests of the working class much more."

Saccomanno is critical of Perón's lifelong flirtation with Fascism, his systematic use of thuggery, his cynical exploitation of fanaticism. He can't, however, bring himself to be critical of the millions of people who are still devoted to Perón, so when the Menem campaign people approached him he signed on, and did his best with the candidate's campaign slogans, although he found them vague. (The key one was "Follow me, I will not deceive you.") On Election Night, after months of hard work, he found himself on one of three floors of the congressional office building where Menem victory parties were being held. The media campaign workers—advertising-agency people, journalists, and writers like Saccomanno, people who had survived the years of the military dictatorship in near-hiding or had had to flee abroad—had a drab sort of party: sandwiches and cheap wine in plastic glasses, and a conspicuous absence of big-name politicians. Menem never showed up to thank them. Saccomanno looked through the doorway at a party on another floor, which Menem did attend. Its host was one of the regulars of the night scene that Menem loves—a man who had got rich managing the

soccer star Diego Maradona. There was champagne and live music and laughter there, and guests of a kind that Saccomanno
would never have expected to see at a Peronist celebration:
"movie stars, oligarchs, and the man we whistled down and
cursed in the campaign room whenever he appeared on television." That man was Alvaro Alsogaray, who was there with his
daughter, María Julia. It was the first real inkling Saccomanno
had that Menem might not be an orthodox Peronist after all.

WHEN I FINALLY MET María Julia Alsogaray, I found her much
more pleasant and intelligent than she appears in the photo lay-
outs she so patiently sits for. Dressed not in a bathing suit or a
slit-to-the-navel evening gown but in a blouse and a short skirt,
she talked in a posh, cluttered private office in the downtown
shopping district while in a neighboring room her aides were trying to decide which type of television program among the several
that were being offered would best suit her image. She issued
brisk orders to a secretary, told an assistant to prepare her costume change for the evening, and stated forthrightly that the reason she and her father were now on such good terms with a
Peronist President was not that they had wavered in their principles but that the President had come around to her father's point
of view on how governments and economies should be run. "The
Peronist Party hasn't changed," she said. "The President changed
despite the Party, and he has made a hundred-and-eighty-degree
change in political direction from Perón. We have met on the
common ground of the idea of a free-market economy and freedom." María Julia thinks that Menem kept his campaign promises
so vague because he actually didn't know what he was going to
do once he got elected. "He's a man with very strong intuitions,
and what he sensed is that for the last forty-five years every government—military or Peronist, or whatever—had done the same
thing, which was to mire the country in bureaucracy," she said.
"The only thing that hadn't been tried was what we have been
upholding with almost sectlike firmness. Once he was in power, he
knew he had the strength to do what was necessary."
   Menem is betting that he will go down in history not as the

king of scandal but as the man who managed to reverse the country's sixty-year economic decline and dismantle an arthritic but
omnivorous bureaucracy by putting virtually everything the state
owns on the auction block. Whether he can accomplish these
feats by hastily selling off the national telephone company to
the Spanish state telephone company without considering other
offers, as María Julia did last year with his approval, remains to
be seen. One can also wonder whether a private sector that has
made fortunes on speculating with the rates of inflation and
money exchange will be willing to bring its capital back from
abroad and risk it in industrial projects. María Julia thinks that
even if Menem is successful in laying the groundwork for a
healthier economy he will pay a political price, and so will her
father's party, the Unión del Centro Democrático. "The project
isn't ready to bear fruit yet," she told me. "And we have elections
coming up in October. At this point, the people who most
strongly support Menem are the people who voted for us, not for
him, but we have also suffered from the scandals and garish
events that are taking place, which our voters don't really go
along with."

I asked María Julia if the Unión del Centro Democrático
would not also continue to pay a price with voters at large because she and her father had always maintained silence on the
issue of the atrocities committed by the military during the
Dirty War.

She crossed and uncrossed her legs and teasingly began speculating on whether she had really had liposuction recently, but
she finally came back to the subject. "There might have been a
problem on the question of openness," she said. "There were
many things the military needed to do, but these things should
have been done openly."

The question of Menem's popularity is more complicated
than María Julia appears to think. I spent a long afternoon with
Felipe Noguera, of the polling firm of Mora y Araujo, Noguera
y Asociados, discussing the charts and graphs of the President's
political health. Noguera thinks that Menem's betrayal of Peronist principles in adopting free-market economics hasn't neces-

sarily cost him a great many potential votes. "When he got elected, he decided that free market was the way to go, and he said, 'What's got to be done has got to be done,'" Noguera told me. "That gave him a lot of popularity. People wanted decisiveness, and they wanted economic change, because there is general agreement that the old system doesn't work anymore." Noguera also disagrees that Menem's outlandish private life is necessarily a handicap; despite the juicy scandals, his popularity ratings have averaged forty-five per cent or so, with occasional dips for hyperinflation or the military pardons. "For one thing, he's more fun than Alfonsín ever was," Noguera said. "But it's obviously a high-risk strategy that depends on his government's continued economic stability."

Noguera, who has been prescient in the past (he's one of the few professional pollsters to have predicted Violeta Chamorro's victory in Nicaragua), thinks that on the whole things look good for Menem, and even for politics in Argentina. Reading the charts, he finds it encouraging that people can show more support for Domingo Cavallo—who was Menem's Foreign Minister at the time of Swiftgate and is now the Finance Minister—and his economic programs than for the President himself. Noguera thinks it is a sign that people are becoming less personality-oriented in their politics. He thinks that part of the reason for the tidal wave of corruption scandals is that people no longer take corruption for granted, as they did during the infinitely corrupting regime of Isabelita Perón, for example. But if the corruption investigations and economic conditions turn against Menem, Noguera believes, he will no longer be perceived as engagingly flamboyant, but as a failure. "Perón had a wise saying," Noguera pointed out. "In politics, one can recover from anything except looking like a fool."

For Daniel Capalbo, the scandals that keep him busy and entertained are definitive proof that his country is "not serious"— a phrase that, like *carnaval carioca*, is one of the most damning ways Argentines can describe a situation. Menem is not serious, Congress is not serious, the press, most particularly, is not serious, Capalbo told me when I visited him at *Noticias* back in May, and he added, by way of example, that the *Noticias* offices were a joke. Indeed, they were spectacularly shabby, particularly when one considered that the magazine was the largest-selling newsweekly around, its circulation having doubled in a year to a healthy hundred thousand per issue. Capalbo, who was editing *Noticias'* political section when I visited him, did not even have his own desk, and another reporter approached me to ask if it were true, as he had been told when he complained to his higher-ups about the phone system, that United States publications like *Time* and *Newsweek* also put out a magazine with the help of only twelve phone lines. Capalbo said that his salary at *Noticias* was "extremely high" by local standards—about fifteen hundred dollars a month—but in fact that doesn't go far in a country where a local phone call can cost two dollars.

In any case, it isn't money that makes Capalbo drag a little more urgently on his cigarette when he talks about the problems of the press. He wants to know how much time reporters in the United States have to work on their stories. It worries him that newspapers and magazines are telling the Menem stories because scandal is good business, and for no other reason. But he is not quite clear himself on the distinction between scandalmongering and muckraking, and he acknowledges as much: "Everything is so corrupt here that we have lost all sense of proportion; we have no parameters for judging a story's seriousness, or worth." Once the *Noticias* photographer had talked María Julia Alsogaray into posing sexily for the magazine, Capalbo feels, it had no choice but to put the picture on the cover—though doing so meant that a major investigative story the magazine had been readying all week was scrapped at the last minute to make room for the María Julia interview. I asked him about a cover story he had written for *Noticias* on the large number of unsupervised landing strips in the corruption-riddled province of Catamarca, next door to La Rioja. His story had stated flatly that those strips were being used for the transshipment of cocaine, and had described so clearly some of the persons alleged to be involved that it didn't make much difference that their names had been left out. I wanted to know if he was worried about a libel suit. "How could they sue?"

he replied. "Everybody in Catamarca can tell you about the strips." And anyhow, he added, libel questions are routinely settled out of court, by means of an even exchange: a publication will react to a public figure's complaint about a nasty article by printing a favorable one forthwith. The real problem, he said, with some bitterness, is that he hasn't seen any of his stories having an effect. "Take the Catamarca issue. It got a lot of comment on the radio talk shows, but the talk wasn't about the story itself—any number of reporters had the same information. It was about the fact that we'd dared to print it."

Capalbo would like to take time off to think about all the stories he has covered since the military dictators released their grip on Argentina, and he would like to work somewhere where reporting is a "serious" activity. Like many of his colleagues, he has migrated through the available range of professional options in the last eight years without finding any of them particularly satisfying. He started at *La Razón*, moved to *Página/12* but found its salary difficult to live on, was tempted by the idea of being an editor at *Noticias* but was disappointed by the working conditions, and has now landed at *Clarín*, as the editor of a weekly political supplement. He was delighted by the professionalism he felt around him on his first day on the job, he told me, but he didn't want to set his hopes too high. "The renewal of hope is always followed by disappointment," he said. "That is why all of us journalists are itinerants." Even the publications seem transitory. With the exception of *Clarín* and *La Nación*, which is the second-largest daily, news publications seem to be in a constant state of flux. That great bastion of gossip *Gente* has seen its circulation wither, while that of the two-year-old *Noticias* has doubled. Timerman's *La Razón* folded, and *Página* bloomed. But, for all *Página*'s energy and intelligence, it is hard to imagine the same irreverent publication coming out regularly for ten years—the minimum length of time one would think was necessary for it to consolidate as a newspaper. Fleetingness seems part of its charm.

The same thing might be said of democracy, except that Daniel Capalbo doesn't think he's really seen it yet. He's not quite sure what it is, but he has no doubt at all about what it isn't: it isn't impunity for torturers and killers, nor is it related to an economic system that increases rather than erases social inequality. One sees as very Argentine his inability to be satisfied with what are merely notable improvements over past aberrations, yet it's hard to disagree that life and politics in his country could be far better. Certain events that recur with obsessional predictability make it difficult to believe at times that Argentina can ever overcome its past. Right-wing terrorists, possible leftovers from the dictatorship's intelligence services, threaten human-rights activists and intimidate journalists. Jewish cemeteries are desecrated. The noted filmmaker Fernando Solanas, who is unswerving in his commitment to left-wing Peronism and extremely vocal in his disgust for Menem, was shot in both legs recently, presumably by enemies of Menem who would like to pin the blame on him. (No one, including Solanas, suspects the President.) These things are frightening and depressing, but not at all unfamiliar.

When Capalbo is pressed, though, he will admit that there are two areas of life here that look encouragingly like something a proper working democracy might rely on: one is the justice system, which, despite severe manpower problems, appears to be operating with increasing autonomy and self-confidence; and the other—for all its faults and limitations, he says—is the press. Once he has got started on this train of thought, his mood is brighter. "There's something else," he says. "Whatever Menem may think about what we write, nobody gets killed for it. There's no more official torture here, there are no more 'disappeared.' Whatever else may be happening, this is terribly, terribly important."

RIO
1991

"Where is it written that we have to be coherent?"

I KNOW A MAN here who believes that he killed three people. He did not take part in any actual killings, and, in fact, none of these deaths were violent, but he thinks that at the time they occurred he was acting as an intermediary for the Devil, and that in return for his help the Devil got rid of his enemies. Seu Ramos, as he prefers to be called, is a small, round, pink-skinned man with wispy white hair and a benevolent squint that turns sinister when he recounts his experience with telepathic murder. "Thanks be to God!" he likes to exclaim in referring to his deliverance from his heinous past. He has made some radical changes: he no longer drinks, he no longer smokes, he no longer conjures the death of his enemies. Seu Ramos's intense concern with matters of the soul might appear surprising to those who think of Rio de Janeiro as a place where only the body and its pleasures are worshipped, but a fervent and restless spiritual life is something he has in common with most cariocas, or inhabitants of this city. These days, he is a deacon in a well-established Pentecostal church, at peace with the world, and hungry only for more converts to Jesus Christ. He is, in other words, a perfect product of the latest stage of Rio's religious effervescence: a militant crossover from the traditional Afro-Brazilian religions that have

helped define the carioca spirit to the sprouting dozens of fundamentalist evangelical sects that are now at its religious vanguard.

What Seu Ramos left behind was Umbanda, a blend of traditional Afro-Brazilian religions with the still fashionable French
theory of spiritism. From its black roots Umbanda derives a belief
in gods brought from Africa by the slaves, and the practice of
provoking a trance state through ritual dances that allow the
gods to "descend" on their worshippers. From spiritism, which
was first propounded in Lyons by the mystic Allan Kardec in the
mid-nineteenth century, Umbanda borrowed the theory of reincarnation and the pursuit of physical healing and spiritual guid-
ance through communication with the souls of the dead. Like
Haitian *vodoun* and Cuban Santería, Umbanda holds that the spirits are able to influence, and even terminate, human life; but in its
magpie delight in incorporating new spiritual theories and ritual
practices Umbanda is distinctly carioca—flexible, tolerant, and
insatiably curious about new experiences. Umbanda has no central authority and no official statistics, but one can guess that its
followers here number in the millions. It is virtually the official
religion of the city's poor, who are predominantly black but include large numbers of immigrant Portuguese and their descen-
dants—like Seu Ramos—and migrant whites and mestizos from
the impoverished countryside to the north. The most respectable
middle-class neighborhoods are also dotted with Umbanda
temples, however. Politicians and anthropologists consult Umbanda seers, and on New Year's Day the major dailies run big
news stories on the seers' forecasts for the next twelve months.
On New Year's Eve, vast numbers of cariocas participate in one
of Umbanda's central rituals: dressed in white, they gather on the
city's beaches at midnight to light candles and offer prayers to
the ocean goddess Yemanjá. Nonbelievers join believers in the
ceremony, for the same reason that agnostics elsewhere celebrate
Christmas—because it is a lovely and meaningful part of their
history and tradition.

The secretary of public works for the city, Luiz Paulo Corrêa
da Rocha, says that he does not mind at all that his political adversaries call him a Marxist-Spiritist. The question came up while

we were discussing his recent suggestion that a special area be set up in one of the forest preserves surrounding Rio where followers of the Afro-Brazilian religions could deposit their *despachos*, or propitiatory food offerings to the gods. Corrêa had pointed out that among numerous other advantages—tranquillity for the worshippers, contact with the natural forces where the divine spirit resides—such a park would lighten the work load of the already beleaguered street-cleaners, who have to sweep up tons of additional detritus each weekend, after the offerings are set out on street corners and in parks. I was fascinated by his technical and convincing explanation of how food offerings that are made by human beings in this three-dimensional universe can actually get absorbed into a parallel vibratory particular magnetic field—a given god's wavelength—so I asked him what he himself believed in.

"I believe in reincarnation and communication with the spirits," he said. "But I also believe in the founding principles of Marxism-Leninism." He shrugged, smiled mischievously, and added, "Where is it written that we have to be coherent?"

Eclecticism comes naturally to people here. There are large numbers of Catholics who are also socialists—Brazilian bishops practically invented the combination, back in the nineteen-sixties—and Spiritists and Umbandistas don't see why, if Catholics can simultaneously hold high office, preach the need for revolution, and pray to a man who rose from the grave three days after his death, anyone should think it strange that they can talk with the spirits of the dead and concern themselves with social change. By and large, cariocas do not think it strange: in its infancy, in the nineteen-twenties and thirties, Umbanda suffered the same persecution that Rio authorities inflicted on all black social activities, but more recently relations between the Umbandistas and the municipality have flourished. Partly this is because many officials are sympathetic to Umbanda or, like Corrêa, are directly involved in it or in some other form of esotericism. Partly it is because Umbanda and its colorful rituals are seen to contribute positively to the city's image at a time when Rio otherwise seems under siege.

Nearly seven years of electoral democracy, following twenty-one years of military rule, haven't managed to improve most people's standard of living—not that of the miserably poor, and not that of the better-off. A series of ambitious economic megaplans has led only to successive waves of hyperinflation. The latest plan, put in place by President Fernando Collor when he came to power, a year and a half ago, has only aggravated the steepest industrial recession the country has ever known. Thirty years of decay, Corrêa admits, are beginning to take their toll of Rio's patience, although the city's beauty is so extreme and so poignant that one could believe it capable of surviving all the indignities visited on it. The spectacular outcrops of solid granite that punctuate the landscape more than make up for the dreadful modern high-rise buildings in their shadow. Near-permanent traffic jams are more tolerable when they take place along the still waters of the Rodrigo de Freitas Lagoon or the shimmering bay of Guanabara. The breathtaking perspectives from the heights of the city's five hundred or so favelas—hillside slums—can lift the spirits even of the perpetually unemployed.

There may be limits to this tolerance, however. The city is still recovering from the experience of having gone bankrupt under its previous administration. At the time, the governor suspended work on a new section of the Metro which was being built to connect the downtown business area to the glitzy neighborhoods of Ipanema and Copacabana. The gaping holes remain, and now the surrounding buildings are threatening to slide into them—a situation that makes for a certain ill humor in their neighborhood. An underwater sewage main burst the other day, adding its contents to the already polluted beaches. Even lying on the sand has become less pleasurable: bands of favela teenagers maraud the oceanfront despite the efforts of special police detachments that regularly frisk black youths before allowing them onto the beach.

Corrêa pointed out to me that today Rio's finances are sound for the first time in decades, and yet the city's problems are so deep that money can't solve them. "The principal service the citizenry wants is an educational program for children that includes meals," he said. The reasons are clear: some two million of Rio's six and a half million inhabitants live in favelas and improvised squatter camps. Many more live in barely decorous poverty in more established neighborhoods. The number of single-parent households here is known only to be staggeringly high. What parents want, Corrêa explained, is some kind of school that will guarantee their kids more food than they can afford to buy, and will keep kids for a full day so the mothers can work to provide some food themselves. Leonel Brizola, the governor of the state of Rio, instituted such a plan and built sixty schools in the city alone during his previous term, but Corrêa says that building more isn't necessarily a budget problem only. "Where are the people who are qualified to administer the schools, run the cafeterias, fix the plumbing, design the programs, teach the kids?" he asked. "We'd give any percentage of our budget to have them, but there simply aren't enough qualified people to go around."

In outlining the city's problems, Corrêa was drawing a map of its misery, for, as he pointed out, the fact that Rio is back on a sound financial footing doesn't mean that people are less poor. On the contrary, more people who are unable to make the rent are taking up residence in the favelas, he told me. More families are simply living on the street, and more hospitals are increasing their purchases of an intravenous glucose solution to cope with the increasing number of cases of infant dehydration. When he asks the people what they would like most after schools with food programs, they say that they want public lighting, because the rise in drug warfare, kidnappings, assaults, and death squads has made all residential streets unsafe. Assaults and kidnappings can also take place on Avenida Copacabana at noon, but people seem to feel that if there is some public lighting in their neighborhoods after dusk they will at least see what they are dealing with. Clearly, survival under these circumstances calls for imaginative solutions, and religion as it is practiced by the cariocas is nothing if not a triumph of imaginative thought. The gods and spirits of Umbanda that Seu Ramos once worshipped, and that he now calls devils, are proof of this.

• • •

THE GODS ARE ON DISPLAY at the Spiritist Tent of Granny Maria Antonia of the Congo, one of the more successful of many
thousands of Umbanda temples in Rio. The temple is not a tent
at all but a spacious, comfortable two-story house with a long
open-air corridor and a shining tile-walled meeting hall on the
ground floor; it is called a "tent," or tepee, in honor of the spirits
of various Indians—among them the Indian of the Seven Crossroads, the Indian of the Coral Cobra, and the Indian Who Tears
Up Tree Stumps—who are believed to have lived long ago in the
Brazilian jungle. The Granny who is honored in the temple's
name is a well-known Old Black Woman, the spirit of a slave who
was born in Africa and died in Brazil. At this temple, Granny
Maria Antonia is the principal spirit incorporated by Stella Virginia dos Santos Soares, who runs it. She is a tall, imposing black
woman of such extraordinary efficiency in every gesture that one
cannot help having faith in her, and hundreds of people do. She
has dozens of regular initiates, mostly white and quite well off,
and she is also extremely popular among the black slumdwellers
on a hill behind the middle-class neighborhood where her temple stands.

When worshippers arrive for ceremonies that take place every Friday night, they stop in the corridor to pray briefly before
half a dozen shrines, where the gods live. During the years of
slavery in Brazil, which lasted until 1888, blacks managed to worship their own African gods—*orixás*, in Yoruba—only by disguis-
ing them as Catholic saints. Candomblé, a religion that sprang up
in the northern city of Salvador da Bahia, standardized a canon of
camouflaged gods, and Umbanda followers in Rio borrowed it.
St. George, for example, is actually Ogum, the god of wars and
metals, who, like his dragon-slaying Christian counterpart, carries a sword. According to legend, St. Barbara's pagan father, who
sought to have her executed for becoming a Christian, was felled
by lightning, and so Iansã, the warrior goddess of the forests and
of lightning, is worshipped under her name. Yemanjá, the gentle
mother goddess of the oceans, who dresses in blue and white, is
the Virgin Mary—in her incarnation as the Virgin of the Im-

maculate Conception, who wears the same colors. Most of the plaster-cast figurines in the shrines at Granny Maria Antonia's were made specifically for Umbanda worship, and they would look a little strange inside a Catholic church: the colors are too bright, St. George looks too angry, and the Virgin Mary looks strangely buxom and hippy. On a separate altar, the statues of an Indian and an Old Black Man are more recognizable: the Indian is holding an arrow and wears a long headdress of feathers, like Sitting Bull's, and the Old Black Man is portrayed sitting pensively on a tree stump, smoking a corncob pipe.

Although the Indians and Old Black Folks are not *orixás* but mere spirits, their cult is what defines Umbanda. Indeed, the religion is said to have started one evening in 1908, after the participants in a middle-class Spiritist séance refused to allow an Indian spirit to speak. The séance regulars, who were white, were used to communing with the likes of Voltaire and Plato, and when the Indian of the Seven Crossroads tried to butt in he was told that Indians were "forces of darkness," and was asked to go away. The Indian got angry and, speaking through a sickly adolescent, whose vocal cords he had borrowed before, he swore that he would found a religion in which Indians and Old Black Folks would finally have a voice. In Umbanda's religious hierarchy, they are ranked as inferior to the *orixás*, but have a central advantage over them: in Candomblé, when the *orixás* take possession of their initiates they make their presence known by executing characteristic dance movements, but they remain silent. When the Umbanda spirits appear, they talk. Indians, on their allotted night, suggest potions and incantations for the medical problems of their devotees. Old Black Folks, who appear on separate evenings, impart wisdom and spiritual counsel.

On a night when an Indian session was to take place, I found Stella Virginia dos Santos Soares selling soft drinks and chicken empanadas to her followers at a refreshment stand she runs at the entrance to the temple. After the snack, the faithful headed for dressing rooms in the back to change from their work clothes into all-white costumes that looked like hospital uniforms. The resemblance is no coincidence. Stella is a former nurse who loved her work, and she tries to bring as much of its character as possible into her ritual center. "Standard white uniforms are more egalitarian," she told me. "There are very rich and very poor people here, but once they've changed there's no way of knowing the difference." Briskly, she instructed an assistant to show me and a photographer friend to our assigned places for the ceremony, which, with the aid of a clock on one of the shiny, hospital-like walls, was to begin at eight sharp.

Stella summoned everyone into the meeting hall and directed the rest of the seating arrangements. Those who were wearing street clothes—non-initiate suppliants—sat in pews at the back. In the middle, ranged in rows according to rank, stood the white-clad initiates, and they were flanked by white-clad apprentices, who sat on tile-covered benches against the walls, with a gleaming metal spittoon on the floor between every two people. Stella stood at the front, facing the congregation. Behind her, chairs for special guests were on one side, and on the other stood a drummer and half a dozen singers. In the center of the front wall was the altar, topped by an image of Jesus Christ, who appeared to be blessing ranks of Umbanda saints below. With startling speed, the ceremony got under way: the drummer beat out a complicated rhythm, the singers chanted an invocation to each of the saints and then to an Indian named Seu Tupinambá. At that point, Stella's body jerked up, down, and sidewise, and she sank into a crouch. She remained in that position for a few seconds, sighed, and then straightened up and lit a big cigar.

Soon all the initiates had incorporated Indians and lit up. Indian spirits like to smoke and spit, and Stella doesn't like messes—that's why she provides the spittoons. They were in use throughout the ceremony, which proceeded at a breakneck pace and developed a sweaty, dreamy intensity. While the chanting continued, Seu Tupinambá—whom Stella had now incorporated—gave orders. The suppliants at the back were told to come forward seven at a time, barefoot and without their jewelry, and when they were lined up in front of the altar Seu Tupinambá strode past them, waving his arms energetically above their heads. At the end of each pass, he disposed of the evil energies he had absorbed by shaking his hands in the direction of the apprentices on the benches; they received this discharge and howled, metabolizing it into harmless force. When all the suppliants had received this initial cleansing, they were told to line up again, in rows facing the altar, this time one per cigar-smoking initiate. Each initiate blew smoke around the aura of a suppliant and, with loving care, performed healing gestures with his arms. At last, the initiates and the apprentices, their medical mission accomplished, were allowed to attend to themselves. They danced, sang, and went into little spinning frenzies. The apprentices fell into long, suffering trances that shook their bodies and sometimes made them weep, and the initiates took care of them, watching to see that they did not bump into anything or otherwise hurt themselves. Every once in a while, for no apparent reason, Seu Tupinambá or another of the temple elders went up to someone and offered a warm, healing embrace. Then, at a signal from Seu Tupinambá, everyone lined up again, sang farewell to the spirit guests, and shuddered briefly as the otherworldly visitors departed. By ten-thirty, it was all over. The former Indians clustered once again around the refreshment stand to sip beer, laugh, and chatter loudly.

"Why do I do this?" a woman named Gloria said later. "I've asked myself that question a hundred times, and I can't come up with a logical answer." Gloria is part of Stella's high command, a middle-aged woman with bleached hair and a friendly, intense manner. She lives in one of many airy, terraced high rises that dot the temple neighborhood, a bastion of the middle middle class that has gradually settled here since 1900, far away from the frivolity of the oceanfront neighborhoods to the south. There are bakeries, and family restaurants serving heavy Portuguese food, and all-girl schools housed in birthday-cake fin-de-siècle manors. Everything bespeaks respectability, and so did Gloria's attire and that of her husband, who had also turned into an Indian at the earlier session and now sat silent while Gloria speculated about the origins of her faith.

Typically, the couple had first come to Stella's, some fifteen years ago, because Gloria's husband had a health problem that doctors couldn't cure. The sessions helped almost immediately, even though for the first year or so the couple did nothing but sit quietly in the back pews. Then a day came when the spirits arrived and took possession of their bodies, and there was no turning back. "Now, I ask you, how could a couple like us, well-educated, well-off, professionally successful, fall into this?" Gloria said. "You know, there are some sessions when I turn into a child, and when I think of the things this child makes me do I think I must have a screw loose! I jump around, turn somersaults, talk nonsense. But the thing is, even on evenings when we think how much nicer it would be to rent a videocassette and stay home, we know that there are people waiting who need our help. For us to stay away, it would be like a surgeon leaving the hospital waiting. So we don't stay away."

Just about everyone I've talked to who has ever been involved in Umbanda, including Seu Ramos, the lapsed sorcerer, has testified that the religion cured him of some physical ailment that doctors had failed to treat successfully. Stella and other temple heads, though, attach even more importance to Umbanda's ability to deal with psychological disorders. Basically, Stella says, her sessions are "one big therapy," and it's not difficult to understand how they might help. During a session, someone who harbors a sorrow so deep that he may not even know he has it can wail and curse—and remember nothing once he has come out of his trance. Timorous women can turn into powerful Indians. Favela blacks can be transformed into gods, and middle-class whites can feel earthy and uninhibited by turning into black and Indian spirits. (And there is an Amazonian variant of Umbanda in which beleaguered real-life Indians can incorporate a singular family of spirits called *gente fina*, or, roughly, "people of a better class"— whites, presumably. The *gente fina* drink only champagne and soft drinks and act terribly refined.) It is part of Umbanda's genius that it knows how to make room for each person's strongest fantasies.

Stella would disagree with this analysis. She thinks that her religion's healing properties are much more scientific, and go beyond mere catharsis. She believes that emotional distress is

caused largely by "obsessor spirits"—spirits who, unlike the Indians or the Old Black Folks, have not yet reached the enlightened
state that allows them to help humanity. "For example, when my
mother died, I knew I was going to be in bad shape until her soul
found a way to depart into the other world," she told me one
afternoon before the start of a session. "When she appeared in
our sessions, we worked with her, helping her to overcome her
grief and adjust to her new state." As her mother grew to accept
her own death, Stella's depression lifted. There is some evidence
that severe mental disorders can also be helped through the kind
of ritual that Umbanda has perfected. The head of the Umbanda
Federation of Rio de Janeiro, one of several associations that have
been formed periodically to try to bring the thousands of dis-
persed temple heads together, told me that he had been committed to an insane asylum as an adolescent. Now, in his early fifties,
he is a successful lawyer, and he believes that he was cured because a psychiatrist at the asylum put him under the care of an
Umbanda center.

Umbandistas who talk to outsiders such as reporters are careful to stress these aspects of their religion, because another aspect
of it is one that comes up for discussion much more often. That
is Umbanda's commerce with spirits that evangelicals like Seu
Ramos zero in on—a commerce that allows him to say he was
once employed by the Devil. The basis for Seu Ramos's assertion
is Umbanda's commitment to a spirit known as Exu.

Strictly speaking, Exu is not one but many, and he isn't really
the Devil, either, but Umbanda has blurred the difference between Satan and the spirit it represents as a cloven-hoofed, leer-
ing creature with horns. This disturbing figure is responsible for
the only real schism in Umbanda's eighty-year history—between
those who reject his worship and those who accept it. Umbandistas who follow the founding fathers' principles by rejecting the
Exus are very much a minority, dismissed as practitioners of
"white Umbanda" or "Umbanda Lite" by those who keep an altar
for Exu at the entrance to their temples. Traditionally, the Exus
that "black magic" Umbanda borrowed from Candomblé are divine messengers who allow human beings to communicate with

the *orixás*, and who must be propitiated with offerings outside a temple before the ceremony can start within. Even in Candomblé, though, Exus have certain riveting characteristics: they are priapic; they are utterly ruthless; they preside over cemeteries, where flesh is transformed into spirit. In Umbanda, the ceremonies staged in their honor are the hands-down crowd favorite.

At Granny Maria Antonia's one afternoon, Stella proudly showed me a video she had had made of the once-monthly evening sessions she holds in honor of the Exus. The Exu who takes hold of her is called Seu Midnight, and he did not seem at all distressed by the presence of the camera. Wearing a top hat and a black cape with gold tridents embroidered on the back, he stalked about, limping, and hissed commands to the lesser Exus who had taken possession of Stella's disciples. These minions appeared in the form of *malandros*—ne'er-do-wells, rogues, and pimps—and of their female counterparts, the *pombagiras*, who are gypsies and streetwalkers. Just as the Indians resemble cigar-store figures much more than real-life Amazon Indians, who neither live in tents nor smoke cigars, the streetwalkers and pimps who appear at Stella's belong to a Rio underworld that is long gone. These days, prostitutes are into spandex, and the *malandros*, who wear Bermudas and heavy gold chains, are drug traffickers, not mere pimps. But the initiates at Granny Maria Antonia's had dressed for their visitors in the old style, which included white patent-leather shoes and fedoras or straw boaters for the men and flouncy embroidered dresses for the women.

In a sense, the video was disappointing. Although everyone in it appeared to be having a typical carioca good time, swigging ritual beer, dancing, and flirting outrageously, there didn't seem to be anything particularly lewd or sinful about the ceremony. (For one thing, the *pombagiras*, in their layered petticoats and low-cut bodices, were wearing far more clothes than most women here ever put on.) For all the ceremony's friendly cheer, however, the fact remains that Exu is in charge of manipulating evil. It was to him that Seu Ramos turned when he asked for the death of his enemies, and he was granted the favor. When cemetery watchmen find black dogs at the entry gates around midnight, their throats slit and their paws bound in red ribbon, it is a sign that Exu has been asked to make some particularly gruesome and difficult intervention. Lighted candles at crossroads—visible everywhere on Friday evenings—are also requests for his help. Seu Midnight's purpose at Stella's session was not to oversee a great party but to grant equivocal favors to petitioners who in some way wanted to harm or control others. I asked Stella what she made of this.

"The main thing you have to understand about Exus is that they're spirits in evolution," she said. "They're not enlightened, so if you decide to use them you'd better know what you're getting into. I warn people, 'Whenever you ask for something evil, you're going to have to absorb part of that evil yourself.' Whether people want to seek out Exu despite that warning is something I can't control."

Stella seemed more concerned, however, about the impression the Exus might make on her congregation, which, as she frequently points out, consists largely of *gente fina*. She doesn't specifically mention the fact that many of her initiates are white, but a couple of her white assistants did make remarks to me to the effect that Stella was a very good person, even though she was black. The issue of race is present in Umbanda in precisely the same convoluted, fragmented, and deflected way that it is present in all aspects of life in Brazil. Heads of successful temples with large black congregations tell visitors that their temples are not "voodoo" centers, and cite as evidence the fact that many of the worshippers arrive in their own cars. (The rate of car ownership for blacks in Brazil is visibly low.) Practitioners of "white Umbanda" explain painstakingly that Indians and Old Black Folks don't really exist—that they are only the simple, accessible packaging the spirits came up with in order to address themselves to "maids who aren't really capable of understanding a dialogue about metaphysics," "maids" being one of the many code words for "blacks." "White Umbandistas" also explain that the African *orixás* are not really African gods but vibratory magnetic fields, and that their origins aren't really African anyway but Egyptian, or maybe Oriental. They despise the cult of the Exus. Stella, however, thinks that Exus reflect a fundamental part of human nature, and she probably also thinks that they're good business. Her main concern is that they appear in a form that will not unduly shock those white people who come to her temple precisely because it has an Exu. "Exus can be educated, they can be helped," she says. "That's why in *my* sessions no Exu ever uses dirty words."

THE QUESTION OF the Exus' relationship to the Devil is part of the larger question of how Christian churches should relate to Umbanda, and that question has been around for a long time. During its first decades, when it was expanding dramatically, Umbanda was under attack by both the Catholic Church and the civilian authorities, as were Candomblé, samba music, and most other forms of black culture. Official persecution gradually gave way to mass acceptance, but as late as the nineteen-sixties Father Bonaventure Kloppenburg, an influential Franciscan theologian, could write, "In the face of the cult of the Exus, the Catholic's attitude is one of saintly horror, and he will repeat this always with apostolic vigor." For its pains, the Catholic Church found its places of worship increasingly empty, and had to modify its attitude drastically—to one of tolerant understanding. The new fundamentalist evangelical sects are making no such concessions, with the result that they can't build churches fast enough for all the worshippers who wish to cleanse themselves of the Umbanda sin, while even the oldest, most firmly established Umbanda temples are cutting back dramatically on the number of sessions they hold—to one a week, or even one a month. When I asked Átila Nunes, the Umbanda constituency's representative in the Rio state legislature, how Umbanda was doing in terms of growth, he said, "We have entered a phase of qualitative growth, after an initial phase of quantitative growth." In other words, the numbers are terrible.

Mariza de Carvalho Soares, an anthropologist who has studied both the Afro-Brazilian religions and the new evangelical churches, finds it logical that the sects should be taking droves of faithful away from the Afro-Brazilian religions. "The Christian churches are based on an ethic of solidarity, whereas Afro-Brazilian religions are *disgregadoras*—they're all about conflict, enemies, and revenge," she told me on a recent morning. "They are religions that see individuals in permanent isolation and at odds with one another, much the way the *orixás* appear in the mythology." This is a time when Rio's social problems are setting people at one another's throats, she believes, and it would be hard to disagree: would-be passengers fight for the right to hang out the back door of an overcrowded bus; women fight over scarce and wayward men; self-appointed parking attendants fight over a hard-won half block's worth of turf. De Carvalho Soares is a funny, quick-witted, and gregarious woman, and, in the sense that she is both an academic and a homeowner, she belongs to the small minority of the relatively privileged, but in her tiny living room, as she raised her voice to a near-shout to make herself heard over the blast of yet another traffic jam, she seemed to be just another carioca struggling in a misshapen urban environment. "At this particular time, when everything in Brazilian society tends toward individual isolation, conflict, and a struggle for survival, Umbanda's atomizing tendencies are too much for people to handle," she told me.

PASTOR LAIME, one of many preachers who participate in an all-day schedule of services at the main Rio house of worship established by the Church of God Is Love, can't keep track anymore of how many houses of worship his church has. He debated with the receptionist outside his office whether the total was fifty-two hundred or fifty-four hundred, and finally settled on "five thousand and something" in Brazil alone, in addition to about three hundred temples in other Latin-American countries. In his office, separated from the temple itself by three flights of stairs and four electronically controlled gates, it was possible to talk quietly: there was only the sound of air-conditioning and, in the background, the piped-in voice of the pastor who was conducting the service downstairs, and whose sermon was being taped on a professional sound system. Five television screens silently monitored the security gates and the altar. Downstairs, however, the pastor and a multidecibel sound system had to compete with the racket of incessant hammering as a construction crew worked around the clock to build extra balconies, where more pews could be fitted. Most of the newcomers to the church, Pastor Laime said, were fleeing the clutches of Satan. "Every time I hold a baptism—let's say there are fifteen hundred people present, six hundred will be former Umbandistas renouncing the Devil."

Fundamentalist evangelical sects like God Is Love, the Assembly of God, and the Universal Church of the Kingdom of God have been operating in Brazil for several decades. The oldest, the Christian Congregation in Brazil, was founded in 1910, by an Italian immigrant who passed through the United States on his way here and liked what he saw of the Pentecostal rituals in the Deep South. All the sects are invariably referred to as "the new sects," though, because their phenomenal growth has taken place only over the last twenty years, and because this period of growth coincides with the development of a new type of ritual, which is probably unlike that of any Protestant cult ever previously known. They rail against the Catholic Church, which they claim is an invention of the Devil, who hides behind every saint in the form of an *orixá*. At the Universal Church—by far the fastest-growing of the sects—preachers who are former Umbandistas conduct mass exorcisms of the *orixás*. They call the *orixás* demons, but also address them by name ("Come out, Xango! Come out, Ogum!"), and the *orixás* growl and curse more richly than they are ever allowed to at Stella's temple, but finally quit the bodies of their victims and flee the presence of Jesus Christ. In nearly all the new churches, flasks of oil or water are blessed and used for faith healing. At the Church of God Is Love—which also conducts *orixá* exorcisms—the faithful are encouraged to write letters to Jesus Christ requesting a miracle, and the letters deposited on the altar are prayed over by the preacher and a fervent congregation. The sects have made it easy for converts to renounce a lifelong association with Umbanda: they do not have to admit that the *orixás* do not exist—only that they are the Devil, and that God is stronger. And, in this country that so badly needs miracles, the possibility of supernatural benefits cannot easily be overlooked. The preacher shouts over and over at the Church of God Is Love that the only true miracles, the best miracles, the biggest ones, are performed by Jesus Christ.

At nearly any hour of the day, it is possible to find one's way from President Vargas Avenue—the sixteen-lane slice of modernity that cuts through the run-down heart of colonial Rio—to the main house of worship of the Church of God Is Love by following the sound of chanting through the surrounding narrow streets. The stucco-decorated houses along these streets were once among the most delicate and charming in the city, but now their pink or blue façades are faded and crumbling, and they are occupied by electrical-supply stores, garages, and butcher shops. The main temple—a whitewashed warehouse from which songs issue all day long, at the end of a street barely wide enough for one car—blends easily into its surroundings.

When I arrived there in midafternoon a few days after my conversation with Pastor Laime, a preacher was warming up the congregation by lying on the ground behind the altar, so that only his voice, emerging through the sound system's gigantic speakers, held sway. It was hard to understand what he was shouting from this position, but that didn't seem to make much difference to the crowded house. The women sat to the left and the men to the right of the altar, which stands in front of a wall on which a large rainbow has been painted. To judge by the worshippers' knobby bone structure and threadbare clothing, they were among Rio's very poorest, and, to judge by their manner of praying, they needed a break. Some sat weeping silently. Some stood and prayed loudly, with their palms raised to Heaven. Several were kneeling up against the altar with their arms raised high, and others had flattened themselves against the booming speakers in order to feel the preacher's voice vibrating through their bodies.

Ushers—elderly women wearing uniforms and nametags— patrolled the aisles, taking up collections and handing out slips of paper on which the faithful could write letters to Christ. (Periodically, the ushers gathered up the letters in small butterfly nets and deposited them in a cardboard box on the altar, where, the preacher assured everyone, they would soon be answered by Jesus Himself.) I noticed that a heavyset woman in a faded skirt and blouse sitting a few rows in front of me kept turning to stare in my direction. Soon she moved closer, struggling to fit herself and an overstuffed plastic supermarket bag she carried in lieu of a handbag into a small space next to me. "I don't know how to write," she said as soon as she sat down. "Will you write my letter for me?" Then she dictated it in rapid bursts, pausing hardly long enough between thoughts for me to get the words down.

"Dear Lord Jesus Christ," she began. "This is from Maria da Conceição. Please help me find a job. And bless my daughter and tell her to stop screaming and yelling at me. I know it's not her but the Devil that's making her do it, but still she just won't listen to sense. Tell her yourself to stop being an Umbandista; you know she never pays any attention to me. And her husband, who's worthless—at least help him find a job, so that both of them can move out, and so he can earn enough money to help feed the kids. And bless João and Gerónimo and Zé Carlos and Zezinho and Nilse and Ilcemar."

When I later asked Pastor Laime, who is a serious, intensely religious young man, what God Is Love could do to improve the lot of its faithful, he answered straightforwardly that that was not the church's task—that God did not want His worshippers to be more interested in material things than they were in Him. He admitted reluctantly, however, that many people's lives do improve when they quit Umbanda and join God Is Love. He cited himself as proof, saying, "Before I joined the church, I was smoking two packs a day. That's money. You save even more when you stop drinking, and it gets easier to hold down a job. And Umbanda costs a lot of money—all those offerings, the costumes, the parties. They add up."

God Is Love costs a lot of money, too. Believers are expected to turn over a tenth of their income to the church, and also to buy Bibles, hymnals, and records of church music. During the services, collections are taken up constantly, and the preacher will often begin by asking those who want to demonstrate their faith to display a large-denomination cruzeiro bill. ("I want to see four people holding a five-thousand-cruzeiro bill. Let's give them all a round of applause!") In addition, Maria da Conceição told me proudly, it was a major sacrifice for her to put the money together for the suburban train that brought her to the church every day. She showed me the Bible she was paying for on the installment plan—one more sacrifice for God. I asked if someone at home read it to her, and she said the Bible itself talked to her when she prayed to it.

The new evangelicals not only ask for money outright but also boast of their wealth—which is proof of Christ's support—by building larger and larger churches and setting up more and more elaborate television programming, whereas Umbanda principles state unconditionally that "blessings aren't paid for." It is only by charging for "consultations" and by relying on wealthy patrons—who will often make a cash contribution in return for a miracle—that the head of an Umbanda temple can make a living. But love potions aren't as important as jobs, and if someone like Maria da Conceição can begrudge the *orixás* the money her daughter spends for their ritual candles and food offerings, while herself giving unstintingly to the church from her meagre funds, it's because the *orixás* and the Exus don't seem to be able to perform the kinds of miracles that people need these days.

A SELF-EMPLOYED handyman I know says that the help of an evangelical church—the Assembly of God—is what has kept him and his wife not only married to each other for fifteen years but also happy about it. In the favela of Vidigal, where family life is often violent and chaotic, this is a feat so remarkable as to make some of Jamin and Maria Tereza Mendonça Merense's neighbors consider conversion. Jamin, a birdlike, intensely curious and restless man, is lucky in other ways, too. He is well-off even by the standards of Vidigal, which is easily the most prosperous and consolidated of all Rio's favelas. He has a car, which serves him well as he makes the rounds of his clients, most of them well-paying foreigners. True, he has to park the car about half a mile away from where he lives, because that is where the nearest road is, and it takes him about half an hour to coax the aging vehicle out of the steep, hillside chicken yard that serves as a parking lot. Yet there the car is, a venerable American model vast enough to accommodate his entire extended family. He has a house, which he built himself. So do all his neighbors, but Jamin, because he is an exceptionally thoughtful, thrifty, and industrious craftsman, was able to figure out ways of building three stories of fairly stable brick and concrete on top of a one-room brick shack his wife inherited long ago. The house looms skyscraperlike over its neighbors, and from its top story one can see not only the crazy jumble of tilting brick houses, winding alleys, trash dumps, open sewers, and surviving bits of forest which make up Vidigal but also a far more awe-inspiring expanse of beach and ocean than that enjoyed by guests at the Sheraton Hotel, which lies at the foot of Vidigal hill.

Jamin, whom I have known for years, was happy to take me on a tour of his living room, tiled bathroom, master bedroom with balcony (ocean view), and terraced top-floor work-and-play area, where his wife has her knitting machines, and their children—two girls and a boy—have a rusty seesaw and a swing. From the terrace he pointed out less populated areas farther uphill, where the local drug traffickers have their hideaways, and the nearby neighborhoods of Ipanema and Leblon, where many of Vidigal's residents find jobs as maids or construction workers. Leaning against the railing, one small bare foot resting on the instep of the other, skinny arms folded against his chest, he reflected again on his luck, and on where he would be today if he and the beautiful Tereza had not found their way years ago to the Church of the Assembly of God.

Tereza, who has a large capacity for introspection and a seeming inability to paper over unpleasant facts, tells the story more precisely. She met Jamin when she was fifteen years old. He was working as a delivery boy, while she was working in an office, washing dishes and preparing the little cups of coffee that Brazilians drink all day long. She is very black and Jamin is classified as white—a combination that is not unheard of in serious relationships here but isn't common, either. Her friends warned him away: "That girl is insolent. She's going to give you a *bad* time. You're spending too much money on her." She wasn't wild about him, but when she mentioned that she liked to knit he took all his savings and bought her a little knitting machine. They moved in together, but soon Tereza decided that he would drive her crazy with his doglike devotion and suffocating jealousy. She left him, and then she discovered that she was pregnant.

Tereza told me this story while she combed her two lovely daughters' masses of bouncy, ringleted hair and tied it with ribbons. Tereza keeps the girls and the little boy dressed in picture-perfect pastels and sees to it that the children have pleasant manners. There is an orderliness about her—an emotional discipline—that one rarely finds among people in a very poor urban environment, but she told me that she was not always that way. When the first baby was born, she said, she used to keep it locked in the crawl space below the shack, so that she wouldn't have to hear its crying. She would struggle all day to calm her nerves, but when she heard Jamin trudging up the path in the evening, her heart would start beating in anguish. Soon she would be yelling horrible things at him. "She was sarcastic," Jamin recalls. "Whatever plan I came up with, however I tried to please her, she would cut me down. She made me feel worthless." They did not speak to each other except when they were quarrelling.

It was because she was in a complete state of despair that Tereza agreed to let a neighbor take her to an Assembly of God church service one afternoon, and although she didn't like the shouting and the chanting that went on there, she was interested in some pamphlets her neighbor gave her which had to do with the family. She read that women should obey their husbands in everything, and not talk back to them; that they should not go to parties where provocative music is played; and that they should dress modestly. There were instructions on child care. In the favelas, many children are disciplined through beatings, and it is not uncommon for them to be chained for hours at a time, either as punishment or to keep them safe while the parents are at work. The pamphlets forbade child-beating and all other forms of child abuse, along with wife-beating and drinking and gambling. They defined a role for each member of the family and provided instructions on how to fill it.

Tereza took Jamin to the Assembly meetings. She began guitar lessons, and she and Jamin practiced hymns together until late at night. She stopped talking back to him, and noticed that his jealous fits eased almost immediately. They discussed child-rearing methods and the homemaking suggestions in the pamphlets, and applied them. They were so excited by all these new ideas and methods that they hardly noticed that their relationship had changed until, sitting up in bed late one night, they suddenly realized that they had been having their first conversation. They were in love.

Umbanda's strength has been the ability to imagine an alternative reality better than the present dreary one, but to a large extent the evangelical sects' genius is to have helped their followers *change* reality. Never mind that most of the worshippers' most ambitious letters to Jesus remain unanswered; Tereza wears high-cut blouses and below-the-knee skirts and keeps her husband happy, and more and more women in the favelas are becoming convinced that doing that is miracle enough. Converts are instructed in the virtues of formality, punctuality, and self-control, and the lesson has proved so successful that many job interviewers will give "believers" preference in hiring, particularly for unskilled jobs. Despite these clear benefits, Protestant sects are unpopular in the media and among many intellectuals, on the basis of their puritanism and what is seen as their Yankee origin. One intellectual who isn't bothered is Darcy Ribeiro, the near-legendary anthropologist and leftist politician, who, despite surgery to remove one cancerous lung nearly a decade ago, continues to spout ideas, articles, and government projects—he drafted Governor Brizola's plan for daylong schools with two square meals—at an undiminished pace.

"The sects are a form of worship that has found a way to dignify the lower-income sectors," he said cheerily the other day, brushing aside objections that the new churches deal in snake oil and siphon money out of the pockets of people who desperately need it. "This is a class of people who want to discover the values that will allow them a stable family life and respectability. It's a class that suffers enormously from the effects of alcoholism: every Friday night, the husband comes home pickled in *cachaça*, he beats his wife, and then he gets on top of her. Umbanda has no religious morality; basically, it's a lumpen ethic and so, of course, it has had to suffer in the face of this new cult, which is so full of family virtues, protects children, and has a very strong notion of sin. There have probably never been so many virgins in Rio as now! The Catholic Church always preached about the family, but the fact is that there has never been much family life in Brazil; in the upper classes, it's all hypocrisy, and what has prevailed among the poor is the model of the heroic mother raising a family that is poorer with every new child. Also, the new churches have a Brazilian *jeito*—a Brazilian way of doing things. That is particularly true of the Assembly of God, but all the others are nonhierarchical and informal, too. They're growing like weeds."

Actually, the Assembly of God is not growing at the same exorbitant rate as the God Is Love and the Universal Churches, perhaps because its *jeito* isn't quite Brazilian enough. The Assembly combats Umbanda and practices faith healing, but what draws crowds is the rapturous theatrics of its younger competitors. I asked Father Valdelí Carvalho da Costa, a Jesuit priest who wrote a dissertation on Umbanda, why religion in Brazil tends toward the extravagant and the magical, and he answered that this is a reflection of the Brazilian soul. "We live in a mythic universe," he said. "It comes from our African and Indian roots, and it's much more fluid and all-encompassing than Catholicism— which is the official religion. This universe is inhabited by all Brazilians, from the most illiterate slumdweller to a novelist like Jorge Amado, who has been both a member of the Communist Party and a follower of Candomblé. It's as if this mythic mentality were a parallel atmosphere we float in. Everything is always in flux, always changeable. As in the stories about men who turn into jaguars and jaguars who turn into armadillos, transformations are always possible."

"We believe in what we see," I was told by the sociologist

Mariza da Costa, who is an initiate in Candomblé. "I believe in the *orixás* because I see them. The Western perception that one should believe in what one can control is the complete opposite of this. People who come from abroad to look at the Afro-Brazilian religions are always asking me 'Do you really *believe* in this?' I tell them that in those terms one has to make a distinction between belief and faith. I have faith."

THERE WAS TINGLING excitement in the air at the Spiritist Tent of Father Gerónimo one night as the initiates changed out of their white Umbanda uniforms into red-and-black costumes for the Devil-like Exus. Mother Marinete, who inherited the temple from her father, the Gerónimo of its name, had invited me earlier in the day to attend this session, which she was holding at the request of her followers to replace a session she'd had to cancel because of a trip abroad. "The women love the *pombagiras*," she said, grinning. "They wouldn't miss that for the world." All the women looked beautiful when they emerged from the dressing room, ready to receive the *pombagira* spirits: middle-aged or very young, fair-skinned or very black, they had stuck flowers in their hair, rubbed garish red lipstick on their mouths, and added a certain nonchalant sway to their walks as they strolled about the temple in expectation of the spirits. The temple that Father Gerónimo created is certainly a place where magical things can happen. Its courtyard, which is reached through a long, narrow alleyway from a quiet suburban street, is full of shrines where homemade representations of the *orixás* glow in the light of candles set there by their devotees. Two enormous palm trees, which Mother Marinete calls her antennae, poke through the floor of the theatre-size ceremonial hall, which is all white, and through its tentlike ceiling. In the courtyard that evening, the palm fronds framed a full moon.

There aren't many temples like this one left in central Rio, Mother Marinete said, standing in the moonlight in an African tunic, a glittery turban framing her smooth, round face. There aren't many temple heads who can afford all that real estate, she explained. She gave up her law practice to take over the temple after her father became ill, a couple of years ago, and now she makes ends meet through the contributions of tourists, who regularly arrive in busloads from South Zone hotels to watch the sessions, but if she hadn't inherited the temple she probably wouldn't have been able to set one up on her own. Mother Marinete has great faith that there is about to be a second expansive wave of Umbanda, and that this time it will occur abroad, thanks to the influence of people like the foreigners who come to visit her out of curiosity and leave with the seed of Umbanda in them. In fact, the reason she had had to cancel the regularly scheduled Exu session was that she had gone to inaugurate a congress on Afro-Brazilian religion organized by some of her father's disciples in Argentina. She thinks that Argentines and other foreigners are attracted to what they see in her temple because in their own daily lives they have no contact with their ancestors, and that anyone is lost who is out of touch with his past. But she also thinks that she makes converts because people can see for themselves that Umbanda works. "It's all scientific," she said, and she pointed out a woman emerging from the dressing room. The woman was epileptic, she said, but had suffered from attacks much less frequently since she began coming to the temple. Then she spoke of a man who is now one of her principal assistants, and whom her father had rescued off the street when he was alcoholic and crazy. "The point is that we can control access to the trance state through breathing, and proper breathing balances the spirit and allows people to be in harmony with the world," she said.

Nevertheless, Mother Marinete acknowledged, there are major problems with Umbanda in Rio these days. There are hustlers and quacks all over the place, and the evangelical churches have known how to take advantage of people's anger with bad Umbanda. And there is the problem of transmitting Umbanda knowledge. "Most of the temple leaders who have real roots, real traditional knowledge, come from very poor and ignorant backgrounds, and they haven't known how to pass on their wisdom," she said. "But I notice that there is a great surge of young people from academic backgrounds who are coming here and to other

temples to find out what it is we know, and I think the next generation of religious leaders will come from them." She smiled and
shook her head. "It isn't easy. Being a Mother of a Saint"—the
head of a temple, who can initiate people into the cult of the
orixás—"requires a lot of juggling. In the sessions, I very rarely
incorporate my saint, because I am taking care of everyone
else—making sure the novices don't hurt themselves or get
frightened, seeing to it that the people who come in looking for
help find it. And then I have to deal with the outside world.
Things are very crazy in Rio—the city isn't what it used to be. I
have to deal with all these little drug-trafficking kids who come
in here thinking they can expect favors from me. And with mug-
gers who think I have something to steal. And with the people
who want to join the evangelicals and with those who want to
come back. A lot of them do, you know."

Inside the temple, the initiates had covered the altar holding
the statue of Christ with a curtain, so that He would not be
forced to see the Devil having his way. They had laid out a red-
and-black cloth on the floor and set on it cigars, bottles of beer,
red roses, and red and black candles. Now the men began to un-
cork bottles of cider, and every time a bottle popped, a large
crowd of suppliants sitting along the sides of the ceremonial area
applauded joyfully. Then drumming started. A black woman with
a deep, gritty voice sang the praises of Exu Who Clears Paths
and Closes Gates. Soon the spirits arrived. They cackled and
leered inside their worshippers' bodies and lurched around
wildly, calling more spirits in, and even taking possession of non-
initiate suppliants, whipping their bodies about and throwing
them to the floor. The entire congregation became engaged in
the Exus' urgent and mysterious business as the temple took on
the air of an agitated but very friendly insane asylum.

I left the temple and travelled across the city, to a chrome-
and-marble meeting hall in a neighborhood near the lustrous bay
front, where hundreds of sweaty believers prayed loudly to Jesus
for a miracle while on the dais above them three preachers roared
simultaneously into microphones, exhorting the Devil to be
gone. The crowd's fervor virtually guaranteed that a miracle

would occur, and the same was true at the temple of Granny Maria Antonia, where Stella's followers were welcoming the old
slave spirits, who twisted their devotees' bodies with arthritis and
old age and filled their souls with wisdom. A short time later and
a couple of miles away, a small crowd gathered around the miraculous statue of Our Lady of Fátima, brought here by Portuguese
Catholics to make a tour of her churches. She was travelling
through Brazil in a minivan, encased in a Lucite box, and as she
rode into the night her devotees sang farewell and waved goodbye from the steps of a small church. Down the street, on a dark
corner, half a dozen women dressed in white set out an offering
to Exu of the Seven Crossroads, which glowed with the light of
a score of candles until, suddenly, a sharp wind rose and snuffed
them out. It was Friday night in Rio, and all the spirits were at
work.

LA PAZ
1992

"It takes so long to get so little."

ALMOST EVERY EVENT worth noting in La Paz seems to take place along the Prado, a pleasant ten-block stretch of boulevard that cuts straight through the heart of the city. The Prado is a favorite strolling destination, and it is also frequently used for demonstrations. During one of the more violent of several coups that took place in the nineteen-seventies, for example, an armored helicopter swooped down at the northern end of the boulevard and opened fire on thousands of protesters who had gathered at Plaza San Francisco; dozens were killed, to signify that resistance was useless. In July of 1980, paramilitary squads under the direction of General Luis García Meza started a coup by assassinating three leftist labor and political leaders hiding inside the headquarters of the Bolivian Workers Confederation, a graceful old house on the Prado. The squads then blew up the building. The house has been replaced by a parking lot, and modern office buildings and hotels now outnumber the few surviving ornate mansions, but the Prado's daily rituals and rhythms can deceive one into thinking that it has stayed unchanged since it was dedicated, in 1925. The clipped shrubbery and modest statues of Columbus, Bolívar, and Athena remain. Criollo women out for an afternoon of shopping still favor pearls and careful hairdos, and middle-aged criollo men do their strolling dressed in stolid brown double-breasted suits. Indian women still offer goods for sale on the sidewalk, babies slung in hand-loomed *aguayos* on their backs. Tenants don't change much, and old customs linger. The Bolivian Mineworkers Federation, the now ravaged heart of what used to be the powerful Bolivian Workers Confederation, has managed to hang on to a tiny warren of offices at the rear of the parking lot where the confederation headquarters once stood. And every now and then out-of-work miners still march up the Prado toward the seat of government, the Palacio Quemado, or Burned Palace, shouting that they want their back wages, and revolution.

The Indian women are selling L'eggs pantyhose and electronic goods these days—evidence that a revolution is in fact already taking place, though hardly the socialist one that the miners did their best to bring about. Instead, Bolivia is the site of a six-year-old experiment in neoliberal upheaval, and I arrived in La Paz last November in time to witness one more episode in the continuing test—what at first appeared to be a routine municipal-election campaign. Elections here are hardly a routine event: the first free Presidential election in more than twenty years was held in 1985. But, because so many of the actors on the current political scene have been around far longer than any one cares to remember, the electoral process already has something of a used, worn feeling to it. Víctor Paz Estenssoro, who became President in 1985, had already been President in 1952 and again in 1960. In 1964, he was overthrown by a coup, which inaugurated a long sequence of military regimes. The leading contender in the 1985 elections was General Hugo Bánzer, one of the more successful of the military dictators.

The Bolivian constitution requires that, to be elected, a candidate have an absolute majority, which none of the excessively well-known array of politicians ever gets; as a result, the outcome of most recent elections—whether municipal or Presidential—has been decided through back-channel negotiations in Congress. Thus, although General Bánzer actually won the Presidential election in 1985 with a plurality of a few thousand votes, the subsequent dealmaking handed power to Paz Estenssoro. Paz

Estenssoro's political successor won the 1989 election with a similarly slim majority, but the right-wing Bánzer prevented him from becoming President by forming an alliance with the third-place runner-up, his own former archenemy Jaime Paz Zamora, a leftist, who is in power today. (Paz Zamora is a political opponent of Paz Estenssoro, his uncle.) The expectation before the nationwide municipal elections that took place last December was that abstention rates would be high, and that the traditional parties' candidates would square off briefly before settling down to a session of horse-trading.

Nevertheless, the mayoral campaigns in La Paz were colorful and a little desperate. The ruling coalition's candidate, a man with the unlikely name of Ronald MacLean, urgently wanted to win a third two-year term as mayor, to finish up the administrative reform he had been carrying out. (Typically, the only time MacLean attained a plurality, he didn't get to rule, and his subsequent administrations were the result of deals.) His slogan was "All Colors for MacLean," which was a brave attempt to bridge the chasm separating him—he is upper class, conservative, blond, and white-skinned—from the country's Indian majority. Paz Estenssoro's party, the Movimiento Nacional Revolucionario, or M.N.R., just as urgently needed to win in order to regain its slipping hold on national politics. Its candidate, Guido Capra, it was claimed, "Listens and Knows," and because he is a confident, personable civil engineer with an easy style the slogan seemed credible.

Background noise from some lesser political aspirants—leftists, loony arrivistes, a talk-show host—occasionally distracted the attention of the media and the pollsters from the main campaigns, but no one really focussed on the outsiders until the upstart multi-millionaire brewer and aspiring Presidential candidate Max Fernández, of the Unión Cívica Solidaridad, or U.C.S., decided to show the élite of La Paz just how large his political following is. On the Sunday I arrived, he and Juan Ayoroa, his designated mayoral candidate for La Paz, who is a retired general with virtually no political experience, led a caravan of trucks and station wagons stuffed with their supporters up and down the

Prado, at a time when the avenue is closed to traffic and filled with strolling families.

The display struck many people I talked to in the establishment's campaigns as unseemly, but the truth is that none of their candidates had been able to muster a similar crowd, and so by the eve of the elections the people working with MacLean or with the M.N.R. were ready to acknowledge that Ayoroa was a distant but decidedly plausible threat. So was the candidate for the party founded by the talk-show host, which is called Condepa, for Conciencia de Patria, or Awareness of the Fatherland. No one imagined, though, that Condepa's mayoral candidate, an orthodox leftist who makes much of his Indian origins, was about to win the La Paz mayoralty by a landslide, or that throughout the country Max Fernández's candidates would vacuum up almost twenty-three per cent of the vote, two percentage points behind the M.N.R. and just five points behind the ruling Paz-Bánzer coalition. The effects of the neoliberal revolution that had turned Bolivia's economy upside down were extending into politics, although not quite in the way its leaders had hoped.

I first understood the appeal of the man everyone in Bolivia calls Max one drizzly afternoon before the elections, when he attended a campaign event for his Unión Cívica Solidaridad at the central slaughterhouse in La Paz. It is not a pretty place, especially when it rains; as the head of the La Paz Association of Slaughterers repeatedly informed the crowd over a loudspeaker, neither the muddy, fly-infested grounds nor the machinery had been improved since the place opened, half a century ago. Nevertheless, the site had been decorated for the event with flowers and handwoven Indian banners studded with silver objects and dolls, and the crowd added lustre, too. There were folk dancers in gaudy costumes, a brass band playing mournful Andean songs, and plump Indian market women—*cholas*—dressed in their Sunday best: voluminous satin skirts and alpaca shawls, bowler hats worn tilted at a smart angle, and big gold earrings dangling almost to their shoulders. Max, who is a hulking man with a florid complexion, was up on the speaker's platform, his face almost hidden from view by an enormous flower wreath someone had draped over his neck. The head of the slaughterers' association looked near tears as he called Max "a father, who has shown his commitment to us with works," and whom, he promised, "we will do our best to help get to the top, as he deserves."

Brand-new meat-packing machinery from Brazil, piled up in crates at the entrance to the slaughterhouse, and worth about half a million dollars, was the source of the public gratitude. Contrary to his usual practice, Max was not giving this equipment away but had found affordable financing for the slaughterhouse coöperative. Max, who rose to wealth from humble beginnings, is not a graceful or dramatic orator, but his very awkwardness helps make him a convincing speaker for listeners who are as poor and socially outcast as he once was. "Do you think I'm in the business of selling slaughterhouses?" he asked the crowd when his turn came. "I have my own money and I don't need more, but in the U.C.S. we are good citizens who want to work for the good of all Bolivians. How many mayors have passed through this city without doing a thing? And yet we are standing in what could be one of the great breeding grounds for cholera in the city."

Not every man who has made a vast fortune out of nothing, who lives in a smoked-glass-and-cast-concrete fortress with a dozen anxious assistants permanently at his command, decides that the thing to do in his spare time is to travel the country dispensing largesse and running for President. In the headquarters of the Cervecería Boliviana Nacional, which has a massive crystal chandelier in the new marble lobby, Max told me it was his natural constituency that made him get into politics. At one point in his career, he was the owner of a sizable fleet of trucks, and so he already commanded the loyalty of thousands of drivers. Now, as the owner of the Cervecería Boliviana, he estimates that he is responsible for the well-being of some forty thousand families, counting brewery employees, grain suppliers, distributors, drivers, and carriers. In effect, this makes him the single largest employer in Bolivia outside the government, and it was this community, Max told me, that knew how much he had done for the beer factory and was demanding that he do the same for the country. "I'm not a fanatic for politics," he said. "But my people insisted so much, there was so much pressure from so many sectors, I had to do it."

Max acquired a controlling interest in the brewery in 1986, shortly after Paz Estenssoro came to power and embarked on a revolution that he called the New Economic Policy. The overnight restructuring of the country's jerry-built economy sent most businesses into a tailspin; Max, on the other hand, had enough cash at the ready to snap up the shares of the foundering Cervecería Boliviana, which were offered to him at cut-rate prices by a desperate board. He told me that he had started out as a messenger boy in his home province, Cochabamba, some thirty years ago, and that his rise was due to his capacity for hard work and his joyous passion for "planning, finances, and marketing."

Max's detractors—who until very recently included the United States Ambassador here—have often speculated that Max actually owes his fortune to the drug trade, which would then be the source of the financing for the electric generators, the sports fields, and the school and market buildings that Max bestows everywhere on his campaign tours. Bolivia's beer king distrusts the press and is uncomfortable with interviews, but there was no bitterness, defensiveness, or gloating in his manner when I brought up the subject. "There was some tension between me and the Embassy," he said. "Finally, I went to the Drug Enforcement Administration people and showed them documents explaining how I had made my fortune. Everything I possess is registered under the name Max Fernández: cars, buildings, a new tin-can-manufacturing plant in Oruro, which cost me eight million dollars. I have nothing to hide. I think they're satisfied now." Embassy officials later confirmed that the tenor of their dealings with Max had "modified considerably" in recent weeks, because, despite former Ambassador Robert Gelbard's well-known suspicions, the D.E.A. had not been able to prove any of the allegations about Max.

What no one questions is that under Max's ownership the Cervecería Boliviana Nacional has flourished. The payroll is up from three thousand to twenty-three thousand. Distribution is up from nine thousand dozen bottles a day to nearly ninety thousand dozen. Max has imported state-of-the-art canning equipment, which will allow the brewery to begin exporting, and he hopes to travel to Russia this year to see about setting up a brewery there. This, he insisted, was his true passion. Politics was a circumstantial sideline, "for which the only guiding ideology is that wherever a citizen needs bread or health we give it to him, without asking for anything in exchange."

But Max sounded a little put out a few days after the elections, when, having spent close to four million dollars in handouts, and having won close to six hundred city-council seats across the country, in addition to a hundred mayoralties, he declared that he had wanted more. "I've made a great many investments at all levels, but some cities have turned their backs on me," he told the press. "I'm hurt that people should be so ungrateful." Hurt, but not enough to consider leaving national politics. In fact, the establishment's continuing post mortems on the elections are made increasingly gloomy by the realization that the man all the candidates will have to beat in 1993—a Presidential-election year—will, in all probability, be Max Fernández.

AMONG THE PEOPLE gathered in the slaughterhouse yard on the day Max Fernández handed over the new equipment, a number of men were unmistakably identifiable as miners by their livid color and gaunt faces. Several of them told me that they were near fifty or older; the very fact that they were still alive made them a statistical exception—life expectancy for Bolivian males is fifty, but miners often die earlier than that, from silicosis, tuberculosis, or alcohol-related diseases. The miners said that they had been laid off in 1985 from the two most famous of all Bolivia's tin mines, Siglo XX and Catavi. These were discovered and mined by the legendary Simón Patiño, who built up one of the world's great fortunes at the beginning of the century, when the demand for canned food sent the price of tin soaring, and who, having made his fortune and run into tax problems with the Bolivian government one too many times, went to live and die abroad in luxury. Siglo XX and Catavi were also the organizing strongholds of the miners' federation: where the movement to nationalize the mines took hold; where miners conspired and campaigned against one military dictatorship after another; and where their wives barred access to the camps with their bodies whenever a dictator sent the troops in with orders to shoot. It has been several decades since the miners had friends in government, and longer still since they could see the world in terms that were not strictly dictated by Trotskyist or orthodox Communist Party ideology, but times change. They told me they thought that Max could have their vote if they could make a deal with him. What kind of a deal? "Anything," one of the men replied. "A little work, maybe."

When American Embassy officials or representatives from organizations like the World Bank list the achievements of Víctor Paz Estenssoro's fourth term in power, they generally say that he stopped inflation, balanced the budget, and broke the back of the miners' movement. The irony is that it was the miners, more than any other political force, who made Paz Estenssoro the century's most influential politician. In 1952, the M.N.R. rose to power in a widespread popular insurrection, with the Mineworkers Federation at its heart: miners led strikes, plotted, marched on La Paz, built barricades, and cheered their leader, Juan Lechín, who was the only one of the principal revolutionary conspirators to address the crowds during those heady days. Lechín and the miners were able to alter the course of Bolivian history, because they worked in an industry that provided Bolivia's only significant source of foreign income before the advent of the drug trade. They were indispensable. When the insurrection triumphed, Paz Estenssoro carried out a drastic program of nationalization, land confiscation, and ambitious educational and political reforms. When he came to power for the fourth time, in 1985, at the age of seventy-seven, no popular triumph was involved, and he was thus politically answerable to no one: his final four years as President were remarkable both for his achievements and for the systematic assault he launched on his own previous reforms.

Paz Estenssoro, who is said to like order above all things,

inherited a country in chaos. The foreign debt was three billion two hundred and seventy million dollars—the size of the gross national product. The annual rate of inflation was twenty-four thousand per cent. The mining industry was collapsing. Two days after Paz took power, he appointed an emergency task force of businessmen, economists, lawyers, and congressmen to draw up an economic-emergency program. According to a participant in the first meeting, Paz began the session by reminding everyone that he could go down in history as the author of the great 1952 reforms: suffrage for women and illiterates, free primary education, nationalized resources, land for the peasantry. What, he wanted to know, would happen if he rested on those laurels and applied inoffensive solutions to the current crisis? The task-force members thought about this and replied that at the rate things were going Paz might soon guarantee himself a place in history as the man who presided over the world's highest-ever rate of inflation—higher even, probably, than that of Germany after the First World War. "In that case, let's get to work," Paz said.

Three weeks later, Bolivia once again embarked on a revolution—this time, the neoliberal economic one, which knocked over everything the M.N.R. was thought to stand for. With the help of the Harvard economist Jeffrey Sachs, who has since gone on to advise the governments of Russia and Poland on how to create capitalism, Paz decreed a free-floating currency and open economic borders. Shortly after he took power, world tin prices fell, and he saw to it that the state mining corporation, Comibol, got rid of more than two-thirds of its thirty thousand miners and other employees. Then he promised to reverse the most important symbolic achievement of his first administration: the state's appropriation of the mining industry, which even in its dilapidated condition remains Bolivia's treasure. The country is still reeling. And the laid-off miners, the heroes of their century's revolutionary epic, are stunned, bitter, broke, and defeated.

The intended benefits of the straitjacket policies that Paz Estenssoro and his advisers applied to the economy are clear: the end of inflation and the consequent possibility of designing an orderly economic policy; a new, shrunken role in the economy

for the government; the timid beginnings of an efficient and independent business sector. The social costs of a program so ruthlessly applied are also clear. Bolivia now rivals Haiti as the
country with the lowest standard of living in the hemisphere:
unemployment and underemployment hover at around forty per
cent. But, like the initial collapse of the business sector, this devastation was predicted and taken into account by the planners.
It's the unwanted side effects that have everyone dumbfounded:
the general cynicism about traditional politics; the rise of Max
Fernández; and the disreputable ways that people forced into unemployment have found to make ends meet. Some have taken to
begging, some to sidewalk peddling. In the first months of the
programmed misery, as official unemployment climbed to nearly
twenty-five per cent, thousands of desperate people—including,
of course, the miners—headed for the tropics and set themselves
up as coca farmers. Given that the illegal cocaine trade was
slowly destroying the Bolivian social body—and that it remains
Bolivia's principal problem vis-à-vis the United States—this may
have been the most unwanted side effect of all.

BEYOND THE SNOW-COVERED volcanoes that guard the dry
brown altiplano is a second Bolivia—semitropical, rich in oil and
natural gas deposits, sparsely inhabited, and psychologically
very distant from the tradition-bound highlands. It is here, in the
prosperous industrial and agricultural province of Santa Cruz—
where Max Fernández made his fortune—that the cocaine trade
is said to have started, almost two decades ago. The late Bolivian
journalist René Bascopé believed that in the mid-nineteen-
seventies, when a severe financial crisis hit the wealthy cotton
growers of Santa Cruz, many of them turned to the nascent Colombian cocaine trade to offer raw materials. Coca grown in Colombia was not of high quality, and the traffickers there, who
were beginning to manufacture cocaine in laboratories, needed
Peruvian and Bolivian middlemen who could guarantee a steady
supply of coca leaves. This was provided by a trickle of *colonos*,
or settlers—both peasants and former miners—who were leaving the desolate altiplano in search of a better life and settling in

the province of Cochabamba, next door to Santa Cruz. A lot of these migrants found that the Chapare, an area of river-crossed subtropical flatlands, was a good place to grow coca and that, thanks to the cotton growers, coca was an increasingly profitable way to make a living. When the economic crisis provoked by the New Economic Policy hit, in 1985, large numbers of out-of-work miners—a majority, according to some estimates—joined the *colonos* in the coca fields.

The leaf of the coca bush provides only one of the essential ingredients for the manufacture of cocaine, but this ingredient is the toxin that gives the drug its kick—cocaine alkaloid, which is processed to obtain cocaine hydrochloride, the white powder. For centuries before the laboratory process for precipitating cocaine hydrochloride was developed, coca leaves were used in the Andes for ritual purposes; chewed with small amounts of ash, they act as a sensory suppressant and a euphoriant. After the Conquest, the Spaniards learned to provide coca leaves in large amounts to the enslaved Indians in the mines and on the haciendas; chewing the leaves enabled workers to endure constant hunger, exhaustion, and despair. *Pij'cheo*, the practice of chewing coca, is both legal and customary today among Indians and the very poor—categories that are virtually synonymous. Bolivian miners receive a daily coca ration as part of their salaries. In all the Andean countries, significant amounts of coca are grown legally for domestic consumption, and a small quantity is sold legally to pharmaceutical companies and then to the Coca-Cola Company, which extracts the flavor for its soft drinks. What is *not* legal is buying coca for the purpose of manufacturing cocaine, and it is the nebulous quality of this distinction—and the political and military difficulties of enforcing it—that makes the Chapare the quagmire for drug-interdiction policy that it is today.

The Chapare is where I first had an inkling of the difficulties involved in getting coca farmers to sympathize with the United States' war on drugs. I had spent the day travelling through the region with José Chile, a former miner who is now a coca grower and a leader of a local growers' association. Much of our time was spent tracking down a few sacks of cement that Chile was transporting in stages to his home district, where he hoped to build a rudimentary clinic, in the further hope of persuading the government to send a doctor to staff it. The cement had been a donation from a local government office, but since Chile had no transport he and his neighbors had had to rely on one friendly driver and then another to nudge the shipment down the main Chapare road from village to village over the past several days. While we were looking for the cement's latest stopping place, Chile suddenly commented that foreigners tended to be more charitable than Bolivians. Would I know, he wondered, of any international aid association willing to donate money for his clinic? I said that foreigners—of the type that go in for international good works, at any rate—tend to despise the cocaine trade and would probably be disinclined to donate money to coca growers, and Chile looked first stunned and then devastated at this notion.

I had met José Chile the day before, in the city of Cochabamba, in a sparsely furnished building that houses the Special Federation of Farmers of the Cochabamba Tropics, which represents about twenty-five thousand coca growers and their families. Although miners are a minority among the Chapare settlers, they are quite active in the coca growers' five associations. Chile introduced himself as the federation's finance secretary, and, without wasting any time on chitchat, he agreed to join me in the Chapare for a day and talk about the coca farmers' life there.

Surrounded by other former miners in the federation's headquarters that afternoon, Chile seemed efficient and dignified. When I saw him next, at three in the morning of the following day, trotting alone out of the shadows of the shantytown where he stays when he is in the city, he looked small and shrunken. I had rented a jeep, and our driver, also an Indian from the altiplano, appeared towering and robust next to him; José Chile had taken on the distinct look of a miner—the drawn, sere aspect of someone who has spent a lifetime working underground. But despite his harrowed look and a dour reserve before strangers, Chile turned out to be a sociable and cheery man, and found nothing to complain about in the fact that it was before dawn and we were travelling quickly up into freezing temperatures, along a rutted dirt road in a vehicle with hardly any springs.

The steep, low range we were climbing is buffeted by cold altiplano winds on its western side. The eastern slope looks toward the Amazon basin, and the climate is more temperate. As we came up and over the last promontory, we felt the air grow warmer. Day broke as we drove down canyons guarded by tall, mist-covered peaks that were wrapped in dense green vegetation except where ferns and spidery trees parted to make way for streams of rainwater racing toward the rivers below. After a four-hour drive, or about a hundred miles, the two-lane gravel road flattened out, the air became steamy, and we reached Villa Tunari, a very small town at the entrance to the Chapare sub-Amazonian lowlands. A short while later, we stopped at Eteramasama, where the Chapare farmers' two principal means of making money from coca can be found within a hundred feet of each other. Here, a block from the main road, is one of the three main coca exchanges for the region, and here also, on this particular day, was a travelling delegation from the government's Department of Agricultural Reconversion, which pays farmers two thousand dollars for every hectare of "legal" coca they uproot; that is, coca planted before new plots were outlawed, in 1988.

The coca exchange is a large open-sided warehouse where buyers flock to appraise the merchandise and haggle over the best lots. Sometimes they are purchasing on behalf of the Coca-Cola Company. (The D.E.A. says it always knows when it has managed to bring down prices through interdiction, because the soft-drink company's resident Bolivian buyer makes an appearance.) Most often, they are purchasing for the drug trade, but on this point Chile became untypically reticent. I asked him how, with special anti-drug troops stationed just down the road, buyers for the drug trade could appear, make their purchases, and carry away their merchandise unseen, and Chile said only, "Who knows?" This was the same unsurprising answer provided, rather more tensely, by two employees at the government reconversion office. They also offered an explanation of how the program works. Farmers wishing to receive two thousand dollars for an uprooted plot get two visits from a reconversion inspector, who measures the coca plot before and after the uprooting and testifies that eradication has indeed taken place. The reconversion office then sends a check, along with a certificate that qualifies the grower for alternative-development aid from the government and the United States Agency for International Development. Despite the best efforts of A.I.D. and a host of other international agencies, like the United Nations Drug Control Program, the reconversion employees said that most farmers eradicated only part of their coca holdings, generally when there was a family emergency, or when coca prices were low.

To some degree, José Chile has a vested interest in seeing his fellow-farmers resist reconversion. He is a union man, and for him union work is a matter of life-and-death confrontation with an endlessly hostile state. In 1965, Chile participated in the Mineworkers Federation's feverish attempt to take over the tin mines at Oruro and Catavi, which ended with a military offensive that left twenty-four people dead. (Chile himself drank too much the evening before and overslept as a result, missing the bloodshed.) He has marched and conspired, joined hunger strikes, manned barricades. He left the mines before the 1985 mass dismissals, but after wages had sunk so low that he couldn't keep his family alive on them. A brother had gone into coca farming in the tropics before him, and at the time it was possible to make around seven thousand dollars a year by farming a couple of hectares. In the Chapare, Chile immediately became active in his federation's local *sindicato*, which acts as a grass-roots administrative system for the settlers. Shortly after Chile arrived, coca prices suffered their first major collapse, and the *sindicato* became even more important as a mutual-help-and-support organization. When the United States and Bolivia embarked on their first joint military offensive on coca, during the Paz Estenssoro regime, even the most apolitical farmers were terrified and outraged. The *sindicato* acquired a new edge; it acquired, in effect, a miner personality, and is now militantly committed to getting rid of the United States military presence in the region and defending the legality of coca production.

• • •

WHAT THE GROWERS are defending is a livelihood that is now
barely above subsistence level. Although coca prices rise and fall,
the days of seven-thousand-dollar yearly incomes are long gone.
Buyers are paying around a hundred and sixty bolivianos a load
these days, or about forty-five dollars, which Chile says is a good
price; he can harvest four crops a year on one hectare for a total
earnings of about seventeen hundred dollars. Still, the signs that
we were travelling through a region in economic recession were
everywhere. We were in the prime-real-estate zone of the Chapare, an area that has a road, some water and electricity, and, as
of last year, the rudiments of a sewer system. (The very poor, like
José Chile, live several days' walk from the road and the public
services.) Yet even in this privileged place there were dozens of
shacks with "For Sale" signs tacked up on the plank walls.

In the hot shade of a restaurant at Isinuta, where the road
ends, we finally caught up with Chile's neighbors and fellow former miners, who told him that the cement for the clinic had arrived safely this far, and that now all they had to do was wait for
the river, swollen by heavy rains, to subside so they could cross
it and continue on their way home, carrying the cement on their
backs. They had been waiting already for a couple of days, but,
since the rains had stopped, they thought that they would be
able to cross any time now. We sipped some of Max Fernández's
beer and watched the rare traffic along the road: a bicycle, a
pickup truck carrying passengers in the back, a four-wheel-drive
vehicle carrying international reconversion technocrats and project supervisors, a nonarmored personnel carrier filled with Bolivian special forces. The miners spat on the ground at the sight.
"They grab our bicycles, our radios, our coca, and half an hour
later we see their girlfriends trying to sell it all," one of the men
said.

Chile is also used to seeing operatives from the Drug Enforcement Administration. For all practical purposes, the D.E.A.
runs the Bolivian government's anti-drug program, providing a
rare patch of ideological common ground for poor Indians like
Chile and the white urban middle classes of La Paz, whether con-

servative, liberal, or radical: they are united in their loathing of the gringos' interference in local affairs. The D.E.A. first moved into Bolivia in a major way in 1986, when it staged the showy display that radicalized so many coca farmers; this was Operation Blast Furnace, in which Bolivian and United States troops helicoptered into jungle laboratories and torched them in view of dozens of photographers and many more local residents. The M.N.R. regime of Paz Estenssoro later decided that allowing Blast Furnace had been a mistake, and so did Paz Estenssoro's opponents in the Revolutionary Left Movement, President Paz Zamora's party. In the early days of his administration, Paz Zamora swore that he would not tolerate a United States military presence here, and that he would not give in to American pressure to militarize the drug fight by involving local troops. Yet since May of 1990, thanks to determined lobbying by the United States Embassy, Bolivia has accepted a significant American military presence, and the drug fight is no longer being left to the police. United States troops are training Bolivian Army conscripts, although it is not clear whether the Bolivian soldiers, many of whom are teen-agers, are supposed to take on the elusive drug mafia or get involved in confrontations with the coca growers.

The United States spent about thirty-five million dollars in direct military assistance here last year, and dozens of American military instructors were in the country to train Bolivian antinarcotics troops. Despite the years of United States military and police assistance and intense local involvement by the D.E.A., there are still almost forty thousand families making a living from coca farming in the Chapare alone. Having lived through the delinquent regime of General García Meza, the narco-President, who ruled with brazen and ruthless use of force from 1980 to 1982, La Paz residents are virtually united in their conviction that the one thing Bolivia's military doesn't need is an opportunity for further corruption. Ernesto Machicao, an articulate young congressman from the M.N.R., told me of another concern: the local drug élite, which has thus far been extremely reluctant to use violence, may resort to Colombian-type tactics if pressed too far. People here also worry about the effect of bringing down coca prices so much that cocaine—or, at least, the highly addictive and harmful crude coca paste—becomes affordable for the local population. Already, and as a result of the decline in coca prices, many Chapare farmers who previously had little or no association with the drug side of the trade are processing their own paste at home, to make extra money. And people worry about the contradiction in United States foreign policy, which, as Machicao pointed out, supports democracy with one hand and strengthens the military with the other. "It's not as if military strikes against civilian regimes were unusual here," he said.

Of course, there have been periodic successes: huge laboratories burned down in the Beni region; the surrender of seven leading traffickers under a no-extradition guarantee last year; the dismissal, at D.E.A. insistence, of Colonel Faustino Rico Toro, the man President Paz Zamora had appointed as head of the special anti-drug forces. Rico Toro was dismissed because he had long-standing and very public links to General García Meza. But United States officials fear that this last affair is noteworthy less as a drug-interdiction triumph than as a demonstration of how high corruption goes in the Paz-Bánzer government.

The Paz-Bánzer administration has committed itself to eradicating about thirty-five thousand hectares of coca cultivation by 1993, and the United States has linked the payment of hundreds of millions of dollars in aid to the success of the program. However, the voluntary eradication is running behind schedule. So far, none of the miner-farmers who are José Chile's neighbors have eradicated any coca, because they have worked out the figures, and the figures don't make sense. Theoretically, eradication is only the first step to making a decent living by growing something else, but Gustavo Camargo, an agronomist who was hired jointly by the coca farmers' associations to advise them on alternative crops, pointed out to me that few crops grow easily in the Chapare, and that profitable ones are expensive. "Take pineapple, for example," Camargo said. "It is adaptable to soil and climate conditions here, and a single hectare of export-quality pineapple can yield thirty thousand dollars a year. But a farmer needs twenty thousand dollars to plant forty thousand pineapples in a start-up hectare, not to mention the costs of agro-inputs and of training farmers."

There are other problems. Sitting in the muggy restaurant at Isinuta, Óscar Arias, a miner who has the same harrowed look as José Chile, said that coca was the only product with buyers willing to send planes to take it out. He had oranges, bananas, yuca rotting at home, he said, because he had no way to get his crops to market. "The only people really benefitting from eradication are the program's employees and their cronies," he went on. "We miners have shown that we can start from nothing and build a lot. We've known how to bring in drinking water, health clinics, roads, all through our own effort, but the government knows only how to make promises."

We left him and Chile's other neighbors at the river and headed back toward Eteramasama, where Chile stopped at a hopelessly underequipped clinic to ask the new doctor if she would come to his district for a vaccination campaign. She agreed, and Chile proceeded to draft an announcement of the campaign, to be broadcast by the local radio station. So far, he seemed highly pleased with the day's progress, but when we got back on the road he said something that surprised me. "It takes so long to get so little," he said. "What I need to do is figure out how to get in touch with Max Fernández. He can help."

TWO DAYS LATER, Fernández's Unión Cívica Solidaridad got about a third of the Chapare's votes, and most of them appear to have been cast by deserters from Víctor Paz Estenssoro's M.N.R. Nobody was more worried about this in La Paz than the current head of the M.N.R., Gonzalo (Goni) Sánchez de Lozada, who in his own way is quite as bizarre a politician as Max Fernández.

There are many compelling reasons that Sánchez de Lozada should never be President, and he takes perverse pleasure in listing them. First, there is the question of the accent: because his father, a left-wing politician, lived with his family in the United States—first as a diplomat and then in exile—from the time that Goni was one, and because Goni did not return to Bolivia until he was twenty-one, and because he has a tin ear, he speaks Spanish with what sounds like a parody of a gringo accent, and also makes grammatical mistakes, which he enjoys quoting to others. Then, there is the question of attitude: he *thinks* like a gringo, favoring efficiency and results over history and process to a degree that often maddens even his followers. There is his corrosive sarcasm, and the fact that he likes to say what he thinks. He doesn't remember names *or* faces. There is some debate whether he is the wealthiest or the second-wealthiest man in the country. By rights, he should never have made it to Congress, but in fact he has already been elected President of Bolivia once. He is the man who, as Paz Estenssoro's neoliberal Minister of Planning, brought inflation down from twenty-four thousand per cent to about fifteen per cent in 1985. In gratitude, a small plurality of the electorate—twenty-six per cent—gave him their vote in 1989, despite the fact that Paz, jealous and querulous, virtually refused to campaign for him. He is also the man who, as head of the Senate, lobbied successfully to have Paz Estenssoro named President over General Bánzer, the actual winner of the 1985 elections, and it was he who was robbed of his own victory by Bánzer's pact with Paz Zamora four years later.

We talked in a wealthy suburb of La Paz, in the den of Sánchez de Lozada's comfortable, rambling house, which contains a wonderful collection of colonial art. Sánchez de Lozada wants very badly to be President of Bolivia, but, at the age of sixty-one, with his moment of historical significance receding fast, he may find that the 1993 elections will be his last chance. Hugo Bánzer will run again in 1993, with President Paz Zamora's support, and Sánchez de Lozada would like to believe that Bánzer will get fewer votes than he did the last time, because people are unhappy with the Paz-Bánzer alliance. But Max Fernández could easily win enough votes to turn the contest into a three-way race, and between him and Bánzer they could deal Sánchez de Lozada out of the Presidency yet again. Once, people voted for him because he beat inflation, but now that the full consequences of the readjustment program are being felt, he acknowledged, "people are extremely doubtful about the famous neoliberal model." He went on, "If you ask people if they're better off today than they were, and if they will be better off soon, the answer is no. I'm completely convinced that the reforms were inevitable, that there was no alternative, but it is undeniable that as a result Bolivia is at a very difficult crossroads."

When I asked him why he and Paz Estenssoro had dealt so ruthlessly with the miners, he answered, "It wasn't our intention." The mass dismissals at the mines, he insisted, were the inevitable result of the collapsing tin market, but others remember a more complicated chain of events. I talked to one man who was deeply involved in the planning and execution of the New Economic Policy, and who believes that the mining measures were as much the result of necessity as an integral part of the economic revolution. "The metal content in the mines was very low," he said. "The world price collapse was beyond our control, and the government was also under great pressure from the international finance and development organizations. It was the most efficient thing to do." He wonders if the dismissals had to be carried out so indiscriminately, though. "The government could have started with the younger, unmarried workers first, for example. It could have been a surgical operation, but it was carried out with a butcher knife. Forty-six-year-old men with families were fired— men who didn't stand a chance of finding a job again in the few years they had to live." Morales says that he made these points to the N.E.P.'s designers, "but they felt very strongly that they would lose credibility if they showed any softness."

Sánchez de Lozada has been puzzling over the reform plan he supervised and its consequences in ways that sometimes make it sound eerily as if he were criticizing someone else's program. Now that the mass dismissals are over, and thousands of campesinos have left their land, unable to compete with the cheaper prices of imported produce that flooded in as a result of the N.E.P.'s free-trade policy, he muses on the fact that people coping with quadruple-digit rates of inflation find it almost impossible to survive once inflation comes down to a mere ten or fifteen per cent. "It's difficult for technocrats to understand that hyperinflation creates its own mechanisms for survival," he said. "A lot of people fall back then on what is almost a barter economy. When you take those mechanisms away, you'd better make sure that inflation goes down to absolute zero. If in the United States a single inflation point gets people worried, imagine what it does to people here, who are living on the edge."

At this stage, Sánchez de Lozada thinks, something other than neoliberal orthodoxy is called for. Unusually for a politician, he is given to self-criticism and reflection, and it is perhaps these qualities which make him the favorite candidate for 1993 of almost every middle-class person I spoke to. But he understands very clearly that his chances are slipping. "In the M.N.R., we're a little like the Red Queen, running to stay in place," he said. "We know we need answers to structural problems, but we don't have them yet. I'm trying. What I know is that we need a two-tiered economy, with one level that is export-geared and highly productive, and another that addresses the needs and limited capacities of the traditional peasant economy, which can exist only with very low production costs. We have to combine the capacity to charge a reasonable level of taxes with mechanisms to address the critical needs of the majority—and stay free of the excesses of the welfare state. The thing is, in countries as destitute as this, you have to address the problems simultaneously. I don't have the answers yet, but I know that that is the general direction, and I'm working on it. The problem is that people aren't interested in terribly sophisticated solutions; they need immediate answers."

And he offered the hard political truth that he says he and Víctor Paz Estenssoro learned when their government was in power: "If the price of tin goes down overnight from five dollars and sixty cents a ton to two dollars and forty cents, and you're a good manager, you fire half your workers. But if you're in government and you do that you lose the next elections." He should know: one of the places that Max Fernández trounced the M.N.R. in December was the city of Potosí, where the Party has traditionally been strong, but where some three thousand mineworkers were dismissed in 1985.

• • •

THE HILL THAT OVERLOOKS Potosí, which is the capital of the province of the same name, will probably be the grave of the miners' movement, but it was also its cradle. It could even be said that the Cerro Rico, or Rich Hill, of Potosí was the cradle of Bolivia itself, for without the staggering amounts of silver that Indian peons hacked out of its bowels in the sixteenth century the Spanish Crown would never have thought to make a separate administrative unit of the vast, frozen, infertile, endlessly hostile region that it baptized Upper Peru, and that became economically viable as "Bolivia" only because of the wealth of Potosí. The hill's silver contributed to the genesis of world capitalism, and helped fuel Europe's first great inflationary crisis, but in Potosí the silver booms that came and went left nothing behind except a near-feudal system of injustice and a town plaza surrounded by a few cobbled streets of exquisite charm. Later, when the hill's silver reserves seemed exhausted at last, along came the tin boom. Once again, thousands of workers flocked to the mines, and once again the explosion of wealth failed to produce anything but misery for the area. In this commemorative year of the five hundredth anniversary of the Spanish Discovery, Potosí has become a favored recipient of international aid, but not even the money lavished on it by the Spanish government and the various international development agencies has managed to dent the atrocious infant-mortality and life-expectancy statistics for destitute campesinos and the miners who remain, most of whom are self-employed. The province of Potosí is one of the poorest regions in the world—so impoverished that there are fewer than five thousand motor vehicles of any kind in it, for a population of nearly seven hundred thousand. There is no system of paved roads, and no commercial flights go in or out of its tiny airport.

What used to be Potosí's most prosperous government-owned mine, the Unificada, is now all but abandoned. An elevator still takes an occasional worker to the stiflingly hot inner tunnels, where a little tin and some associated metals are being mined, and once in a while a rail car clatters down the tracks that used to carry Potosí's wealth to the refinery twenty-four hours a day. Out of what was once a work force of twenty-five hundred, there are four hundred workers left, few of whom are actually miners. The countless massacres of the miners by both civilian governments and military dictatorships were unsuccessful in turning them from their stubborn vision of socialist revolution, but the Paz Estenssoro regime managed to do away with the miners, their union, and their dreams by the simple expedient of firing most of them. I found a few of the survivors in the repair room, a gloomy cavern deep in the mine. There Alejandro Gutiérrez, a former secretary of the Bolivian Mineworkers Federation, raged against Víctor Paz Estenssoro, the United States, the current government, and the ruin of Potosí. What was the future of Bolivia, he wanted to know—to sell its greatest wealth to Yankees? To see the best, the bravest of its workers peddling imported cigarettes on the streets of La Paz, or growing coca for the drug trade in the Chapare, or digging for silver in frighteningly primitive private mines—bare holes in the earth, really—which have turned the Cerro Rico into a landscape of unstable and deadly pits? Where, he demanded, were the benefits of capitalism?

The repair room's walls were plastered with militant posters showing heroic workers, outlined in red, greeting the socialist dawn. A couple of miners, great lumps of coca leaves wedged between tongue and cheek, came in for repair work on their drills. "We're all Communists here!" Gutiérrez roared, but I wondered if his compañeros had been among those who voted for Max: the benefits of capitalism were not to be found in the Cerro Rico, yet belief in Communism hadn't got the miners very far, either. The two miners listened quizzically to Gutiérrez, and did not join in. He was listing the miners' historic battles against the dictatorships, their role in bringing down one after another of the hated generals, which prompted me to think of the miners' last great struggle, in 1983, when they destabilized the transitional civilian government of President Hernán Siles Zuazo by staging a violent, unruly protest in La Paz, marching down the

Prado and exploding sticks of dynamite in the air to demand an end to inflation.

Outside the mines, there is general agreement that the march signalled the end of the miners' union as a vanguard force in Bolivian politics, and I asked Gutiérrez whether the violence displayed by the miners on the Prado, the attempt to polarize Bolivia at a time when people were glad simply to be rid of the military, had not backfired on them. "Not at all!" he roared again. "We made people afraid of us! We stopped traffic! We set buses on fire!" And then, more reflectively, "We used the only weapons we had. Workers don't have bullets, the government does. We have our dynamite, and it was a poor defense."

THE MINERS AT PORCO, one of a dozen mines owned or administered by the Comsur corporation, whose principal stockholder is Gonzalo Sánchez de Lozada, no longer know whether they agree with Gutiérrez or not. Porco, which lies a couple of hours' drive through the mountainous desert that leads from Potosí to the tin mines of Oruro, was the very first silver mine exploited by the conquistadores, before an Indian told them of the amazing treasure hidden inside the Cerro Rico. Probably as a result of the Cerro's wealth, Porco was neglected and mismanaged for centuries after that, but today prosperity is evident from the moment one approaches the mine, which Comsur has rented from the government since 1965. Comsur has broadened and built up the shafts, installed tracks everywhere, and brought in high-tech drilling equipment. It is also constructing a sixteen-million-dollar zinc mill to expand its processing capacity. (There has been no significant investment in any government-owned mine since long before the 1952 nationalization.)

The most striking difference between Cerro Rico and Porco is in the miners themselves. The base wage is higher at Porco, but most of the men prefer to hire themselves out to the mine on a contract basis, and by working sixteen-hour shifts some miners earn as much as two thousand bolivianos, or about five hundred and forty dollars, a month—five times as much as a government schoolteacher. They don't look like miners—in fact, most of them are local campesinos driven off the land by the New Economic Policy, and by a drought that has now lasted for five years—but the difference is due chiefly to the Comsur management's obsession with safety regulations. Hard hats, boots, and dust masks are mandatory. (The miners at Cerro Rico do not wear dust masks, and they would probably scorn the suggestion that they do so.) The pits are well lit throughout, with signs everywhere pointing to little hollows in the wall, where one can wait for the railroad car to pass, or to the way out. Support timbers are carefully shored up, floods are instantly dealt with, ventilation is good. I toured the mines with the safety inspector, Juan Aguilar, and he told me proudly that there had not been a single fatality in the mine all last year. Small wonder, then, that when I talked to a young man who is a former union representative he was in a state of high confusion.

"The truth is, our relations with management are very cordial," he said, a little guiltily. "They treat us well, they respect us." He told me that there had been only one work stoppage the previous year, over the delayed delivery of some tools. (No one even bothers to count the stoppages and strikes at the state-owned mines anymore.) "The state miners must see things differently, because they say that we are exploited, and, of course, it's true that the state can't exploit the workers, because only capitalists can, but then that must mean that workers have to try harder to make the mines successful." The strain of reconciling the different arguments in his head kept him sitting tensely on the edge of his chair, and when I asked him if such disagreement with the state miners could lead to a division in the Mineworkers Federation he was so flustered that he started to answer and then stopped to ask whether I would mind giving my opinion first.

"There's some discussion of a division," he acknowledged. "The state miners have had all the union leadership positions locked up for a long time, but now there are actually more of us here at Porco than there are at Cerro Rico, for example; there are nearly five hundred workers here, of whom more than three hundred are miners. We could form a union, but then we would be splitting the workers' movement, and no one could ever recover from that blow." He paused as a counter-argument forced its way through. "How can we keep on with the struggle, though?" he asked. "How can we keep obeying the calls for one more strike? No one pays attention to that anymore. The fact is that the state didn't know how to make a success of mining, and the workers' movement has already been damaged, because it's just ideology now. I think that perhaps unionism in Bolivia is already dead."

JUAN LECHIN, the man who led the miners over nearly four decades of revolutionary effervescence, hasn't been back to Potosí for a while. These days, he sees visitors and kibitzes with acquaintances in the Club de La Paz, a dark-wood-and-mirrors café just off the Prado, where every client seems to be at least sixty years old. Lechín is approaching eighty (he will not reveal his age) but is still dapper and hale. His detractors, who are legion, say that his very longevity is proof that he was never a miner or even saw the inside of a pit, that he climbed to fame on the shoulders of the miners—thanks to his skills as a soccer player, which made him a hero to them. (In his youth, he was captain of the revered La Paz team, the Strongest.) They say that he has fortunes squirrelled away in Venezuela, and that while he was, first, Paz Estenssoro's most direct source of popular support, then his Minister of Mines, and then his outspoken critic, he consistently betrayed the miners and his own principles in the name of expediency. All this could well be true, but what is also evident is that the miners knew who and what Lechín was when they made him their leader, and that they must have realized that a spokesman from their own ranks—small and Indian-looking, stumbling over awkward phrases in Quechua-accented Spanish—would have got them nowhere in the corridors of power. It was Lechín they needed, with his soaring gift for public speaking, his boulevardier charm, his legendary courage, and his wily skills to match the corrupt talents of the establishment.

We had lunch in a fancy rooftop restaurant on the Prado, staring out at the dun, treeless shantytowns that line the ancient crater in which La Paz is nestled. Lechín does not look like a prosperous man; his jacket, though natty, was a little threadbare. He doesn't own a car, and he lives in a single room in his sister's house, as he has for years. He resigned from the leadership of the Bolivian Workers Confederation in 1987, after every attempt to force the government to reverse its mining policies failed, and now he makes a living as an adviser to the "informal sector," in which so many former workers have ended up. He still cannot understand why the miners' movement should be so reviled. "We changed Bolivia," he said. "I remember that before the 1952 insurrection there was a peasant who managed to put himself through teachers' college, and he tried to set up a little school for the peasants in his district. A month hadn't gone by before the landowners had him lynched. Look how many rural schools were built after the revolution! They say the miners created a labor aristocracy, but you can't compare the miners' needs with anyone else's. Inside the mines, a worker lasts three years before he begins to get sick. The union demanded good-quality subsidized foodstuffs, because our workers deserved it. We created solidarity; people became capable of going on strike—we had no strike funds yet, mind you—to support the demands of miners in a different district. The Paz Estenssoro regime destroyed all that in 1985. Now you have all these little technocrats running around saying that they fought for democracy—where did they fight? I never saw any of them risking their lives to overthrow a dictatorship. I never saw any who had the ability to call two thousand people out on a protest march. We did that."

We said goodbye on the Prado, after I asked him if he thought that the last great miners' march, the one along this street, when the marchers set off dynamite, had been a mistake.

"What kind of mistake?" he asked. "You know very well that a successful leader never really leads, but follows. Miners' wages at that time were barely seven dollars a month! Do you think I could have stopped them from doing what they did?"

IT WAS THE DAY BEFORE the elections, and also the close of the school year in La Paz, a time when the strollers and the *cholas* are joined on the Prado by graduating high-school students and their families on their way to the graduation ceremonies, which take place at a cinema on the bottom end of the boulevard. The previous evening, I had had dinner with a group of middle-class intellectuals who had been pondering the difficulties of writing an official history text for young students that could last for more than one regime. How would a Bánzerite author explain the achievements of Paz Estenssoro's 1952 revolution? Or write the account of his return to power? How could an objective account of the post-M.N.R. regimes, on the other hand, deal with Bánzer without risking military unrest? What favorable, patriotic light could be cast on García Meza, the narco-President? How could national pride be built on a history filled with misguided and bloody wars, which had led, in 1884, to the loss of Bolivia's shoreline to Chile and, in 1935, to the loss of most of its eastern territories to Paraguay?

The evening turned into a reflection on prominent figures in Bolivian history, like the fabled nineteenth-century dictator Mariano Melgarejo, who built the few roads that Bolivia still has only after he had decided to march at the head of his troops to the defense of Napoleon III and realized how impassable his native land was. And who once went to surrender to the man who had led an uprising against him but instead shot him dead, and appeared on the balcony of the Presidential palace to face the waiting hordes outside shouting, "The king is dead! So who's alive now?"

The intellectuals recalled the experience of an acquaintance who had been named Information Minister of an incoming government sometime during the turbulent seventies; he showed up for his first day of work after a night of hearty celebration only to be told that the regime he supported was no longer in power. They told stories about Saúl Salmón, the mad, Argentine-hating *radionovela* scriptwriter on whom a major character in Mario Vargas Llosa's autobiographical *Aunt Julia and the Scriptwriter* is based, who returned from a long exile in Peru (where Vargas Llosa met and worked for him) and became briefly—and wildly—the mayor of La Paz. They contemplated a future in which Max Fernández, in power, might generate even more extravagant stories. After the laughter died down, the mood was decidedly gloomy, and in the silence one man burst out, "I think we should invent an official history for ourselves that would serve us better than the real one! Everything we learned in school about Bolivia has to do only with defeats."

In this context, Bolivia's very recent history, full though it is of devastation and loss, looks more dignified than most of its entire past, and, indeed, the graduating students who were gathering that afternoon outside the cinema on the Prado to have their pictures taken said that they were immensely proud to be Bolivian and proud of their own achievement. "This is the most important moment of any family's life," a happy young man said. He was there to attend the graduation of his friend José Luis Ignacio, who was dressed in a black suit, white shirt, and pointy black shoes, and who only reluctantly admitted that the Indian couple in traditional dress standing next to him were his parents. "Nobody wants to dress like that anymore," said his sister, who was wearing fashionably ripped bluejeans and lots of makeup. "Only tourists like that." José Luis was his family's first high-school graduate, but his sister did not think that she would be able to follow in his steps. "The only way we can get by, with the economic situation the way it is, is by selling something on the street," she said. "That's what always gets us Bolivians the food we need each day." José Luis, however, had aspirations. He thought that life had got just a little easier in the last couple of years—he is sixteen, and he couldn't really remember what life in Bolivia was like during the final years of the Paz Estenssoro regime, except that it was hard—and he said that if the economy continued to improve he would be able to pursue his dream of attending technical college and graduating as an electrical engineer. "You're nothing these days if you're just a high-school graduate," he pointed out. "You stay a messenger boy forever."

Then he excused himself and went to pose for a photograph with other black-suited graduates and their families in Indian dress in the shadow of the Prado's grandest statue. It is a representation on horseback of Marshal Andrés de Santa Cruz, an idealistic follower of Simón Bolívar, who led the Bolivians into practically every one of the very few battles they have won, who administered the state fairly and honestly, and who, overthrown by his enemies, spent the rest of his life in exile.

Postscript, La Paz

GONZALO SÁNCHEZ DE LOSADA and his party, the M.N.R., won the June, 1993, elections with thirty-five per cent of the vote and an absolute majority in the Senate. Despite this signal triumph, his right to govern was by no means assured immediately after the elections. It took General Hugo Bánzer, the former dictator now born again to democracy, some days to decide that his twenty-two per cent of the vote could not be usefully parleyed into a majority alliance with other sore losers. He conceded defeat at last in the face of what was a very audible demand by civil society that the majority vote be respected. Max Fernández, the beer king, spent the days following the election pondering the meaning of his third place in the race—a mere fifteen per cent of the electorate cast their vote for Max's U.C.S., despite lavish campaign spending nationwide. When he emerged from his retreat, he declared himself ready to enter into an alliance with Sánchez de Losada, a move that guarantees the M.N.R.-U.C.S. coalition two-thirds of both houses of Congress.

In 1992, for the first time in many years, Bolivia had a real growth rate: one per cent. The mood in the country as Sánchez de Losada prepared to take power was decidedly optimistic.

PANAMA CITY
1992

"The day that made George Bush weep."

THE TEARGASSING OF George Bush in the Plaza Porras last June 11th, at the start of what was supposed to be an easy, feel-good photo op for his ailing reëlection drive, may have been a public-relations fiasco for the White House, but it had the effect of an earthquake on his hosts. Any number of Panamanian politicians and political groups had been competing for the benefits that such an important visit was supposed to confer, and ever since the fumes cleared they have been anxiously trying to scrape the blame off themselves and fling it on their opponents. The country that George Bush had previously tried to save by invading it is very small, with fewer than two and a half million people, and the kind of vicious infighting that goes on among its leaders rarely focusses on substantial issues. The debacle at the plaza was a real event—and a big one—and to the degree that it provided real grist for everyone's mill it could be said that it was almost welcome. The flood of recriminations, counter-accusations, and indignant editorials that followed has kept everyone so busy that hardly anyone has had time to notice that once again, as always, Panama came politically alive only because the United States cast a passing glance in its direction.

The welcoming committee on the platform at the Plaza Porras represented a cross-section of the victors in the struggle against Manuel Antonio Noriega that preceded the December, 1989, invasion by United States forces. They included Mayor Omaira (Mayín) Correa, of Panama City, a tough former journalist and vehement opponent of Noriega; Second Vice-President Guillermo (Billy) Ford, whose bloodied face had become famous around the world following his beating by Noriega's thugs in the aftermath of the 1989 elections; several founders of the Civic Crusade, an organization of private-sector and community leaders that took to the streets in an attempt to force Noriega to acknowledge his defeat in those elections; Deane Hinton, the United States Ambassador, who was appointed in January, 1990, to oversee the present transitional period in Panamanian democracy; and the Panamanian President, Guillermo Endara, and his wife. In a country where members of the ruling class routinely refer to each other in public and in print by their baby names, the rotund, affable Endara carries no diminutives, but in private Panamanians love to call him Pan de Dulce, or Honey Bun. No one has yet hit upon a suitable nickname for his wife, the former Ana Mae Díaz Chen, an outspoken twenty-five-year-old who met him three years ago while he was engaged in a hunger strike to defend his right to the Presidency. The union between a ruling-class widower and a lower-class part-Chinese woman stunned the country's élite, but Mrs. Endara is an eye-catcher. She stood out even at the teargassing, attired in what a White House pool reporter described as a "cocktail dress" worn under something that looked like a see-through baby-doll top. There was no First Vice-President on the welcoming committee. Ricardo Arias Calderón, who, representing the Christian Democrats, held that post in Endara's coalition government, was kicked out of the Cabinet a year ago last April. Although he says that more substantial issues were involved, the common perception is that he and his Party cohorts were dismissed after he crossed Ana Mae's path once too often.

Bush's stopover, on his way to the Earth Summit in Rio de Janeiro, was announced—indeed, it was decided on at the White House—only a few days before the event. According to the hastily planned program, the President was to arrive in Panama in time for welcoming ceremonies, lunch in the lovely old Palace of the Herons, on the colonial waterfront, and a speech on democracy at the Plaza Porras, a pleasantly old-fashioned downtown square. The visit occurred on the day before Bush's birthday, and subsequent editorials bemoaned the risk at which local grade-schoolers had been put when they were ferried to the plaza to wave flags and sing "Happy Birthday" with "no regard for their innocent lives." They didn't get to sing. Within minutes of George and Barbara Bush's arrival at the plaza, the skirmishing that had been taking place since the previous day between protesters and the police swelled into a melee. Someone threw a tear-gas bomb upwind of the dais. The Mayor gasped through her speech. The Presidents sniffled. The Secret Service sprang into action and hustled Mr. and Mrs. Bush into a limousine. Even as editorialists decried this day of shame and (local) Presidential spinelessness, they also referred to it, not without a touch of pride, as "the day that made George Bush weep."

Who *was* to blame? From the safety of a United States Air Force base outside Panama City, President Bush said that it was "a tiny little left-wing" group of demonstrators who had ruined the day, but no one here paid the slightest attention to that, because several of the rowdier demonstrators were too well known; they turn up frequently at public events, and include members of both the Norieguista and the anti-Norieguista opposition, to which the categories of right and left simply do not apply. The point was: Who had handed them such a golden opportunity? In the heated debates that followed the teargassing, the government's defenders put the blame on Mayor Correa, maintaining that she has Presidential ambitions and recklessly insisted on an open-air event for her own greater glory. The Mayor blamed the police, declaring that they had failed to keep the demonstrators at a safe distance and then had used tear gas and unnecessary violence when the situation got out of hand. In the continuing uproar, President Endara ordered an official inquiry, to be headed by Justice and Interior Minister Juan Chevalier—who, it was pointed out, has jurisdiction over the police force and was thus being asked to investigate himself. At a crowded press confer-

ence, Chevalier announced listless sanctions against five police
officials who had failed to act with sufficient energy; the dismissal
of a cop who had turned up, in civvies, among the rock throwers;
and the tentative official version of an account that had been
making the rounds for a few days. Its main point was that it was
the White House planners who had insisted on having the visit
include a public event—a cheerful crowd scene for the campaign
back home. Embassy and military personnel here had warned
Washington that the time had not yet come in Panama for such
a display, but they had been ignored. Panama's officials, for their
part, had wanted to avoid the possibility of protests, but Bush's
people had said no, a little protesting would be fine—it would
show the world that there was democracy in Panama at last.

The aftershocks of the Bush visit—which took place a
month before Noriega was sentenced, in Miami, to a forty-year
prison term on drug and racketeering charges—provided as
good an opportunity as any to see what has happened to Panama
since the invasion. Indisputably, the country is better off. With
occasional lapses, there is press freedom, in which any number
of dreadful tabloids revel. The National Assembly has approved,
in record time, a package of sensible changes in the Constitution.
The oppressive atmosphere of the final days of the Noriega era
is gone, and there is probably not a Panamanian alive who doesn't
feel free to make fun of President Endara. The economy is recovering, with an astounding growth rate last year of 9.3 per cent—
an impressive figure, even if a lot of the growth is drug-fuelled
and none of it has so far had any impact on the poorer half of
the population, which is in terrible shape. But what the visit, specifically, revealed is that the body politic is in disarray—the various members of the coalition that formed to overthrow Noriega
are now at each other's throats, and public disaffection with the
government is running perilously high. Endara is viewed at best
as incompetent, at worst as corrupt. And the citizens' always ambivalent feelings about the United States seem more tangled than
ever. A lot of people here argue that the painful consequences of
the United States' intervention—the military and civilian deaths
and the destruction of entire neighborhoods; the rampages of

looting which took place under the indifferent eyes of United
States soldiers; and the very indignity of the invasion itself
(which no Panamanian had requested)—were compensated for
by the joy of getting rid of Noriega. But others, including many
Panamanians who supported the invasion wholeheartedly, are
surprised to hear themselves saying now that a lot of things were
better in the old days.

A MIDDLE-CLASS WOMAN I know told me that the main thing
she regrets these days is her loss of influence. Like her neighbors,
she is constantly figuring out how to make ends meet, and now
that her electric bills have increased to eighty dollars a month
(even though she gets no electricity after 10 p.m.) she has no one
to turn to. In the past, she says, whenever she had a complaint
she would get in touch with someone at the National Defense
Forces—Noriega's Army. "Let's say that the neighbor had a
washerwoman who was married to the shoeshine man who polished some captain's shoes at the barracks every morning—you
could say, 'Hey, why don't you tell your husband to tell the captain that no one has come around to check the meter, and that
the bills are too high?' It would happen. You had to slip the guy
a little tip, of course. But the problem got looked after. The thing
about Noriega is that he stole but he let other people eat, too,
and everyone knew someone who had access to the levers of
power. Now this country is being ruled by a small group that
keeps all the power to itself. Hardly anyone has access to the
levers." And she repeats a line I've heard everywhere—that
people expected things to move forward after the invasion, and
instead the country seems to be right back where it was in 1968,
when a group of young military officers headed by Omar Torrijos
overthrew President Arnulfo (Fufo) Arias and embarked on an
authoritarian program of social reform.

Twenty-one years elapsed between Torrijos's rise and Noriega's fall. The civilians who are back in power now refer to that
time as La Dictadura, but that isn't what they called it then. By
and large, the business class had a tolerant view of Torrijos, who
dominated Panama's political landscape until he died, in a plane

crash, in 1981. Torrijos rewrote the banking laws so they were like Switzerland's, and turned Panama into a major financial center. He also negotiated, in 1977, an alternative to the onerous in-perpetuity Canal Treaty that Teddy Roosevelt had imposed on Panama when he instigated its revolution and its secession from Colombia, in 1903. Torrijos created a bureaucracy that may have strained the state's resources unreasonably, but he also reduced unemployment to respectable levels for the first time in the country's history. He significantly reduced illiteracy and child-mortality rates, and made a lot of Panamanians proud of his role as a major player in the turbulent regional politics of the time. In the course of all this activity, Torrijos grew wary of the power he wielded by fiat. "Power is like a snake," he liked to say. "When you try to hand it over to someone, one of the two of you is bound to get bitten." A former close associate of his told me that Torrijos also said he had no fear of a coup, because he had No-riega to watch his back. On being asked what he would do if he found out that Noriega himself was plotting against him, he said, "Put a gun to my head." When Torrijos died, Noriega was widely suspected of having engineered the plane crash.

Torrijos, who played around arbitrarily with press freedoms and citizens' rights, and who, in the early years of his rule, was directly or indirectly responsible for most of ninety or so politi-cally related deaths that human-rights monitors attribute to the military regime, was nevertheless deeply loved by large numbers of Panamanians, and they maintain to this day that he opened the doors of society and politics to the middle class and the poor. Noriega, though he kept the barracks doors open for people who had problems with their electric bills, and could count on the explicit and reiterated backing of the United States for much of his career, never commanded any affection—not even from hun-dreds of businessmen who prospered more than ever when he first came to power. He was not friendly, and, in a country that dotes on gossip, he shared his secrets with no one. By the end of his rule, he was widely despised and politically outgunned, but if his opponents were unable to mobilize a popular insurrection against him, and if the party that Torrijos founded, the Partido

Revolucionario Democrático, or P.R.D., continues to give shelter
to a number of Norieguistas who have managed to get themselves elected to the National Assembly, it is because Noriega
always distributed corruption democratically.

Part of what people mean when they say that Panama has
gone back to 1968 is that it is again ruled by the very men who
were in power when Torrijos and his populist associates took
over from President Arias, and that it is ruled in the same style.
Endara was Planning and Economic Policy Minister to Arias, who
was his mentor. (Arias, who was Panama's leading civilian politician for decades and was elected President three times, died only
in 1988, at the age of eighty-seven.) First Vice-President Arias
Calderón and Second Vice-President Billy Ford came of age politically during the Arias years. More than individuals, though, a
concept of society is what seems to be in fashion again. Those in
power today live in glamorous oceanfront apartment towers in
what is known as the Golden Stretch. The men wear designer
shirts, and their wives wear big gold jewelry and short, tight,
double-breasted linen suits. These people make up the lily-white,
cosseted, English-speaking élite known collectively as the *rabi-
blancos*, or whitetails—an incestuous set whose obsession with
race, class, and family lineage turns virtually all society gossip
into a discussion of genetics. This obsession accounts for a significant proportion of the élite's disaffection with Endara, because
of his wife's racial origins. (For the same reason, Mrs. Endara has
the makings of a popular following. That became clear early this
year when she led a street protest against the Attorney General
for his slow progress in improving the appalling conditions in the
country's justice and prison systems.)

The ruling élitism harks back to the pre-1968 period, but so
do social conditions that, according to Aurelio Barría, who heads
the government's Social Emergency Fund, or F.E.S., have not
been this bad in a long time. Barría, a businessman who left his
job as manager of the local Christian Dior office to found the
Civic Crusade, in 1987, is the only one of its leaders currently
serving in the government. Although he is reluctant to criticize

Endara, he does acknowledge that his contemporaries in the Crusade are impatient, and feel that a government handed such an extraordinary opportunity to break with the past is once again engaged in shopworn economic thinking, cronyism, and intrigue. I had lunch with Barría the other day in a chic nouvelle-cuisine-ish restaurant in the glittery heart of the financial center, and he laid out the figures. "It *is* time for new solutions," he said. "We live in a two-economy country—those of us who live within the Golden Stretch don't even know about the poverty that exists in the other Panama. We have one of the highest per-capita incomes in Latin America, yet we also have one of the lowest levels of income distribution. Fifty per cent of the population lives below the poverty line. Malnutrition is everywhere. In Colón"—the twin port city on the northern, Caribbean end of the Canal—"unemployment is near fifty per cent. In the countryside, the poverty is unbelievable. I have to admit I had no idea what Panama was like before I took this job." Nevertheless, he added, now that twenty million dollars provided to the F.E.S. by the United States Agency for International Development has run out, his program is facing a shutdown. The funds were a onetime grant to help reverse the damage done to Panama's economy by the United States' two-year-long economic siege of Noriega, which paralyzed the banking system and made the gross domestic product drop by fifteen per cent in 1988. Barría is generally given high marks for his handling of the A.I.D. money, but the grant, which amounted to eight dollars per citizen, was not enough to make a dent in the overall poverty level. (The Panamanian government took over the F.E.S. this year, but so far its contribution to the budget has only been three million dollars.)

A POPULAR LINE has it that Noriega's removal from the government signified the departure of Ali Baba but not of the Forty Thieves. Most opinion makers stop short of accusing Endara directly of corruption, and say instead that he is too pleasant and too weak to deal firmly with the larceny going on around him. "Endara was really not supposed to be President," Barría said. "He was the least controversial choice to head the coalition of parties that ran in 1989 just to show the world how Noriega would steal those elections. Endara was a not very prominent Arnulfista, and it was decided that he could stand as a buffer between Billy Ford's party, the Molirena, and Arias Calderón's party, the Christian Democrats, and keep the movement united." Barría himself belongs to the Molirena, whose most prominent figure is the current Comptroller-General, Rubén (Chinchorro) Carles. Chinchorro is a crusty old man whose voice makes him sound like Vito Corleone. He used to be the local vice-president of Chase Manhattan, and he is known to administer his present office with a stern, watchful eye for the bottom line. He is also presumed to be the real head of the Endara government—a supposition he dismissed when I asked him if he agreed with the frequent cartoon depiction of Endara as a fluffy, wide-eyed pussycat. "Don't be fooled," Chinchorro warned. "He has claws, and he rules. Ask the Christian Democrats, who got kicked out of the government when they messed with La Presidenta." But several political insiders later assured me that it was Chinchorro himself who had forced Endara to dismiss Chinchorro's archenemy, First Vice-President Arias Calderón, on the not very credible grounds that Arias Calderón was plotting a coup and was having his Christian Democrats stockpile weapons.

Chinchorro, who has a sterling reputation for financial honesty, was dismissive when I asked him about corruption—and, specifically, about the general belief that money laundering and drug trafficking have continued unabated despite the removal of Noriega. "There is a difference," he said. "Before, cocaine transshipment and money laundering used to be a government-protected enterprise. It should be no surprise that the most successful Latin-American multinational operation"—he meant the drug trade, of course—"should continue to operate now, despite this government's efforts. The United States would like us to do things it doesn't even do itself. Narcodollars circulate through its financial system—how do they expect them not to circulate through ours? We are capturing more shipments of cocaine and drug dollars than ever before, but the United States wants us to put limits on our banks' acceptance of cash deposits. We just can't limit our country's economic possibilities like that."

BECAUSE IT WAS Washington's rage over Noriega's involvement in drug trafficking that led to his downfall, the question of drug-related corruption under the new regime is taken very seriously here. I heard about the increase in the cocaine trade from, among others, a skinny, much-weathered transport artist called Yoyo. Yoyo, who is black and comes from Colón, paints portraits of famous beauties on the rear door panels of buses, and mountain landscapes or vistas of the Canal on the small arched panels between the doors and the roofs of buses, and, sometimes, along the buses' sides. Most buses in Panama are decorated, inside and out, with work by painters like Yoyo, at a cost to fleet owners that would be hard to factor into a normal chart of income and profit. But Yoyo claims that, because Panamanian people are strange, they prefer to ride in a bus whose art they like, and that they will actually wait for the bus with their favorite decorations to come along. "Long time ago, I painted a bus with a painting that was called 'El General,' " he says, in Caribbean English, which is what black people in Colón speak. "That was back in Torrijos's day, and it was a very big success. The school kids only wanted to ride on 'El General.' " Yoyo found Jesus some years ago, but he still has a jive walk, and addresses people as "Baby" or, in Spanish, as "Nené" and "Nena." Because he is considerably well acquainted with drugs, which led him into trouble in the past, he still keeps an eye on the market, and he is certain that cocaine is a more serious problem for Panama today than it ever was under Noriega. "In the time that I was doing cocaine, it cost forty dollars a gram, and plenty of people tried to sell you all kinds of junk for that price," he says. "Now it's one dollar a hit. One dollar! And it's pure." He sees addiction spreading among the children in his neighborhood, as they scavenge cans and bottles to get the money for coke, and he sees the police as much less effective than they have ever been before. He is convinced that Torrijos presided over "the best government there ever was," while this one is made up of a bunch of rich men engaged in corruption greater than what even Noriega fostered. "I wasn't in love with the man," he says. "I could take him or leave him. But I'm telling you, he was better than this. Cocaine couldn't have taken over my neighborhood under him."

Ebrahím Asvat, an equable Christian Democrat politician, who supervised the formation of a post-Noriega police force until Endara kicked his party out of the government, does not think that the police are necessarily accomplishing less than they used to, although he admits that they are demoralized and haven't been overwhelmingly reformed. (Most of the policemen are re-hires from the Noriega regime, for in the end only the top officers were purged.) He does think that drug trafficking is on the rise, and finds evidence of the increase in some interesting figures having to do with the current economic recovery. A significant proportion of the boom in productive activity is related to construction, as even the briefest walk along the Golden Stretch will show. High-rise luxury apartment buildings are going up everywhere, but the striking thing about them is that at night there are very few lights on: the buildings are largely unoccupied. Asvat showed me the figures for new-construction loans last year and the year before: the total remained steady, but the value of the actual construction, in dollar terms, skyrocketed way out of proportion to the loans granted, rising more than three hundred per cent. The point is that most of these empty buildings are being paid for in cash, and Asvat suspects a scam. "Maybe there are one or two people here who are wealthy enough to pay cash," he explained, "but the inescapable conclusion is that most of the money is illegitimate—this is how it's being laundered." There may not be much demand for the buildings now, but, for someone who can afford to park his money for a while, new construction in Panama is a sound investment. "The demand will grow," Asvat feels. "The United States is already relocating some of its high-ranking personnel from the military bases into Panama City, and paying high rent for these apartments." And there is the steady influx of bankers as well. In a few years, money launderers will not only be in a position to recoup their investment, they will have become part of the local moneyed élite.

One of the very few people here who openly challenge the President on the issue of corruption is Tomás Cabal, a correspondent both for ABC television and for the Spanish newsweekly *Cambio16*. He is a corpulent, tense man, and some of his tension may be explained by the fact that for the past year or so he has been documenting Endara's links to the Colombian Cali and Medellín cartels.

According to documents reproduced by Cabal and never challenged by the President, who is a former corporate lawyer, Endara helped set up at least six companies that were money-laundering fronts for a United States–based drug ring allegedly headed by two Cuban-Americans, Guillermo Falcón and Salvador Magluta, who have been indicted by a Miami court on drug-trafficking charges. In addition, Endara served on the board of the Banco Interoceánico, commonly known as Interbanco, and owned two per cent of its stock. This bank has lent over twelve million dollars to Celso and Manuel Fernández Espina, whose alleged drug-related activities in their native Spain have been the subject of an ongoing investigation by Spain's best-known prosecuting judge, Baltasar Garzón. The money went to finance the reconstruction of the Hotel El Panamá, the country's largest, and of three other business-class hotels.

The charges against Endara originally surfaced in April, 1991, when a National Assembly representative of the P.R.D., Torrijos's old party, released a United States Drug Enforcement Administration agent's leaked report on the President to journalists. Shortly after that, Endara publicly answered questions on the allegations for the last time. At a press conference, he stated that he had never met with any of the people involved with the corporations he set up or lent money to, and that, since he was a corporate lawyer, setting up companies constituted a routine part of his activity. Furthermore, he said, he had agreed to set up these companies at the behest of "a very good friend of mine," a Cuban-American lawyer named Juan Acosta. Tomás Cabal later found out that the lawyer was known for his connections to the Medellín drug trade, and had been assassinated in Miami in 1989.

Cabal told me that he is currently focussing on the activities

of the Attorney General, Rogelio Cruz, who served as a director
of another bank, the First Interaméricas Bank. It was owned by
the head of the Cali drug traders, Gilberto Rodríguez Orejuela,
who was in jail in Spain at the time Cruz served on the bank's
board. Cruz, who has had a falling-out with the President since
he was appointed, but who remains in office, has called Cabal
into his office and warned him to stop his stories, and, according
to Cabal, has also threatened to file a suit against him. Cabal, a
careful journalist, points out that all his stories are supported by
documents in the possession of Spanish and D.E.A. investigators.
Nor is he the only reporter making the charges. Similar stories,
about both Cruz and Endara, have appeared abroad, notably in
the Spanish daily *El País* and in the Baltimore *Sun* and *U.S. News &
World Report*. The Panama office of the D.E.A. denied my request
for an interview (it is the only D.E.A. office in Latin America that
routinely denies press interviews), but the *U.S. News* story printed
the reply of a State Department official who was questioned
about Endara's involvement with drug-related corporations. "We
took the position that if it turns out Endara did something
naughty, he'll have to live with it," the official said.

I was hoping to ask Endara directly how he viewed his earlier
business links to drug dealers when I went to one of his weekly
press conferences at the Palace of the Herons, which is so called
because several of these birds stalk around the central fountain
in the palace's Moorish-revival tiled courtyard. The conference
actually took place at a press center across from the palace, overlooking the bay, and it was an odd event. The conference room
is dominated by an enormous portrait of the happy President and
his bride. Under the portrait, a couple of dozen reporters laughed
openly almost every time the President answered one of their
questions, which were sometimes insolent. Endara gamely attempted to address their concerns, but he is not a gifted speaker,
or fast on his feet. The central question was whether a referendum scheduled for November to approve the package of constitutional reforms passed in late June by the National Assembly
would be seen by Panamanians as a referendum on his government, and thus be voted down. "Anyone who thinks that the No-

vember vote is a referendum on my government is really out of it, but I mean, really, really out of it," Endara replied, bouncing up and down for emphasis. The reporter next to me tucked his head behind his coat lapel and sniggered. After the press conference, I followed the President out and asked for an interview. "He's not granting any," a handler said, and hustled him away.

WASHINGTON'S UNABATED SUPPORT for Endara has sparked a surprising reëvaluation of the need for the 1989 invasion, which earnest young United States officials have insisted be called *la liberación*, to no effect. Chinchorro was among those who justified the invasion to me, saying that "Noriega was the gringos' creation, and it was their job to get him out." Others, however, are now expressing bitterness about the fact that the welfare of Panama was only one of the four reasons—and not even the first—given by the White House to justify the invasion, the others being the defense of American lives, the security of the Canal, and the war on drugs. The president of the Panamanian Human Rights Committee, Roberto Troncoso, argues that even if one feels that the protection of Panamanian democracy was a legitimate cause for a full-scale invasion, there is a troubling disproportion between the total of ninety-odd lives lost during the entire twenty years of the military regime and the three hundred civilian lives lost during the invasion.

The intensive and highly negative United States press coverage that preceded the invasion, much of it fuelled by United States government officials, was intended to demonize Noriega. The truth is that he was nasty, treacherous, occasionally murderous, and thoroughly corrupt, but no more so than any of the other dictators the United States had in the past been pleased to call "*our* son of a bitch." Even his drug dealing now seems relatively modest, at least in cash terms. According to John Dinges's thoroughly documented book *Our Man in Panama*, the total amount that Noriega took in bribes for looking the other way while cocaine was shipped through his country en route from Colombia was at most fifteen million dollars—not a huge figure by the standards of Latin-American graft. In any event, Dinges adds, the evidence is that Noriega's dealings with drug lords came to an end in 1985, after which he coöperated with D.E.A. officials and received public praise from them for doing so.

Nothing that emerged in the Miami trial contradicted Dinges's conclusion, which may be why not even the most clued-in political observers I've talked to have been able to explain Washington's sudden, extreme hatred of Noriega. Perhaps it was his brazenness in dealing with and double-crossing intelligence agents in both Washington and Havana. Perhaps it was the exception he took to having his leash yanked, or the energy with which, having taken exception, he yanked back. Perhaps it was truly that, after years of lobbying, Noriega's opposition at last gained an attentive ear in Washington. This is not a strongly convincing explanation, even to people like the editor of *La Prensa,* Roberto Eisenmann, who was the opposition's most prominent Washington lobbyist. Panamanians have a natural attraction to conspiracy theory, so it was widely believed here that Noriega himself would provide an explanation for his misfortune during his seven-month trial. But Noriega's rambling statement during his sentencing hearing, on July 10th, gave no evidence of any secret deals or betrayals involving him and Washington which could have explained the White House's obsession with him, and major political figures were left to ask, as they have asked me, in mid-interview, "Why do *you* think George Bush had it in for Noriega?"

Washington's association with Noriega goes back to the nineteen-sixties, when he was merely a regional Guardia Nacional intelligence chief who got United States counter-intelligence training and coöperated with United States military personnel. By the early seventies, as Dinges's book documents, he faced accusations that he was involved in drug and arms trafficking, but those were overlooked in Washington, because he had proved to be a valuable intelligence asset. When he became head of the Guardia, in 1983, and thus de-facto head of state, the United States Ambassador grew concerned and wanted an investigation, but he was overruled by the C.I.A. station chief, who valued Noriega's coöperation. Over the years, Noriega travelled to Washington several times and was received courteously, and even enthusiastically, at the C.I.A., the Pentagon, and the State Department. In 1983, when, as Vice-President, George Bush travelled to Panama and met with Noriega, he limited his private statements to brief admonitions on the dangers of money laundering. When Noriega's Presidential candidate won the 1984 elections through fraud, the Reagan Administration continued to support Noriega. For the next two years, the opposition's efforts to find a receptive ear in Washington were fruitless. Even as the United States media began to publish accounts of Noriega's illegal activities, Oliver North and his mentor, William Casey, who was then the C.I.A. chief, were interceding in his favor before the Drug Enforcement Administration.

It was only in mid-1987, long after disaffection with Noriega had become widespread and vocal in Panama itself, that Washington changed course. Vice-President Bush announced financial sanctions, looked into possible coup options, and, through back-channel negotiations, offered Noriega an easy way out: all he had to do was resign, and Washington would even see to it that the drug indictment being prepared against him in Miami was dropped. The deal fell through, and in the Presidential elections in May, 1989, Noriega again claimed a fraudulent victory for his candidate.

TUCKED IN AMONG the hotels of the Golden Stretch is an American-style coffee shop (it has a rotating display case for pies and Jell-O desserts) where the last of the Noriega faithful gather every morning for coffee and a schmooze. At the unofficial center of this little circle is Assemblyman Mario Rognoni, a witty and highly intelligent man, who became familiar to television viewers in the United States as the bulky, smooth-talking explainer of Noriega on "Nightline" in the days when Washington first turned its fiery stare on the General. Now that most people of any reputation belong to what is known as the I Never Even Knew Him Club, Rognoni is still loyal to El Hombre, for unfathomable reasons of his own. By any of the genetic measurements employed here, he qualifies as a *gente decente*: he is white, and is fluent in English, and a street has been named after his father, who was an eminent physician. He could be eminent himself, but he prefers the company of the unsavory types who frequent the coffee shop, like a former Norieguista radio announcer who arrived there the other morning and ordered a beer-and-tomato-juice on ice for his massive hangover, or a thuggish former P.R.D. leader who once tried to serve an arrest warrant in absentia on the U.S. Generals Maxwell Thurman and Marc Cisneros, and whom the radio announcer described admiringly to me as "serious business, a guy who used to go around throwing contact bombs and starting brawls."

Rognoni wishes that Noriega had followed his advice and got out before he turned into the Rosemary's Baby of United States foreign policy, and while Washington was still offering deals. "It wasn't as if he didn't have the political instincts to know that that was the thing to do," Rognoni said. But he thinks that Noriega was held back by the upper-echelon officers in his Army. "The truth is that Noriega's senior officers had become completely corrupt, and they were saying, 'Noriega can get out with his own goods, but what's going to become of us?'" Rognoni said. "Toward the end, he was living from coup to coup. He couldn't stay, but he couldn't leave." Right to the end, according to Rognoni, Noriega refused to believe in the possibility of an invasion, but when it finally happened he and every other Panamanian understood immediately that his winning streak was over. "From the moment the first bomb fell, on December 20th, no one believed we could win," Rognoni said. "The only question was how long we could last." At the very beginning, Noriega realized that his private walkie-talkie channel was intercepted (thanks to a member of his guard who sold a radio to United States Army Intelligence, Rognoni believes). With his communications gone, he moved from safe house to safe house, with a million-dollar dead-or-alive price on his head, waiting for the promised Latin-American brushfire, which never happened. "We had so many promises that if the United States touched him the region would go up in flames," Rognoni recalled. "But when the time came our so-called allies couldn't get out of Panama fast enough. The Cubans left on a shrimp boat. The Salvadorans *swam* out of here. And we waited and waited for the United Nations to intervene, but it announced that the General Assembly wouldn't meet to consider the Panama case until December 29th. There was no way we could last that long. Noriega had reformed the Army, turned the National Guard into the National Defense Forces. The troops looked very pretty when they marched—we all loved to watch the parades—but it turned out that they couldn't fight worth a damn." Noriega himself joined the flight, leaving behind in his freezer mysterious wrapped packages that were initially described by invasion flacks as cocaine but turned out to be a stash of tamales (street value unknown). The narcotamales incident was followed by the United States Army's death-by-rock-and-roll siege on the Nunciatura—the Vatican Embassy—where Noriega and a few of his aides had sought asylum. The Nuncio—a Basque priest, who was being kept happy by the inspired cooking of one of Noriega's bodyguards, who had learned his technique from a Basque terrorist with gourmet leanings—was himself the protagonist of two mind-boggling episodes: at the gates of his Embassy, he persuaded General Maxwell Thurman, who wanted to storm the Nunciatura, that the only thing standing between the Vatican Embassy and Thurman's encircling tanks was God; and then he convinced Noriega that the only thing standing between him and the lynch hordes—which were not really so large, reporters recall—was the Nuncio himself. On January 3rd, Noriega, following the Nuncio's advice, surrendered to the occupying troops, and it was all over.

"I DIDN'T EXPECT the invasion would be like this," a Venezuelan woman who married into Panamanian society told me. "We knew something was going on, because we were driving over the Bridge of the Americas one day and we saw all these planes landing at Howard Base. But we thought it would be a matter of surrounding Noriega's headquarters with a few HummVees and forcing him out." Instead, there were the terrifying bombing runs over the city, the tracer bullets lighting up the night sky, test combat flights of the new Stealth attack planes, the mass graves, the looting, and a three-month-long occupation by United States military forces, whose objective had been not just the capture of Noriega but the destruction of his military apparatus.

In the days that followed the invasion, no other group of people was the object of so much foreign press coverage or national concern as the residents of Chorrillo, a neighborhood of some fifteen thousand surrounding the headquarters of Noriega's National Defense Forces. Even in the first few weeks of euphoria, when United States troops were still being cheered on the streets, and *la liberación* was not just United States Embassy newspeak but an accepted description of what had taken place, the fate of Chorrillo was a raw and charged issue. A festering warren of two-story wooden houses just a few blocks from the Palace of the Herons, it was most often described in the foreign media as a slum or shantytown, but that is not all it was. It was also mysterious and beautiful, in the way the Casbah is. The houses were painted in a crazy quilt of bright colors, salsa music blared from the balconies, and geraniums potted in tin cans spilled over the bannisters. Chorrillo had looked this way since the beginning of the century. Construction workers lived here, and maids who served the residential area. In what has always been a rowdy port city, Chorrillo embodied some of its most enduring traditions: prostitutes and pimps, burglars and pickpockets fanned out from here. When Torrijos came to power, he won the Chorrilleros' devotion with small favors and significant public works, but Noriega was reportedly enraged when, in the 1989 Presidential elections, his candidate lost the vote in what he, too, had considered a sure bastion of popular support.

Seven hours after the official start of the invasion, while some United States troops were still patrolling the area with loudspeakers, urging people to evacuate it, a fire began to spread. About a third of the inhabitants took refuge in the local church; others fled in every direction. Within hours, the entire neighborhood was in flames. Eventually all the Chorrilleros ended up in a sports stadium operated by United States emergency-relief personnel. They spent their days in the glaring sun and their nights in flimsy tents. When they finally did return to their neighborhood, weeks later, the Chorrilleros, the poorest of the city's poor, found that they had absolutely nothing left in the world. All that remained in the entire neighborhood was the church, a couple of concrete buildings, and Noah's Ark, a two-story compound of wooden shacks raised on stilts over a layer of reeking mud. The compound's residents felt lucky at the time, but today they wish their compound had burned, too.

The man who told me about the compound is Darío Ospina, a sort of unofficial leader of the forty-seven families that live in it. Most afternoons, when he and his wife can get the money together to buy a box of deep-fried dough cakes, which are known here as tortillas, he earns his living by walking around the downtown area selling them to people looking for an afternoon snack. Mornings, he turns up regularly at the National Assembly and hangs around the offices of the P.R.D. It doesn't matter to Ospina that the party that Torrijos founded and Noriega inherited no longer rules; in his mind, it is still the place where people of his class and degree of desperation stand some chance of getting a hearing. What Ospina would like the P.R.D. to do is convince someone that just because his decrepit home was spared by the fire doesn't mean his family is not entitled to a better apartment. A deeply religious man—it was he who first called the compound Noah's Ark—Ospina doesn't like to give up hope, but on the morning I met him in the P.R.D. offices he seemed to feel he wasn't getting anywhere. He had spent months pestering functionaries at the Housing Ministry, but they had stuck to their guns: he had a house to live in and should stay there.

The Agency for International Development was not so mean-spirited. A.I.D. provided funding for the construction of some two thousand housing units. A quarter of those are on the site of what was once Chorrillo. The apartments are rudimentary and stiflingly hot, but they are an immeasurable improvement over what existed before: they have bedrooms, running water, indoor toilets and showers, kitchen facilities, and even play areas. After some initial delay in getting the funding and the plans approved, they were built quickly and were turned over, on a one-per-family basis, with a minimum of fuss. Most people believe that this was the least the United States government could do to repair the damage to Chorrillo, since its troops were presumed responsible for the neighborhood's destruction, and A.I.D. has chosen not to argue with that conclusion. But the most credible evidence shows that the fire that destroyed Chorrillo was the work not of United States troops but of Batalloneros—members of Noriega's Dignity Battalions.

The only person I met in the Chorrillo area who was willing to say that he saw a Batallonero pouring gasoline on some wooden constructions in front of the parish church and igniting them with kindling was so terrified that he asked me at least ten times not to mention his name or identify him in any way. Mainly, he was afraid that the virtual strongman of Chorrillo, a former world-class soccer player called Héctor Avila, would take revenge on him. Avila is the president of the Chorrillo neighborhood association, but the word around the neighborhood is that he had not lived there for years—that, in fact, he had been living in Ecuador at the time of the invasion, and that when he came back and set up a tenement squat in an abandoned half-finished construction right on the edge of the barrio he invited in a number of raffish families who were not Chorrillo residents, either, and they constitute his shock troops today. By early last year, he had emerged as the leader of the neighborhood's displaced families, and they had learned from him that the most effective lobbying technique of getting the homes they needed was to set tires on fire and close off the Pan-American Highway at the Bridge of the Americas, just outside the capital. Avila and his followers were not at the Plaza Porras on the day it became famous—a rare miscalculation on his part.

When I talked with Avila, in his new, A.I.D.-financed apartment, he appeared to be in such a state of rage that he could hardly sit still. Every two or three minutes, he would break off a sentence and prowl briefly around the small apartment and out into the hallway, while his two little girls went on with their games and his wife went on equably with her cooking. Then he would return to his chair and discuss again, in barking, disconnected sentences, how the Endara government had stolen the

A.I.D. money, and how paltry the reparations have been for all that the neighborhood suffered. In reality, though, he has not come out badly: his former neighbors at the squat he founded are still there, but he has a new apartment. He pops in and out of jail, but when I attended Endara's press conference the President described his relations with Avila as "excellent" and sent compliments to Avila's mother as well.

When I asked Avila how he had missed being on hand for the demonstration at the Plaza Porras, he told me he had figured that his group would have a greater effect if they massed around the Palace of the Herons, where Bush was having lunch, and heckled him from there. He added, with a whiff of sour grapes, "We didn't make the headlines, but he heard us better."

"The point is, the government listens to us because we make life difficult for it. When we close the bridge, it hurts the government economically. We deserve more help than anyone else, because we suffered most from the invasion, which can never justify the thousands of dead and the rape of our sovereignty." Though the most reliable estimate for the number of civilian dead is far lower, of course—just three hundred—Avila wants a higher rate of carnage, because if there were "only" three hundred dead, and if less than thirty of those deaths occurred in Chorrillo, and if the fire that destroyed the neighborhood was not the fault of the invaders, he doesn't have many arguments with which to rouse the Chorrilleros and demand more aid.

Roberto Troncoso, the president of the Panamanian Human Rights Committee, who has been a steadfast critic of the invasion, says that during the first few days after the burning of Chorrillo all the witnesses his office interviewed stated freely that they had seen the fires started at various points around the neighborhood by men whom they either knew as Batalloneros or, because of something indefinable in their aspect, identified as such. There is no good explanation for why the Batalloneros would have wanted to start a fire, but then there is no explanation for why United States forces would have wanted to, either. The United States had a great deal to lose from a heartless attack on civilians, but Noriega had much to gain from making it appear that such an attack had taken place. "The bottom line, though," Troncoso says, "is that it's much more advantageous for everyone now to believe that the United States did it, because there's more money involved that way."

Unfortunately for the residents of Noah's Ark, there is no argument they can muster to turn themselves into either victims or beneficiaries of the United States, and so their lives continue in the Ark as if they and it were invisible. In what was once a colorful barrio, they are now surrounded on all sides by apartment buildings. There are two tall towers that Torrijos put up years ago, which were heavily damaged by the fire and were repaired by the United States; there are the new A.I.D. blocks, where Avila's people rioted a couple of weeks ago to protest the construction of a children's park, on the ground that it would be a superfluous luxury; there are lower apartment buildings on the edge of Chorrillo, where Avila is organizing people to demand the suspension of all utilities payments, on the ground that it wouldn't cost the government much to pick up the expense; and there is a whole new set of buildings going up on a stretch of land close to a muddy inlet of the city's bay. When I spoke to Darío Ospina, he said he thought there was a chance that the government might finally relent and give residents of his tenement some apartments there, but when I visited his wife, Marilyn, in Noah's Ark, she said she didn't think the deal would come off. "They're demanding a minimum income of three hundred dollars a month to live there," she said.

It's doubtful whether any of the residents of the Ark, where parasitic intestinal worms are visible in the overflowing public latrines, will be able to meet the new buildings' requirement. Mrs. Ospina knows that her husband cannot guarantee that income. Their life, she feels, has reached the breaking point, and she, too, said that since the barracks burned down there is no one to help. "In the past, we could always go over there and someone would give us a blank slip to get the medicines we needed, or a scholarship for the kids. Now we're desperate." Over the months, the Ark has become something of a favorite cause, but Mrs. Ospina and two of her neighbors, courteous and friendly teen-agers, said that they have grown weary of posing for pictures with politicians in the hope that it will help. "We're tired of being used," Mrs. Ospina said.

LESS THAN THREE YEARS after the restoration of democracy, a recent *La Prensa* poll has found, political apathy is at an all-time high and the President's approval ratings are singularly low: barely twelve per cent. Apathy guarantees stability, since no one I've talked to, including the Ospinas, seems to have the energy to do anything about Endara except giggle. On the other hand, apathy bodes ill for those looking forward to a change in 1994, when the next elections are scheduled. Thirty-one per cent of those polled said they didn't like any party at all, and the most popular party, the Christian Democrats, got barely 10.5 points. The figures have led to a popular parlor game, centered on the question "Where's our Fujimori?"—meaning "Where is the unknown candidate who, like Peru's Alberto Fujimori, will sweep all others before him?" At this stage, the bottle tends to stop spinning at the name of the singer and composer Rubén Blades, who has promised for some years now that one day he will quit his singing career and move back here from the United States to run for President. This time, he has gone as far as to found a movement—the Papa Egoró, which means "Mother Earth" in the Emberá language—and he had the distinction of running second to "Nobody" in the recent poll as the candidate most people would choose. But this means only that he has a personal-popularity rating of 11.3 per cent. So far, he's not even a Perot, let alone a Fujimori. More worrisome still, some argue, is the fact that Blades's intricate, demanding, and sophisticated music is hard to dance to—a flaw that could prove fatal in a country that, by my informal count, has twenty-seven first-rate Afro-Caribbean radio stations. No wonder the leaders of the P.R.D. brandish the *La Prensa* poll and point to their own third place (after "None" and the Christian Democrats) in the ratings: it only translates as 8.5 per cent, but it beats Endara's Arnulfistas by almost a full point. As a P.R.D. leader told me, it means that even after Noriega, even after the invasion, he still has reason to hope.

The apathy that the Panamanians feel toward their own government does not extend to El Gigante del Norte. No other Latin-American country has Panama's history of dependency on the United States. People here expound constantly on the nature of this relationship, reaching for metaphors that are often painful in their intensity. I asked Roberto Eisenmann at *La Prensa* how he thought people now felt about the United States and the invasion, and he said, "The love part of our relationship has to do with the advantages our unique association brings: the Canal, our trade situation, and so on. The hate part is like what a teen-ager feels about his overprotective father: he knows he should love him, but he wishes that his father would just leave him alone for a while." Ebrahím Asvat, the former head of the restructured police force, put it differently: "We feel like a woman who loves her husband, but he beats her up all the same."

When I visited Asvat, in his law offices, I remarked to him that, apart from the fact that Bush had planned his visit around a birthday party for himself and not around a commemoration for the civilians who died in the invasion, and the fact that Ambassador Hinton is unduly fond of telling Panamanians exactly what he thinks they're doing wrong and precisely what they ought to be doing instead, there didn't seem to be much cause for tension between the two countries right now. After all, I pointed out, the economic siege against Noriega was followed by grants and indirect assistance programs totalling a billion dollars—far more than Nicaragua, say, has received to repair the damage of the Washington-sponsored Contra war. Besides, the Endara government and the Bush Administration are in fundamental agreement on matters of economic philosophy, and United States businessmen are bidding eagerly for the state-owned companies the government is privatizing.

Asvat shook his head. "It's in the control," he said. "What we resent is the control. The Embassy people have any number of ways of putting pressure on us to do things the way they want: they can stigmatize a given individual they don't like; they can shut off the funding valves; they can stop hiring Panamanians to work in the Canal Zone; they can hold back on a loan or halt an

investment program or keep critical intelligence about something to themselves. They don't even have to do any of these
things; it's enough to know they're possible."

THE CANAL REMAINS one of the engineering wonders of the
world. From any high point in Panama City, one can look out to
the gorgeous bay and see ships interspersed among the islands,
lined up and waiting their turn to pass through the three sets of
locks that make it possible to navigate the narrow stretch between the Pacific and the Caribbean. I joined a crowd of Panamanian and foreign tourists at the Miraflores locks, less than an
hour's drive from the capital, to gawk as the ships plowed
through, as big as buildings, on the Canal's two narrow lanes. The
locks filled with water from the lake that United States engineers
created long ago at the Continental Divide, and the ships rose
and fell smoothly on this brief tide before continuing on their
way to sea. A guide explained the steps involved with appropri-
ately impressive statistics: it takes fifty-six million gallons of water to raise and lower the ships through the three sets of locks.
The gates that make this possible weigh hundreds of tons each,
yet are moved by a forty-horsepower electric motor.

   The Canal today is a wonder not only of engineering but of
administration and maintenance, and it is still the central bond
in the extraordinary relationship between the two countries. But
not for much longer: on December 31, 1999, the Panama Canal
will revert in its entirety to the country on whose soil it was built.
The deadline seemed very far away in the heady days when Torrijos used to proclaim, with characteristic panache, that he didn't
want a place in history—he just wanted the Canal. Now, under
the gradual-reappropriation terms of the historic treaty worked
out between him and President Jimmy Carter in 1977, a good bit
of the land and the installations surrounding the Canal belong to
Panama, and eighty-seven per cent of the work force is made up
of Panamanians. Less than forty per cent of the high management
positions are occupied by Panamanians, however, and nowadays,
when it is the treaty signing that seems the remote event and
the millennium that looms frighteningly near, what worries the

Panamanians—what turns them into the apprehensive teen-agers of Eisenmann's description—is whether they will be ready to assume responsibility when the time comes.

After all, their experience so far with nationally administered foreign enterprises has been one of dismal failure, and the evidence is highly visible: residential districts turned over to Panama have been allowed to run down and become overgrown. Administration offices have been systematically scavenged. The Canal's future is so worrisome that a seminar on the subject held in June by the Panamanian Business Managers' Association drew a standing-room-only crowd of some of the country's most influential men. The Comptroller-General was there, and the Foreign Minister, and Nicolás Ardito Barletta, who used to be a respected World Bank figure before he became Noriega's puppet President. There were also representatives from A.I.D., and dozens of prominent businessmen.

Throughout the meeting, these normally boisterous men, much given to backslapping, loud laughter, and trumpeting conversations, listened in almost Quaker silence to the speakers. Notes were taken. Thoughtful questions were written out and passed to the podium. During coffee breaks, the factional hatreds that divide the power élite were kept in check. I had the initial impression that I had arrived at the wrong meeting—one that was taking place in a different, and more boring, country. Then I caught an edge of excitement in the air, and asked about it. "This is the first time the issues of the Canal have been debated seriously among Panamanians," one of the speakers explained. "It certainly wasn't a topic for discussion during all the years the United States had complete control. And what Torrijos did was to talk, barter, decide, and sign the treaty all by himself."

Now the Canal was almost in the conferees' possession, and several of them spoke eagerly of the possibility of privatizing it, charging high tolls, and turning it into a profit-making corporation. Wasn't that, after all, what capitalism was all about? And wasn't it what Uncle Sam wanted? Fernando Manfredo, who served for years as the top Panamanian administrator on the Panama Canal Commission, quashed that view. "One of the problems I see is that there is very limited knowledge regarding the terms and conditions of the treaty," he said, and he read one of the *entendimientos* wedged into the treaty by the United States Senate at the last minute, in 1978. In suitably roundabout language, the *entendimiento* makes it clear that the United States will always be able to object if the amount of the toll stands in the way of "a maximum increase of international trade."

But could Panama, and the Canal, survive on toll fees based exclusively on operating costs? The lowest-paid Panamanian workers in the Canal Zone—janitors or line handlers, for instance—receive around seven hundred dollars a month through the Panama Canal Commission, and their contracts are regulated by unions affiliated with the A.F.L.-C.I.O. A well-paid Panamanian government employee—a policeman, say—earns barely three hundred dollars a month. Can the country continue to treat one part of itself as a colonial enclave, with the segregation and privilege that that implies? The Canal is supposed to be self-sustaining, but its worn equipment is increasingly expensive to maintain, and what used to be the most important part of the Canal's income, a flourishing marine-services enterprise, has withered. The question was suddenly urgent, and troubling: Can Panama afford the Canal?

In one form or another, a second, and even more highly charged, question came up time and again from the floor: Will Panama know what to do with the Canal? Finally, one conferee ventured an anxious joke: "If the Canal is eighty-seven per cent local staff now, why don't we just keep it that way? Look at what happens to enterprises that are one hundred per cent Panamanian, like the government." The question was met with silence.

One of the most profound changes in the country's recent history, the abolition of the Army, which was approved in June by the National Assembly, brought other questions: How can the Canal be defended? Whom would it be defended against? Can it, in fact, be defended, Panamanian Army or no? "Is it coherent to have no national Army and yet continue to have United States military bases?" one speaker asked. But the most frequent question of all was: How can we persuade Washington to keep the bases here, along with the two hundred million dollars in wages and the one hundred million dollars in local purchases that they represent? Teddy Roosevelt's ghost might have smiled. Once again, Panamanians were tangled in the ribbons of their relationship with the United States.

MEXICO CITY
1992

*"This bleeding, burning, conquered, crunched, roasted, ground,
blended, anguished heart."*

MEXICANS KNOW that a party has been outstandingly successful if at the end of it there are at least a couple of clusters of
longtime or first-time acquaintances leaning on each other
against a wall, sobbing helplessly. The activities one normally
associates with a party—flirting and conversation, and even the
kind of dancing that leads to an amnesiac dawn in a strange
bed—are considered here mere preludes to or distractions from
the ultimate goal, which is weeping and the free, luxurious expression of pain. A true celebrant of the Mexican fiesta will typically progress along a path that leads from compulsive joke-
telling to stubborn argumentativeness to thick-tongued foolery,
all in pursuit of a final, unchecked, absolving wash of tears, and
a casual observer of this voluptuous ritual might conclude that
the essential Mexican *fin de fiesta* cannot happen without alcohol.
Not so. It cannot happen without *ranchera* music. People may cry
admirably with little help from booze, but a drunk who begins
to whimper without the benefit of song produces only mediocre
tears. He cries out of self-pity. The man or woman who, with a
few tequilas packed away, bursts into tears to the strains of a
ranchera hymn—"Let My Bed Be Made of Stone," for example—
weeps for the tragedy of the world, for a mother, for a father, for
our doomed quests for happiness and love, for life. Sorrow on

such a magnificent scale is in itself redeeming, and—an added benefit—its glory leaves little room for embarrassment the morning after.

Now that Mexico is carpeted with Kentucky Fried Chicken, Denny's, and McDonald's outlets, and Coca-Cola is the national drink; now that even low-paid office workers are indentured to their credit cards and auto loans; now that the government of President Carlos Salinas de Gortari has approved a North American Free Trade Agreement, which promises to make Mexico commercially one with its neighbors to the north, there is little scope for magnificent sorrow in the average citizen's life. In the smog-darkened center of Mexico City, or in its monstrous, ticky-tacky suburban spokes, the average citizen on an average day is more concerned with beating the traffic, making the mortgage payment, punching the clock. Progress has hit Mexico in the form of devastation, some of it ecological, much of it aesthetic. Life is rushed, the water may be poisoned, and the new industrial tortillas taste terrible. Favorite ornaments for the home include porcelain dogs and plastic roses, and for the two-thirds of the population which is confined to the cities recreation usually takes the form of a couple of hours with the latest imported sitcom or the local *telenovelas*. Hardly anyone knows anymore what it is to live on a ranch or to die of passion, and yet, when it comes to the defining moments of *mexicanidad*, *ranchera* music, with its odes to love, idyllic landscapes, and death for the sake of honor, continues to reign supreme.

It is a hybrid music. Sung most often to the accompaniment of a mariachi ensemble, *rancheras* generate tension by setting the classic formality of the trumpets and violins against the howling quality of the vocals. The lyrics of many of the best-known songs—"Cielito Lindo," say—include verses that were inherited in colonial days from Spain. Many of the rhetorical flourishes— "lips like rose petals," "eyes like stars"—are Spanish also. But when *rancheras* turn, as they do obsessively, to the topics of death and destruction, alcohol and defeat, and the singer holds up his dying heart for all to see, or calls for the stones in the field to shout at him, he is bleeding from a wound that is uniquely Mexican.

The spiritual home of *ranchera* music is in the heart of Mexico City—in a raucous plaza surrounded by ratty night clubs and forbidding ancient churches. The plaza, which is not far from where I grew up, is named after Giuseppe Garibaldi, the nineteenth-century Italian revolutionary, but the central statue is of José Alfredo Jiménez (1926–1973), who wrote more songs about weeping, alcohol, and women than any other *ranchera* composer. José Alfredo's statue is wearing mariachi costume, because that is what he wore when he sang, and because the plaza is home to dozens, if not hundreds, of men who are themselves mariachis, and who stroll the plaza at all hours of the day and night, singing José Alfredo's songs and those of other *ranchera* composers to anyone who pays to listen.

On three of the plaza's irregular sides are vast cantinas and a food market, where vats of highly seasoned soup are sold throughout the night to ward off or cure hangovers. At the plaza's dissonant center is a constantly moving swarm of blurry-eyed revellers and costumed mariachis. The people in mufti stroll, wail at the moon, stagger into each other's arms, or gather around a group of musicians and sing along with them, striking defiant poses as they belt out the words. The mariachis tag after potential customers and negotiate prices, play checkers with bottle tops, shiver in the midnight cold, and, thirty or forty times an evening, play their hearts out for the revellers. Here and there, an electric-shock vender wanders through the crowd, offering a brightly painted box of programmable current to those who, for the equivalent of a couple of dollars, want to take hold of a pair of wires and test their endurance of electricity. A gaggle of tall, goofy-looking foreigners applauds and smiles at the mariachis who have just finished playing for them, and the mariachis smile, too, because tourists pay well. The people from Stand P-84, a wholesale outlet for guavas and mangoes in city's gigantic central produce market, think the tourists are pretty funny.

Chuy Soto and his guava-selling colleagues arrived here

around eight o'clock on this particular drizzly evening, and now, five hours later, they have reached the euphoric, sputtering stage at which the spirit invariably moves a Mexican to reach for extravagant metaphors and sing the glories of his country. There is a little pile of plastic glasses and empty bottles to mark the site where Chuy's group has been standing all this time, and the singer for the mariachi ensemble that has been accompanying them has just about lost his voice, but Chuy and his friends are full of vigor. "We come here to sing, and after a while emotions come out of us, and Mexicanness," Chuy says, blinking and pursing his lips as he struggles to focus. An adolescent tugs at my elbow, teary-eyed and anxious to share his own thoughts, but he can't get out a single coherent phrase, and he vanishes. One of Chuy's warehouse partners is trying to dance with a plump young woman whose acquaintance he has just made, but he's holding on too tight, and she pushes him away. The woman's friend is singing along with the mariachi (the name refers both to the group and to its individual members), for perhaps the fifth time, a song called "Dos Almas" ("Two Souls"), but by now she can't get anyone to listen to her and she weaves off in a huff. The amiable Chuy is still explaining Mexicanness to my companion, who is Peruvian. "A Mexican's heart is always open and full of music," he stammers, but a buddy of his, who spouts profanity and has in general a sharper-edged vision of things, butts in. "A Mexican knows that life is worthless," he declares.

The mariachi singer Ismael Gutiérrez and his group charge twenty-five thousand pesos, or about eight dollars, per song, but they offered Chuy and his friends the wholesale rate after serenading them with thirty *rancheras*. This meant that for a lucky evening of solid work each of the members of the Mariachi Real del Potosí, as the group Gutiérrez belongs to is called, got about thirty dollars. The group is small, and not first-rate. There's only one of each of the essential components of a mariachi: a violin; a guitar; a trumpet; a *guitarrón*, or fat bass guitar; a *vihuela*, or small plinking guitar; and the singer—Gutiérrez. Like many of his fellow-musicians who have land or a family trade in the provinces, Gutiérrez comes to Mexico City every fortnight or so from his home state—San Luis Potosí, in his case—and puts up at one of the scarred buildings around the plaza, where, he says, the old-fashioned, high-ceilinged rooms are crowded with bunk beds stacked as many as five high. There, he makes sure he gets at least eight hours' sleep a day, to keep his voice going. That is also where he stores his costume, which is as essential to his occupation as any instrument.

In the old days, before the movies, mariachis used to dress like what they were: peasant musicians. But when the Mexican movie industry began producing musicals, back in the thirties, mariachis in Indian dress—big white shirts and trousers, and straw hats—came to seem too ordinary, and someone decided to outfit them in the elegant *mestizo* dress of the *charro*, or horseman. Its basic elements are a broad-brimmed felt hat, a short, fitted black jacket, and tight black trousers with double seams running down the outside of the leg. For show, *charros* decorated the seams with brass or silver fittings and with fancy embroidery. Mexico's Hollywood kept the ornaments and the embroidery and added color. The majority of Garibaldi's mariachis wear silver-trimmed black, but now they do this to signify that they are free-lancers, which means that if a customer approaches a *guitarrón* player, say, requesting a song, the musician has to pull an ensemble together from the other black-clad free-lancers standing around. Ismael Gutiérrez is a significant step up in the hierarchy: he belongs to a formally constituted group, and all the members of his Mariachi Real wear sober Prussian blue. Gutiérrez—stout, cheerful, courtly, and equipped with a remarkable handlebar mustache—looks reassuring in his outfit, like a character out of an old-time movie.

Because Gutiérrez belongs to an established mariachi, he has been able to weather a disaster that has affected Garibaldi since the beginning of the year: construction of a new subway line began then, shutting off the main access road to the plaza and cutting down the number of potential customers so drastically that on any given Friday night the ratio of mariachis to revellers appears to be almost one to one. Gutiérrez and his mates have discovered the advantages of business cards, and by handing them out (printed with a more prosperous relative's phone number) around local office buildings and to friendly customers, they have been able to make up for the loss of walk-by trade. Not so the free-lancer Jesús Rosas. Although he plays what his colleagues describe as "a very pretty trumpet," all he can do now is dream of joining a group or landing a permanent job with the mariachis who play inside one of the huge cantinas, such as the famous Tenampa, that face on the plaza. Rosas is only twenty-five, but he has been playing Garibaldi since he left home, more than a decade ago. He used to be in demand, because he plays well, knows a lot of songs, and has a particular affability, at once alert and courteous, friendly and firmly reserved, that is much prized by Mexicans. Now times are bad, but he is stubborn. While dozens of lesser mariachis are coping with the subway crisis by heading for the Reforma, a few blocks away, to flag down cars and hustle for customers, Rosas, who finds such a procedure completely undignified, remains in Garibaldi. "The plaza is here," he says, but that means that by noon on most days he is already cruising it, his trumpet protectively cradled in a beat-up vinyl carrying case, trying to make up in long hours for the clients he has lost.

Mexico's subway is a tremendous achievement: it is now one of the longest urban railroads in the world; it allows millions of people to crisscross the sprawling city to get to work on time every day; it did not collapse, or even buckle, during the earthquake that shattered much of the city seven years ago; it is clean; it runs smoothly. Its expansion has forced dozens of shop owners along the path of its construction into bankruptcy and brought the Garibaldi mariachis to the brink of despair, but if everything goes according to the official plan, once the station opens in 1993 Garibaldi will be overrun by *ranchera* devotees, and mariachi income will soar. Gutiérrez doesn't think this will happen, because people who can afford mariachis travel by car. Nevertheless, this is the kind of promise that Mexico's rulers are constantly making to their subjects these days: severe sacrifices are being asked, and times are hard, but the country is being modernized, and when modernity arrives it will bring great rewards.

• • •

"MODERNITY" IS THE BUZZWORD, and, although hardly anyone knows how to define it, even the people in Garibaldi can
recognize its presence in their lives. Modernity is what makes the
mariachi Guadalupe González—a man who boasts that he beats
his woman regularly, out of a traditional sense of duty ("She
misses it if I don't," he explains)—welcome the subway that Jesús
Rosas dislikes. *"Hay que modernizarse,"* he admonishes Rosas, citing
the contemporary imperative. Modernity is what makes Rosas
look uncomfortable at the mention of wife-beating by his elders,
and it is also what makes his young fellow-mariachis finish their
ranchera practice and immediately tune in a rock station on the
radio, to Rosas's distress. Modernity is the guiding impulse behind the latest gambit by the travel agencies, which consists of
bringing tourists to Garibaldi by the busload to be serenaded by
musicians permanently under agency contract, instead of letting
the tourists wander about in time-honored fashion until they find
a mariachi who strikes them as *simpático.* It used to be, Guadalupe
González says, that first-rate mariachis like him could deliver the
traditional *ranchera* serenade outside the window of a house where
a party was going on, and then prove their versatility by playing
boleros, polkas, and even cha-cha chas for the partygoers to
dance to. Now, thanks to modernity, mariachis deliver their serenade and are waved away, and the party continues to the sound of
a rock band, a *cumbia* group, or, worst of all, one of those tootling
electronic organs with programmable rhythms and sound effects.
Modernity, as it is understood here, means speed and high pro-
ductivity and the kind of cost analysis that leads to one electronic
organ rather than half a dozen friendly but expensively thirsty
mariachis. Now that a finished text of the proposed North American Free Trade Agreement has been initialled by the trade ministers of Canada, the United States, and Mexico, the arrival of full-
scale modernity is assumed to be imminent. The terms of the
treaty state that fifteen years after its final approval all tariffs and
barriers to trade between the three countries will disappear. In
effect, this means that the continent will become a single, gigantic market, and government officials are already trumpeting the

estimated benefits: great tonic shots of foreign investment that
will make the economy roar. Less powerful people worry that
they, like the mariachis, will lose their jobs to electronic substitutes. But a more common undercurrent of worry and doubt, in
the endless private jokes, offhand conversational references, editorial cartoons, and television chat-show allusions to the free-
trade treaty, is more abstract, and strikes deeper. What people
want to know about the coming onslaught of modernity is: How
Mexican is it to be modern? Or, rather, since everything modern
comes from a large, powerful country to the north, how Mexican
is it to be like the United States?

There is nothing new about such fears of cultural takeover,
of course: Mexico has been under invasion from the United
States in one form or another since the war in 1847 that cost the
country half its territory, and since then the arrival of each new
fad or technological improvement has been used by pessimists to
herald the death of Mexican tradition. Rosas's worry that the
ranchera is a dying form is hardly original, but it is not paranoid.
Rock-music stations *are* increasingly numerous. Mariachi sere-
nades *are* far less frequent. This doesn't mean that Rosas's rock-
humming contemporaries are less Mexican than he is; it simply
means that their culture is more fragmented. The remarkable psy-
chic sturdiness shared by the inhabitants of a city that often looks
like the morning after the apocalypse may or may not owe something to cultural coherence, but, as every Latino teen-ager in Los
Angeles knows, the combination of cultural fragmentation and
social disadvantage can be poisonous. To the whiz kids from
Harvard and the Sorbonne who are currently running the Mexican government, though, the diversification of Mexican culture is
also rich with promise. Nationalism and tradition are *retardatarios*,
cosmopolitanism is creative, and what used to be called cultural
imperialism is now known as "the inevitable future."

THE OBSESSION WITH MODERNITY springs directly from President Salinas de Gortari. Now only forty-four, he was in his
mid-thirties when, as Secretary of Planning and the Budget, he
masterminded the plan that pulled Mexico out from under its

foreign-debt crisis and into full-tilt privatization and liberalization of the economy. He is a "son of the Party"—a second-generation hierarch in the Partido Revolucionario Institucional, or PRI, which has been in power for most of this century. The revolution the Party's name refers to occurred from 1910 to—depending on how one counts—about 1929, and in it Indian peasants, an angry and modernizing northern bourgeoisie, and an urban intelligentsia fought against the dictatorship of Porfirio Díaz and then against each other. Over the decades, the survivors of this bloody game have evolved into what some consider the wiliest guardians of the status quo since the time of the Pharaohs. The system the PRI perfected has been particularly successful in dealing with a problem that the former Soviet Union, for one, never solved: every six years, there is an orderly transition of power, in which the ruling President designates a meticulously trained successor to run in what has been a largely uncontested election. The virtues of the resulting *estabilidad monolítica* have long been a favorite topic of the system's bards, and, in truth, during all the decades that the rest of Latin America was convulsed with insurgency, stability was the keynote for the country ruled by the Institutional Revolutionary Party. A sly newspaper columnist has taken to printing the Party's name "P[RI]" whenever it appears, but actually that is unfair, because if any government in the past sixty years has shaken things up to a degree that could nearly be described as revolutionary it is the government of Carlos Salinas de Gortari.

Like *glasnost*, Salinas de Gortari's quasi revolution has had as much to do with making changes as with opening up the country to the possibility of even greater—almost inconceivable—change. He has opened up the electoral process to serious contenders from what were once token opposition parties, despite the fact that he barely won his own Presidential election—or perhaps even lost it, if the opposition is to be believed. He has, despite charges of fraud regarding this election and others, opened up the government itself, forcing an increasingly irate PRI to recognize the electoral victories of three opposition gubernatorial candidates. He has opened up the traditional, PRI-

controlled union structure to what some see as ruthless depreda-
tion by transnational corporations and others see as full capitalist
relations. And, even before the treaty, he opened up the country
to greatly increased commercial exchange with the United
States. The political *apertura* is based on the premise that the PRI
can face a limited electoral challenge without putting its ultimate
power at risk, and the economic *apertura* on the belief that Mexico
can face barrier-free trade with an economy twenty-five times its
own size and survive. A big, mustachioed truck driver I fell into
conversation with one evening at the Tenampa, in Garibaldi, reminded me that this is not an unreasonable hope. "I'm from the
north, from the state of Chihuahua!" he shouted over the din of
competing mariachis. "And, unlike those of you from farther
south, I know what it is to be intimate with the United States."
He pointed to his cowboy boots, his ten-gallon hat, his jeans.
"All my clothes are from the United States, but does that mean
that I don't look Mexican? As for trading with the gringos, I can
tell you that that's nothing new. Remember *fayuca?*" He meant
contraband. "There's always been trade between Mexico and the
United States. The only difference is that, before, it wasn't free."
He rubbed thumb and forefinger together to indicate the bribes
that were paid as a matter of course to bring in anything from
nail polish to cars. "I'm for the free-trade treaty," he declared, and
then, to make it clear that he did not suffer from any lack of
patriotism, he called a mariachi over and sang "México Lindo"
with them for me.

As everyone knows, though, the north is not *el México pro-
fundo*, and that is so precisely because of its dangerous proximity
to the source of all cultural contamination. The white-skinned
north is industrialized, optimistic, open to foreign influence, and
vastly more prosperous than the Indian south. Though *norteños*
sing *rancheras*, they also have music of their own, which is not at
all tormented but, rather, cheery and literally upbeat, being based
on the polka. The essayist Carlos Monsiváis calls *norteño* music
"the soundtrack for modernity," and it may be that its booming
nationwide acceptance is a sign that non-*norteño* Mexicans are becoming willing to see life as something other than one long train-

ing session in pain. Perhaps it is also true that neither *norteños* nor any other Mexicans have anything to fear from a treaty that allows foreign manufacturers to come pouring over the border, but whether economic *apertura* will lead to a final drowning of Mexican culture in United States sauce is not an entirely idle question—at least, not when one is sitting in a Kentucky Fried Chicken outlet and eating some of the first fast-food tacos that Taco Bell is hoping to find a mass market for in Mexico City.

BOTH KENTUCKY FRIED CHICKEN and Taco Bell are subsidiaries of Pepsico, and five months ago, when Pepsico decided that Mexico was ready for a gringo taco, it chose one of its more successful Kentucky Fried Chicken fast-food outlets to test-market the idea. Fast food is a privilege of the middle class here: it's something hygienic and slightly exotic to eat on a weekend with the family before heading out to the country, say, or at lunchtime on those weekdays when the fare at the local *fonda*— vegetable soup, rice à la mexicana, veal birds, and flan, for example—seems too commonplace, or when a better restaurant is too slow and pricey for the occasion. The Kentucky Fried Chicken outlet now offering a sampling of the Taco Bell menu stands at a busy intersection of an upwardly mobile middle-class neighborhood and boasts Rufino Tamayo reproductions on its walls. About half of the well-dressed customers sitting at *típico*-style wooden tables were having the Colonel's batter-fried special, and the rest were having tacos and nachos, that dubious Tex-Mex contribution to the world of food. I asked a pretty, densely made-up young woman and her date what I should have, and they recommended the shredded-beef taco and, less warmly, the pork carnitas, which turned out to taste precisely like ground-up, very salty paper sautéed in chicken fat. The shredded-beef taco had better seasoning, and the tortillas were surprisingly good, but the nachos—over which I had been instructed to pump a chrome-yellow substance that had the consistency of tooth-paste—were inedible.

When spokesmen for the company are asked to explain why residents of one of the great culinary capitals of the world might be interested in Mexican fast food, they have replied that the one thing Mexico lacks is somewhere to get a clean, cheap, fast taco. This is patently untrue, and shows surprisingly flabby work on the part of the market researchers, for, while it is true that no Mexican taco stand looks like a NASA food-preparation station, many such stands are clean, all of them are cheap and fast, and even the chain-food taco stands (there are several, including one down the street from Kentucky Fried Chicken) feature a variety of selections far beyond the scope of the Taco Bell menu: chorizo tacos, squash-flower quesadillas, fresh-mushroom-and-poblano-chili soft tacos, and chicken hard tacos served with heavy cream, chopped onions, and lettuce are all standard. At the Kentucky Fried Chicken outlet, I asked a well-dressed couple who had come in from the suburbs why they had decided to have a Taco Bell lunch, and they replied, in effect, that it was because the place was cheap, clean, and fast. "But I'm a little disappointed," the woman added. "This doesn't taste like the real thing, does it? What I wanted was those big taco shells stuffed with salad and Kraft cheese and all *kinds* of stuff, like what you get in Texas. But I asked the manager, and he says they're going to start making them soon." In other words, Taco Bell tacos sell because they're American, and, to judge from the size and enthusiasm of the clientele, they sell very well indeed.

I WENT TO SEE the postmodern *ranchera* singer Astrid Hadad's show a few days after my Taco Bell lunch, and as she worked her way to a tiny stage through the crowded bar where she was performing she peddled tacos from a basket. "What kind would you like?" she asked her customers. "Now that we have the free-trade treaty, I can offer you hamburger tacos, hot-dog tacos, chili-con-carne tacos. . . ." For her presentations, Hadad likes to wear red lipstick with carnival glitter in it—on her eyelids—and a Jean Paul Gaultier-like cone-shaped bra, which she later rips off and replaces with a big, anatomically accurate foam-rubber heart. Her show, which has been attracting ever more loyal audiences over the last four years, relies heavily on the nostalgia value of *ranchera* music and on its inherent campiness, but it would not be

so energetically appealing if her powerful voice were not a perfect vehicle for *rancheras* or if her understanding of a *ranchera* prototype—the brassy, hard-drinking, love-wounded dame—were
not intuitive. Hadad belted out, "As if I were a sock, you step on
me all day," and her audience howled with laughter and the acid
pleasure of recognition. When, in a frenzy of Mexican passion,
she asked what would become of her heart—"this bleeding,
burning, conquered, crunched, roasted, ground, blended, anguished heart"—a couple of people in the audience rose to give
her a standing ovation. Hadad had come onstage with peasant-
style braids and wearing a typical *china poblana* embroidered skirt.
Now she loosened the braids, tore off the skirt to reveal a slinky
black dress underneath, removed the heart from the dress's strap-
less bodice, added long gloves, checked her image in an empty
mirror frame, and retold the well-known myth of Quetzalcoatl,
the god-king of Tula, and his rival Tezcatlipoca, or Smoking Mirror. "Tezcatlipoca is jealous because Quetzalcoatl is blond, so he
gives him some pulque. Quetzalcoatl gets drunk, screws his own
sister, wakes up with a terrible hangover, and sees his image in
Tezcatlipoca's mirror. He heads for the beach and sets sail, and
as he leaves he promises to return. So he does, the blond, blue-
eyed god, and that's how we discovered the joys of"—here
Hadad licked her lips lasciviously—"cultural penetration."

Offstage, Hadad turned out to be a tiny woman with a sharp
Lebanese profile (it is a curious fact of cultural life here that many
of the most devoted *mexicanistas* are themselves—like Hadad and
like Frida Kahlo—first- or second-generation Mexicans) and an
intellectual manner. Not surprisingly, she declared that what first
attracted her to *rancheras* was that they are so essentially Mexican.
"I think it has to do with the attitude toward suffering that we
inherited from the Aztecs," she said. "It's not that we have an
extraordinary capacity for suffering—everyone does. It's the way
we *relish* it. I think only Russians compare with us in that. And
then there's the element of machismo. Again, it's not that men
here beat their wives more, because I'm sure that Germans do it
just as much; it's that here they boast about it. Obviously, I'm
very critical of that, but what keeps me coming back to the music

is the passion. Now that we're all becoming so rational and sensible, it's getting harder and harder to find passion in our lives; I think that's what we all seek in the *ranchera*."

I asked Hadad why she cracked so many jokes about the Free Trade Agreement in her show, and why she thought her audience was so responsive to them, and she said it was because of the enormous apprehension that people are feeling about it. She pointed out that even the great Mexican movie goddess María Félix had taken the unusual step of speaking out publicly against the treaty, warning that it might cause Mexican values—not to mention factories—to collapse. Like nearly everyone else who is fearful of the treaty, Hadad confessed that she had no idea what was in it. "But it seems obvious to me that the little guys—us— are not going to be the ones calling the shots," she said. "The government gets all excited describing the wonderful things that will result from the treaty, but I say '*What* wonders?' As far as I can make out, all it means is that in the future we're going to be more like South Korea and less like us."

THIS IS, IN FACT, precisely what one of Salinas de Gortari's bright young intellectuals described to me some time ago as his best hope: that if Mexico's debt situation remains stable, if its workers can be persuaded to let wage increases remain just below the rate of inflation, if monetary policy and inflation itself continue under tight government control, enough foreign investment will land here "to turn this country into South Korea, or maybe Taiwan."

It won't be easy to make that happen. Over the last decade, Mexico's financial planners have brought the economy back from the brink, but that doesn't mean that the country is in marvellous shape. Ten years ago, the world learned that Mexico was on the verge of collapse when the Secretary of Finance announced that his country would not be able to meet the commercial banks' schedule of payments. Today, the public-sector debt is down from its 1987 high, eighty-one billion dollars, to seventy-four billion, and combined private- and public-sector debt represents only twenty-nine per cent of the gross domestic product. (It represented seventy-eight per cent of the G.D.P. as recently as 1986.) On the home front, though, things are shakier. Workers would have to receive at least a thirty-per-cent wage increase to recover even the ascetic standard of living they enjoyed when the crisis began, but such increases are out of the question, partly because the government wants to keep wages attractive for foreign investors, and partly because so many businesses and industries, large and small, are either heading straight for bankruptcy or barely making ends meet. Whatever the real causes of the business collapse may be, several trade associations are laying the blame for their woes on the huge wave of United States imports that a liberalized tariff policy has made possible, and they are fearful that the treaty will bring in foreign competition at unbearable levels. In any event, a punishing wage policy, severe budget cutbacks, and tight money appear to be the only measures capable of preventing the kind of three-digit inflation that plagues so much of Latin America. The government always promises lower levels, but so far it has been unable to keep inflation below fifteen per cent.

For Salinas de Gortari and his economic advisers, there is just one way out of this economic gridlock, and that is the Free Trade Agreement. I talked about the treaty with the novelist, historian, and magazine editor Héctor Aguilar Camín, who is perhaps the most outstanding of the pro-Salinas intellectuals. The last Mexican President to have a respectable set of house intellectuals was Lázaro Cárdenas, who nationalized the petroleum industry in 1938 and practiced a fervent leftist nationalism, which subsequent Presidents paid skillful lip service to. Salinas de Gortari's thinkers are remarkable not only for high I.Q.s and fancy educations but also for a self-proclaimed freedom from the bonds of nationalist thought. Aguilar Camín, for example, is completely unconcerned about the fact that the treaty will open the doors to investment capital from abroad. The point is, he told me, that Mexicans' standard of living will not improve unless at least twenty million new sources of income are created, and that will not happen with the country's available investment capital. The treaty, which is seen across the border as a potential threat to

United States jobs, is seen by people like Aguilar Camín as a crucial guarantee of economic, and thus political, stability in a country that could well export twice as many illegal aliens (and illegal drugs) if things don't improve.

"If the treaty isn't signed, economic expectations will fall, and so will investment," Aguilar Camín said. "This could lead to a very high budget deficit and a consequent devaluation of the peso. There's not much more that can be trimmed from the budget without causing enormous social pain. But if there were a devaluation, even if it were only a moderate one of, say, twenty per cent, the political impact would be devastating; once again, we'd be seeing capital flight abroad, and a completely destabilized business climate." Indeed, the treaty's eventual ratification is so important for the business climate that the Mexican Bolsa, or stock exchange, which only last year was one of the fastest-growing stock exchanges in the world, has been losing points steadily since June, largely as a result of jitteriness over the possible election of Bill Clinton to the White House and a possible rejection of the treaty by his administration. After Clinton spoke out in favor of the treaty, the Bolsa soared.

The highly technical trade and tariff treaty that Aguilar Camín was describing was an entirely different kind of beast from the culturally ominous one that frightens Astrid Hadad and María Félix, and I found him to be sharply impatient with any discussion of cultural imperialism. "The more Americanized we become, the more the idea scares us," he said. "But the fact is that United States culture is already part of our landscape and our way of being. The élite is bilingual, ten per cent of our population lives in the United States, and the tribulations of Woody Allen and Mia Farrow are like a family affair to us. Our greatest writers were weaned on United States authors. Perhaps the United States is the enemy, but it is also our big opportunity, and, while I think that with the free-trade treaty we will have more fights than ever with the United States, these will be about things like tomato and broom quotas, and not about the twisted rhetoric that for years had us saying fantasizing, idiotic things on the order of 'They have the know-how, but we have civilization.'

A fundamental rhetorical change has taken place: in the nineteen-seventies, Mexico was supposed to be 'proudly Third World,' but today, we want to belong to the First World."

AGUILAR CAMÍN, bright and urbane and at ease with power as he is, doesn't seem to be the type who gravitates toward controversy. Yet his role as a supervisor and co-author of a newly revised official history textbook for Mexico's grade schools has people in the greatest uproar about the Salinas de Gortari government and its modernizing intentions that his Presidency has seen. The scandal began percolating in the back pages of the local press about a week before I met with Aguilar Camín, and rapidly moved to the front pages.

The new textbook project was announced at the beginning of the year as part of an educational reform package that was given the full, glorifying treatment accorded to major Presidential initiatives: there were decrees, signing ceremonies, adulatory press stories, and a succession of what are known as adhesion speeches (in which the speaker, by means of flattery, attaches himself firmly to the initiative and its foreseeable rewards). Aguilar Camín and a flotilla of top-of-the-line intellectuals got to work. Then, in August, teachers, parents, and education reporters opened the brightly colored new textbooks and discovered a history that was both subtly and radically different from the one they themselves had learned in school. The priest Miguel Hidalgo, whose fiery call to arms in 1810 for independence from Spain became the touchstone of all nationalist sentiment, is described cursorily. The account of the traumatic war with the United States is rendered in reassuring understatement. Emiliano Zapata, the southern leader of Mexico's agrarian revolutionary tide, who was finally betrayed and assassinated in 1919 by the norteño revolutionaries, is portrayed not as a pure and heroic peasant but as merely one leader among several warring factions. Earlier generations learned that the dictator Porfirio Díaz, who first came to power in 1877, was guilty of genocide against the untamable Yaqui Indian nation, and that he ruled tyrannically and unswervingly in favor of a small white-skinned percentage of the population who lived off the sweat of an impoverished Indian majority. In the new textbooks the reviled dictator—whose stubborn hold on power led directly to the revolution that the PRI honors in its name—turns out not to have been such a bad guy after all. "Porfirio Díaz's long rule created a climate of peace and encouraged the country's economic development," the section on him concludes. "His government diminished individual liberties, concentrated power in a few hands, and put a brake on the development of democracy."

Aguilar Camín is not the only modernizing academic to see the PRI's favorite villain as a progressive dictator who created the infrastructure that made a twentieth-century Mexico possible. But he is the only one who is on such friendly personal terms with a President whose own rule invites so many comparisons to Díaz: "Don Porfirio" started out in politics as a supporter of the ultraliberal Benito Juárez, then ruled in favor of a tiny, conservative élite. Salinas de Gortari, for his part, has turned his back on the party that brought him to power. He is currently "refounding" it with policies that are often anathema to the Old Guard and very pleasing to the PRI's most threatening opposition, the conservative Partido Acción Nacional, which also welcomes the refurbishing of Díaz's image. Banks have been reprivatized, a decade after President José López Portillo, in a fit of pique, appropriated them for the state. The Revolution's keystone, the Agrarian Reform Law, which assigned inalienable communal lands to millions of peasants (and kept most of them desperately poor), has been modified to permit private sales. Legislative restrictions have been loosened to allow foreign investment greater leeway than at any other time since the dictatorship. Even though they are patently sensible, these moves have the left and the traditional PRI in an uproar, because of the larger ideological issues that are perceived to underlie them. But the textbook rehabilitation of Porfirio Díaz rubs the wrong way even for people who don't care much about politics. This is not primarily because Díaz was a dictator—there is nothing particularly democratic about the PRI people live with and often support. Nor is it just because Díaz presided over a society even more contemptuous of its great un-

washed than the present one. It is, rather, because, even though
Porfirio Díaz started out in life as an impoverished, Mixtec-
speaking *mestizo*, he has always been perceived as profoundly un-
Mexican in his impact on society. He modernized the country,
but did it by bringing in foreign capital. He turned Mexico City
into one of the loveliest in the world, but Frenchified it. He presided, as the textbook says, over thirty years of stability, but did
so wearing a tricorne hat and a ridiculous tin-pot-general's uniform. It may seem foolish—or suggest a pathetic insecurity—for
a whole nation to go around worrying that reading good things
about such a man or eating lunch at Taco Bell will somehow diminish its Mexican essence. The point is, though, that nationalism is still the great common meeting ground of a society that
might otherwise be as tragically riven as any in Latin America. It
is not in the voting booth but in the Zócalo on Independence
Night, surrounded by mariachis and showered in confetti, that
the vast mass of the *pueblo* feels like citizenry. It is in the kitchen,
where lowly cooks prepare glorious food for the children of the
middle class, that Mexicans forge a common heritage. It is in
Garibaldi, bellowing out *ranchera* songs, that rich papa's boys out
on a spree and truck drivers in from the road can be equal.

I FLEW FROM MEXICO CITY to Tijuana, a scorching-hot border
town that can be seen either as the hideous, seedy product of
more than a century of cultural penetration or as the defiant,
lively result of a hundred years of cultural resistance. Just a few
miles south of San Diego, Tijuana reigns as the world capital of
Spanglish, shantytowns, and revolting souvenirs, yet, despite it
all, remains completely Mexican. The United States may be just
an imaginary line away, but on this side of the line driving becomes more creative, street life improves, bribes are taken, and
hairdos are more astonishing. I thought Tijuana would be a good
place to catch a show by Juan Gabriel, a singer and prolific composer who is the most unlikely heir to the mantle of *ranchera*
greatness that could ever be imagined.

Juan Gabriel likes to perform at *palenques*, or cockfight arenas,
which are a traditional element of state fairs. When I arrived at

the Tijuana *palenque*, around midnight, several hundred people were watching the last fight, perched on chairs in a coliseumlike arrangement of concrete tiers surrounding a small circular arena. Those in the know say that hundreds of thousands of dollars' worth of bets are placed in the course of a fight, but all I saw was half a dozen men with little notebooks standing in the arena, catching mysterious silent signals from the audience and scribbling down figures, while the two fighting cocks were displayed by their handlers. After a few minutes, the men with notebooks left, and the cocks, outfitted with razorlike spurs, were set on the ground. The cocks flew at each other, spurs first, while the audience watched in tense, breathless silence. In a matter of minutes, one of the animals lay trembling on the ground, its guts spilling out, and the other was proclaimed the victor, to a brief, dull cheer. Instantly, Juan Gabriel's roadies moved in.

The instruments they set up—electric organ and piano, two sets of drums—are not the ones normally associated with *ranchera* music, but then Juan Gabriel is not what one would think of as a typical mariachi singer. For starters, he is from the border himself—from Ciudad Juárez, where he was born, and where he was raised in an orphanage. When he burst on the pop-music scene, in the early seventies, radio audiences often mistook his high-pitched voice for a woman's. His fey mannerisms became the subject of crude jokes. He has been press-shy ever since a scurrilous book by a purported confidant fed hungry speculations about his sexual preferences. Yet, in this nation of self-proclaimed machos, Juan Gabriel has been able to perform before a standing-room-only crowd in the Palacio de Bellas Artes, Mexico's Carnegie Hall. He lives in Los Angeles, uses electronic backups and percussion, and writes songs that never mention drunkenness or two- or three-timing women, but when men in Garibaldi drink and fall into the confessional mode these days their musical inspiration invariably includes songs composed by Juan Gabriel.

As the first, wailing *ranchera* chords tore through the din and Juan Gabriel emerged from the bullpen, there was a roar from the *palenque*, and in the roar there was a call for blood. The composition of the audience had changed: a majority of women, mostly middle-aged and in girls'-night-out groups, had filled the stands, along with a large minority of romantic couples and a dense sprinkling of men in groups. A lot of the men were wearing big *norteño* hats, and in the front row a group of couples and male buddies in big hats and heavy gold chains had set up beer cans and bottles of tequila along the concrete ledge that defined the arena space. The women in the audience were shouting their love for Juan Gabriel hysterically, but a couple of men behind me were shouting something quite different, and so were a lot of the men in big hats. "*Marica!*" and "*Jotón!*" they yelled, meaning "Fag!" or "Queer!" They yelled this over and over, and, because the cherub-faced Juan Gabriel in his graying middle age has put on something of a paunch, someone improvised an insult that was quickly copied: "You're pregnant, you faggot! Go home!" The men had paid between forty and sixty dollars a head to indulge in this pleasure, and Juan Gabriel, circling the arena slowly to acknowledge the majority's applause, also acknowledged this generosity with a small, graceful curtsy before he began to sing.

His music is proof of the fact that the *ranchera* has changed as much as Mexico has, and that in doing so it has survived. His backup singers at the *palenque* were two skinny, curvy black women in tight dresses: they chimed in on the chorus as required, but with distinctly gringo accents. Standing between them and his electronic band, Juan Gabriel sang and twirled to music from his pop repertoire, punctuating some of the jazzier songs with belly rolls and shimmies that drove the women and the machos wild in opposite ways. There was rather a lot of this cheerful music, and then he slowed down and began to sing a real *ranchera*, a song of bad love, loss, and pain, in which the composer makes abject offers to his departed love. In case the fugitive should ever decide to return, Juan Gabriel sang, "You'll find me here, in my usual spot, in the same city, with the same crowd, so you can find everything just as you left it." By the second verse, there was no need for him to sing at all, because the members of the audience were chanting the words for themselves with the rapt reverence accorded an anthem. "I just forgot again," the audience sang, "that you never loved me." I glanced at a couple of the big guys sitting in the front row, armed with their bottles of tequila, who had earlier folded their arms protectively across their chests and smirked whenever Juan Gabriel wiggled in their direction. Now they were singing.

A dozen fawn-colored *charro* hats wobbled at the entrance to the bullpen, and the audience, seeing the mariachis arrive, roared itself hoarse with welcome. Gold decorations along the musicians' trousers caught the light. The men lined up facing Juan Gabriel's band, adjusted their hats, took up their instruments, and filled the *palenque* with the ripe, aching, heart-torn sound of the mariachi. Juan Gabriel, singing this time about how hard it is to forget, was now not queening at all. The big guys sitting across from me leaned into each other, swaying companionably to the music, like everyone else in the audience. Behind me, the last heckler had finally shut up. Juan Gabriel sang a lilting *huapango* and a couple of *sones*, without pausing once for chatter. He segued from one song to the next or went through long medleys, the doo-wop girls bursting in occasionally with a trill or two. Then the girls left the stage, and so did the band. Juan Gabriel, alone with the mariachis, slowed down for the introductory chords of a song that begins, "Podría volver," and, recognizing these, the audience squealed in ecstatic pain. "I could return, but out of sheer pridefulness I won't," the lyrics say, in what is perhaps the most perfect of a hundred *ranchera* hymns to the unbending pride of the loser. "If you want me to come back, you should have thought of that before you left me." Here and there, his listeners yelped as if some very tasty salt had just been rubbed into their national wound. Life hurts. I hurt. The hell with you: I'll survive, Juan Gabriel sang. In the front row, the two big guys looked immensely happy, and just about ready to weep.

LIMA
1993

"How difficult it is to be God."

A JOURNALIST I KNOW in Ayacucho, where the ultra-Maoist revolutionary group Sendero Luminoso, or Shining Path, got its start, tells a story about the guerrillas that he heard from a friend of his, a local military officer. The officer had captured three members of the Communist Party of Peru, which is the official name of Sendero, and proceeded to torture them in what is, in this country, routine fashion. Eventually, one of the three captives died. As a second captive seemed to be struggling for his life, the third intervened. "I will coöperate," he said. "But if you let my compañero live he will let the word out that I talked, and I'll be a dead man. Kill him first, and then I'll talk." The officer accepted the deal and murdered the second man, but at that point the prisoner who had promised to talk in exchange for the killing began insulting his captors more fiercely than ever, kicking out at them and provoking even worse treatment. The officer, astonished, reminded him that he had promised to coöperate. "I'll never talk," the man said. "I'm a member of the Communist Party of Peru. The other man was just a collaborator, and I saw he was beginning to crack and would have put our compañeros in danger. Now he won't talk, and you can kill me."

In its harshness, horror, and unyielding fanaticism in the face of brutality, this possibly apocryphal story reflects perfectly what

Peruvians know about the organization that has terrorized their country for the last thirteen years. During that time, the fundamentalist revolutionaries of Sendero Luminoso have been engaged in a steadily intensifying effort to demoralize and undermine the Peruvian state, and make it ripe for a violent takeover. Peru, with a population of twenty-three million, has a standing Army of a hundred and thirty thousand; generous estimates put Sendero's total of full-time militants at six thousand. Defense and security take up forty per cent of the national budget; Sendero attacks with shotguns, revolvers, and even knives. There have been twenty-five thousand or so deaths—mostly civilians—in the violent struggle between the Army and Sendero; of these, Sendero has been responsible for nearly half. The group operates throughout the country, and has forced the military to stretch itself past any reasonable limit just to patrol—ineffectually— areas challenged or dominated by Sendero. The Army is constantly in a reactive, defensive mode, while Sendero has never once been obliged to engage in combat. Instead, it has bombed police headquarters and municipal offices, gas stations and middle-class apartment buildings, think tanks and public schools. It has paralyzed the country with so-called armed strikes, and set fire to bus drivers who defied its orders to stay home on strike days. It has murdered peasant families and leftist leaders. Most often, the victims are killed in full view of their family or community. Sometimes they are hanged and sometimes shot, but often an execution-squad member—in many cases a woman—delivers the coup de grâce with a knife. Sometimes the tail of a live cat will be set on fire and then the animal will be let loose in a field of corn ready for picking. Sometimes a man who has just finished casting a mandatory vote in a national election will have the finger with the telltale electoral ink hacked off.

Despite its omnipresence, Sendero has until recently remained almost entirely opaque in the public mind, and the journalist's story about the three captured guerrillas illustrates part of the reason. Besides, for years the war took place in the most inaccessible villages of the Andes, and thus had little or no impact in the cities; this was particularly true of Lima, where a quarter of the country's population lives. Beginning in 1989, however, Sendero moved the war to the capital, first consolidating its hold on the shantytowns and then, last year, announcing its presence among the middle class with a series of spectacular car bombings. Still, the organization remained magically elusive.

This perception changed dramatically last September 12th. At 8:30 p.m., members of the Dirección Nacional Contra el Terrorismo, or Dincote, an independent branch of the national police, arrested Carlos Abimael Guzmán, the fifty-seven-year-old Fourth Sword of Marxism and the chairman of the Communist Party of Peru. Guzmán is not only the leader and strategist of Sendero. In his incarnation as Presidente Gonzalo, as he is now known, he is its godhead: its creator, patriarch, and single source of inspiration. It is he who moves his followers to self-immolation, and he who authorizes the car bombs and the mutilating punishments. He is the sole proponent of something called Gonzalo Thought, which initiates see as a dazzling intellectual construct by means of which the wisdom of Mao is adapted to conditions in Peru, and Marxist theory as a whole is further advanced. There are songs to Gonzalo, and poems. When he is depicted in murals or in easel paintings, he is shown wearing glasses, as befits a scholar, and rising out of the mountains or shining from the sky like the sun. His apparent invulnerability was central to his mystique; between the day in 1980 when a small group of university students descended on a voting station in an isolated Andean village and set fire to the ballot boxes, thus beginning Sendero's military operations, and last summer, when all Lima appeared to be under siege by a force that blew up entire city blocks in fashionable neighborhoods, none of his followers had been persuaded to reveal his whereabouts. On September 12th, though, he was arrested swiftly and with a minimum of fuss in a quiet Lima neighborhood, on the second floor of a house whose first floor functioned as a modern-dance studio. In the days following that arrest, transfixed television viewers feasted on images of the man who in his writings fulminated against "reactionaries who unleash their bloody claws upon the people and shred their flesh," who claimed to speak with the people's "voice of angry thunder"—the scourge of Peru, the exterminating angel.

There is Guzmán on the screen at the moment of his detention—owlish, bearded, riddled with psoriasis—in a tape that was not intended for public consumption but got leaked anyhow. Sitting next to his companion, Elena Iparraguirre, in the book-lined study where he was arrested, he addresses his captor, General Antonio Ketín Vidal, who is the head of Dincote. "You can kill a man, but you can't kill this," he declares emphatically, tapping his head. "And when we die, this will live on." Vidal, a character straight out of Simenon, is clearly not listening. Dressed casually in a leather hunting jacket and dark-gray slacks, slightly built, with an intelligent, beaked face, he is standing next to his prey, looking down on him in amazement, trying to comprehend the fact that he, Vidal, has just bagged the Minotaur. Still blinking in similar shock, viewers sucked information off the screen, veering dizzily between a sense of historic moment and a recognition of absurdity: Look at his paunch! Look at how calm he is! Look at how much like a nun Elena Iparraguirre looks, and how defiantly she stares at the camera! And look at the little red flag with a hammer and sickle that she keeps waving protectively over Guzmán's head! Look at how comfortable the room they are sitting in seems!

There were other tapes, these willingly released by the government: Guzmán taking orders from his captors, removing his clothes, so the psoriasis showed, then methodically getting dressed again. And the very first one, the one in which Guzmán and seven persons arrested with him were presented to the press. A young woman I know was called out of the shower that morning by an urgent scream from her mother. Rushing to the television set, she arrived in time to scream, too. "Maritzita!" she cried, staring at the screen, where her high-school chum Maritza Garrido Lecca, the star pupil, the fervent Catholic, the ballet student turned bohemian and modern dancer, was being identified as a terrorist agent who taught Nickolaus-technique alignment exercises on one floor of her rented house and kept Guzmán hidden on another. Maritza, it turned out, was the niece of an ex-nun of Welsh descent, Nelly Evans, who had been captured two years earlier. The aunt is reported to have handled Sendero's sizable bank accounts abroad, and is presumed to have given over some of her other housekeeping activities to Maritza. Maritzita's friend tried to recognize the nice girl she knew in the blazing-eyed woman with the set jaw who, with a fist clenched in the air, kept shouting "Long life to Presidente Gonzalo and the Communist Party of Peru!," but the images of Maritzita past and present did not add up.

Really, none of it does, still. The startled, mildly ironic Guzmán on the leaked arrest tape, who objects to his captors' request to pat him down ("What do you think I have on me, a *gun*?"), is hard to reconcile with the barking maniac who was presented to the world twelve days later, dressed in cartoonish prison stripes and confined in a *Silence of the Lambs* cage in the Lima police courtyard. And the image of the man who has inspired thousands to suicidal struggle hardly meshes with the performer in the cage, either. The speech he delivered there was a model of retro revolutionary rhetoric and structural incoherence, swerving crazily from exhortations to his adherents to follow up the achievements of the Third Central Committee Plenum with the launching of the Sixth Military Plan, to a cursory account of imperialism in Peru, and then to dire warnings that unnamed forces were trying to divide the country. Having finished with a throaty "Honor and glory to the Peruvian people!" Guzmán marched toward the door of his cage, obviously expecting to be led away in oratorical triumph. Instead, his captors refused to open the door. Glaring at the horizon with his fist raised, Guzmán stuck stubbornly by the door while an increasingly frenzied crowd of local reporters jeered and then, in a fit of patriotism, burst into the national anthem. Guzmán responded by lighting into the "Internationale," but he either forgot the words or realized too late that he had missed a unique opportunity to look patriotic. Silent once more, he stood with weakly clenched fist until his captors tired of the circus and ordered the journalists out of the courtyard.

Some days later, I discussed the Guzmán tapes with a bright, ambitious young woman from the provinces who is here in Lima trying to make a career for herself in marketing. "There is such wisdom in everything that man says!" she said. "I have no sympathy for Sendero, but I got goose bumps in the scene where he taps his head and says you can't kill a man's ideas. In just a few words he'd said all that is important!" Maritzita's friend, having taken her first good look at Presidente Gonzalo, responded similarly. "Sendero is a terrorist organization, but one has to acknowledge that he is an incredibly well-prepared man," she said. Giovanna Peñaflor, who runs a poll-taking organization that is small but asks interesting questions, found that twenty per cent of her respondents felt "compassion" when they saw the caged Guzmán.

THE WEIRDLY POSITIVE RESPONSE of so many Peruvians to a man who traffics in brutality, whose writings are few and unimpressive, and who in the flesh turns out to be flabby, splayfooted, and solemn, says something about the desperate state of Peruvian politics. President Alberto Fujimori himself is said to have come up with the idea for Guzmán's cage and stripes, but the attempt to make his top prisoner look foolish was at best a mixed success. In order to appear really foolish to Peruvians, Presidente Gonzalo would at the very least have had to equal the performance of the members of Congress who in the summer of 1991 famously spent three days in a rowdy discussion of whether the official spelling of an ancient city in the Andes should be "Cusco" or "Cosco." At that time, Peru was having one of those weeks in which the final breakdown of the ruling order seems barely hours away: Sendero had stepped up its terror campaign against the cities; every single one of the country's teachers and nurses was on strike; police were threatening to go on strike, too; and the chronic water and electricity shortages that keep Lima in a state of unshowered, refrigeratorless stress were worse than ever.

President Fujimori cites this episode whenever he feels compelled to explain why, on April 5, 1992, he suspended the writ of habeas corpus, announced a complete purge and restructuring of the judiciary, and closed down Congress—an *autogolpe* that left him, in effect, with dictatorial powers. Fujimori, who shares with

Presidente Gonzalo an extreme contempt for Peruvian politicians, has a hunger for revenge and a pronounced authoritarian bent—most vividly expressed in the April coup—along with a popularity that many find inexplicable. Having leaped out of nowhere to gain an astonishing electoral victory over the novelist Mario Vargas Llosa two years ago, Fujimori went on to enforce a drastic package of neoliberal reform measures. He can claim, with justice, that the reforms have been effective: no one believed that it would be possible to bring yearly inflation down from more than seven thousand per cent in 1990 to a mere fifty per cent and keep it there, but he has. He has also restored the nation's reserves to almost two billion dollars. He has renewed payments to the international banking community, which were suspended by his predecessor, and, by successfully concluding negotiations with hundreds of private banks that had lawsuits pending against Peru, he has opened up the international money flow again. He has balanced the budget, primarily by dismissing thousands of employees from a fat bureaucracy, putting dozens of state-owned enterprises up for sale, and reducing government investment to nearly zero.

The President is less forthcoming when it comes to discussing the incidental expenses of what is known as the Fujishock. Two and a half years ago, the number of people living below the poverty line—unable to afford rent, utilities, and food staples—was seven million. Today, the number is twelve million—about half the population. The number of government-assisted soup kitchens has risen from one thousand to four thousand in Lima alone—a figure that does not include many thousands of communally operated kitchens, where a majority of shantytown residents get their only real meal of the day. A cholera epidemic that broke out after the Fujishock left thousands dead in 1991. Last year, the incidence in Peru of tuberculosis—a disease directly related to poverty—was for the first time higher than that in any other country in Latin America, and recently even cases of bubonic plague have been reported. The G.N.P. keeps shrinking. Comparable statistics elsewhere in the hemisphere have caused riots and brought governments to their knees, yet Fujimori, though he has lately begun to subside in the polls, nevertheless retains a high overall popularity rating, and the cleverest political analysts and newspaper columnists are hard put to it to give reasons. There are at least some partial explanations. His hatred of politicians helps a great deal; the more or less unbroken record of official corruption, cynicism, and incompetence here makes for embarrassing reading. The loathing for him expressed by an increasingly disoriented and impotent white establishment also helps; the President's outsider status as a descendant of Japanese shopkeepers and as a former agronomy professor is much appreciated by the brutally marginalized poor, who suffer a burden of racism and exploitation rarely equalled in Latin America.

After the April dictatorial decrees, Fujimori's opponents thought that they had more than enough moral ammunition with which to bring him down, but it turned out that most people liked the *autogolpe,* because Fujimori closed down Congress. The coup has been followed by a series of increasingly arbitrary Presidential statements and measures, and by a sweeping campaign against virtually every national politician—a grab bag of people who detest each other but whom the President now accuses, unconvincingly, of conspiring with dozens of military officers who appear to have wanted to overthrow him and, Fujimori says, assasinate him. One result of all this heavy-handedness is that Fujimori, who used to be known everywhere as El Chinito—the Little Chinaman—is now referred to, more respectfully, as El Chino. Even among his opponents, there is an unaffectionate but steady conviction that, unlike his predecessors, he at least gets things done. Fidel Castro used to say that revolution is like a bicycle: if you stop pedalling, it falls down. In that sense, El Chino knows how to ride a bike. He issues decrees with great frequency, keeps a firm hand on the economy, overturns institutions at the drop of a hat, and delights in the kind of effrontery that, for example, led him recently, at graduation ceremonies for Navy cadets, to point out to the new officer corps just how corrupt their institution is. Of course, Fujimori has the other Presidente to thank for a good part of his popularity: Guzmán's arrest may have made him politically unassailable for all time. Yet, in what Guzmán would no doubt leap to point out as a dialectical unity of opposites, it can also be argued that Fujimori's economic program—the pauperization he has enforced on the already very poor—accounts for a good part of the measurable support for Presidente Gonzalo, and for Sendero's swift growth in the last couple of years.

AYACUCHO, an impoverished town surrounded by bare rocks, dry streams, and empty fields, is where it all began a quarter of a century ago. I flew there in November on the day before nation-wide elections, scheduled by Fujimori, for a Constituent Assembly that has replaced the closed-down Congress. I was told to travel light, for Sendero traditionally protests elections by calling armed strikes, whose most immediate target is public transportation. On such days, Ayacuchanos who have to travel know that it is preferable to walk the mile or so between the town and the airport, luggage in hand, rather than risk a Sendero reprisal. In the event, the strike either was not called or was only feebly enforced—no one seemed to know which—and I was able to take a taxi to the Hotel de Turistas, which these days is inhabited mostly by local officials, who live in the heavily guarded hotel because they do not feel safe from Sendero in their homes.

Carlos Abimael Guzmán was hired as a philosophy professor by the University of San Cristóbal of Huamanga, situated in the Ayacucho town square, in 1963. He had earned a doctorate in philosophy and practiced law in his home town of Arequipa, a lovely and prosperous city a world away from the upper Andes, and then had travelled around the country, teaching here and there, until fate delivered him to the one town in Peru where backwardness and an eagerness for modernity, and vast social rancor of poor against rich, Indians against whites, and provincials against Limeños, were most poisonously concentrated.

Guzmán harbored some rancor of his own. He was the polite, studious, and illegitimate son of a prosperous importer, who he appears to feel slighted him—treatment he is said to resent to this day. He was also a *provinciano*, which meant that in Lima,

despite his doctorate and a weighty thesis on Kant, he was condemned to remain always a scrofulous outsider, a hick in a funny
suit and a bad haircut trying to make it in the world of people
who count. In Ayacucho, however, it was he who was from
the big town: no one at the university had read more books or
could quote from them more impressively. The current rector of
Huamanga, Pedro Villena Hidalgo, who in the mid-nineteen-
seventies played a significant part in the ouster of Sendero Luminoso from its academic power base, was among the few who were
not star-struck. Late one afternoon, I talked to him in his office,
which is presently his home as well, because, like everyone else
who has crossed Guzmán in the past, he fears for his life; he
leaves the relative safety of his guarded administrative compound
as seldom as possible. It was a holiday, and was nearly dark; every
time the outside door creaked, he shifted uneasily in his chair.

When Villena arrived from Lima, in 1973, to teach chemical
engineering, Ayacucho had just acquired its first air link to the
capital, in the form of two rattletrap commercial flights a week.
He found temporary living quarters near the plaza, in a run-
down, ancient house with a dirt courtyard and no running water,
where the owner felt it necessary to place one of her indentured
servants, or *pongos*, at Villena's disposal. Until Villena protested,
the *pongo* slept on the slag-stone floor outside his bedroom every
night, ready to bring a glass of water or empty a chamber pot. In
these and other ways, Ayacucho struck Villena as semifeudal. In
reality, however, it was undergoing drastic changes: electricity,
water-treatment plants, and television-transmission stations were
finally being put in, along with a stadium and a cultural center,
and changes were being made in the university itself. Headed by
a progressive rector and with bright young leftist teachers hired,
like Guzmán, largely from around the provinces, Huamanga ac-
tively recruited students from among the sons and daughters
of the *pongos*—students who were first-generation literates, put
through school, at huge sacrifice, by their families.

Villena didn't think much of the academic level. "Guzmán's
second-in-command used to teach that 'communism' was a derivative of 'commune,' and that was about as far as theory got," he

recalls. Yet for the proud, ambitious new students the lessons about dialectical materialism, evolution, and matter in motion were world-changing events. "You have to realize that until the day we graduated from high school all of us believed that the first man was Adam and the first woman was Eve," a former student of Guzmán's told me. "Once we had learned that the Bible could be wrong, everything was up for grabs." Guzmán taught this student that Marxism was the culmination of fifteen billion years of evolution, leading from the first gestation of matter to the amoeba, the dinosaurs, pithecanthropus and the French Revolution, right through to dialectical materialism and the unity of opposites. And he reminded him and the other students constantly that the fact that they were at the university made them privileged but that, this man added, "in Lima they would always look down on us, because we were from the provinces."

Guzmán at the time was no more radical than any of the other teachers who were convinced that socialist revolution was the only way to dynamite Peru out of its cruel, idiotic stupor, but he was the only one equipped with such gravitas or with such a comely, intense, and fervently ideological wife. Augusta La Torre, who graduated from the Ayacucho nuns' school, was the daughter of the local Communist Party leader, and the legend that surrounds her speaks of her mad determination to escape the suffocating provincialism of Ayacucho by waging war on it. She is said to have had herself sterilized, so that she would never be distracted from her revolutionary task by succumbing to the temptation to have children. And she also made other crucial decisions in her life based solely on their revolutionary worthiness, according to a man who loved her so much that he still catches his breath at the mention of her. "She told me that she would not marry me, because Guzmán was the one who was destined to carry our revolutionary task to completion," he said to me. "He was the one with the theoretical grounding. She wanted to keep on seeing me anyway, but that was something I couldn't do as a man." The frustrated lover became wistful. "What I know about Augusta is that she was fulfilled politically, but she wasn't happy as a woman." Like other people in Ayacucho who knew the couple well, he is convinced that Guzmán would never have propelled himself and his group of followers into armed struggle if he had not been constantly urged on by La Torre. She was the group's most persistent and most successful organizer, and work that she did in the nationwide teachers' union provided the base that has allowed Sendero to influence, and even recruit, school-children, whom Senderistas see as the only noncorrupt force in society. Five years ago, after she began to suffer from a serious heart condition, La Torre committed suicide rather than leave the country for treatment. She is the greatest hero in Sendero's pantheon.

The road from the university to revolution was long: there were years spent by Guzmán building up a power base in the Revolutionary Federation of Students, or FER, which was essentially a Communist Party front organization; there was the 1963 Sino-Soviet split, which in Peru took the form of a long discussion at a secret meeting of the Partido Comunista Peruano, Sector Ayacucho, in which Guzmán doggedly refused to back down from a demand that, as Mao would have wished, Stalin be included in the list of honorary members of the presidium, along with Marx, Lenin, and José Carlos Mariátegui, a Peruvian socialist visionary. (This split gave rise to the name by which the Communist Party of Peru is now generally known: the FER split also, and Guzmán's followers, to distinguish themselves from the revisionists in the pro-Moscow FER, appended the tag line "Down the Shining Path of José Carlos Mariátegui" to their name.) After the split came a long trip by Guzmán to China, sometime between 1965 and 1968, followed by an even longer, comfortable stint as head of personnel for Huamanga University. For six years, from a tiny office that sat like a guard post directly opposite a fig tree in the university's cobbled patio, Guzmán determined staff appointments, kept a close watch on who taught what, and supervised the school cafeteria and dormitories, with their vitally important subsidies for the campesino students. It was during these glory days that Sendero Luminoso, in all seriousness, came up with the theory that Huamanga University was "objectively" destined to be the seedbed of the Peruvian revolution.

There were setbacks; in 1969, Guzmán and his disciples were expelled from the pro-Maoist Communist Party he had helped create. Then, in the mid-seventies, they were ousted from the university bureaucracy by a coalition of anti-Maoist, anti-Guzmán leftists, and had to take their organizing work into the surrounding countryside, where some Sendero anthropologists and schoolteachers had established contacts.

Even in the bad years, though, the cult of Guzmán continued to grow. Carlos Tapia, who was then another Huamanga firebrand and is now one of Guzmán's most perceptive critics, recalls that one day he was invited by a friend to a baptismal celebration. Referring to Guzmán by his nickname, which reflected his acknowledged brainwashing skills, the friend said, "Shampoo Guzmán is the godfather, and there will be lots of food and drink." Tapia found that the *chicha* and barbecue were indeed plentiful at the party, but he saw no sign of a baptized baby. Eventually, it was explained to him that the host, a man named Juan Alberto, was celebrating his own baptism: in honor of the man he admired more than any other, he had gone to the civil registry and had his name changed from Juan Alberto to Juan Abimael. "And Guzmán seemed to think that this was an unremarkable and entirely appropriate thing to do," Tapia says.

"From the day I met Abimael, I knew that he was incapable both of walking a whole city block and of killing a man, and when I saw him on television the other day I knew I had been right." Thus the man who loved Augusta La Torre stumbled on what is probably the principal source of Shampoo Guzmán's appeal: the Guzmán of the leaked arrest tapes, like the Guzmán of Ayacucho memory, is placid and solicitous of his inferiors; possessed of great book learning and a dense, professorial self-esteem; incapable, in his monumental dignity, of causing hurt of any kind. But this unthreatening, physically lax side of Guzmán, while attractive, would not account for his ability to hypnotize if it were not for an added element of danger. In Ayacucho, he was not only ponderous and courtly; he was also a *misti*—a powerful white man. In Lima, he was quite literally invisible until the day of his arrest: throughout the bloody decade that followed

Sendero's armed début, in 1980, the organization released no photographs of its leader, and, with one lengthy exception, he gave no interviews—not to the local press, not to influential international media, and not to any of the friendly publications from the many solidarity groups that were springing up in Europe and the United States. In this void, a private, monstrous image of Guzmán took shape in each Peruvian's mind—an image that was powerfully reinforced when the caged madman in prison stripes was finally put on display. A psychotherapist friend of mine confessed that following the caged press conference, she, too, like her patients, was having nightmares about him. Then *that* image was blurred, contradicted, and made infinitely more potent by the leaked arrest tapes, which showed Guzmán gravely asking about the welfare of his fellow-prisoners, and guarded by the love of his compañera. That Presidente Gonzalo was able to combine in his single person the attributes of Guzmán the Avenger and Guzmán the Kindly Uncle is without a doubt the luckiest thing that ever happened to Sendero.

By 1980, Sendero was ready to go to war. In May, the group trashed the ballot boxes in the Ayacuchano village of Chuschi during the first democratic elections held in the country since 1964. By 1982, it was a presence in the Andean countryside. In the years since, Peruvians who once scorned Sendero as simply another mad leftist organization, and Peruvians who once paid it no mind, have spent many painful hours examining its formative period, sifting through the record of its failures and of Ayacucho's centuries of neglect, compiling anecdotes on the growth of Guzmán's ego and the parallel increase in his resentment—all in an attempt to explain the transmutation that took place in a group of university radicals in the nineteen-seventies and caused them to emerge from the Ayacucho crucible as a band of fundamentalist *justicieros*, ready to tear Peru apart in order to save it.

CARLOS IVÁN DEGREGORI, a Senderologist whose essay titles make good reading in themselves (one, on Guzmán, is called "How Difficult It Is to Be God"), in attempting to account for the bloodthirsty fundamentalism of a movement that began as a backcountry intellectuals' revolt, once described Sendero as a phenomenon in which the claustrophobic density of the Ayacucho environment generated a concentration of energy and mass out of all proportion to the group's apparent size or merit. The black hole created by this concentration of energy, the logic goes, devoured the Senderistas' reason, sense of proportion, and basic respect for life, whether their enemies' or their own. Perhaps this is enough to explain the years of rage and insane murder that followed—the disembowelling of children, the gouging out of young women's eyes, the castrations and hangings, the human bonfires.

In Peru, the years between 1983 and 1986 are outstanding chapters in the world annals of war and desolation which have been compiled by organizations like Amnesty International and Human Rights Watch. Thousands were butchered—by the Peruvian military or by Sendero. Entire villages emptied out. Hundreds of thousands of Quechua-speaking campesinos descended on the provincial capitals and then on Lima, fleeing Sendero's terror and the Army's horrific forms of blanket revenge. In Ayacucho, on the day after I talked to the rector of Huamanga University, I asked to be taken to a nearby village. All the nearby villages were abandoned, I was told, and no one was willing to take me as far as an inhabited one, because of fear of being seen on the road with a foreigner and ambushed by Sendero. Lima, always dysfunctional, is now virtually paralyzed by overload. Agricultural production has undergone trauma, and so has the national culture. One day in November, I went to an open-air "colosseum"—four back yards fenced together—in a poor Lima neighborhood where the Andes' greatest "scissor dancers," or ritual acrobatic performers, were competing for a prize. All the audience members I talked to were from the Andean region, and all had come to Lima fleeing the war. So had the dancers. Similarly, the country's best weavers, retablo artisans, and carvers are nearly all in Lima now, and only the luckier ones can continue to make a living at their craft.

From Sendero's singular point of view, the apocalyptic years in the mid-eighties were a triumph; by 1988, it was ready to stage a Great Party Congress to celebrate its successes and ponder the next move. A captured videotape of that meeting has allowed Peruvians a brief glimpse of Presidente Gonzalo at the moment of his crowning glory. His theories have just been elevated to the category of Gonzalo Thought, on a par with Mao's. Criticism and self-criticism have taken place, and although a de facto tenet of self-criticism is that the leader never engages in it, there has been, at the conclusion, an implicit acknowledgment by the Presidente that mistakes have been made, that perhaps the un-ending violence has been off-putting to people Sendero would like to consider *masas*, or followers. In the future, the goal will be to "broaden mass work"—that is, build up support organizations and kill more selectively—and move the focal point of the strug-gle from the country to the city. In the meeting room of the Party Congress, the floor is littered with cigarettes. On red-bunting-covered tables there are empty glasses, and Presidente Gonzalo, sitting at the center of the main table, is clearly a little buzzy, as happy as any of his comrades, a surprising number of whom are women. They are severe, nunlike in their dark Mao suits, but one is glowing radiantly, alight with love. She is Elena Iparraguirre, a middle-aged, middle-class widow and longtime militant whom Guzmán installed as his companion following Augusta La Torre's death. In the video, their relationship seems brand-new. Teas-ingly, she asks him to dance and, muttering "Let's see if I remem-ber how," he follows her onto the cigarette-strewn floor as the theme song from *Zorba the Greek* begins to play. There are little exclamations of surprise and pleasure from his audience as he moves into the music with the fluid solemnity of a walrus. He dances with great conviction and good rhythm while Iparraguirre encircles him with dainty steps and a shower of glances that are at once flirtatious, tender, and protective. His followers watch adoringly. One could almost wish them well.

Within months of this happy evening, Sendero's campaign against the cities began in earnest, and a self-effacing, sombre police colonel who would have preferred to be a psychiatrist, Antonio Ketín Vidal, joined the Dirección Nacional Contra el Terrorismo, a seven-year-old agency that was being given greater

power by the government of Alan García on the off chance that
it might have better luck against Sendero than the rampaging
troops who were earning Peru such a dismal human-rights reputation abroad but accomplishing little else. Vidal had been fascinated by Sendero for years—ever since, as a young intelligence
officer, he had met one of the group's high command and realized
how different the man was from the average leftist revolutionary.
But when Vidal arrived at Dincote he discovered that the agency
was equipped with only two telephone lines, a handful of operatives, and not a single computer to keep track of its files. Vidal
was obsessed with files. Night after night, he sifted through
them, updating and correcting, tracing networks and interrela-
tionships. His admiration for Guzmán—for his commitment, for
the efficiency with which he used scarce resources, for his learning, and for his disciplined attention to security—grew apace.
Vidal slept little, ate little, and listened to Wagner and Chopin
for relaxation. He might have made progress, but three months
after he joined Dincote he was abruptly—and inexplicably—
dismissed.

It might have been possible to capture Guzmán back then.
For years, he had been living much as he was living at the moment of his arrest: in Lima, shuttled between safe houses in the
trunk of a car, usually driven by one of the women who so loved
to take care of him. Investigators who traced Guzmán's steps for
years confirm that, contrary to rumor, he neither drank heavily
nor womanized—he worked. Although, as the organization
grew, he had increasing difficulty overseeing as many aspects of
it as he would have liked, he appears to have been responsible
for its general strategy and specific plans throughout. He read
newspapers, received reports, and, occasionally, wrote tracts—
although, if the published record is any indication, he is neither
an inspired nor a perceptive theoretician.

Oddly, a long slog through his collected writings and
speeches does not reveal even any instinctive feeling for or empa-
thy with Peru: the country's ethnic diversity, its racism, its heart-
stopping mountain vistas, its maddening bureaucracy are nowhere mentioned. Nor is the word "Quechua," or the unflinching

industriousness of its people. Just as the attempts at art produced by Sendero look like copies of old propaganda photographs from *China Reconstructs*, so the texts of Presidente Gonzalo read like bad Mao. He always begins his expositions with an imitation of the neutral, pedagogical tone that Mao mastered, but he has none of Mao's epigrammatic gift, and his rhetoric is alarmingly, perhaps even psychotically, inconsistent. Just minutes after beginning a calm exposition of the state of the nation, he will lapse into the barking, bloodthirsty mode for which he is best known: "The people, enraged, arm themselves and rise in rebellion . . . tear the reactionaries' flesh to shreds, and these black tatters it will sink into the bog, what remains it will set on fire and throw the ashes into the wind."

In practice, these exhortations translated into the murder of a woman I once met briefly, María Elena Moyano, and the take-over of a series of organizations that she and other members of the nonviolent left had built up painstakingly over the years. Moyano was an original member of Peru's largest squatter settle-ment, Villa El Salvador, which currently has a population of about three hundred and fifty thousand and a place in the history of social movements as a brilliant example of grass-roots organiz-ing. Moyano was active in the Women's Federation in Villa, as it is known, whose members organized soup kitchens and ran day-care centers and health clinics, and she was also a founder of the Villa branch of the Vaso de Leche, or Glass of Milk, movement. Vaso de Leche depends on donated food supplies—milk, primar-ily—to provide a nutritious breakfast for children who would otherwise eat very little; but supplies, and particularly those do-nated by the government, are fitful. Vaso de Leche's members have become expert at persuading the government to coöperate: whenever the authorities get negligent, the women take to the streets of downtown Lima, and, after a fairly well-established rit-ual involving tear gas, high-pressure water hoses, and police clubs on the part of the authorities and much jeering and dodging on the part of the women, the supplies are usually resumed.

The last time I saw María Elena Moyano, a forceful, strongly built black woman with a golden smile, was at one such demonstration a couple of years ago. She was too busy yelling into a megaphone about the obscene, scandalous increases in the cost of staying alive, and about the government's bald attempts to co-öpt her organization, and about the rage that every mother taking part in the march felt at watching her children go hungry, to pay much attention to me and my questions. It is strange now to see this militant, radical woman proclaimed a heroine, and "one of the best generals in the war," by the very establishment that used to despise her and her fellow-activists as rabble and curse them for tying up traffic. But she is an official hero now, because the powers that be have come to understand with urgent clarity that the only thing separating the vast mass of the poor from Sendero Luminoso is the radical but nonviolent left represented by the likes of Moyano. This conclusion is so unassailable that even Sendero agrees with it.

I recently went to the place in Villa where, last February, Moyano was murdered. My guide was a nun who happened to be about a block away when Moyano, returning from a rare day at the beach with her two small sons and a twelve-year-old nephew, stopped for a meeting with fellow-members of the Women's Federation. The women were gathered in one of the communal halls that are a feature of all of Villa's carefully de-signed "social areas"—arid, graceless spots that nevertheless in-clude a playground, a clinic, a soup kitchen, and a day-care center, as well as the meeting hall. From the playground, an un-known woman approached, gun in hand and backed by several youths, who were also armed. Moyano's friends tried to form a protective circle around her when they saw the intruder, but she said, "This is for me," and stepped out to deal with the armed woman. She was shot. Her weeping nephew tried unsuccessfully to prevent the murderer and her accomplices from igniting a stick of dynamite they had tied to Moyano's body. When the nun I spoke to arrived on the scene, a few minutes later, there was nothing to be done except say a final prayer.

At the time of her death, Moyano was deputy mayor of the Villa municipality and was considering running for mayor of Lima. Last month, the man who succeeded her as deputy mayor,

Ramón Galindo, was himself slain—shot six times as his family looked on. Today, the current mayor of Villa lives surrounded by bodyguards and in fear of his life, and someone who is close to him told me, in a voice strained by months of tension, that virtually all the community organizations that used to be a part of Villa's exemplary political structure are under Senderista control. "Go visit them," she said, "but don't tell them you've spoken to us, or you'll be the enemy." I did as she suggested, and found myself travelling through Villa in the company of a woman who claimed to have no connection with Sendero but made sure I cleared every checkpoint in the slum where youths stopped our taxi and demanded to know my business there. "All the old politicians have failed us," the woman said. "Like Moyano, they lied and stole from us and acted as informants for the government, saying we were Senderistas. She deserved to be killed, and now we have taken power into our own hands."

SHORTLY AFTER MOYANO was killed, Guzmán changed safe houses for the last time, to the comfortable quarters directly above Maritza Garrido Lecca's modern-dance studio. It is not clear whether Maritza was originally recruited by her aunt, Nelly Evans, who used to do community work in shantytowns like Villa El Salvador, and who, practically from the day she left the convent, some twenty years ago, began recruiting for a nonviolent Maoist group with links to Sendero. Perhaps Maritza was recruited instead by her husband, a tense young architect who, around the time he began his relationship with her, is said to have approached a friend, full of anguish because he wanted to leave Sendero but didn't know how. It is unlikely that Maritza, who, as a dancer, had a demanding life of her own in what might be considered a frivolous and self-centered occupation, was a very high-ranking Sendero member. More probably, she was simply a young woman looking to make sense of the mindless chaos that is Peru, taking up Senderismo as acquaintances of hers took up herbal medicine or massage therapy, and being used eagerly by Sendero, which saw her occupation as an excellent cover for Guzmán. There is another videotape—of Maritza in her studio,

giving an introductory lesson in Nickolaus technique to an unseen student, and then crossing the dance floor on the diagonal,
in a Graham-technique plié run. Her shoulders are too tense and
high, the spiral of her back has little flow to it, and instead of
looking up and out into the distance she seems to be staring
straight up at the ceiling, toward the room overhead where Guzmán is hiding.

General Vidal, who three years after his removal from Dincote had been appointed to head the agency by the Fujimori government, is said to have had no idea that it was Guzmán himself
he was tracking down in the little dance studio in the Surquillo
neighborhood, just off a small park where mothers bring their
children to play. On his return, Vidal had found a more professional agency with a slightly bigger budget, a few more phone
lines, and even a computer. Within weeks, he raided a house in
which Guzmán had been hiding only minutes before, and a few
months later—last August—he acquired several more computers, as a result of his first major strike against Sendero: his men
raided a college and captured several members of Sendero's Central Committee, in charge of logistics for the entire organization,
along with several of its computers and dozens of diskettes
loaded with Sendero files. As Guzmán himself admitted later, this
was a stunning blow, from which the organization was still recovering at the time of his own arrest. Dincote has a reputation for
avoiding what are known here as "scientific interrogation" techniques. Its success is due instead to its reliance on investigative
procedures that in hindsight seem obvious: Dincote officers followed the relatives and friends of captured Senderistas on their
way back from jail visits; they sifted through trash, and studied
discarded reading material; they networked; and, inspired by
Vidal's single-minded dedication, they refused to take bribes.

There is some confusion regarding the precise sequence of
events that led to the moment on September 12th when some
forty Dincote agents crashed into Maritza Garrido Lecca's studio
and arrested her, her husband, two terrified family visitors, and,
upstairs, Guzmán and Iparraguirre along with two other high-
ranking Senderistas. The National Intelligence Service, which

has been made to look somewhat ineffectual by the arrests, would like to take some credit for them, and sources close to the service insist that its office had captured and "scientifically interrogated" Elena Iparraguirre's brother, and that his testimony led to the discovery of Guzmán days later. This seems unlikely: Why would the intelligence service have handed the information over to a rival agency? What definitely did happen is that minutes before the raid on the Surquillo house a separate detachment of Dincote agents raided another, and found in it large quantities of Sendero documents and other sources of information. Minutes later, the detachment led by Vidal himself burst into Garrido Lecca's house and seized Guzmán, who, seeing them, commented mildly, "Yes, it was my turn to lose. Congratulations."

IT USED TO BE that journalists in Lima who wanted to interview Senderistas had only to hail an ancient VW taxicab—the Peruvian national vehicle—and head for Canto Grande prison, where a special cellblock was reserved for captured Shining Path militants. The prisoners kept the floors there spotless. In the women's pavilion, little curtains of neatly patched-together newspaper hung between the cots. In the courtyard, murals decorated the clean walls. Smiling compañeras offered biscuits. Others explained the revolution's goals. Songs were sung. Chants were chanted. Praise was voiced for the universal struggle of the proletariat. The world and its disasters were explained in simple paragraphs. Often the women performed a song-and-march routine straight out of the Cultural Revolution, with red caps, Mao suits, and red flags, and one could understand how powerful was the dream of perfect order which fuelled the Senderistas, how great their need to create a utopia as much unlike the dismal real Peru as possible.

Today, such easy access to the revolution is no longer possible: Sendero, which lately began to express a new eagerness for international publicity and press contacts, is in hiding. Much of the Central Committee is in prison. Last May, a government attempt to retake the Sendero wing of Canto Grande prison was successful only after thirty-six Senderistas were killed.

A great many people have been lulled into the conviction that Sendero is as dead as it is out of view, but this is to ignore one of the most interesting problems the organization faced in the last couple of years, which is that, as of its move into Lima, Sendero grew at a phenomenal rate—so much so that the rigid control the Central Committee had normally exercised became difficult. In the shantytowns and at all levels of the education system, Sendero is—if not exactly the mass organization its members aspire to—very definitely a force to contend with. I looked for Sendero cadres all over Lima, and probably found them.

In a highly politicized squatters' settlement plunked in the middle of an expanse of sand dunes, I talked with an anxious young woman whose husband, hauled in by the Army several times for questioning, had finally been surrounded on the street one day by men in uniform and never seen again. Other people were in the room where the woman told her story: there was the compañero head of the local block organization, the compañera head of the food kitchens, and a compañero who slipped into the meeting halfway through, offered a memorably sweaty hand-shake, and kept his face turned away, an ear cocked toward me, for the rest of the session. There was a compañero lawyer who came to me with information about human-rights violations against suspected Senderistas, who had an equally damp hand-shake, and who worked himself into a froth when I asked him about certain gruesome murders committed by Sendero. "Human-rights organizations care only about the rights of the bourgeoisie," he said, biting on each word. "But what about the rights of the thousands of children who die of malnutrition every year in Peru?" And there was a compañera *profesora* and teachers'-union organizer, who also talked about human rights and then reacted with fury at the sight of a few scribbled and torn-up note-books her students had left lying about the schoolyard. "Even children so young are corrupted by the system and show no re-spect at all for our efforts!" she exclaimed in disgust. I gave her a ride downtown, and on the way we passed a recreation center for the national police whose walls were covered with Coca-Cola signs. The schoolteacher, barely able to contain her enthusiasm, told me that the walls were a Sendero victory of sorts. Despite the best efforts of the police, she said, Senderistas used to cover the walls of the center with graffiti night after night. In the end, the red-and-white Coca-Cola logos were the only way the police could insure that Sendero's slogans, which are always painted in red, would at least not be visible. Because of the circumstances in which we met, and what I knew about her already, there was no doubt in my mind that she was a Senderista, but, like the others, she would not reveal herself in that role to me.

Julián, when I made contact with him, was pleasingly different. We talked in a cafeteria in San Marcos University, the nation's largest, which is currently surrounded by tanks and constantly patrolled by soldiers. A couple of years ago, this campus, which is operated on a skeletal budget by the government, looked like a nightmare set in the New York City subway system. Revolutionary posters and graffiti covered every wall of overcrowded classrooms and hallways. Periodically, Sendero would stage mass rallies, which sometimes would take place in the evening, in coördination with the dynamiting of electrical pylons, so that while the city was plunged into darkness torches set out in the shape of a hammer and sickle on the campus hillside would shine in the night. Now that the Army has come, San Marcos's walls are clean, there are no demonstrations, and Julián and I were free to chat comfortably while I took notes and he made no effort to keep his voice down. He was cheerful and dry-palmed, was obviously intelligent, and, despite his teen-age looks, was endowed with self-confidence and an unmistakable gift for leadership. He wished to be identified only as a compañero *democrático*, who could not speak for the Party, but soon "we"s and "our"s were flying through his conversation, particularly when he explained how truly democratic Sendero is. "We all coexist here peacefully," he said. "And even though we're the majority, we respect everyone else. They say we beat the students up, but we don't just beat up anyone. Say someone from the opposition wants to put up one of its posters next to one of ours. That's pluralism, and we tolerate it. But say they *tear down* one of our posters to put up one of theirs. That is an attack against our organization, and it must be punished. And if they persist, then they must be annihilated."

He talked on and on, full of confidence in the perfect logic of everything he said. Could I disagree that in Peru the vast majority live lives that are an affront to human dignity? Or that whether dictators ruled or whether elected demagogues were in power has made little difference to the poor? Could anyone object to the sacrifice he himself was making, living on the run and in virtual certainty of a horrid early death just so the people could at last be free? Yes, undeniably, people were afraid of Sendero at first, but once the masses became familiar with it they accepted Sendero's work. "The left in this country has always promised everything. My father himself was involved in the union movement for a long time, but where did that get him? Through our very radicalism, people understand that we are here until final victory. And they come to understand that our justice is right. Everyone here knows someone in the Glass of Milk program who is stealing the supplies, everyone now understands that María Elena Moyano was an enemy. Didn't the establishment press call her one of its best generals? What more proof do you need of her miserable nature?"

I asked him whether, now that Guzmán had been captured, he remained convinced that his leader was infallible.

Julián hesitated. "Perhaps as a person he may have made mistakes," he finally said. "That's only human. But in his thinking Presidente Gonzalo has shown a magisterial interpretation of our reality. People say that we repeat phrases like parrots, but what is wrong with repeating scientific truth? If his theory hadn't been proved in practice over and over again, would it have been elevated to the category of Gonzalo Thought? Of course his capture has been a blow for us, but it was not a surprise; we always knew that he could be captured, or that he could die, like any human being. What is important is that the Party is in place. Presidente Gonzalo once said that as long as a single member of the Central Committee remains alive, as long as a single Communist remains alive, victory will be ours. Now the eyes of the world's proletariat

are anxiously on us, waiting to see how history is being made. As
Presidente Gonzalo said, we are condemned to win."

TOWARD THE BEGINNING of Presidente Gonzalo's caged presentation in September, there was a moment when he interrupted
himself to address his press audience's demand that he answer
questions instead of making a speech. "If you want an interview,
put in your requests with the government, and then we'll see," he
shouted back. Twelve days earlier, at the time of his capture, he
had congratulated General Vidal on his skill and, as the video
cameras rolled, delivered a short statement to the effect that fate
can make enemies of two men who pursue different paths in life,
but that "this does not mean that they can't respect each other."
One can guess what he was thinking as he addressed his extraordinarily polite and deferential captor: in the future, there would
be captivity, yes, but there would also be time to read, and reflect
on the great events coming to pass, and—why not?—to indulge
Vidal in a little fireside game of chess, two geniuses facing each
other across the board.

A few weeks ago, the newsletter *Peru Report* published an account of Guzmán's current situation. Fifteen days after Guzmán's
arrest, the military won a frenzied bureaucratic skirmish with Vidal's Dincote for custody of Peru's most illustrious prisoner, and
made it clear that in Guzmán's future there would be no room for
press interviews or civilized respect for one's enemies. Following
a three-day military trial, Guzmán has been sentenced to spend
the rest of his life in a windowless basement cell at the San Lo-
renzo Island naval base, off the coast of Lima. Presidente Gonzalo has no access to books or newspapers and is under constant
surveillance. He has grown irritable, the newsletter says, and suffers from the psoriasis now left untreated and compounded by
the stress of his imprisonment. He may die soon. One of the first
priorities for the newly elected Constituent Assembly—in which
Fujimori has a majority—is to authorize the death penalty. It
would be unconstitutional to make that penalty retroactive in order to apply it to Guzmán, but the Constitution, after all, has
been suspended by Fujimori, who is known to be very keen on

Guzmán's death. In fact, there were widely circulated rumors that he was irritated with General Vidal for having failed to kill his captive on the spot, which may help explain why Vidal was summarily relieved of his post on January 4th.

There is a rare video portrait of Sendero in a documentary that was broadcast last year by England's Channel 4, and which is now distributed in home video format by Sendero's solidarity committees in the United States. In the film, a few dozen campesinos are shown marching through the countryside, carrying a red banner, in one of the guerrilla group's Andean "support bases." The peasants are native Quechua speakers, desperately poor, traditionally dressed, unsmiling, and slightly stooped. As the peasants approach on the screen, the first words the audience hears from them are "Long live the Strategic Equilibrium!" in heavily accented Spanish. One can imagine the dizzying thrill of empowerment that lies in pronouncing such scientific, modern words, and in explaining that they refer to the balance of force achieved under Presidente Gonzalo's leadership in Sendero's battle against a corrupt and rotten state.

Strictly speaking, of course, they should be shouting not "Viva" but "Muera" to the Equilibrio Estratégico, since it is not meant to perdure. In the beginning, the Senderistas spoke sagely of a struggle that might take generations, and, calling forth images of the millenarian patience of the peasantry, stated that they were in no hurry. But the very real urgency of their masas has overtaken Sendero, as have their own striking successes and the stubborn inclination of the Peruvian state to keep heading for the void. That Sendero may be able to triumph, now or in the next generation, remains an inconceivable thought, but every aspect of Peruvian reality seems inconceivable. In his sombre prison cell, the Fourth Sword of Marxism continues to imagine things that cannot be, and his children—the multiplying squadrons of Juliáns spawned by Gonzalo Thought—strain to catch his dreams and obey them.

Postscript, Lima

ON OCTOBER 6, 1993, just one year after his arrest and trial, Presidente Gonzalo once again appeared before astonished television viewers. With Elena Iparraguirre at his side, the leader of the Shining Path read an open letter to President Alberto Fujimori whose terms and wording evoked Fujimori's pedestrian style more than the other Presidente's extravagant rantings.

"Events show that your Administration has achieved objective advances," Abimael Guzmán told the camera. "And in what refers more directly to us . . . under your political direction, you have developed a systematic and coherent strategy on several levels, especially in the field of intelligence, attaining real successes, principally the capture of cadre and leaders, including the undersigned. . . . Thus, in the Party's current circumstances, just as yesterday we sought to start the people's war, today with equal firmness and resolve a Peace Agreement must be struggled for."

Three weeks later, on October 31st, Peruvian voters approved a new Constitution that will allow Fujimori to run for reëlection and remain in power until the year 2001, and possibly for an additional term after that. The new Constitution also approves the death penalty for terrorists, but given Guzmán's performance on television, he is not likely to suffer the effects of this reform.

RIO
1993

"Brazilians discovered virtual reality years ago."

ON TUESDAY, DECEMBER 29TH, 1992, Fernando Collor de Mello became the first President in Brazil's history to be impeached, accused of standing by while his éminence grise fleeced an impoverished population of millions upon millions of dollars on his behalf. The Senate's vote to remove him from office had been preceded by a lengthy investigation, and by a wave of protest that put hundreds of thousands of people on the streets to demand his ouster. Depending on how one looked at it, Fernando Collor's congressional indictment represented either a new and thrilling empowerment of a population no longer willing to put up with reckless arrogance on the part of its leaders or a depressing watershed in this country's long search for decent government. In any event, the nation's future hung in the balance. Unfortunately, the people of Brazil, and particularly the people of Rio de Janeiro, were too distracted to pay much attention while history was being made. Less than twenty-four hours before the final Senate vote, which decided the President's fate, a television starlet had been found dead on a roadside on the outskirts of Rio de Janeiro, her body perforated by sixteen stab wounds. It was this news that galvanized the nation.

The murder of Daniella Perez—twenty-two, conventionally pretty, and irrelevant to the fate of the country—was merely one

287

of almost four thousand homicides that take place in Rio every year. But the widespread shock and outrage at this particular crime completely overshadowed not only the Senate's impeachment vote but Fernando Collor's face-saving letter of resignation. The substance of the nightly newscast on all the networks was devoted to Daniella. Headlines screamed her name. Foreign correspondents covering the impeachment in Brasília fumed at missing the real story in Rio. On the Sunday following the murder, the main papers published special impeachment supplements; at the beach, Brazilians by the thousand tossed the special sections into the garbage and settled down to read the latest on Daniella Perez. Collor was, after all, merely an unloved politician; Daniella was—and remains—a cherished family member for the forty million souls who tuned in every evening at eight-thirty to watch her in her first big role, in the *telenovela* "De Corpo e Alma" ("Body and Soul").

She was not even the star—just a featured player in one of the multiple subplots on which *telenovelas* depend to keep a story going for at least a hundred and eight daily (except Sunday) chapters. She played Yasmin, a sweet young ticket-puncher on a Rio bus line, whose life was occasionally made difficult by the obsessive, threatening jealousy of her boyfriend, Bira, the bus driver on the line. Within hours of the crime, Guilherme de Pádua, a moody, wooden actor who played Bira, confessed to detectives that he was Daniella's killer. Soon the press was feasting on other ghoulish coincidences between reality and melodrama: One of the subplots featured an older woman who gets involved with a male stripper; it turned out that Guilherme was himself a former male stripper. Guilherme and Daniella were brought together on the set by Daniella's mother, Glória, who is one of the better-known *telenovela* authors, and whose script for "Corpo e Alma" was notoriously lurid. She approved Guilherme de Pádua for the bus driver's role. The romance between the ticket-puncher and the bus driver was initially presented as light comic relief for otherwise *escabroso* goings on, but Glória Perez's own inclination toward the heavily dramatic, and perhaps something she sensed in Guilherme's nature, made her write a disturbing and conflictive screen relationship between him and her daughter, full of jealous confrontations and near-violence.

"Brazilians discovered virtual reality years ago," a friend of mine said recently, commenting on the national reaction to the Daniella Perez murder. "They never know when they are entering the screen and when they are leaving it." The blurry confusion in the public mind between reality and fantasy when it came to the murder scandal—had Guilherme de Pádua killed Yasmin, or was it Bira who had killed Daniella Perez?—turned into full-fledged delirium at Daniella's funeral. It took place the day after the murder, just hours after Fernando Collor de Mello submitted his resignation, and on the kind of sweltering day when everyone in Rio who can afford the bus fare is normally at the beach. Vera Holtz, who in "Corpo e Alma" played the demure, fortyish housewife who falls passionately in love with the male stripper, has vivid memories of the day. "Absolutely everyone from the television company showed up—the stars, the featured actors, the bit players. And then there was the public"—so many people they literally didn't fit. Vera Holtz, who is an exuberant, lively woman, completely unlike the character she played in "Corpo e Alma," laughed and shook her head in dismay at the ludicrousness of the scene. "You know, in Brazil even funerals turn into parties—the corpse is out there in the living room, and in the kitchen there are mountains of food and everyone's telling jokes. Well, there was that multitude, and they had come to mourn, but the stars kept arriving, one by one, and the audience applauded, and asked for autographs, and climbed over the gravestones to get a closer look. 'There's So-and-So! Look at how handsome he is!' they'd scream, and then everyone would go rushing over to see him, knocking the gravestones down and breaking them, and it was broiling hot, and the photographers were in your face. The security people finally squeezed me out of there, but Glória Perez and Daniella's husband had to take refuge in a little chapel. Apparently, Glória had just found out from the police that it was Guilherme who had murdered her daughter. It was a great tragedy. The day that Daniella was murdered and Collor was impeached was the day of the great Brazilian tragedy."

The murder took place on a Monday; it was reported, along with Collor's impeachment and resignation, that Tuesday. By Thursday, the nation's emotional reserves were virtually spent on the past days' sorrows and horrors: Collor had resigned, Guilherme had confessed, Daniella's funeral had turned into a mob scene. But there was more to come, for on that day it became known that the material author of the murder may not have been Guilherme at all but his pretty, pregnant teen-age wife.

One may as well admit that a little *frisson* of delight crept into the national mood at this stage of the true-life drama. It was not just the inevitable guilty pleasure anyone might take at the profusion of gorgeous stars, ghoulish coincidences, and cliff-hanging to-be-continueds; it was the possibility of dreams come true. The statistics of misery in Brazil are well known: more than half the population is chronically hungry, seventy per cent has less than a sixth-grade education, and so forth. Less familiar is poverty's intersection with television viewing, which is a national passion. *Telenovelas* substitute for all the pleasures that most Brazilians cannot afford: the movies, the theatre, the circus, or, for that matter, the carnival parade or a soccer game, since the tickets are priced for tourists. (Even playing soccer is increasingly out of the reach of the poor; the empty lots and fields where geniuses like Pélé and Garrincha forged their technique have been swallowed up by urban development.) The prevalence of poverty, the national genius for fantasy, and the genius of one man—Roberto Marinho, the creator of the Globo television network and of the huge *telenovela* industry—have combined to make the hours between six and nine-thirty in the evening the most meaningful in Brazilian national life. Unlike television stations in the rest of Latin America, which subsist largely on dubbed series from the United States, during prime time TV Globo offers exclusively Brazilian *telenovelas*—glossy, lavishly produced melodramas written by some of the country's most highly respected authors and featuring its best actors. In this tropical country, more homes have television sets than have refrigerators, and from the apartment building in Ipanema where I am staying I can look out in the evening and see the screens' colored lights twinkling in every window: they flicker in the bedrooms of the high-rise luxury towers to my left and right; and in the hillside favela directly in front of me they glow brightly in shacks where an entire family often sleeps in a single room.

TV Globo officials like to point out that the program with the highest average audience share remains the half-hour evening news, but that program is not the one that gets discussed the following morning at the office. The news features characters like Collor de Mello or his replacement, the odorless, flavorless Itamar Franco, who seems incapable of more than pained expressions of dismay as the great ship of state sinks slowly into a mudbank. On the news, executives are kidnapped and murdered, state enterprises go bankrupt, drug lords wage war in the favelas, and sewer systems erupt in the streets, all of which is to say that in Brazilian terms nothing happens. In the *telenovelas*, executives are kidnapped and drug lords wage war in the favelas, but then the kidnapper is caught, the drug lord meets a nice girl and goes straight, the crooked executive's righteous son inherits the family business, and moral order is restored to the world. Things *change.* They change in precisely the same fashion in every single *novela*, which is as it should be, and during the daily three hours of first-run *telenovela* programming viewers can fantasize that the real Brazil is not the hopeless swamp of moral confusion and economic chaos that it sometimes feels like—not the place where citizens can freely and directly elect a President for the first time in twenty-nine years only to have him turn around and thumb his nose at them, for example—but a place where family values withstand all assaults, the poor eventually find jobs and always have enough to eat, and even the wicked can be redeemed. And, in that sense, the murder of Daniella Perez, the eerie resemblance between events onscreen and off, was thrilling, breathtaking evidence that reality could, even if only once, resemble the marvellous, lavish universe of the *telenovela*, so filled with potential and with the liberatingly unrealistic.

By general critical consent, "Corpo e Alma" was one of the more truly awful *telenovelas* ever presented, a compendium of the form's faults rather than its virtues. The saga of a woman with a heart transplant who falls in love with the lover of the heart's original owner, it played shamelessly to the audience's lust for soft porn and evildoing; it presented a universe in which decent souls are endlessly preyed upon by nasty manipulators, sexual perverts, kidnappers, and obsessively possessive lovers; it was violent; it was completely arbitrary in its plot outlines; it was, with few exceptions, plagued by mediocre acting. In the wake of the Perez murder, the Primate of Brazil, Dom Lucas Moreira Neves, wrote an unusually fierce editorial in the *Jornal do Brasil*, Rio's élite newspaper, accusing *novelas* like "Corpo e Alma" of fomenting violence through their exploitative story lines. "Who killed a young actress a few days ago?" the Primate wrote. "It would be ingenuous not to indict one of the co-authors, Brazilian television. The evening *telenovela* in general and—it pains me to say— the *novela* 'De Corpo e Alma.'"

The *novela* continued for two months after Daniella's murder, and, once all the scenes she had taped were used up, the producers and the author continued to present her in flashbacks. Reviewing the final episodes of the *telenovela*, in March, a reporter for the country's principal newsweekly, *Veja*, wrote, "There are no limits to the bad taste and scurrilousness which surface in the cast stuffed with models who failed their school acting classes and in the vulgarity of the bouncing male buttocks of the strippers." Despite such reviews, "Corpo e Alma" was an enormous success with the public. In fact, with rare exceptions, most TV Globo *novelas* are enormous successes, capturing as much as ninety per cent of the IBOPE, the local equivalent of Nielsen ratings. This is due partly to Globo's virtual stranglehold on the television industry, and partly to the skill of its *novela* production line, which turns out melodramas that, exploitative and manipulative as they may be, look like nothing else produced on television anywhere in the world.

IT WAS IN 1965 that Roberto Marinho—Doctor Roberto, as his employees tremulously address him—founded TV Globo. He was already known as the owner of Brazil's largest national daily, *O Globo*. Marinho, who, at the age of eighty-eight, remains fully in control of his empire and of his ability to inspire fear in the meek and the powerful, is a small-boned, wrinkled man who wears suits that look starched. Now that he has been elected to the Brazilian Academy of Letters—on the strength of a collection of his articles and the Academy's sincere hunger for patronage—he will also get to wear the fraternity's plumed hat and medal-studded cutaway.

Marinho rarely gives interviews, but in a recent moment of candor he did tell the journalist Mac Margolis, "Rightly or not, I always had a certain enthusiasm for the military governments." In a sense, his television network was a child of the 1964 military coup that turned Brazil into a military dictatorship for the next twenty-one years. Marinho shared the Generals' belief in order and progress, and their faith in capitalism—capitalism in its most corporatist, heavily state-sponsored form. Under the protective shadow of a strongly interventionist regime, the station grew at a phenomenal rate. Today, eight years after the generals stepped down, there are five television networks in Brazil, and they are theoretically competitive, but Globo has an estimated seventy per cent of the advertising and, at prime time on a bad day, thirty per cent of the audience. It has ninety-four affiliates—thirty-two more than its closest competitor. The half-hour evening news program, sandwiched between the second and the third of the three prime-time *telenovelas*, steadily captures fifty per cent of the audience share; that is about forty million viewers, out of a total potential audience of eighty-three million. Nearly three-quarters of Globo's broadcasting time is taken up with its own productions, while the other stations have had to make do with imported Mexican *novelas* and with Geraldo Rivera, dubbed into Portuguese. When a rival station, SBT, in a desperate move to make money, set up a lottery, TV Globo followed with its own version—promoted by no less a star than Xuxa, the very famous m.c. of a children's program here—which crushed the competition. Making money with a dubious variant on gambling was not the object, but, rather, preventing SBT from doing so. Globo routinely hires whatever talent is around, if only to keep it idle and dry up the rival pools. The most significant rival network, TV

Manchete, which is currently struggling with bankruptcy, produced three winning *telenovelas* over the years. One, "Pantanal"—
a sort of eco-fantasy full of long shots of beautiful naked women
bathing in unpolluted rivers—was one of the most successful of
all time. But all the actors, directors, and authors involved are
part of the Globo stable, which includes nearly six hundred
actors and thirty-one *novela* writers, every one of them on salary.

I met with the managing director of Globo's international division, Jorge Adib. A gruff sort of man, who talks in a gritty voice,
smokes big cigars, and favors broad lapels and mesmerizing ties,
Adib paid far less attention to me than to a European Cup soccer
match on a giant screen behind me, but his answers were tren-
chant. When I asked him what made Brazilian *telenovelas* different
from those in the rest of Latin America, he explained that the
lachrymose Mexican *telenovelas*—the pioneers that set the standard for the form—are static and studio-bound, as if they were
still reproducing the *radionovela* format that shaped the genre,
back in the nineteen-thirties. "They give emotions with words,"
Adib said, focussing momentarily on me. "We do it differently—
we create visual emotion. And so every time we have an emotion
we spend money. We spend an average of a hundred and twenty
thousand dollars per daily *novela* chapter. You think that's money?
We charge fifty-three thousand dollars, fifty-four thousand, for
every thirty-second commercial. We have an enormous market.
We have practically the entire audience in Brazil, and that's equal
to practically all the money in Brazil. And all the money in a
country of a hundred and forty million people is a lot of money."

ALL OF GLOBO'S MONEY and its considerable marketing skills
cannot avoid the occasional dud. There is one screening every
evening now, in the 7 p.m. slot, called "O Mapa da Mina" ("The
Map of the Mine"), which concerns a young novice who has had
the map to a treasure trove of diamonds tattooed on her buttocks.
Despite this promising beginning, the *novela* sank immediately,
and desperate rewrites and the emergency hiring of proven stars
have failed to bring it up from ratings bottom. At its best, however, the genre can produce masterpieces like "Roque Santeiro,"

a howlingly funny account of small-town religious hustlers and their ambitious wives and big-time plantation owners and their uncontrollable lusts. The performers in "Roque Santeiro" went so recklessly for broke, and the production values were so engagingly nostalgic and the story line so affectionately knowledgeable that movie houses and theatres throughout Brazil had to readjust their schedules around "Roque Santeiro"'s screening time to avoid bankruptcy.

The most beautiful four hours of television ever produced in Brazil are probably the opening chapters of the 8:30 p.m. *novela* that replaced "Corpo e Alma." It is called "Renascer" ("Rebirth") and is the saga of a cocoa baron—or *coronel*, in Portuguese—who is first seen as a youth staking his claim to a section of the dense tropical forests along Brazil's northeast coast, where cacao trees grow dense with leaves and cocoa pods in the shade of magnificent tall ceibas. We are in the nineteen-forties, a time when a world cocoa boom made land claims a matter of life and death in the region. The youth is threatened with lynching by rival stakers and is saved by an itinerant Lebanese salesman. The young man kills his would-be murderers, wins a beautiful child bride from her lustful father, and makes the land prosper. In the fifth chapter, set in the present day, the youth reappears as a widowed patriarch, struggling to keep his *fazenda* and his family together as cocoa prices collapse. It is here that the real *novela* begins. The widowed *coronel* marries the young, sexy granddaughter of his mortal enemy. One of the *coronel's* four sons divides his affections between his father's bride and the daughter of another of his father's enemies. This girl, for her part, decides to rebel by reopening a whorehouse that both her father and the *coronel* used to frequent. Another of the patriarch's sons leaves his wife for a beautiful hermaphrodite.

At a cacao plantation near Ilhéus, at the foot of a gently rolling hill overlooking a waterfall, and, behind it, a stretch of dark-green jungle, it took the director, Luiz Fernando Carvalho, forty-five minutes to get a final, perfect take of a single travelling shot that started with the cocoa-crushers' feet, passed over the fermentation vats, and ended with the camera's lingering examination of a skinny old black man—his beakish face, knobby hands, splayed feet, an overall stillness and grace. This is Carvalho's first big directing opportunity after ten years of assistant-director jobs at Globo, and he immodestly wants to do something revolutionary with the genre. "I want to present an image of Brazil that is not simply a postcard," he told me. "I want to get as close as possible to the soul of Brazil, and I want to redefine *o brasileiro* as a heroic being, someone who is always pushing the limits of things—is always between life and death, droughts and floods. I see him as mythical, full of grandeur." Carvalho is as tall and lanky as a basketball player, good-looking enough to be a *novela* star himself, and very intense. He has filled "Renascer" with the region's scrawny music, its feast-day dances, and its farming rituals. It seemed unnecessarily unkind to ask him how the character Buba—the model-thin hermaphrodite who falls in love with the cocoa baron's son and then tricks the patriarch into thinking she is bearing him a grandson (who in fact may be incubating in the womb of a street urchin who may in the end turn out to be the Lebanese vender's long-lost daughter)—fits into the great heroic scheme of things. Carvalho thinks that, for all its flaws, television can have a more positive influence on Brazil than any other single force. "For better or worse, the Globo network is one of the extremely few things that work in this country," he said. "If we can make it engage in a dialogue with the viewer— with the tens of millions of viewers—we can help it provide hope, culture, self-confidence for the people, who need so badly to stop being ashamed of themselves, of their fate."

　　I later brought up the question of television's role in a culturally famished society with Antônio Fagundes, the protagonist of "Renascer." He is graying and a little paunchy, his face is pleasant rather than beautiful, and in "Renascer," as in all his other roles, he is surrounded by some of the most perfectly chiselled men in the country, but he radiates such warmth and relaxed sensuality, such keen Brazilian liveliness, that women consistently crown him their favorite in the fanzine polls. "TV Globo has become Brazilian society's scapegoat," he said, bushing aside any suggestion that the station is a corrupting force. "In this county, the *novela* scriptwriters are among the few prominent figures who do not present themselves as the saviors of the fatherland, and yet television dramas have become the only common point of discussion of our national reality. You can find critical points of view here that not even literature has. Television has been premonitory. When I played the villain in 'The Owner of the World,' Collor had just declared that all the savings accounts in the nation would be confiscated to help the economy. I said publicly then that the Brazilian people had been raped by power, that I had been raped by power, and people thought it was an exaggeration. But look at what happened!"

When I asked Fagundes what it felt like to be a star, he laughed and pointed out that he wasn't one.

"I don't earn like a star, I'm not treated like a star, and if I took it into my head to satisfy any of the whims that real stars appear to have, I would be publicly humiliated," he said. "A real star is forever, like Garbo or Monroe. Here, if you stop working you disappear from view. My vanity is reduced to the fact that if you turn on the television at prime time you're likely to see me there. A lot of people see what I do, and that puts a lot of responsibility on me. Real stars are free of responsibilities."

But if *telenovela* actors are not stars, I persisted, how could something like the murder of Daniella Perez have had such astonishing impact?

"This is a country that has a very hard time maintaining its memory," Fagundes said. "So far, it has proved incapable of telling its own history: it mixes up myths with things that really happened, and confuses the boundaries between events and fiction. When an accident like the murder of Daniella Perez happens, it is easy to get the categories mixed up."

ONE GIGANTIC QUESTION about the Daniella Perez affair remains unanswered: What, precisely, was the nature of the relationship between the victim and her murderer? Central to the myths spun on a weekly basis by the thriving fanzine industry is the promotion of offscreen romances—adulterous or not—between onscreen lovers. In the weeks preceding the crime, there

hadn't been a wisp of such a rumor regarding Daniella and Guilherme de Pádua. According to the soap magazines, she was happily married to a handsome, pleasant actor, also a member of the
regular TV Globo stable, whom she had in fact, in the best fanzine style, met three years earlier, while she was playing a bit part
in a *telenovela* in which he was the leading man. A former member
of an experimental modern-dance troupe, Daniella found her
way easily into TV Globo, thanks to her *telenovela*-writing mother,
but there can be no doubt that she justified Glória Perez's choice
by engaging her audience's affections almost immediately. She
was the perfect *telenovela* ingénue: sweet and sexy, with a baby's
round eyes and plush lips. Now that it is impossible to find anyone to speak well of Guilherme de Pádua, it is easy to say that he
was her diametrical opposite, the very embodiment of a *chato*—
an overbearing and persistent bore. "He had no talent," his colleagues say, but the fact is that in the space of three years he
made the transition from a bit-part actor from the provinces to a
TV Globo featured actor.

Four nights a week, a couple of hundred people—dating
couples, both gay and straight, groups of women, lonely-looking
men—crowd into the front rows of the looming Galeria Alaska,
a theatre on Copacabana Avenue, in a state of high expectation.
The theatre smells, as a friend who went with me commented,
like feet. When tinny music starts up and the curtain rises, a
dozen muscular young men come out, one by one, in leopard
masks and spotted bikinis, doing their best to prowl. The young
men, locked into their muscles as they are, can barely move
through a series of oddly staid, not quite full-frontal stripteases,
and the only entertaining moments occur when Rogéria, a famous transvestite, comes onstage and sings, but the audience
waits stoically for the payoff: five minutes before the curtain falls,
the young men appear again, and, in the equivalent of a tightrope
act, walk from stage right to stage left and back, and then, all
together, from upstage to down, nude and in a state of full (or,
sometimes, perilously flagging) erection. These are the *garotos de
programa*, striptease dancers whose duties often widen into prosti-

tution, and whose profession was featured so prominently in "Corpo e Alma."

To state that Guilherme de Pádua, who is now twenty-three, found his way to the Alaska stage as a *garoto* when he first arrived in Rio from Minas Gerais a few years ago in pursuit of an 'acting career is simply to recount a fairly typical chapter in the biography of many young men trying to get a start in the entertainment world here. One of TV Globo's more desperate requirements is for young, fresh flesh, and one of the places where casting directors look for it is at the strip shows. Guilherme's leap from the Alaska theatre to stardom was not direct, however. He first got featured roles in a few undistinguished plays, and in two of the plays—one was called *Pasolini: Life and Death*—he played a murderer. There were also destitute times when he is reported to have lived as the guest of this or that theatre director or author. Last year, he got lucky: first, he landed a feature role in "Corpo e Alma," and then, despite his reputed lack of talent or charm, the chemistry between him and Daniella proved compelling. He evidently remained a *chato*, though, and cast members insisted loudly to the press that despite the onscreen chemistry, there was no relationship between Daniella and Guilherme other than the normal cordiality expected on the set. How, then, did it happen that on the night of December 28th, after the day's session at the TV Globo studios was wrapped up, Daniella Perez agreed to follow in her black Escort as Guilherme, driving his father-in-law's Santana, led her from the studio to the highway that crosses through Rio's upper-class beachfront suburbs? And why did she agree to pull over, sometime after nine-thirty, onto a weedy patch of ground along one of the highway's dark side roads?

According to the prosecution, which has based its case on Guilherme's confession, and, more complicatedly, on the disputed subsequent confession of his wife, the teen-age Paula Thomaz, Guilherme parked his car next to where Daniella's had pulled off the road, approached the Escort, began a violent discussion with Daniella, and strangled her until she was unconscious. Then he dragged her behind the cars, out of sight of any passersby, and attacked her with a pair of scissors while his wife egged him on. In the initial press stories, the pregnant Thomaz emerged like a figure in a nightmare from her hiding place in the back seat of Guilherme's car, screaming for revenge and wielding the murder weapon in an orgiastic attack of rage, but at this point she stands accused simply of providing "moral encouragement" to Guilherme.

Guilherme, Paula, and their prosecutors are all agreed that the motive for the murder was jealousy, but they disagree on whose. According to Guilherme, it was Daniella who besieged him, seeking a real-life relationship with him, and perhaps even threatening that she would use black magic on him if he didn't agree to be unfaithful to his wife. Tired of her incessant erotic pursuit, Guilherme accepted a meeting. During the confrontation, in the course of which Guilherme once again rejected her attentions, Daniella grew hysterical and violent. Her death was the unfortunate result. In this version, Paula was not present at the scene of the crime. She and her husband claim that Guilherme dropped her off early that afternoon at a nearby shopping mall, and that, despite her pregnancy, she spent the next six hours there, wandering from shop to shop without buying anything. Then Guilherme, the murder over with, picked her up and drove her home. But the prosecution claims that it was Paula who was jealous, and that Guilherme drove her to the spot on the side of the road so that from her hiding place in the back seat she could hear for herself how Guilherme rejected Daniella.

For most actors, the kind of reckless passion that leads to murder normally happens only in *telenovelas*, but Guilherme and Paula clearly wanted to live lives worthy of the screen. Married only a few months, they were simultaneously obsessed with and paranoically suspicious of each other, and in an attempt to seal their love in a way that might be truly binding they had had each other's names tattooed on their persons: Paula on her bikini line and Guilherme (more committed? more imaginative? aware that his love had a shorter name?) on his penis. One can imagine the crises and recriminations that such attempts to bond might produce, and can even imagine that, as the prosecution claims, Paula completely failed to distinguish between the offscreen and the onscreen activities of her actor husband, and came to believe that the passionate kisses he exchanged with an actress in front of tens of millions of viewers translated into a betrayal of their own vows. But perhaps Paula was indeed absent from the scene of the crime, and it was only the tattooed Guilherme, a small-time actor with big dreams and a certain demonstrated tendency toward exhibitionism and punishing ritual, who failed to distinguish between a grand, theatrical gesture involving a pair of scissors and the murder of another human being.

Paula Thomaz was not arrested until three days after the murder. Instead, police investigators, in what might be described as a kidnapping, held her, her mother, and a family friend for more than six hours, first in a police car and then in a municipal parking lot where garbage trucks are kept. There, according to the police, Paula confessed her participation in the crime, between sobs and disjointed mutterings about remodelling problems in her apartment. Despite this confession—which she has since consistently denied making—she was released. The next day, she was picked up at a clinic, where she was being treated for symptoms of a possible miscarriage, and taken to a police station for arraignment. By that time, Glória Perez had authorized TV Globo to broadcast the chapters featuring her daughter in "Corpo e Alma," and had agreed to continue writing chapters until the novela's scheduled end. Glória has since founded a movement of relatives of crime victims, and she is conducting her own tenacious investigation of her daughter's murder.

THE REASON THAT Daniella Perez's mother was able to determine the fate of "Corpo e Alma" is that Brazilians think the soul and essence of a telenovela lies not with its much-loved stars, like Antônio Fagundes, or with skillful directors, like Luiz Fernando Carvalho, but with the author. Some of the authors are recognized members of the intelligentsia and belong, like Roberto Marinho, to the Academy of Letters. Others, like Benedito Ruy Barbosa, who wrote both the ecofantasy "Pantanal" and the cacao epic "Renascer," have made their names primarily in the novela world. Almost without exception, they are political activists who campaign for the very issues and candidates that make Roberto Marinho blanch.

Virtually the entire stable of Globo actors and authors were known to be sympathetic to Luís Inácio da Silva (known as Lula), the radical-leftist candidate in the 1989 Presidential elections, and many campaigned for him. Lula might have won, had it not been for the decisive intervention of TV Globo, which systematically cast the leftist candidate in a bad light, most memorably during the second of two televised debates, which was held just before that election. By then, Lula looked dishevelled and frazzled, and TV Globo edited the material for its newscasts to make sure that he looked his worst. Three days later, Collor won handily. It is all the more ironic, then, that Gilberto Braga, one of the most radical and most highly respected Globo authors, should have written a miniseries (twenty chapters, as opposed to a *novela*'s hundred and eighty plus) that by nearly all accounts played a direct role in the downfall of the Collor Presidency.

The other day, when I called at Gilberto Braga's apartment, on Flamengo Beach, his manservant led me through elegantly decorated rooms and down a spiral staircase to the author's private study, a chrome-and-wood-panelled affair filled with books and first-rate paintings by contemporary Brazilian artists. Braga himself, when he appeared, was not wearing a cut-velvet dressing gown to match his surroundings but, rather, plaid Bermuda shorts and sandals, and he turned out to be tall, gangly, nervous, immensely polite, and rather shy. He has worked for TV Globo for the past twenty-one years, and he ascribes this durability to what he calls his "realism."

"I have never suffered from any limitations on my work," he explained, "but I am aware of the fact that when I sign a contract with TV Globo I am, in effect, as a person on the left, accepting limitations. Like many other artists and intellectuals, I am sensitive to the reality of my country, and I believe that the only solution for its suffering is socialism. Within the limitations of the system, I do what is possible to work for that change with my chosen vocation."

In 1986, Braga explained, he wrote a miniseries about teen-
agers in the sexually repressive world of the nineteen-fifties,
which was called "Os Anos Dourados" ("The Golden Years"). "It
was a very big success, because it dealt with sex and the Brazilian
family," he said. "And so it provided a way for people in today's
families to start talking honestly about sex among themselves for
the first time." Gradually, he began to toy with the idea of a second miniseries, about the frenzied, fervent, nineteen-sixties, centered on a hero who bears a composite resemblance to several
youths who became guerrillas, and who coördinated the kidnapping of, among others, the United States Ambassador in 1969.

Braga called the series that evolved from those noodlings "Os
Anos Rebeldes" ("The Rebel Years"), and with it he transported
an entire generation of teen-agers back to the euphoria of the
sixties. From the very first chapter—which opens with a guerrilla
bank robbery and flashes back to the dutiful, studious, idealistic
teen-agers who try hard not to go all the way with their girlfriends and fail to understand why the son of a doorman should
have different opportunities in life from the son of a factory
owner—the audience was hooked. The series offered the exhila-
ration of living on a heroic scale, the thrill of danger and a worthy cause, and the real drama of the increasingly rigid and joyless
hero, who thinks only of revolution, and his long-suffering and
terrified girlfriend, who wants to know why he can't think of her
every once in a while. Braga believes that the main reason for its
success was that the history of the early years of the dictatorship
and of the struggle to overthrow it remains unknown even to
most Brazilians who lived through that time, and certainly to the
younger generation. Once again, in the way that *novelas* tend to
do, "The Rebel Years" made it possible for families to discuss a
fraught and hidden subject openly at the dinner table, Braga says.
That is certainly true, but there was more than that to the new
series' astonishing impact on national life. In contrast to the standard *novela* plot—that of "Corpo e Alma," say—"Os Anos Rebeldes" dealt with characters who were not a group of tormented
individuals pitted against one another in a contest for life and
happiness but a community of idealists who, even in the course

of making the most dreadful mistakes, were motivated by a deep faith in the common goodness of mankind. It was this sense of shared purpose and solidarity that electrified Brazil's listless, aimless teen-agers. Whether they would have taken to the streets in hordes to demand the overthrow of Fernando Collor de Mello if "Os Anos Rebeldes" had not been showing at the time is debatable. When they did, in July of last year, Collor had been in power twenty-eight months. He had come to the Presidency through yet another of the nationwide waves of hope that Brazilians project onto their politicians. Once in power, he claimed to modernize the economy, wore a great many beautiful suits, failed to stop inflation, travelled widely and lavishly through Europe, and gradually become as deeply despised a politician as Brazil has ever produced. Now, as a fictional corrupt and power-mad politician, he is the thinly veiled protagonist of a miniseries called "The Maharaja," produced by Globo's only real rival in the *novela* field, TV Manchete. In it, the snakelike Collor character is played by an actor who had previously won fame with his Collor impersonations. This is the first time a President of Brazil has become the hero of a farce. (Collor has taken TV Manchete to court to block its release.)

BEFORE COLLOR TURNED INTO a miniseries, he was a national disgrace, and his removal from power last year was a national crusade. Before that, he was a hugely popular, good-looking, karate-black-belt Presidential icon who promised to bring Brazil into the twenty-first century, and before that he was a politician from Alagoas, a state in northeastern Brazil with the size, the economy, and the demographics of a Central American country—an area so poor that most of its families don't even own televisions: they listen to the radio, and are thus easily reached by the Collor family, which owns the principal newspaper (*A Gazeta de Alagoas*), a television station, and three radio stations. This mini-empire was founded by Fernando Collor's father, Arnon de Mello, who, as a loyal supporter of the military, was repeatedly elected to the Senate—even after he shot another senator dead in the course of a dispute over a matter of honor. The murder was officially ruled an accident (Arnon actually intended to shoot somebody else), and unofficially it was understood that death was just an instrument of politics in the northeast, where hired killers can still be easily had for fifty or so dollars a job.

By 1989, when the self-proclaimed modernizer of Brazil leaped into the Presidential race from this state, and this political tradition, he had been the military-appointed mayor of Maceió, the state capital, and the elected governor of Alagoas. And he had divorced his first wife and acquired a new wife and some remarkable in-laws. There were plenty of stories about his second wife, Rosane Malta Collor, and about the Malta clan, who ruled over the most backward part of backward Alagoas. Rosane, who is now twenty-eight, has a little brother, Joãozinho, who in 1988, at the age of fifteen, put a bullet through the neck of a political rival of his family. (As a minor and a first offender, he did not have to serve time.)

The members of the Collor family, who like to talk about their most recent trip to Paris and boast gently of their knowledge of French, were appalled by Fernando's choice of spouse, not so much because there was a murderer in her family—that was, after all, something they had in common—as because Rosane, blond and toothy, with terrible posture and a slack-jawed backcountry smile, is the type of person who thinks that Switzerland and Europe are two geographically distinct places. ("We vacationed in Switzerland and then went back to Europe.") It was known in Maceió that the Collors detested her, and humiliated her at every opportunity, just as it was known that Fernando Collor had been the type of mayor who, according to legend, authorized a road-building project, paved both ends of the road, filmed them, and declared the project finished. It is not unusual for a Latin-American politician to bilk taxpayers out of a public-works project; what was original was the mediagenic use that Collor was supposed to have made of the fraud, and people liked to chuckle about it in Maceió.

But these were not the pictures or the stories that Brazil became familiar with during the Presidential campaign. Roberto Marinho and his TV Globo had been scouting the country for candidates long before the elections and had liked what they saw of Collor, who had run for governor promising to put an end to the rule of Alagoas's "maharajas," or corrupt bureaucrats. Collor was as sleek as a borzoi, articulate, sincere-looking, modernizing, and, above all, a highly palatable contrast to his rivals on the left. Fernando's younger brother, Pedro, was the head of the family's Globo-affiliated station in Alagoas, and the network used him as a liaison with Fernando. Even before the Presidential campaign got officially under way, Globo stationed a news team permanently in Maceió. It proved a brilliant decision. Fernando, barely forty at the time, had an instinctive grasp of television politics; the sound bite, the made-for-the-camera crowd event, the magic of a snazzy logo were as familiar to him as if he had invented them, or as if he had grown up in the United States. Brazilians were charmed. In the words of the actor Antônio Fagundes, "Collor had all the attributes of power: he was good-looking, he wore beautiful clothes, he knew karate, he had a good car. He looked like a President." Soon the rest of the media picked up the Collor anti-maharaja stories, and by the time the 1989 campaign got into full swing Collor was nationally known.

The media could have easily examined the real record of the governor of Alagoas; they could have looked into Collor's dealings with his campaign treasurer, a bald, roly-poly character named Paulo César Farias, who was known around Maceió mainly for his dubious business practices; they could have reported the fact that Governor Collor signed a law exempting the Alagoas sugarcane growers from taxes for ten years, thus eliminating up to sixty per cent of the state's tax base, according to some sources, and they could have wondered just what Collor might have obtained in exchange for such benevolence. But they didn't. Mario Sergio Conti, the managing editor of *Veja*, who seems to inhabit a permanent dense cloud of cigarette smoke and gloom, provoked largely by his country's misfortunes, readily acknowledges that the media had their least fine hour during the 1989 campaign. "We covered Collor according to the dazzling image that he projected, and we covered Lula, who is a former steelworker and union leader, according to the prejudices that society has about workers—that they are ignorant, that they are illiterate," he said when we had lunch recently at a Rio restaurant. "But here's the thing: we didn't know how to do Presidential campaigns, because we had no experience with them. And it wasn't just that we failed to investigate Collor; we didn't investigate anyone." He gave a little snort of despairing mirth, and added, "Next time, we won't leave a single candidate standing."

The first year of the Collor government left Brazilians dizzy. Their President went skiing, scuba diving, car racing. Every Sunday, when he went jogging, he had a new slogan stamped on his T-shirt—an eco-slogan or a just-do-it exhortation. He announced privatizations of state-owned industries all over the map, and the Minister of Science and Technology he appointed finally overturned Brazil's long-standing and much violated ban on foreign computer technology. He dismantled Brazil's nuclear program. He said friendly things about the Indians in the Amazon, and even doubled the territory allotted to them. He cut the number of ministries from twenty-three to twelve and fired about a fifth of the bureaucracy. It was all terribly modern, and wonderfully telegenic, and even my friends on the left, Lula backers all, talked about how maybe this great nation, with its gigantic gross domestic product (the ninth-largest in the world), was about to lumber, at last, out of its perpetual backwardness. Collor appointed Rosane to head the national charity institute, and his campaign treasurer, Paulo César Farias, to serve as liaison in unspecified ways between the government and powerful people with money, and those appointments seemed all right, even though Rosane was given to shopping sprees and fits of temper, and Paulo César Farias, known as "P.C.," who went in for gold chains and wore his shirt open to the chest hairs, seemed a little undignified.

Then there were signs of trouble. In August of 1991, Fernando Collor showed up at a press conference and made a point of displaying a hand that no longer wore a wedding ring. My Brazilian friends attributed the apparent separation to Fernando's reputed womanizing, or to Rosane's penchant for wearing color-coördinated shoes and handbags with her miniskirt tailleurs. In

Brasília, there was even some muttering that it might be Rosane who was having an affair. The media speculated that the separation might be related to mounting evidence that the Maltas were using the charity institute—the Legião Brasileira de Assistência, or L.B.A.—as their own private kitty, but nothing came of this. Although Rosane renounced day-to-day management of the L.B.A., she retained the title of honorary president, and soon Fernando was wearing the wedding ring again. There were accusations that Paulo César Farias was on the take, extorting from the major Brazilian corporations sums so vast as to defy credibility. In November of 1990, Renan Calheiros, who, as the head of Fernando Collor's tiny party, the Partido de Reconstrução Nacional, was the leader of the Câmara dos Deputados, resigned, alleging that corruption was sinking the government in "a sea of mud." Collor was losing popularity, and there was a general sense that once again Brazilians had put their faith in a savior who had no miracles to offer. Then, in May of last year, the President's kid brother, Pedro, gave an interview to *Veja*.

There are diverse explanations of why Pedro Collor decided to talk, and none of them would be out of place in a *telenovela* script. One is that Fernando, in his days as Governor, had had an affair with Pedro's wife, Terezinha, who is the exceedingly pretty daughter of an Alagoas sugar baron, João Lyra. Pedro Collor has repeatedly gone to great lengths to deny this rumor, pointing out that whenever his brother wanted some private time with a woman of his acquaintance he would signal this to his secretaries at the Governor's palace by turning off the light in his inner office. During the one three-hour visit his wife paid Fernando at the palace, he says, the Governor's secretaries assured him that the light was left on the entire time. Pedro says he decided to talk out of an elemental sense of decency, spurred on by the discovery that Fernando and P.C. were plotting to set up a rival media group to the Arnon de Mello empire, which Pedro had managed lovingly over the years.

In contrast to the moody, vain Fernando, Pedro, now forty, is talkative and modest. He has his brother's features, pulled slightly out of kilter, and a stare that can appear unfortunately wild-eyed. Twice in the preceding months, Pedro Collor had raised hackles in Brasília by telling *Veja* about P. C. Farias's involvement in corrupt deals, but, perhaps because of his slightly loopy manner, and perhaps because no businessman had come forward to denounce P. C. Farias for extortion, and because there was no proof, Pedro's accusations did not stir the media or rock the government. P. C. Farias held no official position in the Collor administration, after all, and it was hard to believe that a garrulous small-time operator and failed businessman from Maceió could have significant influence on the Presidency. For good measure, Fernando Collor had proclaimed as soon as the first corruption rumors surfaced that he had last seen P.C. six months after taking power. Pedro, in his third, history-making *Veja* interview, not only restated his claim that P.C. was extorting in the name of the President but said that Fernando had been a frequent cocaine user, that P.C. was his front man, that an apartment in Paris that was nominally an office for P.C.'s business associates had in reality been bought for Fernando, that it was P.C. who paid for Rosane's extravagant shopping sprees, and that P.C. and Fernando had conspired to steal the Alagoas gubernatorial election from Renan Calheiros, the congressional leader who had resigned denouncing the mudslide of corruption, in order to hand it to a less independent candidate who happened to be related by marriage to the Malta clan.

"I was involved with drugs when I was very young, led on by Fernando," Pedro stated. "He was a constant cocaine user, and I learned from him, and from the people he introduced me to." And he continued, "Fernando is incapable of saying 'I need money for my campaign; help me.' He can be naked and not have shoes to wear and still he won't ask for help. P.C. takes the help he needs. If possible, he leaves you standing naked." Pedro then detailed P.C.'s modus operandi, recalling how a professional friend, Laíse de Freitas, had called him in some alarm to say he had been approached by a hit man for P. C. Farias. De Freitas had several government construction contracts, and part of the money for those jobs was being held up. P.C.'s man told him that the money would not be authorized by the state unless de Freitas paid a bribe. "Paulo César would say, 'Seventy per cent is for the boss, and thirty per cent is for me.' He would tell everyone that," Pedro declared. He made these charges on tape, and then, for good measure, the *Veja* team had him restate them on video.

Within days, on June 1st, the special investigative commission appointed by Congress to look into Paulo César Farias's dealings with the government called its first witness.

IT WAS A FEW DAYS before Gilberto Braga became aware of what was happening in the streets of Rio de Janeiro and São Paulo and Curitiba and every other major city in the country. It was July, and "Os Anos Rebeldes," his miniseries about guerrillas and the anti-military struggle in the sixties, was about halfway through its run. The story's transitions were stitched together with international newsreel footage from the era: Beatles concerts and Martin Luther King's speeches, Twiggy and Vietnam, the début of the miniskirt and protest marches in Washington. Braga was spending most of his time in the Globo studios in Rio, doing last-minute editing on "Anos Rebeldes" and adding the music, which, in addition to the theme song, "Alegria, Alegria," by Caetano Veloso, an anthem of the period, included songs that Braga was contributing from his own considerable record collection. He was staying up nights and sleeping well into the afternoons, but one day his manservant shook him awake around the time of the midday news program. "There is a protest march on television!" he said. "Come see!" The protesters were a mass of bouncing teenagers, equipped with anti-Collor signs and slogans, and one of the signs said, "Anos Rebeldes: Último Capítulo." They were calling for the real-life Collor *novela* to end now.

By then, the congressional investigative commission on the doings of P. C. Farias was struggling not to drown in a torrent of information. First, a businessman—just one of many who were approached by P.C.—stepped forward to declare that Farias had attempted to extort money from him, and that he had refused to pay. Then, in late June, one of Collor's drivers produced a few fragments of what would soon become a paper trail involving forty thousand checks and more than a hundred pounds of documents. There was evidence that P.C. had stashed millions of dollars away for Fernando Collor in Europe; that he had had dealings with men whose names were linked by investigators to the drug trade in Colombia and Bolivia; and even that Collor had paid the mother of Lula's illegitimate daughter to come forward and denounce him. The media, now hot on the scent, dug deeper, and the Federal Police weighed in with investigations of their own. It appeared that Rosane Malta's charity institute had bilked thousands of Brazil's poor out of emergency food supplies and blankets, that it had billed the government for "appropriate-technology factories" that turned out to be ice-cream and popcorn pushcarts, that it had speculated on truckloads of water brought in for drought-stricken areas and even on children's coffins.

With each new, sickening revelation in the media about the looting of Brazil, the number of protesters in the streets multiplied. TV Globo was now busy denouncing the corruption scandal, and not just in its news programs: a new *telenovela*, called "God Help Us," began screening in the 7 p.m. slot. Behind the credits socialites and businessmen gaily splashed about in a pool of mud, which gradually engulfed them. Although the print media, in particular, dispute the notion that Gilberto Braga's television miniseries played a decisive role in the mass demonstration of outrage, the influence of "Anos Rebeldes" was obviously felt as long as the street marches lasted. "In Chapter Eight, we showed clips of Haight-Ashbury—hippies with flowers painted on their faces." Braga recalled. "At the very next demonstration, the *caras pintadas*—kids with their faces painted with colors and slogans—made their first appearance. Simultaneously, all over the country."

Perhaps the President was not watching television during those turbulent days. How else to explain the sudden dulling of his habitual extrasensory media perception? On a now famous day in August, he addressed a gathering of truck drivers, and, speaking for the benefit of the evening newscast, called for a march in his favor the following Sunday, August 16th. "Let's show that insane minority who is upsetting the country every day that enough is enough!" he shouted, and he asked his demonstrators to wear green and yellow, the colors of Brazil's flag. On that day, all across the nation, millions of marchers spontaneously thronged the streets, and they were dressed in black.

IN ADDITION TO TELEVISION news clips and the yet-to-be-released "Maharajas," there is now a third entertainment about the unfolding of the Collor family melodrama, courtesy of Pedro Collor: he has summed up his experiences in a book called *Coming Clean: The Trajectory of a Charlatan*. The book was launched this April, and immediately after publication I saw it in the hands of sunbathers in Rio and every other passenger on every commuter flight I took. The little brother who overthrew a president offers us a stream of anecdotes and convincingly detailed examples of Presidential corruption, along with answers to questions that were on every Brazilian's mind and also to questions that had never occurred to anyone. Just what did Collor get in exchange for exempting the Alagoas sugar producers from taxes when he was governor? Donations of twelve million dollars that formed the basis of his Presidential-campaign war chest. Why did Fernando suddenly stop wearing a wedding ring in August of 1991? Because Rosane greeted him one day with the news that she was going to have a baby—news that, according to Pedro, enabled his brother to know that Rosane was cheating on him, because he had had a vasectomy after the birth of two children in his first marriage. Why did the wedding ring suddenly reappear? Because Rosane threatened to spill the goods on him if he left her. What goods? Among other details, the fact that Fernando preferred cocaine in suppository form.

Presumably in the interest of marital peace, Pedro spares only his father-in-law, João Lyra, who was once indicted on charges of ordering the killing of his wife's bodyguard when he discovered that the two were having an affair. (The case was adjourned for lack of evidence.) The rest of the Collor family is presented in compelling, and perhaps even reliable, detail. There are endless stories about Rosane's gaucheries and tantrums, rendered in a backcountry accent worthy of "The Beverly Hillbillies." There is a scene of Fernando Collor at an orgy, instructing the family driver, who interrupts it with the news of Arnon de Mello's death, to choose a woman for himself.

Pedro, who dedicates the book to his parents, among others, gives a straightforward account of his father's role in the death of the fellow-senator. He has a more difficult time writing about his mother, Leda Collor de Mello. A steely woman with a sharp eye for business and, according to Pedro, a fervent belief in discipline, Dona Leda was described to me by a friend who is part of Alagoas high society as "very interesting—so interesting that I am entirely willing to believe that Arnon didn't marry her for the money." Arnon de Mello founded his media business with his brains and her money. Although she owns seventy-five per cent of the shares in the Organização Arnon de Mello, she left its management in the hands first of Pedro's oldest brother, Leopoldo, and then of Fernando, who ran it for seven years and, according to Pedro, brought it to the edge of bankruptcy. When Fernando turned to politics, Pedro took over the business. Soon, he says proudly, the company was making enough to keep his mother on a ten-thousand-dollar monthly stipend. "As a result," he writes, "I conquered, even more than respect, a special place in the austere heart of Dona Leda." There is heartbreak in what follows. On the eve of last year's world ecology conference, held in Rio, and before the publication of the historic interview in which he attacked his brother, she wrote him a letter: "At this hour, when a conference is about to begin that will bring together more than one hundred heads of state . . . the medical examination you are submitting to [should] confirm what everyone can clearly see: that your state of profound stress mandates your immediate separation from this fire in which the smoke does not allow you to see your responsibilities clearly." She signed it "Your long-suffering mother," and summarily removed him from command of the family business. In his book Pedro includes an excerpt of what he said was a long tape-recorded conversation between his mother and an unnamed friend. "It's sad," Dona Leda muses on the tape. "I have one son, the President of the Republic, who is a thief . . . and another who is an excellent businessman but decided to transform himself into a stool pigeon."

Pedro writes, "After being betrayed by one's mother, one has few emotions left in one's soul." But there was more to come. On the morning of September 17th, after reading in the paper the latest round of accusations by Pedro against his brother, Dona Leda suffered three consecutive cardiac arrests. She remains in a coma to this day.

ONE OF THE ESSENTIAL CHARACTERISTICS of the *telenovela* format is its infinite expandability, and in this respect, as in so many others, the saga of Brazil's impeached President fits the genre. First came the sex-drugs-and-corruption melodrama of his public ascent, then the national epic of his removal from power, and now Brazil is witnessing "Collor III: The Chase." In this installment, his henchman, P. C. Farias, is a fugitive, having gone on the lam on June 30th, the day a judge issued an arrest warrant for him on charges of tax evasion. The Federal Police, who performed admirably during the impeachment hearings, have now conveniently turned themselves into the Keystone Kops, and have spent the last few weeks bumbling about the country, showing up in Brasília, São Paulo, and Alagoas to detain the country's best-known scoundrel hours or days, or even months, after he vacated the premises. Since Collor's real-life *novela* keeps adding chapters, we may yet get "Collor: The Comeback," but these days Fernando Collor de Mello rarely abandons his beautiful home in Brasília, with the lavish gardens that P. C. Farias had remodelled for him to the tune of nearly five million dollars. The lumbering justice system is proceeding with its trial of Collor, and, presumably, one day he will be judged. But to believe that he will ever live with sixteen other prisoners in a suffocating cell that has musty mattresses lined up on the floor and a noxious latrine in one corner, like any other Brazilian criminal, is to believe in fantasy. For that matter, to think that even one of the captains of industry who connived with the President's gangsters and acquiesced in their own shakedowns should be punished is to invite public ridicule.

• • •

MEANWHILE, COLLOR'S COMPETITION in the real-life-*novela*
ratings, Guilherme de Pádua, *is* wasting away in jail, in a reeking,
overcrowded prison cell, from which he and his fellow-prisoners
were plotting to escape last month. His wife—whose confession,
if it indeed was such, was obtained illegally—also remains in jail,
waiting for a trial that may be scheduled in a year or two. In May,
she gave birth two months prematurely; the birth was no doubt
hastened by a beating she received at the hands of her fellow-
inmates—hard cases, who judged her crime to have been much
worse than any of theirs. A few months before the baby's birth,
when Guilherme and Paula were called into the same courtroom,
they were photographed making eyes at each other and kissing
behind a prison guard's back. In a brief prison interview just before his son was born, Guilherme, bearded and Christlike, allowed himself to be filmed putting on first a saintly expression
and then a sorrowful expression, and saying things like "I only
believe in eternal love." These vows notwithstanding, there are
increasing signs that the couple are not on friendly terms; there
are reports that Paula's family has taken to burning his letters to
her.

Daniella's mother, Glória Perez, has managed to locate a man
who on the night of her daughter's murder was working as a gas-
station attendant near the scene of the crime. On August 3rd, he
declared that he had washed the blood-caked interior of a car
driven by a man he identified as Guilherme de Pádua; the man
was accompanied by a young woman wearing dark glasses, but
he could not positively identify her as Paula Thomaz. His deposi-
tion lends credence to Glória Perez's theory that Daniella was
not murdered on the roadside, in a spontaneous act of violence,
but inside the car, and possibly at some distant location, by
Guilherme and Paula acting in concert.

There are also increasingly open indications from Guilherme's lawyer, Paulo Ramalho, that Guilherme will soon decide
to accuse Paula of participation in the murder, and broad hints
concerning the motive. "Legal experience demonstrates that scissors are typical of women's crimes," the lawyer declared in an

interview to a scandal sheet called *O Dia* on July 21st. "It's typical of someone who is very jealous." Encouraged by an exhortation of Ramalho's to "let public opinion discover" if it was Paula who killed Daniella, one could speculate that Daniella and Guilherme were having an affair and were spied on by Paula, who crawled out of her hiding place in the car to confront and attack the couple. This is not Glória Perez's version, but at least it is a version that makes satisfying melodramatic sense, and allows Brazilians to explain to themselves a real-life *telenovela* that has kept them in suspense for months.

A few weeks ago, I had a long conversation with Maria Tereza Souza Monteiro, who conducts the surveys that allow TV Globo to monitor audience response to a *telenovela* and steer it to success. I asked her why the public had been so fascinated by a starlet's murder and suddenly so indifferent to its President's impeachment, and she answered that there was no indifference involved: "They followed the impeachment proceedings, but the technical ins and outs of the actual legal process were extremely difficult to understand," she said. "It was much easier to understand Daniella's death, and less frightening. People believed that it was their protests that led directly to Collor's departure, and that was scary: they thought, Oh my God, I can overthrow a President!" Guided by the media, millions of Brazilians have now figured out Fernando Collor in a way that is easy to understand, and is not frightening: He is not the corrupt scion of a corrupt political tradition, a crook who connived with other crooks in government and the private sector to do business in a way that it is traditionally done. He is not part of an unworkable society in which seventy million people vote but only seven million earn enough to pay income tax, nor is he the product of a political culture that was weaned on TV Globo and United States marketing techniques. He is the villain of a *telenovela*. Like Guilherme de Pádua, he is merely a Bad Man, and this means that, now that he has walked off the set, there is still hope.

BOGOTÁ
1993

"I can't imagine a future without Pablo Escobar."

It's BEEN FOURTEEN MONTHS now since Pablo Escobar, the world's most notorious drug exporter, fled a prison near Medellín in which he had voluntarily confined himself in June of 1991. The Drug Enforcement Administration estimates that the group of cocaine exporters based in Medellín and headed by Escobar, which used to control nearly eighty per cent of the cocaine shipped to the United States, now accounts for less than twenty per cent. In its July 5th issue this year, *Forbes* kicked Escobar down a notch on its list of foreign billionaires—dropping his estimated worth from two to one billion dollars—largely because most of the drug-export business has been taken over by his bitter rivals in the tropical city of Cali, who appear to be better and, above all, far more prudent businessmen. If present trends continue, *Forbes* warned, Escobar might be dropped from its famous list altogether next year—if he's still around. So many of his closest associates aren't. Since December, one after another of his front men and confidants have turned up in photographs on the front pages of the local papers, their bodies laced with bullet holes, their corpses surrogates for his. Of the key associates who went to prison with him and fled with him thirteen months later, seven are in jail again and two are dead, including a sweet-natured man known as Angelito who served as Escobar's factotum and official food taster, and who was probably the last man in Colombia Escobar could trust unconditionally. His death, in a shoot-out on October 6th, was followed by the discovery of Escobar's best-hidden urban refuges: hideouts worthy of a wildly ambitious B movie, fitted with sliding doors that opened at the turn of a bathroom faucet, and furnished with beds complete with flowered coverlets and shams. On October 11th, the Colombian security forces announced that Escobar had managed to escape yet again, this time from a makeshift cabin that lacked all the comforts of home, and authorities figured he had not run far. An era is ending, but who could have foretold it? Certainly not Don Pablo.

In truth, even Escobar's voluntary incarceration was hardly a defeat; the fact that the government had been unable to arrest him after years of trying was not lost on anyone. When he opted for jail, he called the shots, as he had throughout his career. The bold assurance with which he conducted his battles made him a folk hero for many—in a country where very few people feel any affection for their rulers, the government of President César Gaviria was not the first Escobar humbled—and he could hardly be blamed for the overweening pride with which he took on the Colombian state and as many other enemies as cared to confront him. This time, though, pride appears to have narrowed his options. Caught between the government and an organization called Los Pepes, whose leadership is made up largely of those he betrayed on his climb to power, Escobar may soon hand his eternally fumbling, ham-fisted adversaries their greatest triumph.

THE NATURE OF THE government's limitations in tackling the man who was once Colombia's most gleefully wealthy drug lord were made evident in painful detail in the course of his prison interlude. Following an arduous negotiation process with the government—during which Escobar repeatedly kidnapped members of the Colombian élite and used them as bargaining chips, murdering at least two along the way to strengthen his position—he and fourteen of his closest companions walked into the sylvan prison compound of La Catedral, confessed to a few lesser crimes, and settled down to await trial. Despite enormous controversy, the government had finally agreed to Escobar's terms: he got to choose the prison site, in the hills above his suburban fiefdom of Envigado, and he supervised its security measures. Neither Army troops nor police officers were allowed on the prison grounds, and Escobar personally approved the hiring of half of some fifty guards—the other half to be recruited by the mayor of Envigado—who were to stand watch over him and his associates.

Given those extravagant concessions, it was only natural that from the moment of Escobar's surrender La Catedral became a constant source of speculation and fantasy in Medellín. It was said that the beautiful wooded hillside on which it stood was in fact the former property of Escobar, who had sold it to the municipality of Envigado precisely so that the government could rent the land and build the custom-designed prison on it. It was said that prostitutes and Escobar's employees routinely visited the prison, and that the cells of Escobar, his brother, and his second-in-command were equipped with giant video screens and Jacuzzis, not to mention state-of-the-art radio-communication devices and machine guns. It was said that the constant traffic of goods and visitors was made possible by a series of paper slips—tinted according to their value that were handed to the Army personnel patrolling the compound's perimeter, and were then cashed in by the bearer at an Envigado bank branch. These were delicious rumors, good for enlivening a conversation and honing the sharp contempt that the *paisas*—the natives of the mountainous, isolated department of Antioquia, of which Medellín is the capital—have always felt for the central government. The story that flew around Medellín a year after Escobar's surrender, however—and which turned out to be as true as all the preceding ones—was grimmer: it concerned the unusually large number of tortured and mutilated corpses that had been turning up on the outskirts of town. The rumor was that the dead men were among Escobar's own lieutenants and most trusted business partners, that they had been kidnapped and taken to La Catedral, and that there, under the boss's supervision, at least a dozen of them had been accused of betrayal and then tortured and killed.

This version of events first circulated early in July of 1992, in the form of flyers dropped from a small plane, and made the Bogotá press days later. Most prominent among the dead men were four members of the Galeano and Moncada families, reputable and powerful drug traffickers whose corpses were found on the roadside not far from the Envigado prison. The fateful murders of Fernando and Mario Galeano and Gerardo and William Julio Moncada were to a large degree a result of the sharp downturn in the Medellín trade's fortunes, which had led to niggling. Escobar, who used to run his business through franchises, commanded huge percentages from associates like the Moncada and Galeano families: he not only billed them on the basis of his logistical support for their shipments but assessed taxes for what he used to call "my struggle": As the head of an interest group called Los Extraditables, and under the slogan "Better a grave in Colombia than a jail in the United States," Escobar waged a campaign—through murder, intimidation, and skillful public relations—to have the government repeal laws allowing extradition for criminals. He claimed success when, in 1991, the Constituent Assembly created a new charter which forbade extradition. In the days when a million dollars or three represented a paltry sum for the cocaine exporters in Medellín, the assessed fees were paid eagerly. By 1992, though, times were tough, and the Galeano and Moncada brothers died as a result of a dispute over a few million dollars they did not feel like turning over to El Patrón.

On July 21st, a week after the story first appeared in the press, an internal investigation of the situation at La Catedral alerted the government to the prison killings of the Galeanos and the Moncadas. In a flustered session, President Gaviria and the members of his security council decided to take control of the compound immediately and move Escobar to higher-security confinement, in Bogotá. Having learned of this plan on the evening news, Escobar judged that it was time to find safer quarters, and although some five hundred troops had already encircled the prison in preparation for the emergency transfer, he walked out, with nine of his fellow-prisoners.

THE EXACT DETAILS of Escobar's leap to freedom remain unknown. Whether he stepped out the back door dressed in women's clothing, as some soldiers involved in the transfer operation claim, or actually took the trouble to hike uphill to a waiting van, as was reported in most press versions, is a matter that could not add much to or subtract much from the shame that engulfed the Gaviria Administration once the escape became known. Months after the flight, a member of Gaviria's kitchen cabinet still clutched his head between his hands and shuddered as he remembered its various boggled episodes: the helpless troops; the Vice-Minister of Justice—who was in charge of supervising the prison transfer—held hostage; the many hours that elapsed before Escobar's disappearance was made known by the local Army command. This man claimed, with justice, that the Gaviria Administration's achievements had been significant in the fields of economic, political, and judicial reform, but he felt that none of them were likely to be remembered in the wake of La Catedral. Unless Gaviria managed to recapture Escobar, what people would remember of his Administration was that he was the President who let the world's most vicious drug trafficker build himself a rest home where he could continue his operations in greater safety than he would have enjoyed at large.

"Escobar did not want to escape," President Gaviria's Secretary General, Miguel Silva, acknowledged ruefully when I talked to him earlier this year. "Clearly, if he was able to walk out of La Catedral while it was surrounded by five hundred troops he could have done so before, and he knew that. The reason he didn't want to escape was that, as we found out, things were going magnificently for him in prison. He escaped because he made a stupid miscalculation: he thought that he was going to be killed." Like most members of Gaviria's inner circle, including the Ministers of Defense and Justice—who shared the job of surveillance over Escobar—Silva forms part of a group known as the Kindergarten.

He is in his very early thirties, bright-eyed and eager, in love with technology and modernity and his own informal, efficient way of doing things. The effect of so much youthfulness at Nariño Palace (Gaviria himself is a boyish-looking forty-six) is both refreshing and alarming—rather as if the country were being run by a platoon of little George Stephanopouloses. An afternoon in the Kindergarten's company makes it easier to understand how two years ago they would have scoffed at the notion that any top Army colonel in Medellín might be pulling a fast one on them, sending brisk *"misión cumplida"* memos back to Bogotá while gratefully extending a hand for the latest check from El Patrón. Such rumors were not worth even a fact-finding trip: the situation was under control, because no one would dare cheat on the President. Leaked transcripts of the government's investigation into the escape reveal how misguided the kids' trust was.

There is, for example, the section referring to the prison's director, Colonel Homero Rodríguez, who is now in jail himself. His querulous correspondence with Bogotá in the months preceding the escape, full of complaints that he was being unfairly accused of laxity, makes entertaining reading. During the period in which computers, prostitutes, and workout machines were finding their way into the prison, Rodríguez proudly points out in his defense that one of the people in charge of improving the prison's fence structure, who had come to photograph the existing fences, was denied access, because he did not have a pass for his camera. Shortly before the escape, there was also a telephone conversation that Colonel Rodríguez had with his superior, duly taped, in which Bogotá asked whether various individuals, including Mario and Fernando Galeano and Gerardo and William Julio Moncada, had been seen to enter La Catedral. *"Negativo"* was the Colonel's unfortunate reply. These were, of course, among the men who are now known to have been assassinated on his watch. They are also the men whose relatives banded together sometime this past winter, under the name Los Pepes (short for Persecuted by Pablo Escobar), and vowed to exact Biblical revenge on the murderers.

• • •

ON JANUARY 31ST, the Pepes made their début by blowing up the country home of Escobar's mother. Days later, they set fire to his wife's country home and also to his prized collection of antique cars (including a Pontiac that he bought apparently under the false assumption that it had once belonged to Al Capone). In March, they killed Escobar's most respectable front man, and also kidnapped and shot, but did not actually kill, one of Escobar's lawyers: an autopsy revealed that he had died of fright—a heart attack—moments before being shot. In April, they killed Escobar's cleverest lawyer. In June, they kidnapped and shot one of his brothers-in-law. The Pepes' determination and modus operandi inspire great respect—so much that I feel moved to conceal even the name of the city in which I met with a gracious, amusing antique dealer who has an intimate knowledge of the drug trade and close friends among the Pepes. I had asked to meet Zé, as I shall call him, because, although I could see how difficult it was for the government to sustain its hunt of Escobar, given the fear factor and the infinite opportunities for corruption along the way, I couldn't understand why even Escobar's most powerfully motivated pursuers had been unable to find their quarry. Zé said he'd heard that Escobar had managed to shake his enemies by turning in or murdering his remaining long-term associates and then recruiting new operatives, mostly very young, who were unknown both to the Pepes and to the security forces. There was nothing new in this pattern of betrayal, Zé explained. Over and over, throughout his career, Escobar sponsored subordinates who would painstakingly build up their *rutas* for shipping cocaine abroad; once the contacts and the landing sites were established and had proved to be safe, he would eliminate the subordinate and take over the route himself. This had happened most outrageously in the case of a brother-in-law of the trafficking Ochoa brothers, who are beloved in drug circles and are considered the peaceable and wise elder statesmen of the trade. (Jorge Luis and Fabio Ochoa, having turned themselves in months before Escobar, are currently serving eight-and-a-half-year sentences. A third brother, Juan David, is also in jail, awaiting sentencing.)

• • •

ESCOBAR WAS now in deep hiding somewhere in the Antioquia countryside, Zé speculated, and was operating for the first time in real clandestinity, of which the logistics and controls—so Zé had heard—were being managed by a man who once provided security for the top leadership of the leftist guerrilla group M-19. Zé also spoke, admiringly, of a woman, the sister of the murdered Galeano brothers, who is widely held to be the real Pepa. She is a Medellín-based lawyer called Victoria, and it was she who first broke the underworld's law of silence—by hiring the plane, back in July of 1992, to fly over Envigado and drop leaflets denouncing the killing of her brothers and the Moncadas. Zé felt that it was this unprecedented outing that forced the government to investigate what was really going on in La Catedral, and turned the tide against Escobar.

If it weren't for Los Pepes, it is unlikely that the government could have Escobar so cornered today. Not that the government itself hasn't been active. Having survived the nightmare of his escape, the Gaviria Administration reacted swiftly: the Fiscalía General de la Nación, or Prosecutor General's Office, which was created just before the escape, in an attempt to modernize the paralyzed justice system, took up the task of filing charges against the fugitive that might stick. The government began using new legislation that allows reduced sentencing for the confession of crimes, offered millions of dollars in exchange for information leading to Escobar's capture, and set up a special witness-protection program. The Fiscalía, beefed up by fourteen hundred "prosecuting judges," or investigative attorneys, and a computer system obtained with United Nations assistance, has filed charges against Escobar on major cases, including the 1986 assassination of Guillermo Cano, the pro-extradition editor of *El Espectador*, and the murder of Luis Carlos Galán, the leading candidate in the 1990 Presidential elections and a firm opponent of the drug trade. And, despite fretting by columnists of every stripe (but of the same, moneyed class) that the reward—"betrayal money," they call it—will corrupt the moral fibre of the lower orders, enough legal evidence has been obtained through the informant program to make an ongoing series of arrests and raids.

The most resources have gone to the formation of an ad-hoc combined military-and-police force known officially as the Search Bloc for Pablo Escobar, which, after a long lull, once again appears to be dogging the heels of its namesake. In July, approaching the first anniversary of its creation, the Bloc's spokesman could assert, more or less accurately, that "the Medellín cartel has been taken apart," thanks to thousands of searches and hundreds of arrests. But it was also around that time that doubts about the security forces' continued effectiveness, and their possible infiltration by both the Pepes and Escobar, began to surface in the press. There was a scandal involving some classified information that was leaked by the police to the Cali drug people. Then, on October 5th, following a rocket-grenade attack on the building where Escobar's family was being guarded by the government, under what was supposedly the strictest secrecy, officials recognized that the only people in a position to know how to find Escobar's wife and children were the security forces. Whether it was fortunate coincidence or the result of a swift campaign to counteract the negative public-relations effects of these allegations, the Bloc sprang into action that very day. Its latest triumphs are the killing of Angelito, Escobar's faithful food taster and scout, and the discovery of Escobar's secret hideouts in his safe houses.

ZÉ HAS A FRIEND whom he describes as a very recently lapsed member of Los Pepes, and when I met him this friend told me that the Search Bloc had indeed been stymied by precisely the same obstacle that has beset the Pepes in their effort to catch their prey: infiltration by Escobar's people. This coincidence, he said, could be explained by the fact that the Pepes' troops, for the most part, are also drawn from the police and the military.

I met Zé's friend—Cándido, I shall call him—one morning after Zé picked me up and drove in circles for what seemed like a very long time. Finally, another car screeched up in front of ours, and a personable, muscular young man got out. He looked me over while he bargained with Zé about some item he had seen in Zé's shop, and, apparently having concluded that I did not look like the enemy, agreed to a conversation. After all this hocus-pocus, I found it unnerving that everyone in the posh restaurant where we talked seemed to know him. I took no notes, as agreed, and I have no way of ascertaining whether his claims are true or whether they might constitute part of an elaborate disinformation setup, but at least they make for a coherent and logical account of how the war on Escobar has evolved.

Cándido said that at the time the Pepes began their operations, Medellín was so crisscrossed with Search Bloc patrols and checkpoints that it would have been impossible for any group of Escobar's former associates—most of whom are also wanted by the government, of course—to operate against him undetected. The logical solution was to ask for police and Army volunteers to moonlight against their common enemy. The line separating the security forces from the criminal world of Medellín has often been crossed—most notably by the former head of Escobar's family security, who was a member of the police intelligence services until he switched jobs three years ago. (He was arrested in New York in March on charges of entering the United States illegally.) At this stage, though, the Medellín police are, as a body, firmly aligned against Escobar, largely because between July of 1992, when he escaped, and February of this year he had a hundred of them killed. Cándido, who seemed as boyishly enthusiastic about Los Pepes as if he were still in their ranks, explained that both the Search Bloc and the regular police were frustrated by the legal and logistical restrictions on their operations against Escobar and were eager to join an effective organization like the Pepes, who operate in small patrols, with sure targets and with trial-and-paperwork-free executions to show for their efforts. The police were particularly happy to work under the leadership of Fidel Castaño, a minor drug exporter and one-time diamond smuggler, whom Cándido identified as "a real *verraco*"—a macho—and "a true leader."

I told Cándido that, as it happened, I was familiar with the name. In the gold-mining town of Segovia, in northeastern Antioquia, where forty-five people were murdered at random in the central plaza five years ago, I once talked to a number of persons who had known Castaño well. Like most towns in that part of Antioquia, Segovia is a raffish, gold-rush sort of place, and at one time Castaño had been very well liked there: people spoke with respect and affection of his talent for acquiring money, his martial-arts skills, and his compulsive—but shrewd—gambling. His relations with the town changed in the mid-seventies, however, after one of the various guerrilla groups that plague Colombia kidnapped his father and failed to let on that the old man had died of a heart attack in captivity until after it had received the ransom money. Castaño organized a hunting expedition that butchered every man, woman, and child living along the riverbank where he suspected that his father had been held captive. Thereafter, all leftists were his targets. When, in November of 1988, masked men shot up Segovia's central plaza as punishment for the town's election of a leftist mayor, Castaño's participation was suspected but never confirmed.

"I remember that," said Cándido, who is an experienced veteran of the war against the left, which was fought jointly by the drug traffickers, government security forces, and cattle ranchers whom the guerrillas subjected to extortion. "I was friendly with the commander of the Segovia garrison."

Castaño used to be friendly with Escobar—in fact, the two are both being investigated for the bombing of an Avianca plane in 1989, which killed all one hundred and seven people on board. Having also cultivated a following among cops, Castaño must not have been happy with the war Escobar waged on the Medellín police, beginning in 1990. Then, when Escobar ordered the killing of Castaño's good buddies the Galeanos and the Moncadas, it was the last straw—particularly since Castaño had also been on the guest list at La Catedral for that evening. (To his good fortune, he failed to make the appointment.) According to Cándido, Castaño personally commanded the first and most successful of the Pepes' operations against Escobar in Medellín. But Castaño was too well known, and too badly wanted by the government, to keep that up for long. He withdrew behind the lines, making it easier for the same infiltrators who in the past have ruined the Search Bloc's closest strikes against Escobar to sabotage the Pepes.

The Pepes had announced last June that they were disbanding. I asked if that was why.

Cándido, who was friendly but not relaxed, was still toying with his food. He smiled disparagingly at my question. That announcement, he said, was merely public relations, because the closeness between the security forces and the Pepes was becoming embarrassingly obvious. The Pepes were still active, but they no longer left signs on the corpses of their victims taking credit for their actions and warning others to stay away from Escobar. Indeed, the murder of one of Escobar's most prominent lawyers this July was a fair example of the Pepes' new tack: recognizing that Escobar would be impossible to get at as long as he remained in deep hiding, they were concentrating on exterminating his aboveground network; one result was that there were no longer any lawyers willing to represent Escobar. Following the murder of Escobar's brother-in-law, in June, his family is desperately seeking asylum abroad. (His son and daughter were stopped by the Colombian secret police at the Medellín airport in February as they were about to board a flight taking them to the United States, which they hoped to enter on the multiple-entry visas they have had since the early eighties.)

For his part, Escobar, while very much in hiding, was hardly inactive. Until recently, Cándido said, laughing at the drug lord's effrontery, Escobar's men were making the rounds of the widows and other relatives of his dead associates, demanding contributions from what El Patrón still considered his turf. (The only relative he didn't dare touch, Cándido added with some relish, was the Galeanos' sister, the Pepa.)

Escobar keeps offering to turn himself in; he did so most recently this week in a message to the mayor of Medellín, requesting that the mayor put him in touch with the Fiscalía. But that may no longer be a choice. Asked whether he would prefer to have Escobar dead or alive, the head of the Bloc, Colonel

Hugo Martínez, publicly stated that he preferred the first option. Then he raided the Medellín city hall, looking for his enemy. There is, nationwide, an impression that life will be easier for everyone if the Bloc or the Pepes finally come up with a corpse.

"FROM A PRACTICAL point of view, it might seem that way," Colombia's Fiscal de la Nación, or Prosecutor General, Gustavo de Greiff, told me recently. "But if Colombia wants to be a civilized society, it has to be able to judge a criminal with due process of law—with a judge, and a trial, and also with an opportunity for the accused to defend himself. The government can't stand by and let a situation be resolved by de-facto means." De Greiff, a pipe-smoking man of sixty-four with a face out of *The Potato Eaters*, presides over his small army of prosecuting attorneys from a spacious office with a view of Bogotá's Parque Nacional, and the office is protected by security measures that are certainly not exceptional—at least, by the standards of this terrorized country. Hardworking, dignified, and canny in legal matters, de Greiff has a cheerful habit of speaking his mind—a habit that has often got him into trouble. His first year in office was rough: it was he who carried out the investigation for President Gaviria confirming the killings in La Catedral and recommended that Escobar be transferred to another prison. A few months later, just as he was beginning to earn recognition for his agency's success in bringing drug cases to justice, he tangled with the establishment over a decision to investigate corruption among the élite. He did not appear concerned when I asked him about the spate of negative articles that the decision produced. "The leading class here thinks that it's fine to prosecute *narcos* and criminals, because no one wants to think of himself as part of that world, but the moment you go after the upper echelons they start talking about prudence," he said. Last March, he managed to raise the hackles of the Search Bloc, and the military in general, by his willingness to contemplate the possibility that the armed forces might have been tempted by drug money. If that were the case, the Bloc would merely have fallen victim to "the same inefficiency, cowardice, and corruption that plague the rest of our society," de Greiff observed coolly. When

Bloc commander Martínez stated his preference for an Escobar corpse, the Fiscal quickly called the statement "monstrous."

In our conversation, de Greiff was equally blunt about the effects of drugs on the United States. Having acknowledged that the greatest damage the cocaine trade has done to Colombian society has been "to corrupt every level of it," he pointed out that the trade has also had a corrosive effect on the country that provides the principal market for Colombia's drugs. "One has to assume that many customs officials, antidrug forces, public officials, and airport authorities there have been corrupted," he said, "because, you know, the wholesale and retail distribution of drugs in the United States also requires the coöperation of venal officials."

De Greiff's interlocutors ultimately have no choice but to swallow these hard truths, because he gets results, and because by now there can hardly be a Colombian alive who does not know the price that someone like de Greiff might have to pay for such honesty. In 1984, Rodrigo Lara Bonilla, the Minister of Justice, was killed on Escobar's orders. In 1986, the editor of *El Espectador,* two Supreme Court judges, and the former director of the anti-narcotics police were murdered. In 1987, Enrique Parejo González, a former Minister of Justice, had his jaw shot off in a failed assassination attempt in Budapest. In 1988, the Attorney General, Carlos Mauro Hoyos, was killed on his way to the Medellín airport. In 1989, it was the turn of Luis Carlos Galán, the leading Presidential candidate. In 1991, another former Minister of Justice, Enrique Low Murtra, was murdered. In 1989, when de Greiff's oldest daughter, Mónica, became the Minister of Justice, she received anonymous calls in which would-be kidnappers tracking her bodyguard-surrounded son relayed his progress from school to home: "The car's just left. . . . It's just crossed the Séptima. . . . It's heading for the garage." She quit after six weeks. People have stopped asking the Prosecutor General how he deals with the danger, but when they did ask him he used to reply that he was getting on in years, he'd had a good life, and it was time to do something for his country.

• • •

THE ONE LARGE STAIN on the record of de Greiff's Fiscalía, according to some people, has been its decision to use emergency counterterrorism legislation to prosecute thirteen technicians employed by the national telephone company. The technicians were among the leaders of a strike last year, in the course of which all telephone service in the country was suspended for two days. By charging that this was an act of terrorism, the Fiscalía has been able to assign the technicians' case to "faceless judges" and severely limit the possibilities for the defense, to the consternation of everyone from the technicians' families to the Lawyers Committee for Human Rights in New York. The technicians are currently facing a twenty-five-year prison sentence. Because the telephone employees are being tried as terrorists, they were held for a time in the same high-security prison in Bogotá as several cocaine traffickers, which is how, when I went to visit the phone workers on a recent Sunday, I found myself face-to-face with Colombia's most famous soccer star, René Higuita, who was sharing a cell with them.

Even today, after he has been accused of aiding and abetting a kidnapping negotiation involving Pablo Escobar, it is not clear whether Higuita is better known among his countrymen as an Escobar protégé or as an unpredictable but brilliant goalkeeper. Colombians loved his laid-back way of confounding the enemy by emerging into the middle of a play twenty or thirty yards from his goalposts, and they despaired of him when this daredevil approach cost the national team a crucial goal by Cameroon in the last World Cup. But, because he looks as irresistibly cuddly as he is talented, it is always hard to stay angry with him. A young man of medium height, with a graceful build, he has large, liquid brown eyes and a fleshy mouth that broadens easily into a slow, innocent grin. His trademark is a thick, shoulder-length mop of black ringlets, and when we met I asked if he had a permanent. He smiled and shook his head, and offered me handfuls of hair so I could feel for myself that it was naturally springy and soft. The fact that I was a journalist did not alarm him; indeed, he

appeared as incapable of mistrust or guile as a puppy. No doubt
this quality helped get him off the hook when, a week after Escobar turned himself in for the Envigado rest cure, Higuita was
photographed paying him a courtesy visit at La Catedral. There
was a halfhearted attempt in the media to make a scandal out of
this, but the truth is that no one was shocked. A candy company
that used him in its television ads did not suspend his contract.
After all, as my friends commented at the time, everyone knows
how much Colombian soccer owes Escobar, and at least Higuita
knew how to be loyal.

Colombians had a painful love affair with soccer, unmarked
by world triumphs, or even regional respect, until, it is said, drugs
got into the game. Traffickers funded the development of enough
talent to insure such marvels as a recent 5–0 victory against Argentina in the qualifying round for the 1994 World Cup. Escobar
has defined himself as a patriot throughout his career, which included a famously brief stint as a substitute congressman for his
district, and has proclaimed soccer his great passion. When Fiscal
de Greiff refers to the corrupting influence of cocaine on Colombian society, he is referring partly to the pride his fellow-citizens
feel when they see Colombia taken seriously on the international
fútbol circuit, and their consequent inability to deny the traffickers
their due for this happy state of affairs. Until recently, there was
no proof of a *narco-fútbol* connection, but, even so, rumors were
everywhere. The Cali team was said to operate on funds provided
by Escobar's archenemy, Gilberto Rodríguez Orejuela. (Gilberto's brother, Miguel, was officially listed as the team's president.) The links to Escobar of the Medellín team that Higuita
played with, the Atlético Nacional, were so close that, rumor has
it, he even had a secret dugout, reached by a tunnel, from which
he could watch the games. At the height of the Cali-Medellín
drug war, team executives turned up dead on the roadsides. After
Escobar's escape, the government found snapshots at La Catedral
not only of Higuita but of midfielder Leonel Álvarez hanging out
there with Escobar's chums. But when Higuita was arrested, in
June, and de Greiff let it be known that he was conducting an
investigation into the serious links between the drug trade and

the soccer world, even a friend of mine who is normally sensible about drug issues expressed anger at the meddling Fiscal. "A witch-hunt is what it is," he fumed. "Publicity-mongering." He hadn't seen the papers that morning: they carried a leaked transcript of a monitored phone call, before Higuita's arrest, between Higuita and Escobar's brother, Roberto, who turned himself in last October after fleeing with Pablo from La Catedral and is now in prison near Medellín, along with most of the surviving members of Pablo's high command.

In the first part of the monitored conversation, Higuita, who in November of 1992 was expelled from the Nacional for outrageous behavior, pleads for help in getting back on the team, and Roberto Escobar gives him an avuncular lecture on his poor discipline. "Look at Pambelé," Roberto says, referring to a former boxing champion now in ruin. "Nobody even glances in his direction anymore, except to spit on him and chase him away. . . . You know I'm a serious person, and I feel much esteem and affection for you and for your family. . . . Don't make me look bad, René. I ask you that great favor." Roberto's rather more ruthless jailmate, Gustavo González, then gets on the phone and berates Higuita. "It's not a question anymore of what you said and what they said. It's a question of knuckling under and getting back to work, dickhead. If we see the team without you, where do we stand?" After René offers assurances that he intends to get down to work, a slightly mollified González reminds him, "Half of this cause is that team. Did you hear me, dickhead? So on your toes, yeah? Don't let me down." René promises that he won't. "You sure?" González insists. "All right, son. *Ciao.*"

A second transcribed conversation follows immediately— this one between the jailed Roberto Escobar and an unidentified director of the Medellín soccer team, who explains that he isn't the only one who doesn't want Higuita back; neither do the players. "I'm going to send him over to you," Roberto Escobar insists smoothly. "And you just tell him one thing—that he can't let the Man down—because if he lets him down, what can I say? . . . It's a mess. We have to try to help him even if he isn't allowed to play a match. I really don't care whether he plays or not, because

Higuita's replacement is doing a good job, but we can't leave him out on the street, either, because we'll lose him." The team director promises to comply with Roberto's wish, and Roberto signs off. "All right, son. Say hello to the boys."

When I asked Higuita about the conversation, he didn't deny that it took place. He said, "But what did we talk about? Soccer. What's wrong with that?" Nor did he deny that he had played the go-between in a kidnapping case that involved the teen-age daughter of an acquaintance of his, who was on the outs with Pablo Escobar, and the kidnappers (who were presumably known to Higuita and were operating on orders from Escobar). Higuita said he hadn't known that a recent anti-kidnapping law prohibited private negotiations with kidnappers, and he had felt that it was his human duty to help rescue a child who most likely would never have been found alive by the state. "I handed the kidnappers the money and they turned over the girl. I'm in jail for acting according to my conscience," he said. I asked him if it was true that he had also accepted fifty thousand dollars from the girl's father (who is known as a former money launderer for Escobar and, after his brother died at the hands of the police, as one of the main promoters of the 1990 wave of cop killings). Higuita looked surprised at this question. "But what other way does a rich man have of expressing gratitude?" he said. "The father wrote me a letter afterward saying he would never have given me those *centavitos* if he'd known it was going to cause me so much trouble."

Before his legal troubles began, Higuita was never reluctant to speak openly of Pablo Escobar. He called him a "good man," and praised him as someone who "has managed to put the country's natural resources to good use." Few young men growing up poor in the hillside *comunas* of Medellín, as Higuita did, and given the opportunity for stardom—or, at the very least, for thrills and a decent income—by a man famous for selling something everyone wants have ever felt differently. There was Higuita, in jail at age twenty-seven, thanks to Escobar, but what was clearly more important to him was that thanks to Escobar he was somebody.

The day I saw Higuita was a Sunday, family-visit day in the cell where he and the phone workers were being kept. It was sun-filled, clean, and spacious—more like a schoolroom, really. The guards did not seem to be convinced that the phone workers were guilty, or to care if Higuita was. The phone workers were privileged prisoners, and Higuita even more so. The middle-class, middle-aged technicians were surrounded by clucking aunts with genteel hairdos, and chubby wives carrying baskets of food. Higuita had a flash girl at his side, his wife: prison-visit regulations forbidding stockings, miniskirts, and spike heels had not been applied to her. She seemed surly, and while the other wives gathered in groups to organize the cooking she worked on her manicure, but she got up and wrapped herself around her husband whenever he beckoned. Later, during a special Mass offered by a missionary priest and a nun, Higuita, still reclining in his relaxed way on his cot with his wife while the others knelt and prayed, spoke up to offer his own interpretation of his legal troubles, as an event sent by God to unmask a clownish government before its too credulous citizens. Early that morning, the prison warden, an Army lieutenant who was retiring, had come to say goodbye to the phone workers and Higuita. Now, after the Mass, his replacement arrived to pay his respects and sheepishly asked the soccer star for an autograph. When Higuita told me—with no visible sign of either rancor or vanity—that the government was persecuting him not as an individual but "in my condition as an idol," he was describing himself accurately, and he owed that description to Escobar. I asked him why, if he had no connections to the drug world, he had gone to visit Escobar at La Catedral. "Everyone knows that Pablo Escobar likes soccer," he said. "I went, first of all, to thank him for having turned himself in, contributing to the pacification of the country, and, second, to talk about soccer."

Cándido, the ex-Pepe, had a rather less sporting version of Higuita's *narco* connections. Perhaps Cándido was merely taking advantage of an opportunity to slander Escobar's most beloved protégés, but he claimed that at the height of the drug king's war against the state, when he was murdering Presidential candidates and setting off car bombs that killed as many as sixty-seven people at a time, Escobar managed to foil the myriad Search Bloc checkpoints in Medellín by using soccer players, whose cars would never be searched by their doting fans, to transport weapons and explosives.

ABOUT THREE YEARS AGO, in an outburst of self-confidence, the government announced that its latest manhunt against Escobar was about to be crowned with success. I had a high-spirited, celebratory dinner in Medellín that night with some friends, but, like long-term prisoners about to be released from jail, we had difficulty imagining the new circumstances in which we would be living once Colombia was rid of its leading perpetrator of nightmares. "I can't imagine a future without Pablo Escobar!" one of our party exclaimed, even as the man was slipping through the dragnet yet again.

There is a real possibility that at this stage one of the people who are currently giving Escobar shelter might decide that seven million dollars—the price on his head—is a safer bet than the likelihood of his beyond-the-grave revenge. Or the Search Bloc could get close to him again. The Pepes could get lucky. The Fiscal might finally even get his prisoner. But, even when his enemies are finally dancing on his grave, there may never be a future without Escobar, so pervasive is his influence, and not just in Medellín. Hounded by successive Administrations in the United States, but ever loyal to his loyal market there, he repeatedly closed down many of his operations in his home base and set up business wherever conditions were more favorable. So successfully did he blaze the trail that his disciples—and his rivals—are now reaping skyrocketing profits from heroin as well as cocaine, and doing business through their connections in Brazil and Argentina, Jamaica and Guatemala, and, quite probably, Poland and Russia, too.

His transforming impact has also been spiritual and aesthetic. Along with the rest of the drug trade, he has reshaped the art world, inflating prices for those painters he favors to levels that would be eye-opening even in Paris or New York. (His omnivorous collecting is fuelled by one-upmanship and a quest for social acceptance, which led him to acquire what may be one of the van Gogh *Sunflowers* paintings and then spirit it out of the country when things got dangerous.) In Colombia, he has made his arriviste tastes respectable even in Bogotá, a formerly straitlaced city that observed turn-of-the-century manners and looked down on conspicuous consumption. Now even old-money notables who loathe Escobar's vulgarity return from shopping sprees in New York with matching sets of designer bedwear.

As the head of the drug trade, Escobar also, of course, transformed business, and even the monetary system, in Colombia. The central bank, Banco de la República, estimates that between two and a half and three billion dollars is repatriated by the trade each year, giving the country one of the most stable currencies in Latin America and subsidizing a boom in money-laundering businesses—ranging from art galleries to imported-cigarette stands. Drug money propelled the Colombian economy even in the absence of a majority middle class and long before boom-size oil deposits were found last year. Between them, Escobar, the Ochoa brothers, and Fidel Castaño probably own the best farmland in the country, and lesser traffickers own much of the rest. Drug money dominates the real-estate market so overwhelmingly that even a bishop's niece I know prayed for a trafficker to be among those interested in buying her bachelor pad and to make an offer too good to refuse. It is perhaps mostly in the course of doing business with Escobar and his fellows that so many Colombians have become practiced in the art of looking the other way, and have come to feel that any amount of terror, pain, and loss is tolerable—that one can survive a drug war, and even prosper in it.

There may not actually be a drug war anymore. That war was promoted by successive United States Administrations and fought by Colombians at a cost that is impossible to quantify. Washington failed to see that the best weapon against the drug lords was to freeze their bank accounts, and instead opted for a military strategy to combat a plague whose origins could be found in an alienated and ravenous consumer population back home. It imposed this strategy on Colombia against a majority perception that drugs were a gringo invention and a gringo problem, and against the better judgment of many of the country's best-informed and most concerned analysts, who could not see where the shoot-'em-up approach was intended to lead in a country with a history of chronic violence. More than a decade after the war began, dozens of the country's bravest, most principled leaders—judges, governors, ministers, politicians—are dead, and thousands of others know the silencing effects of fear. On all sides, thousands of Colombians have died—nearly seven hundred cops in Medellín since 1990. Having been convinced that Escobar was their enemy, they paid the price. But now the war is very much Colombia's to fight, because in Washington the Clinton Administration has come around to the view that a military war is futile against a criminal phenomenon whose primary effects are social and economic. When the new head of the White House Office of Drug Control Policy, Lee Brown, visited Bogotá in August, I asked him if he was avoiding the term "drug war" on purpose, and he equivocated, but his press secretary later approached me to clarify his response: yes, Brown has indeed dropped the term from his agency's vocabulary, because it seems to him that when the word "war" is used in reference to a native population—whether of Colombians or of black inhabitants of the Bronx—it is dangerous. There is much sense in this view, but a problem that it does not resolve is that, in the middle of what was turned into a conflagration, it leaves Colombians holding a very small fire extinguisher.

Shortly after Brown's visit, I had a talk with a longtime foreign observer of the Colombian drug scene who has been a defender of the war approach if ever there was one, and found him in a brooding, pessimistic mood. The D.E.A.'s budget and personnel will likely be cut back dramatically, he noted, but he did not see that the Clinton Administration had really come up with an alternative strategy. In view of the fact that worldwide cocaine production is believed to be almost forty per cent higher today than it was in 1989, when the most severe antidrug offensive began, I asked him what was so good about the previous approach. He listed achievements that could hardly be attributed to the D.E.A.'s fire-and-brimstone campaign in what its agents have often referred to as "the jungles of Latin America." One was that in the United States habitual drug abuse is down in many sectors of the population, and that there is a marked decline in the casual use of drugs. "Drug-enforcement officials can pat themselves on the back for that," this man maintained. He added that these downward figures were the direct result of education campaigns. In Colombia, too, the achievements he listed, which were paltrier, could hardly be attributed to the dramatics of drug fighters leaping out of helicopters. The joint United States—Colombia anti-drug effort, he said, "has been able to make substantial inroads into money laundering," and he also praised the accomplishments of a 1993 financial raid against the Cali cartel called Green Ice, which identified and froze money-laundering accounts. "But my concern," he said, "is that, while law enforcement may be good, or better, Colombia as a country is in worse shape today than it was last year, and it was in worse shape last year than the year before that. The power of the traffickers has not been contained." He went on to list the areas of the country that now have their own independent clusters of traffickers, hard even to track down and keep count of, and he dwelt on the fact that in Cali the Rodríguez Orejuela brothers and a man called José Santacruz Londoño are prospering more than ever—"concentrating on fortifying their economic control of the country and on influencing the upcoming general election."

On another occasion, I asked him what he thought of legalization, and he gasped, then paused a long time before answering, as if even to discuss the topic were sinful. In that sector of the Colombian élite which does not look forward to the prospect of an increasingly assimilated and powerful drug class, the idea of universal legalization of all narcotics is gaining currency, as a way of depriving drug traffickers of their income and reducing the violence and corruption—if not the health problems—associated with drugs. This man disagreed; he felt strongly that legal drugs would lead to vastly more widespread drug use in the United States. But the alternatives that he and Washington have traditionally favored (public education, interdiction, drug raids) have not increased their rate of return over the years, and while

they can occasionally lead to the elimination of individual criminals they do nothing to break the power of the drug traffickers
as a group.

IN MEDELLÍN, which is currently enjoying something of a comeback now that Escobar is offstage, I met with the journalist-
sociologist Alonso Salazar. The last time we talked, two years
ago, he had just come out with a chilling oral history of the
pistolocos—the teen-age killers who are Escobar's most memorable contribution to the culture of Antioquia. Now he was in a
between-books phase, having recently published a companion
volume on the brutal and fierce lives of the outlaw girls. Salazar
was in good spirits, because he had spent the last three years as
an adviser on the staff of a government project to make contact
with alienated young people in the marginalized hillside *comunas*,
and he felt that, over all, the project had been a success. Together
with the project's director, he had served as host of a weekly television program, called "Arriba Mi Barrio!," that became an unexpected hit. Along with old movies and self-help advice, the
program's hosts offered *comuna* teen-agers—students, killers, unemployed workers—a chance to come on the show and vent
their feelings freely. Salazar also went up regularly to the *comunas*
and filmed there, and he thought that, what with the vocational
workshops offered by the project, and the outreach programs,
and the family-counselling services, a good number of kids had
felt themselves helped. Most important, he thought that, for
once, a contact had been made between a notoriously weak and
small central government and its most resentful citizens which
had not been mediated by bullets. And he was intrigued by the
unpredictable effects on his native city of the murderous battle
between the Pepes and Escobar. "It has changed things for the
commanding generals of this war, because it has spread its effects
everywhere," he said. "Before, there were always limits—there
were always untouchables—and the commanders operated from
a control tower. Now they're bombing the control tower. Perhaps
that explains the great fatigue I feel spreading in Medellín—that

the war has gone on to the point where everyone is being defeated."

ONE OF THE UNSTATED CONDITIONS of Pablo Escobar's surrender two years ago appears to have been a strict injunction against photographs of him of any kind. On the evening following his helicopter flight into La Catedral, the director of the Medellín prosecutor's office was persistently asked on the evening news what the famous gangster looked like nearly ten years after his last public appearance—whether rumors of repeated plastic surgery were true, and whether he had a beard. The young prosecutor's discomfiture as he refused to provide a description was embarrassing to watch. Following last year's prison escape, however, Colombians were at last able to contemplate Escobar's likeness: it appeared in photographs of himself that he had kept in his room. In one, he was dressed as an Al Capone–type gangster, and in another, wearing bandoliers crossed on his chest and a wide-brimmed hat, he affected the pose of a Mexican revolutionary. Despite these outfits, he looked much as he had before: a paunchy, plump-cheeked middle-aged man with an unsuccessful haircut whom it was difficult to imagine as a youth, and who had something at once slobbish and guarded about his glance. He had looked better in idealized images of him that had surfaced here and there in his years on the lam, like one I saw painted on the back of a bus in the Caribbean resort city of Santa Marta: in it, he appeared next to an image of a helicopter about to crash-land in a jungle. He was holding a cordless phone and was in control of the situation, as the title, "El Comandante," proclaimed. That was Escobar as he wished to be seen and as poor kids from the comunas, like René Higuita, have seen him: the Man, the hero for whom prayers are offered in the slums he helped rebuild, the one to beat, the poor bastard destined for failure who refused to fail and made the system kneel before him.

Over the years, it must have amounted to a kind of loneliness for him to know that in the whole of Colombia there was no one he couldn't buy, terrify, or eliminate. He ruled unseen over a vast portion of the Colombian hinterland, and at the height of his power he could travel unhindered throughout his native Antioquia and then down through the Magdalena River valley all the way to the cities on the Caribbean coast. Wherever he and his business associates didn't own the splendid farmland along that corridor, they were certain to own the farmers' absolute allegiance. And then, in Medellín, there were the loyalties Escobar treasured most: those of his wife and his two children, whom he adored, and of the sixteen-year-old girls from the convent schools for the daughters of the rich, whom, on occasion, he has also favored; those of the hundreds of teen-age hoodlums who went out and killed on his command; those of the businessmen and judges who rendered fealty to him; those of the police chiefs and the soccer players, and even the odd mayor or two. Richer than his closest allies, more daring than his fiercest enemies, he justifiably considered himself peerless. But he was wrong to think himself indispensable. His power was created by the need to satisfy an enormous appetite; whatever the means of his final departure, his successors are already trying on his crown.

Postscript, Bogotá

PABLO ESCOBAR was gunned down in Medellín by members of the government's Search Bloc on December 2, 1993.

Acknowledgements

OVER THE PERIOD OF TIME encompassed by these articles—
1989 to 1993—sixty-four journalists were killed in Latin America
in the course of doing their job, according to figures compiled
by the Committee to Protect Journalists. Among them was my
friend Sylvia Duzán, whose luminous presence and fearless reporting will be missed forever by those who knew her, and two
journalists I never met, Hugo Daniel Chaparro and Jorge Enrique
Torres, Colombians like Sylvia.

Chaparro and Torres were assassinated in 1991 in the town
of Segovia, in an area of Colombia where guerrillas, death-squad
members, drug runners, gold miners, and rampaging soldiers
have conspired with and against each other to bring about hell
on earth. In November of 1988, in the most extreme—but by no
means the only—seizure of violence in that town, four armed
men entered Segovia at dusk, just as the townspeople were gathering in the town circle for a beer and a chat, and opened fire.
Forty-eight people were killed, including several children. The
government's halfhearted investigation revealed that the massacre was the work of professional killers, paid by drug traffickers
and assisted by the local military, hired to bring revenge on Segovia for having voted for a leftist mayor with links to the guerrillas.
I visited Segovia twice in the course of the following year, trying
to write a story that would help me understand the compulsion
to murder that has taken over so many Colombians, but I was
too scared to finish the reporting properly, and the story never
ran. A year after that, Chaparro and Torres arrived in Segovia,
looking for an answer to the same mystery. Within hours of their
arrival, they were stopped, searched, forced to kneel in the street,
and shot in the head point-blank, possibly by paramilitaries try-

ing to get rid of journalists, possibly by guerrillas who mistook them for paramilitaries.

Sylvia Duzán died in similar fashion in 1990, in the town of Cimitarra, which is at the opposite extreme of the Magdalena River Valley from Segovia, but where drug-financed paramilitaries and entrenched guerrillas also wreak havoc on the local population in the course of carrying out their war on each other. She was murdered along with three members of a farmers' coöperative who had tried to negotiate the right to not take sides in a war they had no stake in, and were punished for that attempt with murder. When Sylvia's husband arrived to pick up the body at the Army barracks near where Sylvia and the three others were killed, the soldiers smirked. "What about María Jimena? Didn't she come?" they asked. María Jimena, Sylvia's sister, is also a journalist.

Every story in this book is the result of an enormous reporting effort, to which I have made a very small contribution. Like other correspondents writing about countries in which they do not live, for publications based elsewhere, I have relied in every instance on the friendship, solidarity, professionalism, historical memory, and sheer hard work of people like Sylvia, Chaparro, and Torres. Like the great majority of Latin-American reporters, all three were underpaid, innocent of formal training, anonymous. All three took risks that more prudent, less interesting people would have avoided—solely in order to understand. Without the help of equally brave and righteous Latin-American reporters, I would not even have known how to begin to focus any one of these articles: I am constantly amazed at the patience displayed by my local colleagues with clueless drop-ins like myself, and at their willingness to share the results of their own years of investigative labor. My debt to the reporters in Latin America I have met and been enlightened by knows no limits.

For the first time in fifteen years as a reporter, I recently found myself submitting to an interview. As a result I now would like to extend my thanks to everyone who foolishly and generously has agreed to talk to me while I take notes, scrutinize their every word, and openly take issue with their statements. It is the duty of public officials to talk to the press, a duty they all too frequently avoid in Latin America. Ordinary mortals have no reason to submit to interrogation by a reporter, other than the conviction that important issues are at stake, and that we might all understand each other better by talking. Miners and missionaries, human-rights workers and wealthy adolescents, *violentólogos* and bus drivers have given me their time, and invited me into their homes and into their confidence.

I owe thanks also to Malú Bruno, Pam Booth, and Barbara Sievert, neighbors who made coming back from a trip so much easier. Octavio Gómez, Salomón Kalmanovitz, Ramón Jimeno, Phil Bennett, Sarita Kendall, Richard Boudreaux, Rafael Noboa, Stephen Ferry, and Marjorie Miller are colleagues and dear friends who were always willing to share sources, and read and improve a draft. Mike Smith, Alisa Berzon, César Otoni, Cecilia Valenzuela, Berta Thayer, Gladys Boladeros, and Eloísa Fontes set up appointments, searched for documents, shared their valuable research, and steered me right while providing good company.

The friendship of Ray Bonner kept me going through some very difficult times. And without the prodigious Gloria Loomis this book might never have happened.

At *The New Yorker*, Tina Brown has been unstintingly encouraging of my work. Chris Knutsen and Nancy Boensch cheerfully helped make life on the road smoother. As everyone knows, the main privilege of writing for this magazine is the opportunity to deliver one's clumsy pages to the finest of editors. I count myself particularly lucky to have been assigned to John Bennet, from whom I continue to learn all the time, and to Pat Crow.

In the end, these pieces remain what they were when they first appeared, in slightly different form, in *The New Yorker*: Letters from Latin America. As such, they were written to, and for, Bob Gottlieb, who first brought me to the magazine and patiently made me believe that I had something worth saying, and who then so generously agreed to edit this book.

A NOTE ON THE TYPE

The text of this book was set in Weiss, a type face designed in Germany by Emil Rudolf Weiss (1875–1942). The design of the roman was completed in 1928 and that of the italic in 1931. Both are well balanced and even in color, and both reflect the subtle skill of a fine calligrapher.

Composed by Graphic Composition, Athens, Georgia

Printed and bound by Arcata/Martinsburg, Martinsburg, West Virginia

Designed by Iris Weinstein